Research Methods and Technology
Custom Edition

Research Methods and Technology
Custom Edition

Chapters Contributed from:
Research Methodology 4e: Ranjit Kumar
Research Methods, Statistics, and Applications:
Kathrynn A. Adams, Eva K. Lawrence

Kean University
Research Methods and Technology
GE 2021-2024

Compiled for:
Teaching Faculty of Research Methods and Technology
Kean University

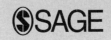

Los Angeles | London | New Delhi
Singapore | Washington DC

Los Angeles | London | New Delhi
Singapore | Washington DC

FOR INFORMATION:

SAGE Publications, Inc.
2455 Teller Road
Thousand Oaks, California 91320
E-mail: order@sagepub.com

SAGE Publications Ltd.
1 Oliver's Yard
55 City Road
London EC1Y 1SP
United Kingdom

SAGE Publications India Pvt. Ltd.
B 1/I 1 Mohan Cooperative Industrial Area
Mathura Road, New Delhi 110 044
India

SAGE Publications Asia-Pacific Pte. Ltd.
3 Church Street
#10-04 Samsung Hub
Singapore 049483

Printed in the United States of America

ISBN: 9781483378930 (paperback)
ISBN: 9781483378923 (web PDF)

This book is printed on acid-free paper.

17 18 19 20 10 9 8 7 6

CONTENTS

How to use this book and its online resources

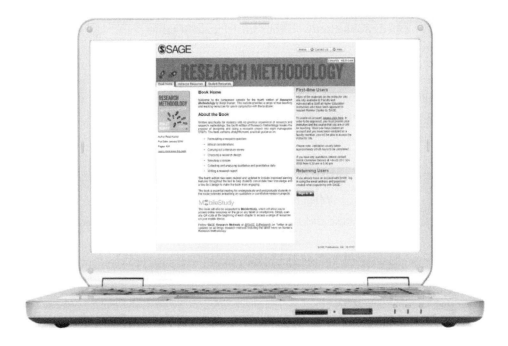

To better support your study, Ranjit Kumar's *Research Methodology, 4th edition* is supported by a wealth of online resources which can be accessed on the book's companion website and on a mobile version of that site called MobileStudy.

Throughout the book you will see the icons below in the margins telling you when additional resources are available online, including:

 Videos containing examples of real world research and advice on how to conduct your research project.

 Further Reading from selected SAGE Journal articles and book chapters allowing you delve deeper into key concepts.

Weblinks to sites offering additional resources to support your study.

Printouts of the exercises and key figures from the book, to use in class or independently to guide you through your research.

Using the companion website and MobileStudy

 If you want to revise using your computer, visit the companion website at www.uk.sagepub.com/kumar4e. If you are studying on the go, scan this QR code to access a mobile optimised version of the companion website called MobileStudy on your smartphone or tablet.

On the companion website and Mobile Study you will find videos, further reading and the printouts highlighted in the margins of each chapter, along with access to a research methods online community called Methodspace, multiple choice quizzes and flashcards to test your understanding.

Lecturers who visit the companion website will gain access to:

Testbanks containing multiple choice questions for each chapter that can be used for student assessment.

PowerPoint(™) Slides of the key concepts of each chapter and of all the figures and tables from the book. These slides can be easily adapted to be added to your own lecture slides.

Instructors' Guide outlining the aims of each chapter with three additional chapter activities ideal for use in seminars and class discussions.

PREFACE

This book is based upon my experiences in research as a student, practitioner and teacher. The difficulties I faced in understanding research as a student, my discoveries about what was applicable and inapplicable in the field as a research practitioner, my development of the ability to effectively communicate difficult concepts in simple language without sacrificing technicality and accuracy as a teacher, and the feedback of many experts who participated in the evaluations carried out by Pearson Australia on the first edition and Sage UK on the second and third editions, have become the basis of this book. Many aspects of methodology were added on the basis of the feedback of teachers of research methods from a number of countries.

Research methodology is taught as a supporting subject in several ways in many academic disciplines such as health, education, psychology, social work, nursing, public health, library studies and marketing research. The core philosophical base for this book comes from my conviction that, although these disciplines vary in content, their broad approach to a research enquiry is similar. This book, therefore, is addressed to these academic disciplines.

It is true that some disciplines and professionals place greater emphasis on quantitative research, some on qualitative and some on both. My own approach to research is a combination of both. Firstly, it is the objective that should decide whether a study is carried out adopting a qualitative or a quantitative approach. Secondly, in real life most research is a combination of both approaches. Though they differ in the philosophy that underpins their mode of enquiry, to a great extent their broad approach to enquiry is similar. The quantitative research process is reasonably well structured whereas the qualitative one is fairly unstructured, and these are their respective strengths as well as weaknesses. I strongly believe that both are important to portray a complete picture. In addition, there are aspects of quantitative research that are qualitative in nature. It depends upon how a piece of information has been collected and analysed. Therefore I feel very strongly that a good researcher needs to have both types of skill. I follow a qualitative–quantitative–qualitative approach to an enquiry. This book, therefore, has been written to provide information about various methods, procedures and techniques that are used in both the research approaches in a simple step-by-step manner, linked to operational steps. In terms of methods, techniques and procedures, as the mixed/multiple methods approach uses qualitative and/or quantitative approaches, I did not consider it appropriate to describe mixed/multiple methods separately. Thus, although Chapter 1 of this book describes three approaches to a research enquiry in social research, the subsequent chapters describe only the two approaches as the third, mixed methods, is covered under them.

Research as a subject is taught at different levels. The book is designed specifically for students who are newcomers to research and who may have a psychological barrier with regard to the subject. I have, therefore, not assumed any previous knowledge on the part of the reader; I have omitted detailed discussion of aspects that may be inappropriate for beginners; I have used many flow charts and examples to communicate concepts; and areas covered in the book follow a 'simple to complex' approach in terms of their discussion and coverage. I have also made a deliberate attempt not to make this book too theoretical. This primarily is a 'nuts and bolts' book that aims to develop elementary skills rather than a theoretical and philosophical knowledge base.

The structure of this book, which is based on the model developed during my teaching career, is designed to be practical. The theoretical knowledge that constitutes research methodology is therefore organised around the operational steps that form this research process for quantitative, qualitative and mixed methods research. All the information needed to take a particular step, during the actual research journey, is provided in one place. The information is organised in chapters and each chapter is devoted to a particular aspect of that step (see Figure 2.3). For example, 'formulating a research problem' is the first operational step in the research process. To formulate a 'good' research problem, in my opinion, you need to know how to review the literature, formulate a research problem, deal with variables and their measurement, and construct hypotheses. Hence, under this step, there are four chapters. The information they provide will enable you to formulate a problem that is researchable. These chapters are titled: 'Reviewing the literature', 'Formulating a research problem', 'Identifying variables' and 'Constructing hypotheses'. Similarly, for the operational step, Step III, 'Constructing an instrument for data collection', the chapters titled 'Selecting a method of data collection', 'Collecting data using attitudinal scales' and 'Establishing the validity and reliability of a research instrument' will provide sufficient information for you to develop an instrument for data collection for your study. For every aspect at each step, a smorgasbord of methods, models, techniques and procedures is provided for both quantitative and qualitative studies (and thus also, by extension, for mixed/multiple studies) in order for you to build your knowledge base in research methodology and also to help you to select the most appropriate ones when undertaking your own research.

It is my belief that a sound knowledge of research methodology is essential for undertaking a valid study. To answer your research questions, up to Step V, 'Writing a research proposal', knowledge of research methods is crucial as it enables you to develop a conceptual framework that is sound and has merits for undertaking your research endeavour with confidence. Having completed the preparatory work, the steps that follow are more practical in nature, the quality of which entirely depends upon the soundness of the methodology you proposed in your research proposal. Statistics and computers play a significant role in research, but their application is mainly after the data has been collected. To me, statistics are useful in confirming or contradicting conclusions drawn from simply looking at analysed data, in providing an indication of the magnitude of the relationship between two or more variables under study, in helping to establish causality, and in ascertaining the level of confidence that can be placed in your findings. A computer is used primarily in data analysis, the calculation of statistics, word-processing and the graphic presentation of data. It saves time and makes it easier for you to undertake these activities; however, you need to learn this additional skill. This book does not include statistics or information about computers.

The fourth edition incorporates a number of suggestions made on the third edition by international experts in social research during a review undertaken by Sage Publications. I have made every effort to incorporate as many of these suggestions as possible, without changing the basic structure of the book. Some of the major changes in the fourth edition are as follows:

- The 'mixed/multiple methods approach' to social research has been incorporated as a philosophy in Chapter 1. To me, a 'mixed methods approach' is a philosophy rather than an approach, unlike quantitative and qualitative, as it does not have its own body of methods and procedures. Therefore, it could not be covered in the same manner as the quantitative and qualitative approaches, that is, by **linking** the methods and procedures that comprise the mixed methods methodology with the operational steps which are the basis of the book.
- A companion website has been developed for the fourth edition to provide additional information. This website can be accessed on your mobile using the QR code at the end of the chapters, or by visiting www.uk.sagepub.com/kumar4e.
- The fourth edition reflects my desire to further break down the barrier between quantitative and qualitative research. Extremely positive reviews and feedback have made me all the more con-vinced that both these methodologies can be described in a common framework. Therefore the fourth edition has much more coverage of qualitative methods than the third. Coverage of quali-tative research has been further strengthened to provide a more balanced picture of both the methodologies.
- Exercises, a part of the appendix, have now been further developed and linked to the appropriate operational steps in the belief that students will learn more if they are given an opportunity to operationalise, in an actual situation, what they have learnt in the chapters.
- Title pages dividing chapters and operational steps have now been redesigned to provide greater clarity as well as informing students in advance what they can expect to learn in a chapter. Also, each chapter has a list of keywords that students will encounter in the chapter.
- In places the language has been changed to enhance flow, understanding and ease of reading.

I am grateful to a number of people who have helped me in the writing of this book. First of all, to my students, who have taught me how to teach research methods. The basic structure of this book is an outcome of the feedback I have received from them over the years. How, and at what stage of the research process, a concept or a procedure should be taught, I have learnt from my students. I thank them all for their contribution to this book.

I am extremely grateful to my friend and colleague, Dr Norma Watson, whose efforts in editing the first edition were of immense help. The book would not have reached its present stage without her unconditional help.

I thank Professor Denis Ladbrook, my friend and colleague, for his continuous encouragement, support and critical appreciation of my writing.

I am also grateful to my friend, Dr Deenaz Damania, a very well-known expert in qualitative research, for her interest, encouragement and help in the completion of this edition.

I am immensely grateful to the international research experts who participated in the in-depth review of the book, undertaken by Sage Publications, and provided valuable suggestions for its further improvement. A number of changes in the fourth edition are a direct result of their feedback. The many reviews on the Sage website by teachers of research from universities in many countries have been very positive and a source of encouragement, motivation and reinforcement for the fourth edition, and I am immensely grateful to the reviewers.

Ranjit Kumar

1

RESEARCH: A WAY OF THINKING

In this chapter you will learn about

- Research: a way of thinking
- Research: a way of looking at your professional practice
- Research and evidence-based practice
- The applications of research
- Prerequisites of a research process
- Types of research from different perspectives
- Mixed methods approach to research enquiry
- Paradigms of research

Keywords

applied research, controlled, correlational research, descriptive research, empirical, explanatory research,	exploratory research, evidence-based practice, interpretive paradigm, mixed methods research, positivistic paradigm, pure research,	qualitative research, quantitative research, reliability, research, structured and unstructured enquiries, systematic, validity.

At the end of this chapter, you should have an understanding of

- The meaning of research and its benefits and applications for your practice
- Situations in which research can be used for practice improvement
- Types of research approaches in the social sciences
- Differences in and the applications of quantitative, qualitative and mixed methods approaches
- The major paradigms of research in the social sciences

Research: a way of thinking

Research is not only a set of skills, but also a way of thinking. Within this framework of thinking, you usually question what you observe, make an attempt to further explore, understand and explain your observations, and draw conclusions and inferences to enhance your practice skills and their knowledge base. It is looking at your practice or work situation inquisitively, critically and analytically to gain an in-depth knowledge of its rationale, relevance, effectiveness and efficiency. You develop an attitude that encourages you to challenge different aspects of your work situation, to question their purpose, relevance and validity, to find their strengths and weaknesses, and to investigate the possibilities and ways for further improvements and refinements. Research develops this thinking, inquisitive perspective in you. Thinking in this research mode, as a practitioner, you develop the ability to ask yourself questions such as: What am I doing? Why am I doing this? How is it affecting my clients or consumers? How can I improve my work? Such questions naturally come to your mind as a practitioner, and as a researcher you make attempts to find their answers. It is to find answers to such questions that you need to have research skills.

Research develops in you a way of thinking that is logical and rational and that encourages you to critically examine every aspect of your day-to-day situation. It helps you to understand and formulate guiding principles that govern a particular procedure in your practice, and develop and test new ways that contribute to the advancement of your practice and profession. This way of thinking develops in you a very different perspective to your work. Research develops this analytical way of thinking in you, and the knowledge of research methodology provides you with the techniques to find answers to your research questions. This research orientation becomes a cycle of your practice which, in turn, encourages you to further observe, question, explore, test and understand various aspects of your practice.

Research: an integral part of your professional practice

Research is an integral part of good professional practice in many professions and has been responsible for greatly influencing the practice procedures and outcomes in these professions. Among many professions such as medicine, public health, psychology, and education, research and practice are well integrated, and practice relies very heavily upon what is discovered through research. As a matter of fact, research and practice are two sides of the same coin that should and cannot be separated. It would be appropriate to say that the greater the integration between research and practice in a profession, the greater the advancement in its theoretical and practice knowledge base. As mentioned, research is a habit of questioning what you do, and a systematic way of examining your clinical observations to explain and find answers for what you observe in your practice, with a view to instituting appropriate changes for a more effective professional service. Let us take some disciplines as examples.

Suppose you are working in the field of health. You may be a front-line service provider, supervisor or health administrator/planner. You may be in a hospital or working as an outreach community health worker. You may be a nurse, doctor, occupational therapist, physiotherapist, social worker or other paramedic. In any of these positions, you may ask yourself or be asked some of the following questions:

- How many patients do I see every day?
- What are some of the most common conditions prevalent among my patients?
- What are the causes of these conditions?
- Why do some people have a particular condition whereas others do not?
- What is the average cost of a service to a patient?
- What is the ideal population–worker ratio for this programme?
- What are the health needs of the community?
- What are the benefits of this programme to the community?
- How do I demonstrate the effectiveness of my service?
- Why do some people use the service while others do not?
- What do people think about the service?
- How satisfied are patients with the service?
- How effective is the service?
- How can the service be improved?

You can add many other questions to this list. At times it may be possible to ignore these questions because of the level at which you work, at other times you may make an effort to find answers on your own initiative, or sometimes you may be required to obtain answers for effective administration and planning.

Let us take another discipline: business studies. Assume you work in the area of marketing. Again, you can work at different levels: as a salesperson, sales manager or sales promotion executive. The list of questions that may occur to you is endless. The types of questions and the need to find answers to them will vary with the level at which you work in the organisation. You may just want to find out the monthly

RESEARCH: A WAY OF THINKING

3

fluctuation in the sales of a particular product, or you may be asked to develop a research and development strategic plan to compete for a greater share of the market for your company's products. You may ask yourself or be asked, for example:

- What is the best strategy to promote the sale of a particular product?
- How many salespersons do I need?
- What is the effect of a particular advertising campaign on the sale of this product?
- How satisfied are consumers with this product?
- How much are consumers prepared to spend on this product?
- What do consumers like or dislike about this product?
- What type of packaging do consumers prefer for this product?
- What training do the salespersons need to promote the sale of this product?
- What are the attributes of a good salesperson?

Again, suppose you are a teacher working in a school. In your day-to-day teaching you are likely to encounter many complex questions and issues, the answers to which could directly or indirectly improve your effectiveness as a teacher. Some of these questions could be:

- What do students think about my teaching?
- What do I need to do to become a better teacher?
- Why are some students good at their studies while others are not?
- What affect does the home environment have on the academic achievement of a child?
- What, in students' opinion, are the attributes of a good teacher?
- Do I have the attributes that make a good teacher?
- What is the attitude of students towards homework?
- What determines students' motivation in their studies?
- Is there a relationship between academic achievement and occupational aspirations?

You can go on adding to this list. Answers to these questions will help you to become a better teacher and develop policies and programmes that will improve the system. In an attempt to find valid answers to these questions you need to have research skills.

To take a different example, let us assume that you work as a psychologist, counsellor or social worker. In the course of your work you may ask yourself (or someone else may ask you) the following questions:

- What are my clients' most common presenting problems?
- What are their most common underlying problems?
- What are the reasons for their problems?
- What is the socioeconomic background of my clients?
- Why am I successful in certain cases and not in others?
- What intervention strategies are more effective for the problems of my clients?
- What resources are available in the community to help a client with a particular need?
- What intervention strategies are appropriate for this problem?
- How satisfied are my clients with my services?
- How can I improve the quality of my services?

As a supervisor, administrator or manager of an agency, again different questions relating to the effectiveness and efficiency of a service may come to your mind. For example:

- How many people are coming to my agency?
- What are the socioeconomic-demographic characteristics of my clients?
- How many cases can a worker effectively handle in a day?
- Why do some people use the service while others do not?
- How effective is the service?
- What are the most common needs of clients who come to this agency?
- What are the strengths and weaknesses of the service?
- How satisfied are the clients with the service?
- How can I improve this service for my clients?

Still, at another level of practice, as a professional who feels a responsibility to contribute to the development and enhancement of your profession, you might be interested in finding answers to theoretical questions, such as:

- What is the most effective intervention for a particular problem?
- What causes X, or what are the effects of Y?
- What is the relationship between two phenomena such as unemployment and street crime; stressful living and heart attack; breakdown in marital relationships and personal communication; and immigration and family roles?
- How do I measure the self-esteem of my clients?
- How do I ascertain the validity of my questionnaire?
- What is the pattern of programme adoption in the community?
- What is the best way of finding out community attitudes towards an issue?
- What is the best way to find out the effectiveness of a particular treatment?
- How can I select an unbiased sample?
- What is the best way to find out about the level of marriage satisfaction among my clients?

Let us now consider some questions from the other side of the desk, that is, from the perspectives of consumers of your service. Recent decades have witnessed a tremendous shift in attitudes in the way consumers expect and accept services. It has changed from an obligatory perspective to the right to have a service. The focus is now not only on the service but also on its quality. Therefore in this age of consumerism, you cannot afford to ignore the consumers of a service. Consumers have the right to ask questions about the quality and effectiveness of the service they are receiving and you, as the service provider, have an obligation to answer their questions. Some of the questions that a consumer may ask are:

- How effective is the service that I am receiving?
- Am I getting value for money?
- How well trained are the service providers?

Most professions that are in the human service industry would lend themselves to the questions raised above and you as a service provider should be well prepared to answer them. Irrespective of your field of practice and the level at which you work, in your day-to-day practice, you will encounter many of these questions and to improve your practice you must find their answers. Research is one of the ways to help you do so objectively.

Research: a way to gather evidence for your practice

EVIDENCE-BASED
PRACTICE

In recent decades evidence-based practice (EBP) has gained recognition as a requirement for a good professional practice. In professions such as medicine it has become a service delivery norm, a requirement and an indicator of practice accountability. Though its origin is credited to medical practice, EBP has become an important part of many other professions such as nursing, allied health services, mental health, community health, social work, psychology and teaching. It is now being promoted as an acceptable and scientific method for policy formulation and practice assessment.

EBP IN NURSING

Evidence-based practice is the delivery of services based upon research evidence about their effectiveness; the service provider's clinical judgement as to the suitability and appropriateness of the service for a client; and the client's own preference as to the acceptance of the service. The concept of EBP encourages professionals and other decision-makers to use evidence regarding the effectiveness of an intervention in conjunction with the characteristics and circumstances of a client and their own professional judgement to determine the appropriateness of an intervention when providing a service to a client. In this age of accountability, you as a professional must be accountable to your clients as well as your profession. It is as a part of this accountability that you need to demonstrate the effectiveness of the service(s) you provide.

PODCAST: BEN
GOLDACRE ON EBP

Research is one of the ways of collecting accurate, sound and reliable information about the effectiveness of your interventions, thereby providing you with evidence of its effectiveness. As service providers and professionals, we use techniques and procedures developed by research methodologists to consolidate, improve, develop, refine and advance clinical aspects of our practice to serve our clients better.

Applications of research in practice development and policy formulation

Very little research in the field is 'pure' in nature, that is, very few people do research in research methodology per se. The use of research skills is mostly 'applied', that is, they are often used in the development of practice skills and procedures, and the formulation of practice policies. All professions use research methods in varying degrees in many areas. They use the methods and procedures developed by research methodologists in order to increase understanding of different aspects of practice in their own profession and to enhance their professional knowledge base. It is through the application of research methodology that they strengthen and advance their own professional knowledge and skills. Examine your own field. You will find that its professional practice follows procedures and practices tested and developed by others over a long period of time. It is in this testing process that you need research skills, the development of which falls in the category of pure research. As a matter of fact, the validity of your findings entirely depends upon the soundness of the research methods and procedures you adopt.

Within any profession, where you directly or indirectly provide a service, such as health (nursing, occupational therapy, physiotherapy, community health, health promotion and public health), education, psychology or social work, the application of research can be viewed from four different perspectives:

EBP IN EDUCATION

1. the service provider;
2. the service administrator, manager and/or planner;
3. the service consumer; and
4. the professional.

These perspectives are summarised in Figure 1.1. Though it is impossible to list all the issues in every discipline, this framework can be applied to most disciplines and situations in the humanities and the social sciences. You should be able to use this to identify, from the viewpoint of the above perspectives, the possible issues in your own academic field where research techniques can be used to find answers.

EBP IN SOCIAL WORK

Research: what does it mean?

The word 'research' has multiple meanings and its precise definition varies from discipline to discipline and expert to expert. Across disciplines and experts, however, there seems to be agreement with respect to the functions it performs, that is, to find answers to your research questions. You can use any of the research methods/approaches to achieve this objective. These methods range from the fairly informal, based upon clinical impressions, to the strictly scientific, adhering to the conventional expectations of scientific procedures. Research means using one of these methods to find answers to your questions. However, when you say that you are undertaking a research study to find answers to a question, you are implying that the process being applied:

1. is being undertaken within a framework of a set of philosophies;
2. uses procedures, methods and techniques that have been tested for their validity and reliability;
3. is designed to be unbiased and objective.

Your philosophical orientation may stem from one of the several paradigms and approaches in research – positivist, interpretive, phenomenology, action or participatory, feminist, qualitative, quantitative, mixed methods – and the academic discipline in which you have been trained. The concept of 'validity' can be applied to any aspect of the research process. It ensures that in a research study correct procedures have been applied to find answers to a question. 'Reliability' refers to the quality of a measurement procedure that provides repeatability and accuracy. 'Unbiased and objective' means that you have taken each step in an unbiased manner and drawn each conclusion to the best of your ability and without introducing your own vested interest. The author makes a distinction between bias and subjectivity. Subjectivity is an integral part of your way of thinking that is 'conditioned' by your educational background, academic discipline, philosophy, experience and skills. For example, a psychologist may look at a piece of information differently than an anthropologist or a historian.

RESEARCH: A WAY OF THINKING   7

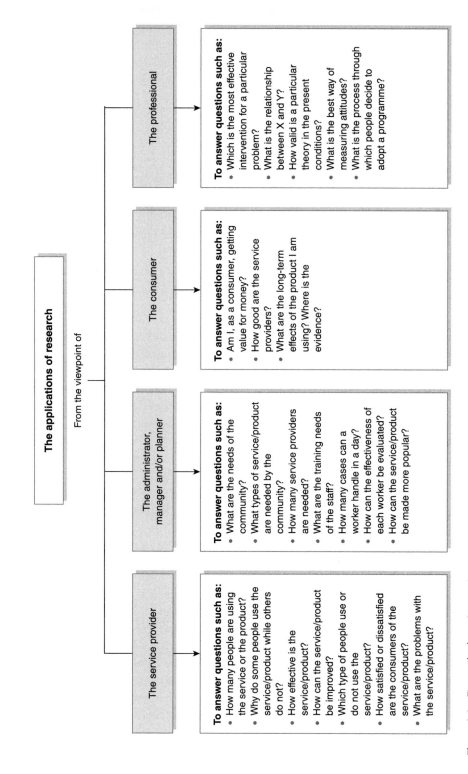

Figure 1.1 The applications of research

Bias, on the other hand, is a deliberate attempt to either conceal or highlight something because of your vested interest. Adherence to the three criteria mentioned above enables the process to be called 'research'. Therefore, when you say you are undertaking a research study to find the answer to a question, this implies that the method you are adopting fulfils these expectations (discussed later in the chapter).

However, the degree to which these criteria are expected to be fulfilled varies from discipline to discipline and so the meaning of 'research' differs from one academic discipline to another. For example, the expectations of the research process are markedly different between the physical and the social sciences. In the physical sciences a research endeavour is expected to be strictly controlled at each step, whereas in the social sciences rigid control cannot be enforced as you are studying the human rather than the material world, and sometimes it is not even demanded.

Within the social sciences the level of control required also varies markedly from one discipline to another, as social scientists differ over the need for the research process to meet the above expectations. Despite these differences among disciplines, their broad approach to enquiry is similar. The research model, the basis of this book, is based upon this broad approach.

As a beginner in research you should understand that not all research studies are based upon complex and technical methodologies and have to use statistics and computers. Research can be a very simple activity designed to provide answers to very simple questions relating to day-to-day activities. On the other hand, research procedures can also be employed to formulate intricate theories or laws that govern our lives. The difference between research and non-research activity is, as mentioned, in the way we find answers to our research questions. For a process to be called research, it is important that it meets certain requirements and possesses certain characteristics. To identify these requirements and characteristics let us examine some definitions of research:

> The word *research* is composed of two syllables, *re* and *search*. The dictionary defines the former as a prefix meaning again, anew or over again and the latter as a verb meaning to examine closely and carefully, to test and try, or to probe. Together they form a noun describing a careful, systematic, patient study and investigation in some field of knowledge, undertaken to establish facts or principles. (Grinnell 1993: 4)

Grinnell further adds: 'research is a structured inquiry that utilises acceptable scientific methodology to solve problems and creates new knowledge that is generally applicable' (1993: 4).

Lundberg (1942) draws a parallel between the social research process, which is considered scientific, and the process that we use in our daily lives. According to him:

> Scientific methods consist of systematic observation, classification and interpretation of data. Now, obviously, this process is one in which nearly all people engage in the course of their daily lives. The main difference between our day-to-day generalisations and the conclusions usually recognised as scientific method lies in the degree of formality, rigorousness, verifiability and general validity of the latter. (Lundberg 1942: 5)

Burns (1997: 2) defines research as 'a systematic investigation to find answers to a problem'.

According to Kerlinger (1986: 10), 'scientific research is a systematic, controlled empirical and critical investigation of propositions about the presumed relationships about various phenomena'. Bulmer (1977: 5) states: 'Nevertheless sociological research, as research, is primarily committed to establishing systematic, reliable and valid knowledge about the social world.'

The research process: its characteristics and requirements

From these definitions it is clear that research is a process for collecting, analysing and interpreting information to answer research questions. But to qualify to be called 'research', the process must have certain characteristics and fulfil some requirements: it must, as far as possible, be controlled, rigorous, systematic, valid and verifiable, empirical and critical.

Let us briefly examine these characteristics and requirements to understand what they mean:

- Controlled – In real life there are many forces that affect the outcome(s) of an event. In the social sciences, a particular event seldom occurs for a single reason. It is the multiplicity of factors that determine the outcome of an event. It is true that some relationships are easy to understand while there are others more complex and difficult. In almost every relationship, simple or complex, most outcomes are a result of the interplay of a multiplicity of interacting factors. In order to reliably establish a cause-and-effect relationship, it is therefore important to design a study in such a way that enables you to link cause(s) with the effect(s) and vice versa. It is important for such studies to be able to isolate the effect of all other factors that are of no interest to you as a researcher but have a bearing on the outcomes. The concept of control implies that, in exploring causality in relation to two variables, you set up your study in such a way that it either minimises or quantifies (as it is impossible to eliminate) the effects of factors, other than the cause variable, affecting the relationship. This can be achieved to a large extent in the physical sciences, as most of the research is done in a laboratory. However, in the social sciences it is extremely difficult as research is carried out on issues relating to human beings living in society, where such controls are impossible. Therefore, in the social sciences, as you cannot control external factors, you attempt to quantify their impact.
- Rigorous – You must be scrupulous in ensuring that the procedures followed to find answers to questions are relevant, appropriate and justified. Again, the degree of rigour varies markedly between the physical and the social sciences and within the social sciences.
- Systematic – This implies that the procedures adopted to undertake an investigation follow a certain logical sequence. The different steps cannot be taken in a haphazard way. Some procedures must follow others.
- Valid and verifiable – This concept implies that whatever you conclude on the basis of your findings is correct and can be verified by you and others.
- Empirical – This means that any conclusions drawn are based upon hard evidence gathered from information collected from real-life experiences or observations.
- Critical – Critical scrutiny of the procedures used and the methods employed is crucial to a research enquiry. The process of investigation must be foolproof and free from any drawbacks. The process adopted and the procedures used must be able to withstand critical scrutiny.

Types of research

As mentioned earlier, to some extent, the definition of research varies from discipline to discipline and expert to expert. This variation in the definition and understanding of research, to a large extent, can be attributed to the different philosophies that underpin research thinking. Your belief in a particular philosophy underpinning the mode of enquiry shapes your opinion about the appropriateness of the methods for finding answers to your research questions. On the basis of the terminology used to describe types of research in the social science research methodology literature, the author has tried to develop a framework for the classification of research from different perspectives (Figure 1.2). The 'mode of enquiry' perspective classifies the research types on the basis of the different philosophies that guide them, while the 'application' and 'objectives' perspectives look at the research classification from the uses and purposes points of view. The three perspectives that form the basis of this classification are:

1. *applications* of the findings of the research study;
2. *objectives* of the study;
3. *mode of enquiry* used in conducting the study.

The classification of the types of research on the basis of these perspectives is not mutually exclusive – that is, a research study classified from the viewpoint of 'application' can also be classified from the perspectives of 'objectives' and 'enquiry mode' employed. For example, a research project may be classified as pure or applied research (from the perspective of application), as descriptive, correlational, explanatory or exploratory (from the perspective of objectives/purposes) and as qualitative, quantitative or mixed methods (from the perspective of the enquiry mode employed).

Application perspective

If you examine a research endeavour from the perspective of its application, there are two broad categories: pure research and applied research. In the social sciences, according to Bailey (1978: 17):

> Pure research involves developing and testing theories and hypotheses that are intellectually challenging to the researcher but may or may not have practical application at the present time or in the future. Thus such work often involves the testing of hypotheses containing very abstract and specialised concepts.

Pure research is also concerned with the development, examination, verification and refinement of research methods, procedures, techniques and tools that form the body of research methodology. Examples of pure research include developing a sampling technique that can be applied to a particular situation; developing a methodology to assess the validity of a procedure; developing an instrument, say, to measure the stress level in

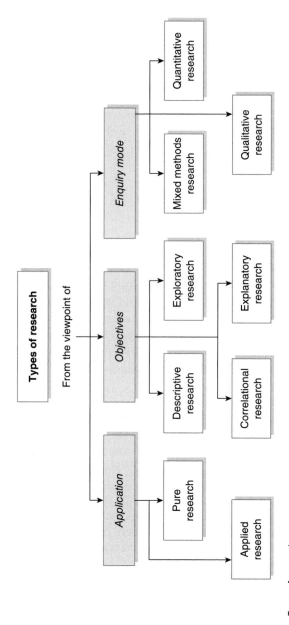

Figure 1.2 Types of research

people; and finding the best way of measuring people's attitudes. The knowledge produced through pure research is sought in order to add to the existing body of knowledge of research methods.

Most of the research in the social sciences is applied. In other words, the research techniques, procedures and methods that form the body of research methodology are applied to the collection of information about various aspects of a situation, issue, problem or phenomenon so that the information gathered can be used in other ways – such as for policy formulation, administration and the enhancement of understanding of a phenomenon.

Objectives perspective

If you examine a research study from the perspective of its objectives, broadly a research endeavour can be classified as descriptive, correlational, explanatory or exploratory.

A research study classified as a descriptive study attempts to describe systematically a situation, problem, phenomenon, service or programme, or provides information about, say, the living conditions of a community, or describes attitudes towards an issue. For example, it may attempt to describe the types of service provided by an organisation, the administrative structure of an organisation, the living conditions of Aboriginal people in the outback, the needs of a community, what it means to go through a divorce, how a child feels living in a house with domestic violence, or the attitudes of employees towards management. The main purpose of such studies is to describe what is prevalent with respect to the issue or problem under study.

The main emphasis in a correlational study is to discover or establish the existence of a relationship, association or interdependence between two or more aspects of a situation or phenomenon. For example, what is the impact of an advertising campaign on the sale of a product? What is the relationship between stressful living and the incidence of heart attack? What is the relationship between fertility and mortality? What is the relationship between technology and unemployment? What is the effect of a health service on the control of a disease, or the home environment on educational achievement?

Explanatory research attempts to clarify why and how there is a relationship between two aspects of a situation or phenomenon. This type of research attempts to explain, for example, why stressful living results in heart attacks; why a decline in mortality is followed by a fertility decline; or how the home environment affects children's level of academic achievement.

The fourth type of research, from the viewpoint of the objectives of a study, is called exploratory research. This is when a study is undertaken with the objective either of exploring an area where little is known or of investigating the possibilities of undertaking a particular research study. In many situations a study could have multiple objectives, that is, some parts of it could be descriptive, some correlational, and some explanatory. As a matter of fact a good study combines all three of these objectives. When the purpose of a study is to determine its feasibility, it is also called a feasibility study or a pilot study. It is usually carried out when a researcher wants to explore areas about which s/he has little or no knowledge. A small-scale study is undertaken to decide if it is worth carrying out a detailed investigation. On the basis of the assessment made during the exploratory study, a full study may eventuate. Exploratory studies are also conducted to develop, refine and/ or test measurement tools and procedures. Table 1.1 shows the types of research study from the viewpoint of objectives.

Although, theoretically, a research study can be classified in one of the above objectives-perspective categories, in practice, most studies are a combination of the first three; that is, they contain elements of descriptive, correlational and explanatory research. In this book the guidelines suggested for writing a research report encourage you to integrate these aspects.

Mode of enquiry perspective

Broadly, from the perspective of 'mode of enquiry', there are three approaches that are used in social research to find answers to your research questions. These are:

- the quantitative or structured approach;
- the qualitative or unstructured approach; and
- the mixed methods approach.

The core difference between the three is the extent of flexibility permitted to you as a researcher in the research process. In the quantitative or structured approach of enquiry everything that forms the research process – objectives, design, sample, the questions that you plan to ask of your respondents – is predetermined. The unstructured or qualitative approach, by contrast, allows you as a researcher complete flexibility in all these aspects of the process. The mixed methods approach has attributes from both the other approaches, that is, some aspects of the research process may have flexibility and others may completely lack it, depending upon the paradigm to which they belong.

The quantitative approach is rooted in the philosophy of rationalism; follows a rigid, structured and predetermined set of procedures to explore; aims to quantify the extent of variation in a phenomenon; emphasises the measurement of variables and the objectivity of the process; believes in substantiation on the basis of a large sample size; gives importance to the validity and reliability of findings; and communicates findings in an analytical and aggregate manner, drawing conclusions and inferences that can be generalised.

The qualitative approach, on the other hand, is embedded in the philosophy of empiricism; follows an open, flexible and unstructured approach to enquiry; aims to explore diversity rather than to quantify; emphasises the description and narration of feelings, perceptions and experiences rather than their measurement; and communicates findings in a descriptive and narrative rather than analytical manner, placing no or less emphasis on generalisations.

The mixed methods approach uses the strengths of both quantitative and qualitative research. It aims to select the best methods, regardless of the qualitative–quantitative divide, to find answers to the research questions. In extremely simple terms, the mixed methods approach to social research combines two or more methods to collect and analyse data pertaining to the research problem. These methods could be either a mix

Table 1.1 Types of research studies from the perspective of objectives

Examples	Aim	Main theme	Type of research
• Socioeconomic characteristics of residents of a community • Attitudes of students towards quality of teaching • Types of service provided by an agency • Needs of a community • Sale of a product • Attitudes of nurses towards death and dying • Attitudes of workers towards management • Number of people living in a community • Problems faced by new immigrants • Extent of occupational mobility among immigrants • Consumers' likes and dislikes with regard to a product • Effects of living in a house with domestic violence • Strategies put in place by a company to increase productivity of workers	To describe what is prevalent regarding: • a group of people • a community • a phenomenon • a situation • a programme • an outcome	To describe what is prevalent	Descriptive research
• Impact of a programme • Relationship between stressful living and incidence of heart attacks • Impact of technology on employment • Impact of maternal and child health services on infant mortality • Effectiveness of a marriage counselling service on extent of marital problems • Impact of an advertising campaign on sale of a product • Impact of incentives on productivity of workers • Effectiveness of an immunisation programme in controlling infectious disease	To establish or explore: • a relationship • an association • an interdependence	To ascertain if there is a relationship	Correlational research
• Why does stressful living result in heart attacks? • How does technology create unemployment/employment? • How do maternal and child health services affect infant mortality? • Why do some people have a positive attitude towards an issue while others do not? • Why does a particular intervention work for some people and not for others? • Why do some people use a product while others do not? • Why do some people migrate to another country while others do not? • Why do some people adopt a programme while others do not?	To explain: • why a relationship, association or interdependence exists • why a particular event occurs	To explain why the relationship is formed	Explanatory research

of quantitative and qualitative or belong to only one paradigm. The approach is based upon the rationale that for certain situations qualitative techniques are better and for some others the quantitative. Hence, to get the best outcome for a research study you need to combine both approaches or use more than one method.

The quantitative or structured approach is more appropriate to determine the *extent* of a problem, issue or phenomenon, whereas the qualitative or unstructured approach is predominantly used to explore its *nature,* in other words, the variation or diversity per se in a phenomenon, issue, problem or attitude towards an issue. For example, if you want to find out the different perspectives on an issue or the problems experienced by people living in a community, then these are better explored by using unstructured enquiries. On the other hand, to find out how many people have a particular perspective, how many people have a particular problem, or how many people hold a particular view, you need to have a structured approach to enquiry. If you need to look into these aspects, you will need to use both approaches, that is, you will need to use the mixed methods approach. Even if your interest is in finding out how many people have a particular problem or hold a particular view, before undertaking a structured enquiry, in the author's opinion, an unstructured enquiry must be undertaken to ascertain the diversity in a phenomenon which can then be quantified through a structured enquiry. Both approaches have their place in research. Both have their strengths as well as weaknesses. Therefore, you should not 'lock' yourself solely into a structured or unstructured approach.

The structured approach to enquiry, as you know, is classified as quantitative research and unstructured as qualitative research, and the mixed methods approach could be either entirely quantitative or qualitative or some sections could be qualitative and some quantitative. The divide between the two is based upon the philosophies of rationalism and empiricism and the difference in attitude towards acquiring knowledge. Rationalism is based upon the belief that 'human beings achieve knowledge because of their capacity to reason' and empiricism upon the belief that 'the only knowledge that human beings acquire is from sensory experiences' (Bernard 1994: 2). Mixed methods, as mentioned earlier, can combine the attributes of both. The distinction between quantitative, qualitative and mixed method research, in addition to the philosophies underpinning them and the structured/unstructured process of enquiry, is also dependent upon some other considerations which are briefly presented in Table 1.2. The choice between the quantitative, qualitative and mixed methods approaches should depend upon:

- the aim of your enquiry − exploration, confirmation or quantification;
- the use of the findings − policy formulation or process understanding.

A study is classified as qualitative if the purpose of the study is primarily to describe a situation, phenomenon, problem or event, that is, if the information is gathered through the use of variables measured on nominal or ordinal scales (qualitative measurement scales); and if the analysis is done to establish the variation in the situation, phenomenon or problem without quantifying it. The historical enumeration of events, an account of the different opinions people have about an issue, and a description of an observed situation such as the living conditions of a community are examples of qualitative research.

On the other hand, the study is classified as quantitative if you want to quantify the variation in a phenomenon, situation, problem or issue; if information is gathered using predominantly quantitative variables; and if the analysis is geared to ascertaining the magnitude of the variation. Examples of quantitative aspects of a research study are: how many people have a particular problem, and how many people hold a particular attitude.

The use of statistics is *not* an integral part of a quantitative study. The main function of statistics is to act as a test to confirm or contradict the conclusions that you have drawn on the basis of your understanding of analysed data. Statistics, among other things, help you to quantify the magnitude of an association or relationship, provide an indication of the confidence you can place in your findings and help you to isolate the effect of different variables.

It is strongly recommended that you do not lock yourself into becoming either solely a quantitative or solely a qualitative researcher. It is true that there are disciplines that lend themselves predominantly either to qualitative or to quantitative research. For example, such disciplines as anthropology, history and sociology are more inclined towards qualitative research, whereas psychology, epidemiology, education, economics, public health and marketing are more inclined towards quantitative research. However, this does not mean that an economist or a psychologist never uses the qualitative approach, or that an anthropologist never uses quantitative information. There is increasing recognition by most disciplines in the social sciences that both types of research are important for a good research study. The research problem itself should determine whether the study is carried out using quantitative or qualitative methodologies.

As both qualitative and quantitative approaches have their strengths and weaknesses, advantages and disadvantages, 'neither one is markedly superior to the other in all respects' (Ackroyd & Hughes 1992: 30). The measurement and analysis of the variables about which information is obtained in a research study are dependent upon the purpose of the study. In many studies you need to combine both qualitative and quantitative approaches. For example, suppose you want to find out the types of service available to victims of domestic violence in a city and the extent of their utilisation. Types of service are the qualitative aspect of the study as finding out about them entails description of the services. The extent of utilisation of the services is the quantitative aspect as it involves estimating the number of people who use the services and calculating other indicators that reflect the extent of utilisation. The mixed methods approach combines the strengths of both paradigms to best achieve the objectives of your research. It replaces those weaknesses of a design had we used methods from one paradigm only.

It is important for you to understand that, as compared to mixed methods, both quantitative and qualitative approaches have well-developed methodologies and methods. In most situations the methods and procedures of both quantitative and qualitative approaches are used in the mixed methods approach. Table 1.2 looks at the differences between the three from different perspectives.

Table 1.2   Differences between qualitative, quantitative and mixed methods approaches

Difference with respect to:	Quantitative approach	Qualitative approach	Mixed methods approach
Underpinning philosophy	Rationalism: 'That human beings achieve knowledge because of their capacity to reason' (Bernard 1994: 2)	Empiricism: 'The only knowledge that human beings acquire is from sensory experiences' (Bernard 1994: 2)	Both are valuable to social research theory and practice. That knowledge can be gained through both the capacity to reason and sensory experiences.
Approach to enquiry	Structured/rigid/predetermined methodology	Unstructured/flexible/open methodology	Can be structured, unstructured or both
Main purpose of investigation	To quantify the extent of variation in a phenomenon, situation, issue, etc.	To describe variation in a phenomenon, situation, issue, etc.	To quantify and/or explore with multiple or mixed methods a phenomenon to enhance accuracy or yield greater depth
Measurement of variables	Emphasis on some form of either measurement or classification of variables	Emphasis on description of variables	Measurement and/or description
Sample size	Emphasis on greater sample size	Fewer cases	Larger sample size for some aspects and smaller for others, depending upon the purpose
Focus of enquiry	Narrows focus in terms of extent of enquiry, but assembles required information from a greater number of respondents/sources	Covers multiple issues but assembles required information from fewer respondents	Narrow or broad, or both, depending upon the methods used
Dominant research topic	Explains prevalence, incidence, extent, nature of issues, opinions and attitude; discovers regularities and formulates theories	Explores experiences, meanings, perceptions and feelings	Both or either, depending upon the methods used
Analysis of data	Subjects variables to frequency distributions, cross-tabulations or other statistical procedures	Subjects responses, narratives or observational data to identification of themes and describes these	Quantitative or qualitative or both, depending upon the objectives
Dominant research value	Reliability and objectivity (value-free)	Authenticity, but does not claim to be value-free	Dominant value of one or both of the paradigms
Communication of findings	Organisation more analytical in nature, drawing inferences and conclusions, and testing magnitude and strength of a relationship	Organisation more descriptive and narrative in nature	Similar to the quantitative and/or qualitative approach

Important note to readers

Both quantitative and qualitative approaches have their own body of theoretical knowledge comprised of their common as well as respective methods, models and procedures. Their respective theoretical knowledge base, in this book, is detailed in relation to the operational steps which provide both the framework and the structure for the book. As the mixed methods approach is of very recent origin, to the best of the author's knowledge and understanding, it does not have an extensive body of methodological literature. It mostly uses methods, models and procedures of the quantitative and/or qualitative approaches. Therefore the book does not detail separately, under each operational step, the theoretical knowledge for the mixed methods approach.

When using mixed methods you first need to decide which methods are most appropriate to best achieve the objectives of your study. Specific methods and procedures that you are likely to use as a part of the mixed methods approach are mostly either quantitative or qualitative, hence, are detailed either as quantitative or qualitative methods and procedures in this book. To learn details about these methods you need to consult the pertinent sections describing quantitative or qualitative approaches.

The next section in this chapter provides details about different aspects such as definition, philosophy, advantages and disadvantages, forms of mixing of the mixed methods approach. It details aspects that will help you to develop a greater understanding of the mixed methods approach per se and provides background information about it as appropriate.

The sole aim of the section below is to provide you, as a beginner in research methods, information sufficient to give you some understanding of the mixed methods approach as such. Also, the emphasis is on providing practical knowledge rather than detailing historical, philosophical and conceptual issues and debates about it. In doing so an attempt is also made not to make things too complicated but simply to make you aware of the mixed methods approach to research enquiry. You can consult books on the mixed methods approach referenced in this book for greater understanding.

The mixed multiple methods approach

Introduction

Though the mixed methods approach in social research has been in use for a 'long time', it has attained its recognition and prominence only during the last two decades. According to Creswell and Clark (2011: xix) 'mixed methods has had its roots over the last 20 years in several disciplines'; however, 'in the past 5 to 10 years we have seen tremendous interest in this approach to research'. According to Teddlie and Tashakkori (2009: 7), 'The [mixed methods] research tradition is less well known than the [quantitative] or [qualitative] traditions because it has emerged as a separate orientation during only the past 20 years'. To the author's mind, it is more than a methodology but a philosophy that has come to be recognised as an approach during the last 20 years or so. It is based upon the assumption that for certain situations, to enhance the accuracy and meaningfulness of your conclusions, to have a complete picture of a situation, and to reconfirm your findings, you need to use more than one method belonging to one or both of the paradigms. The core of the mixed/multiple methods approach is the use of multiple methods belonging to both paradigms, or simply of more than one method from one paradigm. Many research experts (Bernard 1994; Brewer & Hunter 1989; Creswell & Clark 2011; Tashakkori & Teddlie 1998; Teddlie &

WHAT IS MIXED METHODS?

RESEARCH: A WAY OF THINKING   19

Tashakkori 2009) have advocated the use of mixed methods approach in social research. According to Bernard (1994: 1), 'whatever our theoretical orientation, a sound mix of qualitative and quantitative data is inevitable in any study of human thought and behaviour'. According to Brewer and Hunter (1989: 22), 'Since the fifties, the social sciences have grown tremendously. And with that growth, there is now virtually no major problem-area that is studied exclusively within one method.' According to Tashakkori and Teddlie (1998: 5), 'most major areas of research in social and behavioural sciences now use multiple methods as a matter of course'. Such studies that use more than two or more methods, either from one or both the paradigms, to enhance accuracy of the findings, are said to be using a mixed/multiple methods approach.

Defining the approach

TELLING A STORY
WITH MM

According to Creswell and Clark (2011: 2), 'several definitions for mixed methods have emerged over the years that incorporate various elements of methods, research processes, philosophy, and research design'. In extremely simple terms, mixed methods is an approach, rather a philosophy, to social enquiry that uses two or more methods, processes and (in certain situations) philosophies in undertaking a research study. It is based upon the belief that different paradigms and methods have different strengths and, for certain situations, their combined strength would result in improving the depth and accuracy of the findings. The mixed methods approach aims to best achieve the objectives of a study by combining the strengths of different methods and paradigms. According to Teddlie and Tashakkori (2009: 7), 'Mixed methodologists present an alternative to the QUAN and QUAL traditions by advocating the use of whatever methodological tools are required to answer the research questions under study'. According to them, 'mixed method studies are those that combine the qualitative and quantitative approaches into the research methodology of a single study or multi-phased study' (Tashakkori & Teddlie 1998: 17–18). Writers such as Bryman (2004) and Creswell and Clark (2007) also believe that to be called a mixed methods approach the methods you use must be from both the paradigms. According to Creswell and Clark (2007: 5), 'as a method, it focuses on collecting, analysing, and mixing both quantitative and qualitative data in a single study or series of studies. Its central premise is that the use of quantitative and qualitative approaches, in combination, provides a better understanding of research problems than either approach alone.' Tashakkori and Tedllie (1998: ix) define 'mixed methods as a combining of quantitative and qualitative approaches in the methodology of a study'. They consider the mixed methods design as one where you mix quantitative and qualitative methods. Johnson et al. (2007: 113) define mixed methods research as 'the type of research in which a researcher or team of researchers combine elements of qualitative and quantitative research approaches (e.g., use of qualitative and quantitative viewpoints, data collection, analysis, inference techniques) for the purposes, breadth, depth of understanding, and corroboration.'

However, there are others such as Alexander et al. (in Gilbert 2008: 126) who consider an approach to be a mixed methods approach even if the methods used are from only one paradigm, that is, two or more methods could be from both the paradigms or they can be from one of them. According to them, 'mixed methods research seems, self-evidently, to be the use of two or more methods in a single research project (or research programme)'. Writers such as Cronin et al. (2007) also subscribe to the view of Alexander et al. They 'suggest that those studies that even use two different quantitative or qualitative methods can be said to be using a mixed methods approach'.

It is evident from the above definitions that there are two opinions with respect to the definition of a mixed method study (Figure 1.3). The first advocates that the two methods must be from both the paradigms, that is, one must mix quantitative and qualitative methods (Teddlie & Tashakkori 2009; Tashakkori & Teddlie 1998; Bryman 2004; Cresswell & Clark 2007). The second suggests that even if both the methods are from the same paradigm, a study using two methods is considered as a mixed methods study (Gilbert 2008; Chapter 7, Cronin et al. 2007). The present author also believes that for a study to be classified as a mixed methods study, the two or more methods it uses could come from either or both the paradigms.

Though the term 'multiple methods approach' is not much in use nowadays or is used interchangeably with 'mixed methods approach' by some, the author makes a distinction

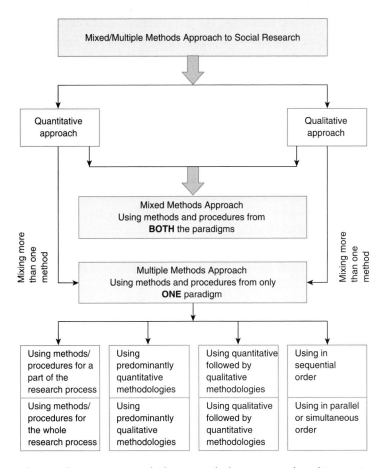

Figure 1.3   Mixed/multiple methods, quantitative and qualitative approaches in social research

between 'multiple' and 'mixed' methods approaches. The term 'mixed methods', according to the author, is used for situations where different elements of the research process are combined from both the quantitative and qualitative approaches, and 'multiple methods' when the methods selected are from one paradigm only.

Combining or mixing of different methods in both these viewpoints is done with the aim of taking advantage of the strengths of both paradigms, and, in the case of multiple methods belonging to the same paradigm, of enhancing and enriching the accuracy, validity and reliability of the findings. There is no single approach that, always and in all situations, can accurately find answers to all your research questions. In some situations you need to use different methods for different research questions or objectives that guide your study. Also there are situations 'in which one data source may be insufficient, results need to be explained, exploratory findings need to be generalized, a second method is needed to enhance a primary method, a theoretical stance needs to be employed, and an overall research objective can be best addressed with multiple phases or projects' (Creswell & Clark 2011: 8). The mixed/multiple methods approach lets you choose the methods that are best suited for your study from within or across paradigms.

There is another consideration you need to keep in mind when defining a mixed methods approach. Many researchers often use two different methods, quantitative and/or qualitative, for only one operational step, that of data collection. For example, you may conduct in-depth interviews with some members of the study population to further understand the issues identified by them in the data collected through the use of a questionnaire. A similar situation is when, for example, you want to develop a questionnaire to ascertain the needs of a community and, to do so, you conduct a number of in-depth or focus group interviews with some of the community members or organise a community forum to establish the diversity of needs. This process of identifying the diversity of needs becomes the basis for developing the questionnaire or interview schedule. The issue is: do you classify such studies as mixed or multiple methods studies where you use more than one method only for collecting data? The complete replication of a study, using two approaches, is quite expensive and hence not common. The author considers a study to be using multiple or mixed methods approach even though it uses more than one method for a single operational step. In the author's opinion the use of more than one method in the following situations will qualify a study to be classified as using a mixed/multiple methods approach:

- Collecting data using different methods for information gathering, that is, you can collect the same data through a questionnaire or an interview schedule (quantitative methods) as well as through in-depth interviews, focus groups or a community forum (qualitative methods). Using multiple methods for data collection will qualify a study to be classified as mixed/multiple methods (depending upon whether the methods are from both or single paradigm). Of course, you also need to use different methods for data analysis and processing to match with the methods of data collection.
- Collecting the required information from different groups of people, for verification and confirmation of findings, drawn from the same study population (different samples). In other words, selecting one sample for administering, say, a questionnaire, selecting another for in-depth interviewing and selecting the third to form a focus group for gathering similar information for validation, verification and greater understanding of the issues.

- Using different ways of data analysis and information dissemination, that is, analysing data with quantitative as well as qualitative techniques to best achieve the objectives of a study.

Tashakkori and Teddlie (1998) differentiate between the two by using two different names. According to them (p. 1), 'mixed methods combine the qualitative and quantitative approaches to the research methods of a study, while mixed models studies combine these two approaches across all phases of the research process'. In the author's opinion it is the use of two or more methods, either quantitative, qualitative or both, for the whole or a part(s) of the research process, that constitutes the mixed/multiple methods approach.

It is important for you to understand that the way you formulate your research problem or subobjective(s) determines the types of method that are appropriate for finding their answers. Let us take an example (Figure 1.4) to further understand the relationship between the way a subobjective is formulated and the types of method that are appropriate to study it and how the methods used determine the typology of the approach adopted. Also note that to achieve different objectives you need to use different research approaches. For some it is purely quantitative, for some purely qualitative and for some it is a mixed methods approach.

Suppose you are interested in the area of domestic violence and want to conduct a study with the following subobjectives (you can select just one subobjective to study if you wish):

1. to determine the prevalence of domestic violence in a community;
2. to understand the nature and extent of domestic violence in the community;
3. to find out what it means for a woman and a man to live in a household with domestic violence;
4. to understand why, in spite of domestic violence, some victims, men as well as women, continue to live in the relationship;

Suppose you are interested in the area of domestic violence and want to conduct a study with the following sub-objectives (you can select even one sub-objective to study if you so desire):

1. To determine the prevalence of domestic violence in a community;
2. To understand the nature and extent of domestic violence in the community;
3. To find out what it means for a woman and a man to live in a household with domestic violence;
4. To understand why, in spite of domestic violence, some women continue to live in the relationship;
5. To describe the types of service available to victims of domestic violence in a community; and
6. To establish the socio-economic demographic profile of people who are consumers of these services.

To achieve these objectives, the study needs to be carried out by using different methods. For example:

Sub-objective 1 can only be studied through methods that fall into the category of quantitative methods (counting the number of households with domestic violence episodes determined by using a predetermined and accepted set of criteria).

For sub-objective 2, you need to use methods that fall into both the paradigms. 'Nature' of domestic violence can best be explored through methods (such as in-depth interviews, focus groups, narratives, oral histories) that fall in the domain of qualitative research and 'extent' through

---

(Continued)

Figure 1.4 (Continued)

methods (such as structured household interview, records of agencies providing services to victims of domestic violence) that are considered to be belonging to the quantitative paradigm.

Sub-objective 3 can best be explored using qualitative methodology (in-depth interviews, group interviews with victims, narratives, oral histories, case studies), as no quantitative method will give you more accurate information on 'what does it mean' to a victim to live in a house with domestic violence.

The reasons for living in the relationship in spite of violence (sub-objective 4), can be investigated through a number of methods belonging to both paradigms (you can conduct in-depth interviews, structured interviews, group interviews, focus groups. You can collect information through one method only or through a number of them).

Similarly 'types of service' (sub-objective 5) can best be studied through a qualitative approach (in-depth interviews with service providers and consumers of the services).

And

The 'profile of consumers' (sub-objective 6), can be better investigated by quantitative methods (questionnaire or interview schedule).

Figure 1.4 Use of mixed and multiple methods – an example

5. to describe the types of service available to victims of domestic violence in a community; and
6. to establish the socioeconomic-demographic profile of people who are consumers of these services.

To achieve these objectives, the study needs to be carried out by using different methods. For example:

Subobjective 1 can only be studied through methods that fall into the quantitative category (counting the number of households with domestic violence episodes determined by using a predetermined and accepted set of criteria).

For subobjective 2, you need to use methods that fall into both paradigms. The 'nature' of domestic violence can best be explored through qualitative methods (such as in-depth interviews, focus groups, narratives, oral histories) and its 'extent' through quantitative methods (such as structured household interview, records of agencies providing services to victims of domestic violence).

Subobjective 3 you can best explore using a qualitative methodology (in-depth interviews, group interviews with victims, narratives, oral histories, case studies) as no quantitative method will give you more accurate information on 'what it means' to a victim to live in a house with domestic violence.

The reasons for living in the relationship in spite of violence (subobjective 4) can be investigated through a number of methods belonging to both paradigms (you can conduct in-depth interviews, structured interviews, group interviews, focus groups). You can collect information using one method only or a number of them.

Similarly 'types of service' (subobjective 5) you can best study through a qualitative approach (in-depth interviews with service providers and consumers of the services).

Finally, the 'profile of consumers' (subobjective 6) is best investigated by quantitative methods (questionnaire or interview schedule).

In the above example you will note that we have proposed different methods for different subobjectives of the study. Studies like this that make use of the strengths of different methods, irrespective of the paradigm they belong to and make use of multiple methods belonging to the same paradigm, are classified as mixed or multiple methods studies. If the methods used are from both paradigms, it is a mixed methods study and if they are from the same paradigm, it is a multiple method study. In brief, any study that uses more than one method belonging to either one and/or the other paradigm for either the total or partial research process, to best achieve the objectives of a study, is classified as mixed/multiple methods study.

Rationale underpinning the approach

The rationale underpinning the mixed/multiple methods approach is primarily based upon two beliefs. The first relates to the ability of the methods of a paradigm to provide accurate answers to all your research questions in all situations. The second relates to the belief that the use of more than one method in most situations will provide a better and more complete picture of a situation or phenomenon than a single method alone. Specifically, these beliefs are:

* The way you formulate your subobjectives determines whether a study would lend itself to a quantitative or qualitative mode of enquiry. Most of the time a study has several subobjectives (Figure 1.4) not all of which lend themselves to be extensively and accurately explored by the methods of a single paradigm. It often happens that some subobjectives are better explored through quantitative methods and others through qualitative methods. In situations like this if you use methods from only one paradigm, you will compromise the quality of your findings. The mixed methods approach is based upon the belief that, in certain situations, use of methods from both the paradigms will certainly enhance the accuracy and reliability of the findings. Openness to the use of methods from both paradigms in a study to best achieve its objectives is the underpinning philosophy of the mixed methods approach.
* In certain circumstances a single method may not provide a complete, detailed and accurate picture of the situation. Or, in some instances, to be absolutely certain you may want to double-check your findings by using another method. The use of multiple methods is based upon the belief that in certain situations the accuracy of your findings can be enhanced by using more than one method from a paradigm.

When to use the approach

Several reasons warrant the use of mixed or multiple methods approach. Some of these reasons are as follows:

* When you want to explore from both perspectives. Qualitative and quantitative research will look at a phenomenon from different perspectives. The qualitative perspective looks at the phenomenon in depth but is based upon information collected from a few individuals, hence, is limiting in making generalisations and broad conclusions. On the other hand, the quantitative approach gathers information from many individuals so that it has the ability to make generalisations but is limited in terms of in-depth analysis. Taking a purely quantitative or purely qualitative approach would give the study the strengths as well weaknesses of the approach. It is to overcome the weaknesses of the approach and make use of the strengths of the other approach that you combine both. By combining both perspectives you can have a more complete picture and understanding of a phenomenon from both perspectives.

RESEARCH: A WAY OF THINKING   25

- **When accurate and complete information from one source is difficult to obtain.** Sometimes there are situations when you are unable to have complete and accurate information about a situation through the use of a single method from either approach. To fill such gaps you need to supplement the information by other methods, thus taking a mixed methods approach. According to Creswell and Clark (2011: 8), 'research problems suited for mixed methods are those in which one data source may be insufficient, results need to be explained, exploratory findings need to be generalized, a second method is needed to enhance a primary method, a theoretical stance needs to be employed, and an overall research objective can be best addressed with multiple phases or projects'. The author was involved in a study to ascertain the number of births and deaths in rural India. To accurately estimate the number of births and deaths two secondary and two primary sources were used. These included: records kept by a government-appointed official responsible for maintaining vital statistics records in rural areas (secondary source); a village midwife who every fortnight was visited by a member of the research team to collect, through informal interviewing, information on births and deaths during the previous fortnight (primary source); ten 'key informants' selected from the residents of the village for the duration of the study and who were contacted every fortnight by a member of the research team (primary source); and the resident midwife nurse, an employee of the research team, who was responsible for sending a monthly report on birth and deaths in her area during the previous month (secondary source). All these reports were compared (tri-angulated) to ascertain the total number of births and deaths in the area. It is in situations like this, where you want to collect factual information on a longitudinal basis and want to be sure of the accuracy of the information, that you need to use more than one method, the mixed/multiple methods approach.
- **A must for good quality research.** Almost every good researcher who aims to undertake a study in order to make generalisations first explores different aspects of the study by undertaking an explor-atory phase which mostly uses qualitative methodology. Everything needed for a quantitative study is usually developed on the basis of an exploratory study. It is also not uncommon that after complet-ing the study you take your findings back to the respondents for explanations and clarifications. In the author's opinion a good researcher always follows a 'qualitative–quantitative–qualitative' cycle of enquiry. Hence, to enhance the quality of your research, you need to mix both approaches and on occasions use more than one method.
- **When you need to make generalisations.** When your aim is to make generalisations on the basis of your study as well as share the findings with the study population, it is good practice to develop issues you want to explore and questions you would like to ask your respondents, in consultation with poten-tial respondents. Development and sharing can best be undertaken by qualitative approaches. In such situations you need to combine both qualitative and quantitative methodologies.
- **When you need to find an explanation for your findings.** There are situations when the findings from a quantitative approach need elaboration as to the exact meaning of the responses given by the respondents. These exact meanings can only be understood when discussed with the respondents. In such situations you need to combine quantitative methods with qualitative ones to further understand the responses. According to Creswell and Clark (2011: 9), 'Sometimes the result of a study may provide an incomplete understanding of a research problem and there is a need for further explanation. In this case, a mixed methods study is used with the second database helping to explain the first database. A typical situation is when quantitative results require an explanation as to what they mean.'
- **When you want to develop a good data collection instrument and ascertain the validity of the questions.** It is a common practice in quantitative studies to develop data collection instruments in consultation with the potential respondents to ensure their relevance. This consultative process entails the use of qualitative methodologies. In addition, this process will ensure the validity of the questions by exploring whether or not the respondents interpreted and understood them as intended by the researcher.

- **When you undertake studies with multiple objectives.** Situations when a study has multiple objectives and not all of them lend themselves to a single approach warrant the collection of data through the use of either quantitative and qualitative approaches or having two sets of data collected through two either quantitative or qualitative methods.

Ways of mixing methods

DEVELOPING MM
RESEARCH

The 'typology' developed here does not strictly reflect the study designs per se but the different ways in which methods and procedures from quantitative and qualitative approaches are mixed with regard to when, what, at what stage, in what order and to what extent. The designs, procedures and methods are primarily those of quantitative and/or qualitative research.

There are several ways in which you can mix methods and procedures belonging to quantitative and/or qualitative paradigms in mixed or multiple methods studies. The types of *mixed methods study design*, as identified by Tashakkori and Teddlie (1998: 18), according to the author, are primarily based upon the way the methods are mixed. The author feels that the classification or 'typology of studies' within mixed and multiple methodologies predominantly depends upon *what* is being mixed (whether mixing is from both paradigms or just one), *when* in the research process the mixing is done (whether mixing is in a sequential or simultaneous order), *at what stage* of the research process mixing is taking place (whether mixing is for a part or whole of the research process), *in what order* mixing occurs (whether it is qualitative followed by quantitative or quantitative followed by qualitative or both together), and *to what extent* (whether predominantly quantitative or qualitative).

In terms of *what*, there are broadly two ways in which you can mix different methods:

- Mix methods belonging to both paradigms either for the whole or a part of the research process.
- Mix methods belonging to only one paradigm either for the whole or a part of the process.

In terms of *when*, again there are two ways:

- Use two or more methods one after the other (sequentially) either for the whole research process or a part of it. Creswell (1995: 177) calls studies using methods one after the other as *sequential studies*.
- Use two or more methods concurrently either for the whole or a part of the process. Creswell (1995: 177) calls studies using methods concurrently *parallel* or *simultaneous* studies.

In terms of *stage*, there are two ways:

- Mix them for the whole of the research process.
- Mix them only for one or some operational steps.

In term of *order*, there are three ways in which you can mix methods:

- Use qualitative methods followed by quantitative.
- Use quantitative methods followed by qualitative.
- Use qualitative methods followed by quantitative followed again by qualitative.

In terms of *extent,* there are two ways of mixing:

- Use both methodologies equally (equivalent status studies: **Creswell** 1995: 177).
- Use one methodology predominantly (dominant/less dominant studies: **Creswell** 1995: 177). When, in conducting a study, the methods are mixed in such a way that one paradigm dominates, with a small proportion of the methods/procedures drawn from the other.

Advantages and disadvantages

The use of mixed methods in a research project has both advantages as well as disadvantages. Some of the main advantages are as follows:

- Enhancement of research possibilities. In situations where you have multiple objectives to achieve in a research study and if not all the objectives lend themselves to be explored with one method, use of multiple methods offers a way to find answers to all your research questions. For instance, in the example in Figure 1.4, subobjective 2 has two dimensions, 'nature' and 'extent'. These two concepts require different methodologies. 'Nature' can be explored more richly through qualitative methods, whereas 'extent' is better explored through quantitative methods as it involves counting the number of households with occurrence of domestic violence. Similarly, suppose you want to ascertain the prevalence of drug use in a community and the process of becoming a drug addict. The first part you can investigate through a number of methods such as structured interviewing or a questionnaire, but the second part is best investigated by unstructured and in-depth interviewing. Thus, the use of mixed/multiple methods approach enhances the research possibilities within the framework of a study.
- Better for more complex situations. Another important advantage of a mixed methods approach is that it provides freedom to use the best methods, irrespective of their paradigm, in more complex situations. We are often confronted with situations with complex structure and dimensions that warrant investigation by multiple methods not only within a paradigm but also across paradigms. A mixed/multiple methods approach provides such freedom and flexibility. According to Creswell and Clark (2011: 21), 'the complexity of our research problems call for answers beyond simple numbers in a quantitative sense or words in a qualitative sense. A combination of both forms of data provides the most complete analysis of problems.'
- Enrichment of data. There are situations when you collect data with one method but for its supplementation or enrichment you need another set of data. The second set of data primarily looks at the issues from a different perspective. This triangulation enriches the information and enhances the accuracy of the findings and is only possible when a mixed/multiple methods approach is used in undertaking a study. Let us take another example (Figure 1.5), in which the author was involved, that used non-participant observation as a method of data collection but with the recording done, on the spot, in two different formats (descriptive and categorical). Though the data was collected by one method, two different methods of observation recording were employed. Some of the subsequent steps – the analysis and communication of the findings – were treated in two different ways appropriate to the manner in which the data was collected. This enrichment of data was possible only because of the use of mixed methods in recording and subsequent steps that followed.
- Collecting additional research evidence. For complex and important situations, where you want further evidence to support or contradict your argument, collection of data by two different methods makes good sense. The second set is used for comparison and confirmation or contradiction of the findings of the first method.

The author was involved in a study designed to develop a service delivery model for maternal and child health services for rural India. To work out the worker–population ratio, data was collected through a 'two-minute-instantaneous' non-participant observation of the activities being carried out by service delivery workers, on randomly selected days, over four years, taking into consideration the periods of fluctuations in the workload due to seasonality. Different categories of health workers, when delivering services in real-life situations, were observed by an observer every two minutes and their activities were recorded in descriptive as well as predetermined service-activity categories (developed on the basis of pre-test phase) by the observers. Information gathered through descriptive recording was thematically analysed to ascertain the activities carried out by the workers and amount of time spent on each one of them. The data gathered through categorical recording was similarly analysed to establish the time spent on each activity. The two sets of data were compared (triangulated) to ascertain the various activities carried out by the workers and the average time spent on each one of them to form the basis of establishing the optimal worker–population ratio for the service delivery model.

Figure 1.5   Mixed/multiple methods study – an example

Some of the disadvantages are as follows:

- **More data means more work and resources**. Collecting data through two or more methods means more data to collect and analyse, resulting in more time, financial resources, effort and technical expertise. Instead of one data set you have at least two data sets to handle for data collection, analysis, processing and information dissemination.
- **Requires additional and diverse skills**. As multi-methods studies use different methods belonging to both quantitative and/or qualitative paradigms, you need to be reasonably well versed in all those methods and procedures that you are likely to use, requiring a wider skill set than for single-method studies. You need to have knowledge and skills in data collection methods that you are proposing to use. Similarly, you need to be competent in data analysis methods suitable for different methods of data collection. Finally, you need to be well versed in data triangulation and information dissemination for different sets of data.
- **Contacting two study populations**. Using a mixed methods design may involve contacting and establishing rapport with two or more different study populations, with all that that entails.
- **Resolving disagreements in data**. You may discover a significant disagreement between the data sets. How do you decide as to the reliability of a set of data?

Considerations to be kept in mind

You need to keep in mind a number of things when using a mixed methods approach:

- Make sure you have sufficient time to complete the additional tasks. Using different methodologies means more work for the whole research project.
- You also need to be sure that you have the required technical expertise to develop and/or undertake different methods and procedures.
- You need to decide how to resolve inconsistencies, if encountered, in the findings.
- How will the findings of different methods be communicated? Will they be triangulated, integrated or communicated in a parallel manner?

RESEARCH: A WAY OF THINKING   29

Situations in which the approach can be used

A number of reasons justify the use of mixed/multiple methods approaches in social research. To illustrate we will take some examples. The overriding reason for using the mixed/multiple methods approach is the desire to enhance the coverage, depth, reliability and validation of your findings through the use of another method(s). Specifically, multiple methods can be used in the following situations:

1. When, in your opinion, an aspect of your study, either methodologically or within the financial constraints, cannot be reliably investigated through the main research approach you have adopted. To gain a deeper, complete and/or reliable understanding of the subaspects of your study, you may need to use another method. Investigation by another method will hopefully provide you with more accurate information about some aspects of your study. For example, suppose you are conducting a study to ascertain the recreational needs of youth in a community and the community's attitudes towards the desirability of those needs. Also suppose you are ascertaining recreational needs by interviewing a random sample of young people. You do not have enough resources to interview a sample of members of the community and, therefore, you decide to set up a community forum for the purpose. In this situation you are using two methods to find out about different aspects of your study that cannot be investigated in the same manner because of lack of resources. Studies like this will be classified as using a mixed methods approach which, in this example, is using both quantitative and qualitative methods.

2. There are situations when you use a particular research approach to find answers to research questions, but, to be doubly sure, you want to compare your findings with the findings determined by another approach. We again take the example of the study designed to determine the needs of youth in a community. To enhance the accuracy and reliability of your findings, you may use a number of methods. For example, you can ascertain the perceived recreational needs of young people by carrying out in-depth interviews of a sample, holding a focus group and holding a community forum. Triangulation of the findings from all three sources will provide you with enriched information. The study will be classified as multiple methods study as it is using three methods, all qualitative, to find answers to your research questions. If, instead of in-depth interviewing, you had used a structured questionnaire or interview schedule (both quantitative techniques), the study, according to the typology suggested by the author, would have been classified as mixed methods study (as you are using quantitative as well as qualitative methods). Such approaches help you to cross-check your findings to ensure their reliability so that you can place greater confidence in your findings, albeit at the risk of creating other problems if there are marked differences between the sources.

Paradigms of research

Although there are two main paradigms (quantitative and qualitative) that form the basis of research methodology in the social sciences, the mixed methods paradigm has also emerged during the last two decades as a third approach. Mixed methods, though considered as an approach to social enquiry, has not yet developed its own body of investigative methods and procedures. It mostly uses the methods and procedures of quantitative and qualitative approaches.

The crucial question that divides the two dominant paradigms is whether the methodology of the physical sciences can be applied to the study of social phenomena. The paradigm that is rooted in the physical sciences is called the quantitative, systematic, scientific or positivist approach to social enquiry. The opposite paradigm has come to be known as the qualitative, ethnographic, ecological or naturalistic approach. The advocates of the two opposing sides have developed their own values, terminology, methods and techniques to understand social phenomena. However, since the mid-1960s there has been a growing recognition that both paradigms have their place, and this has led to the mixed methods approach to social enquiry. The author feels very strongly that it is the purpose for which a research activity is undertaken that should determine the mode of enquiry, hence the paradigm. To indiscriminately apply one approach to all research problems can be misleading and inappropriate. Combining quantitative and qualitative methods is a very powerful methodology and should be used where warranted with full realisation that it entails diverse and/or additional knowledge about different approaches to research.

A positivist paradigm lends itself to both quantitative and qualitative data. The author makes a distinction between qualitative data, on the one hand, and qualitative research, on the other, as the former is confined to the measurement of variables, mostly on nominal and ordinary measurement scales, and the latter to the use of a qualitative research methodology.

The author believes that no matter what paradigm the researcher works within, s/he should adhere to certain values regarding the control of bias and the maintenance of objectivity in terms of both the research process itself and the conclusions drawn. It is the application of these values to the process of information gathering, analysis and interpretation that enables it to be called a research process.

Summary

There are several ways of collecting and understanding information and finding answers to your questions – research is one way. The difference between research and other ways of obtaining answers to your questions is that in a process that is classified as research, you work within a framework of a set of philosophies, use methods that have been tested for validity and reliability, and attempt to be unbiased and objective.

Research has many applications. You need to have research skills to be an effective service provider, administrator/manager or planner. As a professional who has a responsibility to enhance professional knowledge, research skills are essential.

The typology of research can be looked at from three perspectives: application, objectives and the mode of enquiry. From the point of view of the application of research, there is applied and pure research. Most of the research undertaken in the social sciences is applied, the findings being intended either for use in understanding a phenomenon/issue or to bring change in a programme/situation. Pure research is academic in nature and is undertaken in order to gain knowledge about phenomena that may or may not have applications in the near future, and to develop new techniques and procedures that form the body of research methodology.

A research study can be carried out with four objectives: to describe a situation, phenomenon, problem or issue (descriptive research); to establish or explore a relationship between two or more variables (correlational research); to explain why certain things happen the way they do (explanatory research); and to examine the feasibility of conducting a study or exploring a subject area where nothing or little is known (exploratory research).

From the point of view of the mode of enquiry, there are three types of research: quantitative (structured approach), qualitative (unstructured approach) and mixed or multiple methods (structured and/or unstructured approach). The main objective of a qualitative study is to describe the variation and diversity in a phenomenon, situation or attitude with a very flexible approach so as to identify as much variation and diversity as possible, while quantitative research, in addition, helps you to quantify the variation and diversity. The use of mixed methods aims to draw on the strengths of the other approaches, that is, it uses the best of both the paradigms to enhance the accuracy, depth and reliability of the findings. There are many who strongly advocate a combined approach to social enquiry, that is, use of mixed/multiple methods. The author is strongly in favour of the qualitative–quantitative–qualitative cycle of enquiry. The author feels strongly that it is purpose of research rather than the belief in a paradigm that should determine the mode of enquiry.

FOR YOU TO THINK ABOUT

- Refamiliarise yourself with the keywords listed at the beginning of this chapter, and if you are uncertain about the meaning or application of any of them revisit them in the chapter before moving on.
- Consider how you would go about convincing a service provider that evidence-based research might benefit them.
- Identify two or three research questions, related to your own academic field or professional area, that could be answered by undertaking each of the following types of research:

  - ☐ descriptive research;
  - ☐ correlational research;
  - ☐ explanatory research;
  - ☐ exploratory research.

- Consider how the three approaches to research – quantitative, qualitative and mixed/multiple methods – could be applied to improve your practice in your own professional area.

Having worked through the chapter, you should be able to answer the following:

- What is research? What should be the requirements for a process to be called a research process?
- How can research provide evidence for your practice?
- What are the different approaches to research, and what are the differences between them?
- Research can be classified from different perspectives. Describe the typology of research from these perspectives.
- Do you consider mixed/multiple methods approach as a third paradigm of research? Give reasons for your answer.

 Want to learn more? Visit
http://www.uk.sagepub.com/kumar4e
or scan this QR code to gain access to a range of online resources to support your study including practice quizzes, videos, weblinks, flashcards, and journal articles.

2

THE RESEARCH PROCESS: A QUICK GLANCE

In this chapter you will learn about

- The eight-step model for carrying out research
- The different phases of the process

Phase A: Deciding what to research

- Step I: Formulating a research problem

Phase B: Planning a research study

- Step II: Conceptualising a research design
- Step III: Constructing an instrument for data collection
- Step IV: Selecting a sample
- Step V: Writing a research proposal

Phase C: Conducting a research study

- Step VI: Collecting data
- Step VII: Processing and displaying data
- Step VIII: Writing a research report

Keywords

data, data display,
data processing,
empiricism, hypotheses,
interview schedule,
non-probability sample,
primary data,
probability sample,

qualitative research,
questionnaire, rationalism,
reliability, research design,
research instrument,
research objectives,
research problem,
research proposal,

sample, sample size,
sampling design,
secondary data,
study design,
unstructured interview,
validity,
variables.

At the end of this chapter, you should have an understanding of

- The research process and its operational steps
- What it involves to undertake a research study
- The relationship between the research process and the theoretical knowledge needed

The research process: an eight-step model

Research methodology and methods are taught in several ways in many academic disciplines at various levels by people committed to a variety of research paradigms. Though paradigms vary in their contents and substance, their broad approach to enquiry, in the author's opinion, is similar. Such ideas have also been expressed by Festinger and Katz, who in the foreword to their book *Research Methods in Behavioral Sciences* say: 'Although the basic logic of scientific methodology is the same in all fields, its specific techniques and approaches will vary, depending upon the subject matter' (1966: vi). Therefore, the model developed here is generic in nature and can be applied to a number of disciplines in the social sciences. It is based upon a practical and step-by-step approach to research enquiry that at each step provides a smorgasbord of methods, models and procedures to choose from.

Broadly, a research process is very similar to undertaking a journey. Suppose you want to go out for a drive. Before you start, you must decide where you want to go and then which route to take. If you know the route, you do not need to consult a map, but, if you do not know the route, then you need to use one. Your problem is compounded if there is more than one route. You need to decide which one to take. Similarly, for a research journey there are also two important decisions to make. The first is to decide *what you want to find out about* or, in other words, what research questions you want to find answers to. Having decided upon your research questions or research problems, you then need to decide *how to go about finding their answers*. The path to finding answers to your research questions constitutes research methodology. Just as there are signposts along the way as you travel to your destination, so there are practical steps through which you must pass on your research journey in order to find the answers to your research questions (Figure 2.1). The sequence of these steps is not fixed, and with experience you can change it. At each operational step in the research process you are required to choose from a multiplicity of methods, procedures and models of research

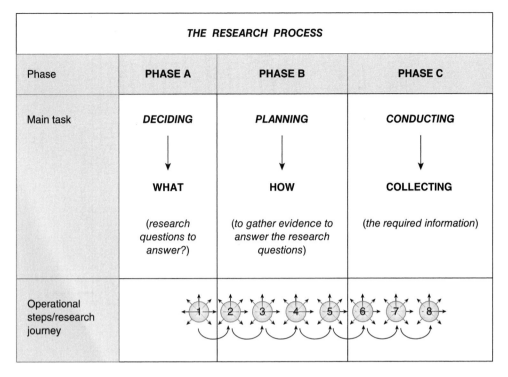

THE RESEARCH PROCESS			
Phase	**PHASE A**	**PHASE B**	**PHASE C**
Main task	**DECIDING** ↓ **WHAT** *(research questions to answer?)*	**PLANNING** ↓ **HOW** *(to gather evidence to answer the research questions)*	**CONDUCTING** ↓ **COLLECTING** *(the required information)*
Operational steps/research journey			

Figure 2.1 The research journey – touch each post and select methods and procedures appropriate for your journey

methodology which will help you best achieve your research objectives. This is where your knowledge base of research methodology plays a crucial role.

The aim of this book is to provide you with knowledge that will enable you to select the most appropriate methods and procedures. The strength of this book lies in anchoring the theoretical knowledge of the steps that you need to go through on your research journey. At each operational step, the book aims to provide, at a beginner's level, knowledge of methods and procedures used by both qualitative and quantitative researchers, though there is an inclination towards the quantitative way of thinking.

Quantitative and qualitative research methodologies differ both in their underpinning philosophy and, to some extent, in the methods, models and procedures used. Though the research process is broadly the same in both, quantitative and qualitative research are differentiated in terms of the methods of data collection, the procedures adopted for data processing and analysis, and the style of communication of the findings. For example, if your research problem lends itself to a qualitative mode of enquiry, you are more likely to use the *unstructured interview* or *observation* as your method of data collection. When analysing data in qualitative research, you go through the process of identifying themes and describing what you have found out during your interviews or observation rather than subjecting your data to statistical procedures. The mixed methods approach to a research enquiry basically uses methods and procedures of quantitative and/or qualitative

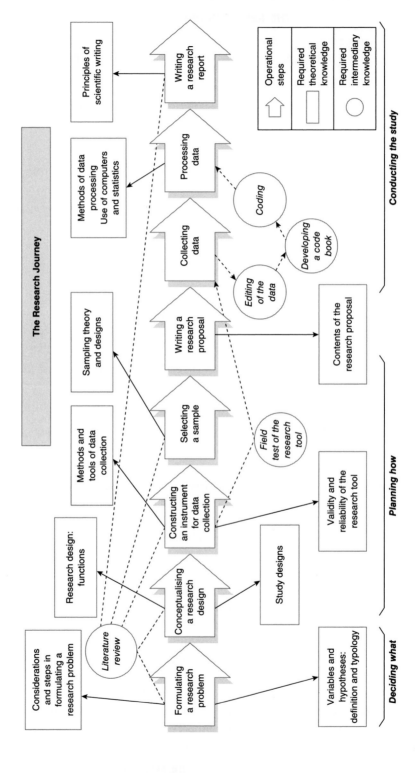

Figure 2.2 The research process

Operational steps and research methodology

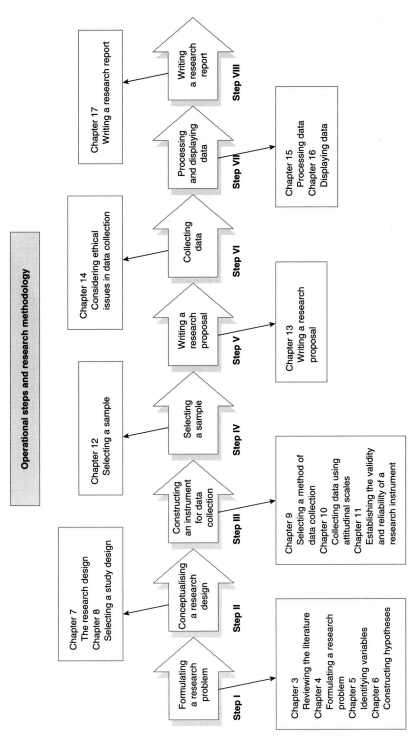

Step I — Formulating a research problem
- Chapter 3 Reviewing the literature
- Chapter 4 Formulating a research problem
- Chapter 5 Identifying variables
- Chapter 6 Constructing hypotheses

Step II — Conceptualising a research design
- Chapter 7 The research design
- Chapter 8 Selecting a study design

Step III — Constructing an instrument for data collection
- Chapter 9 Selecting a method of data collection
- Chapter 10 Collecting data using attitudinal scales
- Chapter 11 Establishing the validity and reliability of a research instrument

Step IV — Selecting a sample
- Chapter 12 Selecting a sample

Step V — Writing a research proposal
- Chapter 13 Writing a research proposal

Step VI — Collecting data
- Chapter 14 Considering ethical issues in data collection

Step VII — Processing and displaying data
- Chapter 15 Processing data
- Chapter 16 Displaying data

Step VIII — Writing a research report
- Chapter 17 Writing a research report

Figure 2.3   The chapters in the book in relation to the operational steps

approaches. Table 1.2 in Chapter 1 compares the qualitative, quantitative and mixed methods approaches to research from different perspectives.

Since, at a number of steps of the research process, the choice of methods and procedures is influenced by the quantitative–qualitative distinction, the methods and procedures discussed in some of the chapters in this book are dealt with separately under qualitative and quantitative sections of the methodology, even though the author does not attach importance to this distinction. The author has tried to minimise this distinction as a number of methods and procedures are applicable to both. Also note that this book is for beginners, it does not cover extensively each method, model and procedure. For a deeper understanding of a method or procedure relating to either, you may wish to consult other books identified in the text or in the Bibliography. You can also visit the companion website for the book on your mobile using the QR code, or by visiting www.uk.sagepub.co.uk/kumar4e where additional information is available.

The proposed research model is shown in Figure 2.2. The tasks identified by *arrows* are the operational steps you need to follow in order to conduct a study, whether quantitative, qualitative or using the mixed methods approach. Topics identified in *rectangles* are the required theoretical knowledge needed to carry out these steps. The tasks identified in *circles* are the intermediary steps that you need to complete to go from one step to another. It is important for a beginner to work through these steps in the proposed sequence, though, as already stated, once you know the route for your research journey you will not need to follow the sequence.

In this book the theoretical knowledge required is written around each operational step and follows the same sequential progression as is needed when actually undertaking a research investigation. For each operational step, the required theoretical knowledge is further organised, in different chapters, around the operational step to which, in the author's opinion, it is most logically related (Figure 2.3). Again, for a beginner, it is important to study this diagram to relate the theoretical knowledge to the operational steps.

The following sections of this chapter provide a quick glance at the whole process to acquaint you with the various tasks you need to undertake to carry out your study, thus giving you some idea of what the research journey involves.

A: Deciding what to research

Step I: Formulating a research problem

Formulating a research problem is the first and most important step in the research process. A research problem identifies your destination: it should tell you, your research supervisor and your readers *what* you intend to research. The more specific and clearer you are the better, as everything that follows in the research process – study design, measurement procedures, sampling strategy, frame of analysis and the style of writing of your dissertation or report – is greatly influenced by the way in which you formulate your research problem. Hence, you should examine it thoroughly, carefully and critically. The main function of formulating a research problem is to decide what you want to find out about. Chapter 4 deals in detail with various aspects of formulating a research problem.

It is extremely important to evaluate the research problem in the light of the financial resources at your disposal, the time available, and your own and your research supervisor's expertise and knowledge in the field of study. It is equally important to identify any gaps in your knowledge of relevant disciplines, such as statistics required for analysis. Also ask yourself whether you have sufficient knowledge about computers and software if you plan to use them.

B: Planning how to conduct the study

Step II: Conceptualising a research design

An extremely important feature of research is the use of appropriate methods. Research involves systematic, controlled, valid and rigorous exploration and description of what is not known, and establishment of associations and causation that permit the accurate prediction of outcomes under a given set of conditions. It also involves identifying gaps in knowledge, verification of what is already known and identification of past errors and limitations. The strength of *what* you find largely rests on *how* it was found.

The main function of a research design is to decide, describe, justify and explain *how* you will find answers to your research questions. The research design sets out the specific details of your enquiry. A research design should include the following: the study design per se and the logistical arrangements that you propose to undertake, the measurement procedures, the sampling strategy, the frame of analysis and the time-frame. (Do not confuse the study design and research design. The study design is just one part of the research design. The research design also includes other parts which constitute the research process.)

For any investigation, the selection of an appropriate research design is crucial in enabling you to arrive at valid findings, comparisons and conclusions. A faulty design results in misleading findings and is therefore tantamount to wasting human and financial resources. In scientific circles, the strength of an empirical investigation is primarily evaluated in the light of the research design adopted. When selecting a research design it is important to ensure that it is *valid, workable* and *manageable*. Chapter 7 provides details about the research design most commonly used in quantitative and qualitative research.

There is an enormous variety of study designs (Chapter 8) and you need to be acquainted with some of the most common ones both in quantitative and qualitative approaches. The chapter does not separately describe study designs for the mixed methods approach as it primarily uses those which are either quantitative or qualitative. Select or develop the design that is most suited to your study. You must have strong reasons for selecting a particular design; you must be able to justify your selection; and you should be aware of its strengths, weaknesses and limitations. In addition, you will need to explain the logistical details needed to implement the suggested design.

Step III: Constructing an instrument for data collection

Anything that becomes a means of collecting information for your study is called a 'research tool' or a 'research instrument', for example interview schedules, questionnaires, notes on field observations, field diaries, information collected from secondary notes, interview guides.

The construction of a research instrument is the first 'practical' step in carrying out a study. You will need to decide how you are going to collect data for the proposed study and then construct a research instrument for data collection. Chapter 9 details the various methods of data collection for qualitative and quantitative studies and the process of developing a research instrument.

If you are planning to collect data specifically for your study (primary data), you need either to construct a research instrument or to select one that has already been constructed. Chapter 10 deals with methods for collecting data using attitudinal scales. The concepts of validity and reliability in relation to a research instrument are discussed in Chapter 11.

If you are using secondary data (information already collected for other purposes), you will need to identify what information is needed and then develop a form to extract the required data. In order to determine what information is required, you need to go through the same process as for primary data.

Field testing (or pre-testing) a research tool is an integral part of instrument construction. As a rule, the pre-test of a research instrument should not be carried out on the sample of your study population but on a similar population which you are not proposing to study. This is covered in greater detail in Chapter 9.

If you are planning to use a computer for data analysis, you may wish to provide space for coding the data on the research instrument. This is explained in Chapter 15.

Step IV: Selecting a sample

The accuracy of your findings largely depends upon the way you select your sample. The basic objective of any sampling design is to minimise, within the limitation of cost, the gap between the values obtained from your sample and those prevalent in the study population.

The underlying premise in sampling is that a relatively small number of units, if selected so that they genuinely represent the study population, can provide – with a sufficiently high degree of probability – a fairly true reflection of the sampling population that is being studied.

When selecting a sample you should attempt to achieve two key aims of sampling: (i) the avoidance of bias in the selection of a sample; and (ii) the attainment of maximum precision for a given outlay of resources.

There are three categories of sampling design (Chapter 12): random/probability sampling designs, non-random/non-probability sampling designs, and the 'mixed' sampling design.

There are several sampling strategies within the first two categories. You need to be acquainted with these sampling designs – the strengths and weaknesses of each and the situations in which they can or cannot be applied – in order to select the one most appropriate for your study. The type of sampling strategy you use will influence your ability to make generalisations from the sample findings about the study population, and the type of statistical tests you can apply to the data.

Step V: Writing a research proposal

Having done all the preparatory work, the next step is to put everything together in a way that provides adequate information about your research study, for your research supervisor and others. This overall plan, called a research proposal, tells the reader about your research problem and how you are planning to investigate it. Broadly, a research proposal's main function is to detail the operational plan for obtaining answers to your research questions. In doing so it ensures – and reassures the reader of – the validity of the methodology to obtain answers accurately and objectively.

WHAT IS A
RESEARCH
PROPOSAL?

Universities and other institutions may have differing requirements regarding the style and content of a research proposal, but the majority of institutions would require most of what is set out here. Requirements may also vary within an institution, from discipline to discipline or from supervisor to supervisor. However, the guidelines set out in Chapter 13 provide a framework which will be acceptable to most.

A research proposal must tell you, your research supervisor and a reviewer the following information about your study:

- *what* you are proposing to do;
- *how* you plan to proceed;
- *why* you selected the proposed strategy.

Therefore it should contain the following information about your study (Chapter 13):

- a statement of its *objectives*;
- a list of *hypotheses*, if you are testing any;
- the *study design* you are proposing to use;
- the *setting* for the study;
- the research *instrument(s)* you are planning to use;
- the *sample size* and *sampling design*;
- the *data processing* procedures;
- an outline of the proposed *chapters* for the report;
- the study's *problems* and *limitations*; and
- the proposed *time-frame*.

C: Conducting a research study

Step VI: Collecting data

Having formulated a research problem, developed a study design, constructed a research instrument and selected a sample, you then collect the data from which you will draw inferences and conclusions for your study.

Many methods could be used to gather the required information. As a part of the research design, you decided upon the procedure you wanted to adopt to collect your data. In this phase *you actually collect the data*. For example, depending upon your plans, you might commence interviews, mail out a questionnaire, conduct nominal/focus group discussions or make observations. Collecting data through any one of the methods may involve some ethical issues, which are discussed in Chapter 14.

Step VII: Processing and displaying data

The way you analyse the information you collected largely depends upon two things: the type of information (descriptive, quantitative, qualitative or attitudinal); and the way you want to communicate your findings to your readers. Chapter 15 describes different ways of analysing quantitative and qualitative data and Chapter 16 details various methods of displaying the data that has been analysed.

In addition to the qualitative–quantitative distinction, it is important for data analysis that you consider whether the data is to be analysed manually or by a computer.

If your study is purely descriptive, you can write your dissertation/report on the basis of your field notes, manually analyse the contents of your notes (content analysis), or use a computer program such as NVivo for this purpose.

If you want quantitative analysis, it is also necessary to decide upon the type of analysis required (i.e. frequency distributions, cross-tabulations or other statistical procedures, such as regression analysis, factor analysis and analysis of variance) and how it should be presented. You will also need to identify the variables to be subjected to these statistical procedures.

Step VIII: Writing a research report

There are two broad categories of reports: quantitative and qualitative. As mentioned earlier, the distinction is more academic than real as in most studies you need to combine quantitative and qualitative skills. Nevertheless, there are some purely qualitative and some purely quantitative studies.

Writing the report is the last and, for many, the most difficult step of the research process. This report tells the world what you have done, what you have discovered and what conclusions you have drawn from your findings. If you are clear about the whole process, you will also be clear about the way you want to write your report. Your report should be written in an academic style and be divided into different chapters and/or sections based upon the main themes of your study. Chapter 17 suggests some ways of writing a research report.

Summary

SUMMARY OF 3 PHASES/8 STEPS OF RESEARCH PROCESS

This chapter has provided an overview of the research process, which has been broken down into three phases (A, B, C) and eight steps, the details of which are covered in the remainder of this book. At each step the research model provides a variety of methods, models, techniques and procedures so that you can select the one most appropriate for your study. It is like a buffet party with eight tables, each with different dishes made from similar ingredients. You go to all eight tables and select the dish that you like the most from each table. The main difference between the model and this example is that in the model you select what is most appropriate for your study and not what you like the most. For a beginner it is important to go through all the steps, although perhaps not in the same sequence. With experience you can take a number of shortcuts.

The eight steps cover the complete spectrum of a research endeavour, from problem formulation through to writing a research report. The steps are operational in nature, following a logical sequence, and detailing the various methods and procedures in a simple step-by step manner.

FOR YOU TO THINK ABOUT

- Refamiliarise yourself with the keywords listed at the beginning of this chapter, and if you are uncertain about the meaning or application of any of them revisit them in the chapter before moving on.
- Reflecting on the differences between quantitative and qualitative research (as outlined in Table 1.2), determine which approach you are more inclined to follow and why. To what extent does this reflect your own underpinning philosophy?

Now, as you have gone through the chapter, try answering the following questions:

- What is the first step in the research process outlined in this chapter? And the last step?
- Critically examine the applicability of this research process to your situation.
- Think about the applicability of the proposed research process for quantitative, qualitative and mixed-methods studies. Are there any differences in how you might approach the eight-step model based on your understanding of the different research approaches, objectives and paradigms in Chapter 1?

Want to learn more? Visit
http://www.uk.sagepub.com/kumar4e
or scan this QR code to gain access to a range of online resources to support your study including practice quizzes, videos, weblinks, flashcards, and journal articles.

STEP I

FORMULATING A
RESEARCH PROBLEM

This operational step includes four chapters:

- Chapter 3: Reviewing the Literature
- Chapter 4: Formulating a Research Problem
- Chapter 5: Identifying Variables
- Chapter 6: Constructing Hypotheses

3

REVIEWING THE LITERATURE

In this chapter you will learn about

- ■ The functions of the literature review in research
- ■ How to carry out a literature search
- ■ The difference between a literature review and a summary of literature
- ■ How to use the Internet for a literature review
- ■ How to review the selected literature
- ■ How to develop theoretical and conceptual frameworks
- ■ How to write a literature review

Keywords		
catalogue, conceptual framework, contextualise, Internet, knowledge base,	literature review, search engines, summary of literature,	thematic writing, theoretical framework.

At the end of this chapter, you should have an understanding of

- The place of the literature review in research
- How to search the literature
- How to develop theoretical and conceptual frameworks

The place of the literature review in research

One of the essential preliminary tasks when you undertake a research study is to go through the existing literature in order to acquaint yourself with the available body of knowledge in your area of interest. Reviewing the literature can be time-consuming, daunting and frustrating, but it is also rewarding. The literature review is an integral part of the research process and makes a valuable contribution to almost every operational step. It is important even before the first step; that is, when you are merely thinking about a research question that you may want to find answers to through your research journey. In the initial stages of research it helps you to clarify your ideas, establish the theoretical roots of your study and develop your research methodology. Later in the process, the literature review serves to enhance and consolidate your knowledge base in your subject area and helps you to examine your findings in the context of the existing body of knowledge. Since an important responsibility in research is to compare your findings with those of others, it is here that the literature review plays an extremely important role. During the write-up of your report it helps you to integrate your findings with the existing knowledge – that is, to either support or contradict earlier research. The higher the academic level of your research, the more important a thorough integration of your findings with existing literature becomes.

In summary, a literature review has the following functions:

WHAT IS A LITERATURE REVIEW?

- It provides a theoretical background to your study.
- It helps you establish the links between what you are proposing to examine and what has already been studied.
- It enables you to show how your findings have contributed to the existing body of knowledge in your profession. It helps you to integrate your research findings into the existing body of knowledge.

In relation to your own study, the literature review can help in four ways. It can:

ROLE OF LITERATURE REVIEW

1. bring clarity and focus to your research problem;
2. improve your research methodology;

3. broaden your knowledge base in your research area; and
4. contextualise your findings, that is, integrate your findings with the existing body of knowledge.

Bringing clarity and focus to your research problem

The literature review involves a paradox. On the one hand, you cannot effectively undertake a literature search without some idea of the problem you wish to investigate. On the other hand, the literature review can play an extremely important role in influencing the nature of your research problem thus conditioning your thinking about choosing your research problem. It is therefore important for you to strike a balance between reviewing the literature and its influence on your research problem. The process of reviewing the literature helps you to understand the subject area better and thus helps you to conceptualise your research problem clearly and precisely and makes it more relevant and pertinent to your field of enquiry. When reviewing the literature you learn what aspects of your subject area have been examined by others, what they have found out about these aspects, what gaps they have identified and what suggestions they have made for further research. All these will help you gain a greater insight into your own research questions and provide you with clarity and focus which are central to a relevant and valid study. In addition, they will help you to focus your study on areas where there are gaps in the existing body of knowledge, and where you can to the existing body of knowledge, thereby enhancing your study's relevance and importance.

Improving your research methodology

Going through the literature acquaints you with the methodologies that have been used by others to find answers to research questions similar to the one you are investigating. A literature review tells you if others have used procedures and methods similar to the ones that you are proposing, which procedures and methods have worked well for them and what problems they have faced with them. By becoming aware of any problems and pitfalls, you will be in a better position to select a methodology that is capable of providing valid answers to your research question. This will increase your confidence in the methodology you plan to use and will equip you to defend its use.

Broadening your knowledge base in your research area

The most important function of the literature review is to ensure you read widely around the subject area in which you intend to conduct your research study. It is important that you know what other researchers have found in regard to the same or similar questions, what theories have been put forward and what gaps exist in the relevant body of knowledge. When you undertake a research project for a higher degree (e.g. an MA or a PhD) you are expected to be an expert in your area of research. A thorough literature review helps you to fulfil this expectation. Another important reason for doing a literature review is that it helps you to understand how the findings of your study fit into the existing body of knowledge (Martin 1985: 30).

In summary, in terms of knowledge base, the literature review is extremely useful for it:

- Helps you to identify what has been established, and what are the gaps in the area of your research, thereby ensuring the relevance and usefulness of your research.
- Acquaints you with methods and procedures used in similar studies, helping you to select a robust methodology for your research.
- Helps you to locate your research questions and findings in the existing literature.
- Helps you to justify the selection of your research questions.
- Helps you to develop, expand and demonstrate your knowledge base in the subject area of your study.

Contextualising your findings

Obtaining answers to your research questions is comparatively easy: the difficult part is examining how your findings fit into the existing body of knowledge. How do answers to your research questions compare with what others have found? What contribution have you been able to make to the existing body of knowledge? How are your findings different from those of others? Undertaking a literature review will enable you to compare your findings with those of others and answer these questions. It is important to place your findings in the context of what is already known in your field of enquiry, that is, to integrate what you have found out with the existing literature.

Difference between a literature review and a summary of the literature

Some people use the terms 'literature review' and 'summary of the literature' interchangeably. However, there is a difference between the two. A summary of the literature is a description of the significant findings of each relevant piece of work that you have gone through as a part of your literature search. The summary basically entails listing, under each pertinent source, the major findings of relevance to your study. The sources searched can be listed in any order. However, in a literature review the main findings are organised around main themes that emerge from your literature search. Different studies in which the same theme is identified are referenced in one place where the theme is being discussed as a part of the literature review. Under each theme the main findings relating to it from all the sources you have searched are mentioned and compared, pointing to similarities and differences between them. This is usually followed by a statement of conclusions with respect to the theme. The themes are then put together in a logical progression. A summary of the literature is a summary of the main findings from each relevant reference you searched. In a literature review you describe each theme that emerged during the literature search, citing its origin, comparing it with others and integrating it in a logical manner with the rest.

How to review the literature

If you do not have a specific research problem, you should review the literature in your broad area of interest with the aim of gradually narrowing it down to what you want to find out about. It is like funnelling your ideas. To start with, these ideas are very broad and vague but as you get more insight into your research problem you narrow and refine them to select something that you are really interested in. Once you have reasonably narrowed your research problem, the literature review should then be focused around your research problem. There is a danger in reviewing the literature without having a reasonably specific idea of what you want to study. It can condition your thinking about your study and the methodology you might use, resulting in a less innovative choice of research problem and methodology than otherwise would have been the case. Hence, you should try broadly to conceptualise your research problem before undertaking your major literature review. Your literature search should concentrate around the main themes of your research problem and should be undertaken as if you are answering the following questions:

- What is already known in the area?
- What is not known or what are the gaps in the existing body of knowledge?
- What questions have remained unanswered?
- Are there any areas of professional conflict?
- What theories have been put forward relevant to your area of research?
- What suggestions have been made for further research?
- What research strategies have been employed by others undertaking similar research?

There are four steps involved in conducting a literature review:

1. Searching for the existing literature in your area of study.
2. Reviewing the selected literature.
3. Developing a theoretical framework.
4. Developing a conceptual framework.

The skills required for these tasks are different. Developing theoretical and conceptual frameworks is more difficult than the other tasks.

Searching for the existing literature

To search effectively for the literature in your field of enquiry, it is imperative that you have at least some idea of the broad subject area and of the problem you wish to investigate, in order to set parameters for your search. You must also have some idea of the study population. For example, you should decide whether your interest lies in studying immigrants, youth, women, students, or residents of an institution. You also need to have some idea as to what it is about your population that you want to study. For example, in the case of immigrants, you might want to study their settlement process, reasons for immigration, or patterns of occupational mobility. Next, compile a bibliography for this broad subject area. There are four sources that you can use to prepare a bibliography:

SEARCHING FOR
LITERATURE

(a) **books;**
(b) **journals;**
(c) **conference papers;**
(d) **the Internet.**

Books

Though books are a central part of any bibliography, they have their disadvantages as well as advantages. The main advantage is that the material published in books is usually important and of good quality, and the findings are 'integrated with other research to form a coherent body of knowledge' (Martin 1985: 33). The main disadvantage is that the material is not completely up to date, as a year or more may pass between the completion of a work and its publication in the form of a book.

The best way to search for a book is to look at your library catalogues. When librarians catalogue a book they also assign to it subject headings that are usually based on *Library of Congress* subject headings. If you are not sure, ask your librarian to help you find the best subject heading for your area. This can save you a lot of time. Publications such as *Book Review Index* can help you to locate books of interest.

Use the *subject catalogue* or *keywords* option to search for books in your area of interest. Narrow the subject area searched by selecting the appropriate keywords. Look carefully through these titles found and identify those books you think are likely to be of interest to you. If you think the titles seem appropriate to your topic, print them out if possible, as this will save you time, or write them down. Be aware that sometimes a title does not provide enough information to help you decide if a book is going to be of use, so you may have to examine its contents too.

When you have selected 10–15 books that you think are appropriate for your topic, examine the bibliography of each one. It will save time if you photocopy their bibliographies., provided it is legal. Go through these bibliographies carefully to identify the books common to several of them. If a book has been referenced by a number of authors, you should include it in your reading list. Prepare a final list of books that you consider essential reading.

Having prepared your reading list, locate these books in your library or borrow them from other sources. Examine their contents to double-check that they really are relevant to your topic. If you find that a book is not relevant to your research, delete it from your reading list. If you find that something in a book's contents is relevant to your topic, make an annotated bibliography. An annotated bibliography contains a brief abstract of the aspects covered in a book and your own notes about its relevance. Be careful to keep track of your references. To do this you can prepare your own card index or use a computer program such as Endnotes or Zotero.

ELECTRONIC
REFERENCING
SYSTEMS

Journals

You need to go through the journals relating to your research in a similar manner. Journals provide you with the most up-to-date information, even though there is often a gap of 2–3 years between the completion of a research project and its publication in a journal. You should select as many journals as you possibly can, though the number of journals available depends upon the field of study. There are a number of ways to find the journals you need to examine in order to identify the literature relevant to your study. You can:

- locate hard copies of the journals that are appropriate to your study;
- look at citation or abstract indices to identify and/or read the abstracts of such articles;
- search electronic databases.

If you have been able to identify any useful journals and articles, prepare a list of those you want to examine, by journal. Select one of these journals and, starting with the latest issue, examine its contents page to see if there is an article of relevance to your research topic. If you feel that a particular article is of interest to you, read its abstract. If you think you are likely to use it, depending upon your financial resources, either photocopy it, or prepare a summary and record its reference for later use. When photocopying, make sure to first seek permission of the appropriate authority.

There are several sources designed to make your search for journals easier and save you a great deal of time. They are:

- indexes of journals (e.g. *Humanities Index*);
- abstracts of articles (e.g. *ERIC*);
- citation indices (e.g. *Social Sciences Citation Index*).

MORE ELECTRONIC
DATABASES

Each of these indexing, abstracting and citation services is available in print, or accessible through the Internet.

In most libraries, information on books, journals and abstracts is stored on computers. In each case the information is classified by subject, author and title. You may also have the keywords option (author/keyword; title/keyword; subject/keyword; expert/keyword; or just keywords). What system you use depends upon what is available in your library and what you are familiar with.

There are specially prepared electronic databases in a number of disciplines. These can also be helpful in preparing a bibliography. For example, most libraries carry the electronic databases shown in Table 3.1.

Select the database most appropriate to your area of study to see if there are any useful references. Of course, any computer database search is restricted to those journals and articles that are already on the database. You should also talk to your research supervisor and other available experts to find out about any additional relevant literature to include in your reading list.

Conference papers

Another important source for the literature review is the papers presented at professional conferences. These can provide you with the most recent research in the area. You should try to get copies of the papers presented at recent conferences in your area of interest.

The Internet

In almost every academic discipline and professional field, the Internet has become an important tool for finding published literature. Through an Internet search you can

Table 3.1   Some commonly used electronic databases in public health, sociology, education and business studies

Electronic database	Description	Printed equivalent
ABI/INFORM	Abstracted Business Information (ABI) contains references to business information worldwide. It covers subjects such as accounting, banking, data processing, economics, finance, health care, insurance, law, management, marketing, personnel, product development, public administration, real estate, taxation and telecommunications	None
ERIC	ERIC is a database of educational material collected by the Education Resources Information Center of the US Department of Education. It covers subjects such as adult career or vocational education, counselling and personnel services, educational management, primary and early childhood education, handicapped and gifted children, higher education, information resources, language and linguistics, reading and communication, rural education, science, mathematics and environment education, social science education, teacher education, secondary education, evaluation and urban education	*CIJE: Current Index to Journals in Education*
HEALTHROM	HEALTHROM provides references and some full-text publications on the environment, health, HIV/AIDS and communicable diseases, aboriginal health, clinical medicine, nutrition, alcohol and drug addiction	None
MEDLINE	MEDLINE contains references to material in the biomedical sciences, including medicine, pharmacology, nursing, dentistry, allied health professions, public health, behavioural sciences, physiotherapy, occupational therapy, medical technology, hospital administration, and basic sciences such as anatomy and physiology	*Index Medicus*
CINAHL	Cumulative Indices to Nursing and Allied Health Literature (CINAHL) provides access to virtually all English-language nursing journals and primary journals from 13 allied health disciplines, including health education, medical records, occupational therapy, physical therapy and radiologic technology	CINAHL

identify published material in books, journals and other sources with immense ease and speed.

SEARCH ENGINES

An Internet search is carried out through search engines. There are many search engines (listed on sites such as http//www.thesearchenginelist.com), and different engines have strengths in searching different areas. Some specialise in business, legal, maps, books, medical, or multimedia; others can be considered as all-purpose search engines. However, the most commonly used for your purpose are *Google, scholar.google.com* and *Yahoo!* Another very useful source on the Internet, particularly to describe and explain terms and concepts, is *Wikipedia*. You can use it for definitions, meanings and other details, though do bear in mind that you may not be able to quote from Wikipedia in your academic dissertations as many universities consider it to be unreliable.

Searching the Internet is very similar to the search for books and articles in a library using an electronic catalogue, as it is based on the use of keywords. An Internet search basically identifies all material in the database of a search engine that contains the keywords you specify, either individually or in combination. It is important that you choose words or combinations of words that other people are likely to use.

According to Gilbert (2008: 73), 'Most search facilities use Boolean logic, which allows three types of basic search "AND", "OR" and "NOT"'. With practice you will become more efficient and effective in using keywords in combination with AND, OR and NOT, and so learn to narrow your search to help you identify the most relevant references.

BOOLEAN
SEARCHING

Reviewing the selected literature

Now that you have identified several books and articles as useful, the next step is to start reading them critically to pull together themes and issues that are of relevance to your study. Unless you have a theoretical framework of themes in mind to start with, use separate sheets of paper for each theme or issue you identify as you go through selected books and articles. The following examples detail the process.

The author recently examined, as part of an evaluation study, the extent of 'community responsiveness' in the delivery of health services in Western Australia by health service providers. Before evaluating the extent of its use, pertinent literature relating to 'community responsiveness in health' was identified and reviewed. Through this review, many themes emerged, which became the basis for developing the theoretical framework for the study. Out of all of this, the following themes were selected to construct the theoretical framework for the evaluation study:

- Community responsiveness: what does it mean?
- Philosophies underpinning community responsiveness
- Historical development of the concept in Australia
- The extent of use in health planning
- Strategies developed to achieve community responsiveness
- Indicators of success or failure
- Seeking community participation
- Difficulties in implementing community responsiveness
- Attitude of stakeholders towards the concept of community responsiveness.

Let us take another example from education.

Suppose you are studying the determinant of high academic achievement among high school students. As part of building your theoretical framework, you might want to focus your literature search on exploring the relationship between high academic achievement and

READING JOURNAL
ARTICLES

- home environment
- peer group pressure
- involvement in sport
- self-esteem
- motivation in studies
- educational background of the parents
- relationship with teacher(s)

Once you develop a rough framework, slot the findings from the material so far reviewed into these themes, using a separate sheet of paper for each theme of the framework so far developed. As you read further, continue slotting the information where it logically belongs under the themes so far developed. Keep in mind that you may need to add more themes as you go along. While going through the literature you should carefully and critically examine it with respect to the following aspects:

- Note whether the knowledge relevant to your theoretical framework has been confirmed beyond doubt.
- Note the theories put forward, the criticisms of these and their basis, the methodologies adopted (study design, sample size and its characteristics, measurement procedures, etc.) and the criticisms of them.
- Examine to what extent the findings can be generalised to other situations.
- Notice where there are significant differences of opinion among researchers, and give your opinion about their validity in addition to putting forward your position, with your reasons.
- Ascertain the areas in which little or nothing is known – the gaps that exist in the body of knowledge.

Developing a theoretical framework

Examining the literature can be a never-ending task, but as you have limited time it is important to set parameters by reviewing the literature in relation to some main themes pertinent to your research topic. As you start reading the literature, you will soon discover that the problem you wish to investigate has its roots in a number of theories that have been developed from different perspectives. The information obtained from different books and journals now needs to be sorted under the main themes and theories, highlighting agreements and disagreements among the authors and identifying the unanswered questions or gaps. You will also realise that the literature deals with a number of aspects that have a direct or indirect bearing on your research topic. Use these aspects as a basis for developing your theoretical framework. Your review of the literature should sort the information, as mentioned earlier, within this framework. Unless you review the literature in relation to this framework, you will not be able to develop a focus in your literature search; that is, your theoretical framework provides you with a guide as you read. This brings us to the paradox mentioned previously: until you go through the literature you cannot develop a theoretical framework, and until you have developed a theoretical framework you cannot effectively review the literature. The solution is to read some of the literature and then attempt to develop a framework, even a loose one, within which you can organise the rest of the literature you read. As you read more about the area, you are likely to change the framework. However, without it, you will get bogged down in a great deal of unnecessary reading and note-taking that may not be relevant to your study.

Literature pertinent to your study may deal with two types of information: universal or general; and more specific (local trends or a specific programme). In writing about such information you should start with the general information, gradually narrowing it down to the specific. Look at the example in Figure 3.1.

If you want to study the relationship between mortality and fertility, you should review the literature about:

- *fertility* – trends, theories, some of the indices and critiques of them, factors affecting fertility, methods of controlling fertility, factors affecting acceptance of contraceptives, and so on;
- *mortality* – factors affecting mortality, mortality indices and their sensitivity in measuring change in mortality levels of a population, trends in mortality, and so on; and, most importantly,
- *the relationship between fertility and mortality* – theories that have been put forward to explain the relationship, implications of the relationship.

Out of this literature review you need to develop the theoretical framework for your study. Primarily this should revolve around theories that have been put forward about the relationship between mortality and fertility. You will discover that a number of theories have been proposed to explain this relationship. For example, it has been explained from economic, religious, medical and psychological perspectives. Within each perspective several theories have been put forward: 'insurance theory', 'fear of non-survival', 'replacement theory', 'price theory', 'utility theory', 'extra' or 'hoarding theory' and 'risk theory'.

Your literature review should be written under the following headings, with most of the review involving the examination of the relationships between fertility and mortality:

- fertility theories;
- the theory of demographic transition;
- trends in fertility (global, and then narrow it to national and local levels);
- methods of contraception (their acceptance and effectiveness);
- factors affecting mortality;
- trends in mortality (and their implications);
- measurement of mortality indices (their sensitivity);
- *relationships between fertility and mortality* (different theories such as 'insurance', 'fear of non-survival', 'replacement', 'price', 'utility', 'risk' and 'hoarding').

Developing a conceptual framework

The conceptual framework is the basis of your research problem. It stems from the theoretical framework and usually focuses on the section(s) which become the basis of your study. Whereas the theoretical framework consists of the theories or issues in which your study is embedded, the conceptual framework describes the aspects you selected from the theoretical framework to become the basis of your enquiry. For instance, in the example cited in Figure 3.1a, the theoretical framework includes all the theories that have been put forward to explain the relationship between fertility and mortality. However, out of these, you may be planning to test only one, say the fear of non-survival. Similarly, in Figure 3.1b, the conceptual framework is focused only on indicators to measure the success or failure of the strategies to enhance community responsiveness. Hence the conceptual framework grows out of the theoretical framework and relates only and specifically to your research problem. The conceptual framework becomes the foundation of your study.

Writing about the literature reviewed

Now, all that remains to be done is to write about the literature you have reviewed. As mentioned at the beginning of this chapter, two of the broad functions of a literature

If you want to study the relationship between mortality and fertility, you should review the literature about:

- *fertility* – trends, theories, some of the indices and critiques of them, factors affecting fertility, methods of controlling fertility, factors affecting acceptance of contraceptives, and so on;
- *mortality* – factors affecting mortality, mortality indices and their sensitivity in measuring change in mortality levels of a population, trends in mortality, and so on; and, most importantly,
- *the relationship between fertility and mortality* – theories that have been put forward to explain the relationship, implications of the relationship.

Out of this literature review you need to develop the theoreitical framework for your study. Primarily this should revolve around theories that have been put forward about the relationship between mortality and fertility. You will discover that a number of theories have been proposed to explain this relationship. For example, it has been explained from economic, religious, medical and psychological perspectives. Within each perspective several theories have been put forward: 'insurance theory', 'fear of non-survival', 'replacement theory', 'price theory', 'utility theory', 'extra' or 'hoarding theory' and 'risk theories'.

Your literature review should be written under the following headings, with most of the review involving the examination of the relationships between fertility and mortality:

- fertility theories;
- the theory of demographic transition;
- trends in fertility (global, and then narrow it to national and local levels);
- methods of contraception (their acceptance and effectiveness);
- factors affecting mortality;
- trends in mortality (and their implications);
- measurement of mortality indices (their sensitivity);
- *relationships between fertility and mortality* (different theories such as 'insurance', 'fear of non-survival', 'replacement', 'price', 'utility', 'risk' and 'hoarding').

Figure 3.1a   Developing a theoretical framework – the relationship between mortality and fertility

---

Note: *Preliminary discussions with some stakeholders revealed that not much was known to them about community responsiveness and therefore it was proposed that the study be carried out in two phases: preparatory phase and actual evaluation phase. The main aim of the preparatory phase was to ascertain the understanding of the concept, identify the strategies that are being or can be used, and developing a set of indicators for measuring its success or failure. This framework became the basis of the first phase of the study.*

The review of literature for the first phase was written around the following theoretical framework which, of course, emerged from the literature review itself.

Community responsiveness: What do the stakeholders (service providers, service managers and the consumers) understand by community responsiveness, why it is needed, and what purpose does it serve?

Historical and philosophical perspectives: Start of the concept, an historical overview of its emergence, philosophical perspective that underpins the concept.

Implementation strategies: What strategies have been used to achieve community responsiveness in the service delivery area?

Attitude of the stakeholders: What are the attitudes of service providers, service managers and consumers of the services towards community responsiveness?

Evaluation of community responsiveness: What indicators can be used to determine the impact of these strategies, what should determine the success or failure of the implementation of the strategies, and by whom and how should it be determined?

Figure 3.1b   Theoretical framework for the 'community responsiveness in health' study

review are (1) to provide a theoretical background to your study and (2) to enable you to contextualise your findings in relation to the existing body of knowledge, in addition to refining your methodology. The content of your literature review should reflect these two purposes. In order to fulfil the first purpose, you should identify and describe various theories relevant to your field and specify gaps in existing knowledge in the area, recent advances in the area of study, current trends and so on. In order to fulfil the second, you should integrate the results from your study with specific and relevant findings from the existing literature by comparing the two for confirmation or contradiction. Note that at this stage you can only accomplish the first purpose of the literature review, to provide a theoretical background to your study. For the second, the contextualisation of the findings, you have to wait till you are at the research report writing stage.

While reading the literature for the theoretical background to your study, you will realise that certain themes have emerged. List the main ones, converting them into subheadings. Some people write up the entire literature review in one section, entitled 'Review of the literature', 'Summary of literature' or 'The literature review', without subheadings, but the author strongly suggests that you write your literature review under subheadings based upon the main themes that you have discovered and which form the basis of your theoretical framework. These subheadings (which will form the basis of your theoretical framework) should be precise, descriptive of the theme in question and follow a logical progression. Now, under each subheading, record the main findings with respect to the theme in question (thematic writing), highlighting the reasons for and against an argument if they exist, and identifying gaps and issues. Figure 3.2a shows the subheadings used to describe the themes in a literature review conducted by the author for a study entitled 'Intercountry adoption in Western Australia'. Figure 3.2b shows themes around which the literature was reviewed for the community responsiveness study.

Intercountry adoption in Western Australia

(A profile of adoptive families)

The literature was reviewed under the following themes:

- Introduction (introductory remarks about adoption)
- History and philosophy of adoption
- Reasons for adoption
- Trends in adoption (global and national)
- Intercountry adoption
- History of intercountry adoption in Western Australia
- Trends in intercountry adoption in Western Australia
- The Adoption Act in Western Australia
- The adoption process in Western Australia
- Problems and issues in adoption
- Gaps in the literature (in this case it was a lack of information about those parents who had adopted children from other countries that became the basis of the study)

Figure 3.2a   Sample outline of a literature review

The literature review for this study was carried out around the following themes identified through the objectives of the study and the literature review.

- Background to the introduction of the concept
- What does community responsiveness mean?
- Historical perspective to the introduction of community responsiveness in W Australia
- Philosophy underpinning the concept of community responsiveness
- Attitudes of the stakeholders towards the community responsiveness concept
- Strategies for achieving community responsiveness
- Measuring effectiveness of the implementation strategies: indicators and methodologies

Figure 3.2b   Main themes from the literature review for the community responsiveness study

THE WRITING
CENTRE

The second broad function of the literature review – contextualising the findings of your study – requires you to compare very systematically your findings with those made by others. Quote from these studies to show how your findings contradict, confirm or add to them. This places your findings in the context of what others have found. Be sure to provide a complete reference for any quoted material, in an acceptable format. This function is undertaken, as mentioned earlier, when writing about your findings, that is, after analysis of your data.

Summary

Reviewing the literature is a continuous process. It begins before a research problem is finalised and continues until the report is finished. There is a paradox in the literature review: you cannot undertake an effective literature review unless you have formulated a research problem, yet your literature search plays an extremely important role in helping you to formulate your research problem. The literature review brings clarity and focus to your research problem, improves your research methodology and broadens your knowledge base. A literature review identifies the main themes from the literature reviewed that are of relevance to your study, whereas a summary of the literature describes the main findings from a reference reviewed without thematic integration and linkage.

Reviewing the literature involves a number of steps: searching for existing literature in your area of study; reviewing the literature selected; using it to develop a theoretical framework from which your study emerges and also to develop a conceptual framework which will become the basis of your investigation. The main sources for identifying literature are books, journals, conference papers and the Internet. There are several sources which can provide information about locating relevant material.

The literature review serves two important functions: (1) it provides a theoretical background to your study, and (2) it helps you to contextualise your findings by comparing them with what others have found out in relation to the area of enquiry. At this stage of the research process, only the first function can be addresed. You can only take steps to address the second function when you have analysed your data and are in the process of writing about your findings.

Your writing about the literature reviewed should be thematic in nature, that is, based on main themes; the sequence of these themes in the write-up should follow a logical progression; various arguments should be substantiated with specific quotations and citations from the literature, adhering to an acceptable academic referencing style.

FOR YOU TO THINK ABOUT

- Refamiliarise yourself with the keywords listed at the beginning of this chapter, and if you are uncertain about the meaning or application of any of them revisit them in the chapter before moving on.
- Undertake a keyword search for a theme or issue that interests you using (a) an Internet search engine, such as Google Scholar, and (b) a library search facility. Compare the results.
- Choose two or three research reports from your search and scan through the summaries noting the theories put forward, the methodologies adopted and any recommendations for further study. Do these reports point to a consensus or differences of opinion in the field?
- Develop a theoretical framework for the theme or issue you selected.

Now, as you have gone through the chapter, try answering the following questions:

- What functions does the literature review perform in a research study?
- Describe the differences between theoretical and conceptual frameworks.
- What is the difference between a review of the literature and a summary of the literature?

Want to learn more? Visit
http://www.uk.sagepub.com/kumar4e
or scan this QR code to gain access to a range of online resources to support your study including practice quizzes, videos, weblinks, flashcards, and journal articles.

4

FORMULATING A RESEARCH PROBLEM

In this chapter you will learn about

- Formulating a research problem in quantitative research
- The importance of formulating a research problem in quantitative research
- Sources of research problems
- Considerations in selecting a research problem
- Steps in formulating a research problem
- How to formulate research objectives
- The importance of establishing operational definitions
- Formulating a research problem in qualitative research

Keywords

concepts, dissect, operational definition, qualitative research, quantitative	research, research objectives, research problem, study area, study	population, subject area, validity, variable, working definition.

At the end of this chapter, you should have an understanding of

- The process of formulating a research problem in qualitative and quantitative research
- Sources and considerations in formulating a research problem
- Formulation of research questions and objectives
- Operationalising concepts and study population

The central aim of this chapter is to detail the process of formulating a research problem, even though the specific procedure that you are likely to adopt depends upon:

- your expertise in research methodology;
- your knowledge of the subject area;
- your understanding of the issues to be examined;
- the extent to which the focus of your study is predetermined; and
- your own orientation to the research methodology – quantitative, qualitative or mixed.

If you are not very familiar with the research process and/or do not have a very specific idea about what is to be researched, you need to follow every step detailed in this chapter. However, more experienced researchers can take a number of shortcuts. The process outlined here assumes that you have neither the required knowledge of the process of formulating a research problem nor a specific idea about what is to be researched. If you have a specific idea for the basis of your enquiry, you do not need to go through this chapter. However, you should make sure that your idea is researchable as not all problems lend themselves to research methodologies.

The research problem

Broadly speaking, any question that you want answered and any assumption or assertion that you want to challenge or investigate can become a research problem or a research topic for your study. However, it is important to remember that not all questions can be transformed into research problems and some may prove to be extremely difficult to study. According to Powers et al. (1985: 38), 'Potential research questions may occur to us on a regular basis, but the process of formulating them in a meaningful way is not at all an easy task'. As a newcomer it might seem easy to formulate a problem but it requires considerable knowledge of both the subject area and research methodology. Once you examine a question more closely you will soon realise the complexity of formulating an idea into a

FORMULATING A RESEARCH PROBLEM 63

problem which is researchable. 'First identifying and then specifying a research problem might seem like research tasks that ought to be easy and quickly accomplished. However, such is often not the case' (Yegidis & Weinback 1991: 35).

It is essential for the problem you formulate to be able to withstand scrutiny in terms of the procedures required to be undertaken. Hence you should spend considerable time in thinking it through.

The importance of formulating a research problem

The formulation of a research problem is the first and most important step of the research process. It is like the identification of a destination before undertaking a journey. In the absence of a destination, it is impossible to identify the shortest – or indeed any – route. Similarly, in the absence of a clear research problem, a clear and economical plan is impossible. To use another analogy, a research problem is like the foundation of a building. The type and design of the building are dependent upon the foundation. If the foundation is well designed and strong you can expect the building to be also. The research problem serves as the foundation of a research study: if it is well formulated, you can expect a good study to follow. According to Kerlinger (1986: 17): 'If one wants to solve a problem, one must generally know what the problem is. It can be said that a large part of the problem lies in knowing what one is trying to do.' You must have a clear idea with regard to what it is that you want to find out about and not what you think you must find.

A research problem may take a number of forms, from the very simple to the very complex. The way you formulate a problem determines almost every step that follows: the type of study design that can be used; the type of sampling strategy that can be employed; the research instrument that can be used or developed; and the type of analysis that can be undertaken. Suppose your broad area of interest is depression. Further suppose you want to conduct a research study on the services available to patients with depression living in a community. If your focus is on finding out the types of service available to patients with depression, your study will be mainly descriptive and qualitative in nature. A study of this type will be carried out using qualitative research methodologies. On the other hand, if you want to find out the extent of use of these services, that is, the number of people using them, it will use mainly quantitative methodologies even if it is otherwise descriptive in nature. If your focus is on determining the extent of use in relation to the personal attributes of the patients, the study will be classified as correlational (and quantitative). The methodology used will be different than the one used in the case of a descriptive study. Similarly, if your aim is to find out the effectiveness of these services, the study will again be classified as correlational and the study design, data collection methods and analysis will belong to the quantitative methodology. Hence, it is important for you to understand that the way you formulate a research problem determines all the subsequent steps that you will have to follow during your research journey.

The formulation of a problem is like the 'input' to a study, and the 'output' – the quality of the contents of the research report and the validity of the associations or causation established – is entirely dependent upon it. Hence the famous saying about computers, 'garbage in, garbage out', is equally applicable to research problems.

Initially, you may become more confused, but this is normal and a sign of progression. Remember that confusion is often but a first step towards clarity. Take time over formulating your problem, for the clearer you are about your research problem/question, the easier it will be for you later on. Remember, this is the most crucial step.

Sources of research problems

This section is of particular relevance if you have not yet selected a research topic and do not know where to start. If you have already selected your topic or question, go on to the next section.

STUDENTS' VIEWS

Most research in the humanities revolves around the four Ps: people, problems, programmes and phenomena. In fact, a closer look at any academic or occupational field will show that most research revolves around these four Ps. The emphasis on a particular 'P' may vary from study to study but generally, in practice, most research studies are based upon a combination of at least two Ps. You may select a group of individuals (a group of individuals, or a community as such – people) to examine the existence of certain issues or problems relating to their lives, to ascertain their attitude towards an issue (problem), to establish the existence of a regularity or occurrence (phenomenon) or to evaluate the effectiveness of an intervention (programme). Your focus may be on the study of an issue, an association or a phenomenon per se; for example, the relationship between unemployment and street crime, smoking and cancer, fertility and mortality, delinquency and street crime, or academic achievement and home environment, carried out on the basis of information collected from individuals, groups, communities or organisations. The emphasis in these studies is on exploring, discovering or establishing associations or causation. Similarly, you can study different aspects of a programme: its effectiveness, its structure, the need for it, consumers' satisfaction with it, and so on. In order to ascertain these you collect information from people.

Every research study has two aspects: people provide you with the 'study population', while the problem, programme or phenomenon furnishes the 'subject area' about which information is collected. This is outlined further in Table 4.1, which shows the aspects of a research problem.

You can study a problem, a programme or a phenomenon in any academic field or from any professional perspective. For example, you can measure the effectiveness of a programme in the field of health, education, social work, industrial management, public health, nursing, health promotion or welfare, or you can look at a problem from a health, business or welfare perspective. Similarly, you can gauge consumers' opinions about any aspect of a programme in the above fields.

Examine your own academic discipline or professional field in the context of the four Ps in order to identify anything that looks interesting. For example, if you are a student in the health field there are an enormous number of issues, situations and associations within each subfield of health that you could examine. Issues relating to the spread of a disease, drug rehabilitation, an immunisation programme, the effectiveness of a treatment, the extent of consumers' satisfaction or issues concerning a particular health programme can all provide you with a range of research problems. Similarly, in education there are several issues: students' satisfaction with a teacher, attributes of a good teacher, the impact of the

FORMULATING A RESEARCH PROBLEM 65

Table 4.1   Aspects of a research problem

Aspects of a study	Information about	Study of	Importance to the study
Study population	People	Individuals, organisations, groups, communities	They provide you with the required information or you collect information from or about them
Subject area	Problem	Issues and problems facing a group of people; description of situations, associations, needs, attitudes; population profiles; service delivery process etc.	Information that you need to collect to find answers to your service research questions
	Programme	Contents, services provided, administrative structure, services outcomes, consumer satisfaction, profile of consumers, profile of service providers, effectiveness, cost benefit, etc.	
	Phenomenon	Cause and effect, relationships, the study of a phenomenon itself, etc.	

home environment on the educational achievement of students, and the supervisory needs of postgraduate students in higher education. Any other academic or occupational field such as marketing research, social work, community psychology, tourism can similarly be dissected into subfields and examined for a potential research problem. Most fields lend themselves to the above categorisation even though specific problems and programmes vary markedly from field to field.

The concept of the four Ps is applicable to both quantitative and qualitative research though the main difference at this stage is the extent of their specificity, dissection, precision and focus. In qualitative research these attributes are deliberately kept very loose so that you can explore more as you go along, in case you find something of relevance. You do not bind yourself with constraints that would put limits on your ability to explore. There is a separate section on 'Formulating a research problem in qualitative research' later in the chapter, which provides further guidance on the process.

Considerations in selecting a research problem

When selecting a research problem or topic there are a number of considerations to keep in mind which will help to ensure that your study will be manageable and that you remain motivated:

- Interest – This should be the most important consideration in selecting a research problem. A research endeavour is usually time-consuming and involves hard work and possibly unforeseen problems. If you select a topic which does not greatly interest you, it could become extremely difficult to sustain the required motivation and put in enough time and energy to complete it.
- Magnitude – You should have sufficient knowledge about the research process to be able to visualise the work involved in completing the proposed study. Narrow the topic down to something manageable, specific and clear. It is extremely important to select a topic that you can manage

within the time and with the resources at your disposal. Even if you are undertaking a descriptive study, you need to consider its magnitude carefully.

- **Measurement of concepts** – If you are using a concept in your study (in quantitative studies), make sure you are clear about its indicators and their measurement. For example, if you plan to measure the effectiveness of a health promotion programme or a programme to rehabilitate asylum seekers in a country or random breath testing programme, you must be clear as to what determines effectiveness and how it will be measured. Do not use concepts in your research problem that you are not sure how to measure. This does not mean you cannot develop a measurement procedure as the study progresses. While most of the developmental work will be done during your study, it is imperative that you are reasonably clear about the measurement of these concepts at this stage.

- **Level of expertise** – Make sure you have an adequate level of expertise for the task you are proposing. Allow for the fact that you will learn during the study and may receive help from your research supervisor and others, but remember that you need to do most of the work yourself.

- **Relevance** – Select a topic that is of relevance to you as a professional. Ensure that your study adds to the existing body of knowledge, bridges current gaps or is useful in policy formulation. This will help you to sustain interest in the study.

- **Availability of data** – If your topic entails collection of information from secondary sources (office records, client records, census or other already published reports, etc.) make sure that this data is available and in the format you want before finalising your topic.

- **Ethical issues** – Another important consideration in formulating a research problem is the ethical issues involved. In the course of conducting a research study, the study population may be adversely affected by some of the questions (directly or indirectly); deprived of an intervention; expected to share sensitive and private information; or expected to be simply experimental 'guinea pigs'. How ethical issues can affect the study population and how ethical problems can be overcome should be thoroughly examined at the problem formulation stage.

Steps in formulating a research problem

The formulation of a research problem is the most crucial part of the research journey as the quality and relevance of your research project entirely depend upon it. As mentioned earlier, every step that constitutes the *how* part of the research journey (Figure 2.1) depends upon the way you formulated your research problem. Despite the importance of this step, there is very little available by way of specific guidance in other books. This task is largely left either to the teachers of research methodology or to students to learn for themselves. One of the strengths of this book is that it offers the beginner a very specific set of step-by-step guidelines in one place, despite the fear of being labelled as prescriptive.

ANSWERABLE
RESEARCH
QUESTIONS

The process of formulating a research problem consists of a number of steps. Working through these steps presupposes a reasonable level of knowledge in the broad subject area within which the study is to be undertaken and the research methodology itself. A brief review of the relevant literature helps enormously in broadening this knowledge base. Without such knowledge it is difficult to 'dissect' a subject area clearly and adequately.

If you do not know what specific research topic, idea, questions or issue you want to research (which is not uncommon among students), going through the following steps will prove to be of immense help in deciding what you want to find out about. They will help you to select and narrow down a subject area that could become the basis of a research problem for your study.

Step 1 Identify a broad field or subject area of interest to you. It is imperative to do this at the very beginning, before starting out on your research journey. Ask yourself, 'What is it that really interests me as a professional?' In the author's opinion, it is a good idea to think about the field in which you would like to work after graduation. This will help you to find an interesting topic, and one which may be of use to you in the future. For example, if you are a social work student, inclined to work in the area of youth welfare, refugees or domestic violence after graduation, you might take to research in one of these areas. Or if you are studying marketing you might be interested in researching consumer behaviour. Or, as a student of public health, intending to work with patients who have HIV/AIDS, you might like to conduct research on a subject area relating to HIV/AIDS. Or you might be interested in becoming a teacher.

Step 2 Dissect the broad area into subareas. At the outset, you will realise that all the broad areas mentioned above – youth welfare, refugees, domestic violence, consumer behaviour and HIV/AIDS – have many aspects. For example, there are many aspects and issues in the area of domestic violence, illustrated in Figure 4.1.

   The more you think or read about an area the more subareas you will identify. For instance, you can go through the broad area of alcoholism (see Step 2 in Fig. 4.2). In preparing your list of subareas you should also consult others who have some knowledge of the area and the literature in your subject area. Once you have developed an exhaustive list of the subareas from various sources, you can proceed to the next stage where you select what will become the basis of your enquiry.

Step 3 Select what is of most interest to you. It is neither advisable nor feasible to study all subareas. From your list, select issues, questions or subareas about which you are passionate. Your interest should be the most important determinant for selection, even though there are other considerations as discussed in the previous section. One way to decide what interests you most is to start with a process of elimination. Go through your list and delete all those subareas, issues or questions in which you are not very interested. You will find that towards the end of this process, it will become very difficult for you to delete anything further. You need to continue until you are left with something that is *manageable*, considering the time available to you, your level of expertise and other resources needed to undertake the study. Once you are confident that you have selected something that you are passionate about and can manage, you are ready to go to the next step.

Step 4 Raise research questions. At this step ask yourself, 'What is it that I want to find out about in this subarea?' Make a list of whatever questions come to mind relating to your chosen subarea and if you think there are too many to be manageable, go through the same process of elimination as in step 3.

Step 5 Formulate objectives. Both your main objectives and your subobjectives now need to be formulated, based on your research questions. The main difference between objectives and research questions is the way in which they are written. Research questions are obviously that – questions. Objectives transform these questions into behavioural aims by using action-oriented phrases such as 'to find out', 'to determine', 'to ascertain' and 'to examine'. Some researchers prefer to reverse the process; that is, they start from objectives and formulate research questions from them. Some researchers are satisfied only with research questions, and do not formulate objectives at all. If you prefer to have only research questions or only objectives, this is fine, but keep in mind the requirements of your institution for research proposals. For guidance on formulating objectives, see the next section.

Subject area   **Subareas**

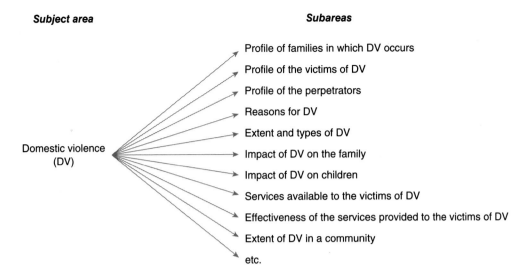

Figure 4.1   Dissecting the subject area of domestic violence into subareas

Step 6   Assess your objectives. Now examine your objectives to ascertain the feasibility of achieving them through your research endeavour. Consider them in the light of the time, resources (financial and human) and technical expertise at your disposal.

Step 7   Double-check. Go back and give final consideration to whether or not you are sufficiently interested in the study, and have adequate resources to undertake it. Ask yourself, 'Am I really enthusiastic about this study?' and 'Do I really have enough resources to undertake it?' Answer these questions thoughtfully and realistically. If your answer to one of them is 'no', reassess your objectives.

Figures 4.2–4.4 operationalise steps 1–7 with examples from different academic disciplines (health, social work/social sciences and community development).

The formulation of research objectives

Objectives are the goals you set out to attain in your study. Since these objectives inform the reader of what you want to achieve in the study, it is extremely important to word them clearly and specifically.

It is important to distinguish between main objectives and subobjectives. The main objective relates to the overall thrust of your study. It is also concerned with the main associations and relationships that you seek to discover or establish. The subobjectives are the specific aspects of the topic that you want to investigate within the main framework of your study.

Subobjectives should be listed numerically. They should be worded clearly and unambiguously. Make sure that each subobjective contains only one aspect of the study. Use action-oriented words or verbs when writing your objectives. The objectives should start with words such as 'to determine', 'to find out', 'to ascertain', 'to measure' and 'to explore'.

Example 1: Suppose you want to conduct a study in the area of alcoholism. In formulating your research problem take the following steps.

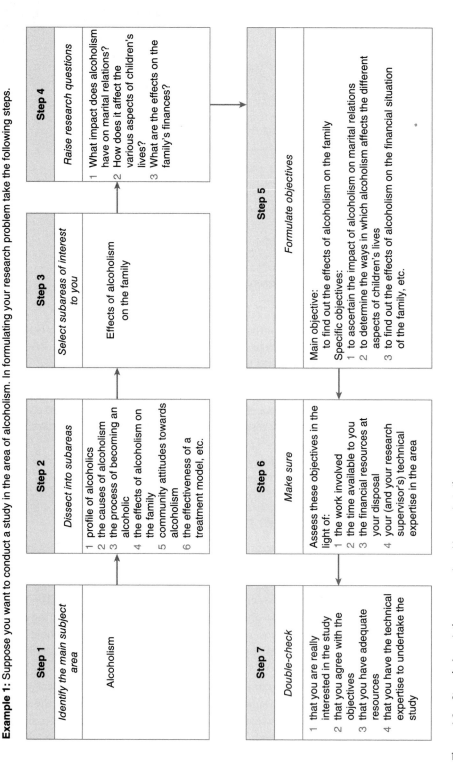

Step 1
Identify the main subject area
Alcoholism

Step 2
Dissect into subareas
1 profile of alcoholics
2 the causes of alcoholism
3 the process of becoming an alcoholic
4 the effects of alcoholism on the family
5 community attitudes towards alcoholism
6 the effectiveness of a treatment model, etc.

Step 3
Select subareas of interest to you
Effects of alcoholism on the family

Step 4
Raise research questions
1 What impact does alcoholism have on marital relations?
2 How does it affect the various aspects of children's lives?
3 What are the effects on the family's finances?

Step 5
Formulate objectives
Main objective: to find out the effects of alcoholism on the family
Specific objectives:
1 to ascertain the impact of alcoholism on marital relations
2 to determine the ways in which alcoholism affects the different aspects of children's lives
3 to find out the effects of alcoholism on the financial situation of the family, etc.

Step 6
Make sure
Assess these objectives in the light of:
1 the work involved
2 the time available to you
3 the financial resources at your disposal
4 your (and your research supervisor's) technical expertise in the area

Step 7
Double-check
1 that you are really interested in the study
2 that you agree with the objectives
3 that you have adequate resources
4 that you have the technical expertise to undertake the study

Figure 4.2 Steps in formulating a research problem – alcoholism

Example 2: Suppose you want to study the relationship between fertility and mortality. Follow these steps.

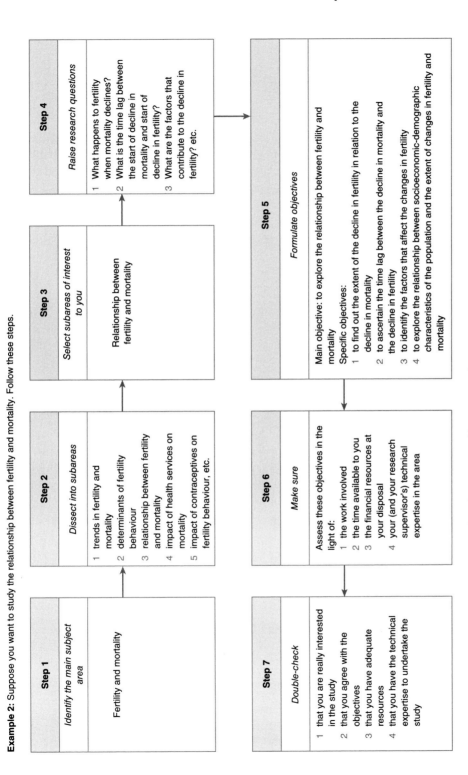

Figure 4.3   Formulating a research problem – the relationship between fertility and mortality

Example 3: Suppose you want to conduct a study in the area of health. Follow these steps.

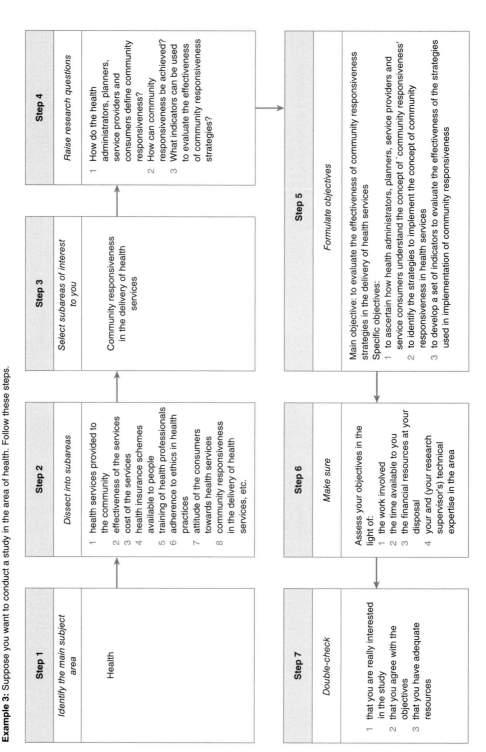

Figure 4.4 Narrowing down a research problem – health

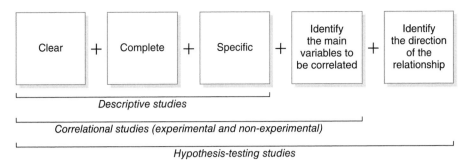

Figure 4.5   Characteristics of objectives

The way the main objectives and subobjectives are worded determines how your research is classified (e.g. descriptive, correlational or experimental). In other words, the wording of your objectives determines the type of research design you need to adopt to achieve them. Hence, be careful about the way you word your objectives.

Irrespective of the type of research, the objectives should be expressed in such a way that the wording clearly, completely and specifically communicates your intention to your readers. There is no place for ambiguity, non-specificity or incompleteness, either in the wording of your objectives or in the ideas they communicate. Figure 4.5 displays the characteristics of the wording of objectives in relation to the type of research study.

If your study is primarily descriptive, your main objective should clearly describe the major focus of your study, even mentioning the organisation and its location unless these are to be kept confidential (e.g. to describe the types of treatment programme provided by [name of the organisation] to alcoholics in [name of the place] *or* to find out the opinion of the community about the health services provided by [name of the health centre/department] in [name of the place]). Identification of the organisation and its location is important as the services may be peculiar to the place and the organisation and may not represent the services provided by others to similar populations.

If your study is correlational in nature, in addition to the first three characteristics shown in Figure 4.5, the wording of the main objective should also include the main variables being correlated (e.g. to ascertain the *impact of migration* on *family roles* or to compare the effectiveness of *different teaching methods* on the *comprehension of students*).

If the overall thrust of your study is to test a hypothesis, the wording of the main objectives should also indicate the direction of the relationship being tested (e.g. to ascertain if an *increase in youth unemployment* will *increase the incidence of street crime*, or to demonstrate that the provision of maternal and child health services to Aboriginal people in rural Australia will *reduce infant mortality*).

The study population

So far we have focused on only one aspect of a study, the research problem. But every study in social sciences has a second aspect, the study population, from whom the information required to find answers to your research question is obtained. As you narrow the research problem, similarly you need to decide very specifically and clearly who constitutes your study population, in order to select the appropriate respondents.

Suppose you have designed a study to ascertain the needs of young people living in a community. In terms of the study population, one of the first questions you need to answer is 'Who do I consider to be a young person?' You need to decide, in measurable terms, which age group your respondents should come from. Is it those between 15 and 18, 15 and 20, or 15 and 25 years of age? Or you may be interested in some other age group. You need to decide this before undertaking your research journey. Having decided the age group that constitutes your 'young person', the next question you need to consider is whether you want to select young people of either gender or confine the study to one only. In addition, there is another dimension to consider: that is, what constitutes the community? Which geographical area(s) or ethnic background should you select your respondents from?

Let us take another example. Suppose you want to find out the settlement process of immigrants. As a part of identifying your study population, you need to decide who you would consider an immigrant. Is it a person who immigrated 5, 10, 15 or 20 years ago? You also need to consider the countries from where the immigrants come. Will you select your respondents irrespective of the country of origin or select only those who have come from a specific country or countries? You need to narrow your definition of the study population as you have done with your research problem. These issues are discussed in greater depth in the next section.

In quantitative research, you need to narrow both the research problem and the study population and make them as specific as possible so that you and your readers are clear about them. In qualitative research, reflecting the 'exploratory' philosophical base of the approach, both the study population and the research problem should remain loose and flexible to ensure the freedom necessary to obtain varied and rich data if a situation emerges.

Establishing operational definitions

In defining the problem you may use certain words or items that are as such difficult to measure and/or the understanding of which may vary from respondent to respondent. In a research study it is important to develop, define or establish a set of rules, indicators or yardsticks in order to establish clearly the meaning of such words/items. It is sometimes also important to define clearly the study population from which you need to obtain the required information. When you define concepts that you plan to use either in your research problem and/or in identifying the study population in a measurable form, they are called operational definitions or working definitions. You must understand that these operational definitions that you develop are only for the purpose of your study and could be quite different from legal definitions, or those used by others. The meanings you assign to the concepts are only for the purpose of your study and are designed to remove ambiguity when selecting or communicating with your respondents. As the understanding of concepts can vary markedly from person to person, your operational definitions will inform your readers what exactly you mean by the concepts that you have used in your study.

Let us take an example from studies where the main objectives are:

1. to find out the number of *children* living below the *poverty line* in Australia;
2. to ascertain the impact of immigration on *family roles* among *immigrants*;
3. to measure the *effectiveness* of a retraining programme designed to help *young people*.

Although these objectives clearly state the main thrust of the studies, they are not specific in terms of either the main variables to be studied or the study populations. You cannot count the number of children living below the poverty line until you decide what constitutes the poverty line and how to determine it; you cannot find out the impact of immigration on family roles unless you identify which roles constitute family roles; and you cannot measure effectiveness until you define what effectiveness is. On the other hand, it is equally important to decide exactly what you mean by 'children',' immigrants' or 'young'. Up to what age will you consider a person to be a child? Who would you consider young? Who would you consider to be an immigrant? In addition, will you consider immigrants from every country or only a few? In many cases you need to develop operational definitions for the variables and concepts you are studying and for the population that becomes the source of the information for your study. Table 4.2 lists the concepts and the population groups to be operationalised for the above examples. Defining these clearly by developing operational definitions will avoid ambiguity and confusion.

Operational definitions may differ from day-to-day meanings as well as dictionary or legal definitions. These meanings may not be helpful in identifying either your study population or the concepts you are studying. Though in daily life you often use words such as 'children', 'youth' and 'immigrant' loosely, you need to be more specific when using them in a research study. You should work through your own definitions.

Table 4.2 Operationalisation of concepts and study populations

| Study | Concept to be studied | | Population to be studied | |
	Concepts	Issues	Study populations	Issues
1	Poverty line	What constitutes the 'poverty line'?	Children	Who would you consider a child?
2	Family roles	What constitutes 'family roles'?	Immigrants	Who would you consider an immigrant?
3	Effectiveness	What constitutes 'effectiveness'?	The young	Who would you consider a young person?
You must:	operationalise the concepts – define in practical, observable and measurable terms 'poverty line', 'family roles' and 'effectiveness'		operationalise the study population – define in identifiable terms 'children', 'immigrants' and 'young'	

FORMULATING A RESEARCH PROBLEM 75

Operational definitions give an operational meaning to the study population and the concepts used. It is only through making your procedures explicit that you can validly describe, explain, verify and test. It is important to remember that there are no rules for deciding if an operational definition is valid. Your arguments must convince others about the appropriateness of your definitions.

Formulating a research problem in qualitative research

QUALITATIVE VS
QUANTITATIVE
RESEARCH

The difference in qualitative and quantitative studies starts with the way you formulate your research problem. In quantitative research you strive to be as specific as possible, attempt to narrow the magnitude of your study and develop a framework within which you confine your search. On the other hand, in qualitative research, this specificity in scope, methods and framework is not required. You strive instead to maintain flexibility, openness and freedom to include any new ideas or exclude any aspect that you initially included but later consider not to be relevant. At the initial stage you may only identify

QUALITATIVE
RESEARCH IN
PSYCHOLOGY

Once I supervised a student who was interested in attention-deficit hyperactivity disorder (ADHD). She wanted to find out, as she put it, 'What does it mean to have a child with ADHD in the family?' Of course my first question to her was 'What do you mean by "what does it mean"?' She paused for a while and then said, 'it means what it means'. I asked her to treat me as one of her respondents and ask the question. She asked me, 'What does it mean to have a child with ADHD?' to which my answer was, 'I do not understand your question. Could you please explain to me the meaning of "what does it mean"?' She found it difficult to explain and immediately realised the problem with the question. What she thought was very clear to her became quite difficult to explain. It took her a while to explain to me what she had in mind. During the discussion that followed, though she could explain some of the things she had in mind, she realised that she could not go to a respondent with her initial question.

The student knew a family who had a child with ADHD from which her interest in the topic had probably stemmed. I suggested that she have a talk with the mother. She did, and, to her surprise, the mother asked her the same question that I had.

I advised her to read some literature on ADHD and also have informal talks with two families who have a child with ADHD. We decided to select one single mother family and another where the father and the mother both take responsibility for the child. She was advised to record all the issues and aspects that reflected her understanding of 'what it means', relating to bringing up a child with ADHD in the family. After going through the above, she developed a list, three and a half pages long, of the aspects and issues that, according to her, reflected her understanding of 'what it means'. She did not construct any specific questions around these aspects or issues. They served as background for her to raise with potential respondents in case respondents did not come up with issues or aspects for discussion in terms of 'What does it mean to have a child with ADHD in the family?'

This list brought immense clarification to her thinking about 'what it means' and served as the basis of her interviews with the families. A number of times during the supervisory sessions she had mentioned that she would not have been able to do much without the conceptual framework. You should not confuse it with the interview guide. The list is a conceptual construction of the thoughts that serve as background and become the basis of discussions in case there is insufficient dialogue with your potential respondents.

---

the main thrust of your study and some specific aspects which you want to find out about. Qualitative research primarily employs inductive reasoning. In contrast to quantitative research, where a research problem is stated before data collection, in qualitative research the problem is reformulated several times after you have begun data collection. The research problem and the data collection strategies are reformulated as necessary throughout data collection either to acquire the 'totality' of a phenomenon or to select certain aspects for greater in-depth study.

This flexibility and freedom, though providing you with certain advantages, can also create problems in terms of comparability of the information gathered. It is possible that your areas of search may become markedly different during the preliminary and final stages of data gathering. During the initial developmental phase, many researchers produce a framework of 'reminders' (a conceptual framework of enquiry) to ensure that key issues/aspects are covered during discussions with the respondents. As the study progresses, if need be, issues or themes are added to this framework. This is not a list of questions but reminders that are only used if for some reason the interaction with respondents lacks discussion.

Look at the example above that details the process of formulating a research problem in qualitative research. In qualitative research you do not formulate a research problem as you do in quantitative research. However, it is of immense importance that you develop a conceptual framework that could serve as a basis for discussing issues with the respondents, especially in cases where respondents are not very forthcoming. In qualitative research you need to be open and flexible in terms of the framework of your enquiry so that you can bring depth and richness to the data.

Summary

The formulation of a research problem is the most important step in the research process. It is the foundation, in terms of design, on which you build the whole study. Any defects in it will adversely affect the validity and reliability of your study.

SUCCEEDING IN
YOUR RESEARCH

There are no specific guidelines, but the model suggested in this chapter could serve as a useful framework for the beginner. The seven-step model helps you to narrow your broad area of interest to enable you to decide specifically what you want to study. It is operational in nature and follows a logical sequence that takes the beginner through the complexities of formulating a research problem in a simple and easy-to-understand manner.

In quantitative research you need to determine the path of your research journey in advance. This navigational map becomes your guide. However, in qualitative research the journey is open, and free from strict adherence to any path.

In quantitative studies it is important to go through the process of narrowing down or zeroing in on the research problem. The path and the outcome are determined by a set of objectives that you formulate. It is therefore important that you articulate the objectives of your study clearly. Objectives – whether the main objective or the subobjectives – should be specific and free from ambiguity, and each one should relate to only one aspect of the study. Use action-oriented words when writing your objectives.

FORMULATING A RESEARCH PROBLEM   77

Formulation of a research problem in qualitative research follows a different path. You do not predetermine the exact nature and extent of the research problem you propose to find answers to. You continue to modify it as you start finding out more about it. However, it will help you if you develop a conceptual framework for the different aspects of the problem to serve as a backdrop for issues to be discussed with potential respondents.

Developing operational definitions for the concepts that you propose to study is extremely important. This enhances clarity about the issues you are trying to find out about and about the study population you plan to gather information from. It is important that you operationalise both the main variables you are proposing to study and the study population.

FOR YOU TO THINK ABOUT

- Refamiliarise yourself with the keywords listed at the beginning of this chapter, and if you are uncertain about the meaning or application of any of them revisit them in the chapter before moving on.
- Identify two or three potential research questions, related to your own academic field or professional area, that would fall under each of the four Ps (as outlined in Table 4.1): people, problems, programmes and phenomena.
- For each of these hypothetical research questions, identify which concepts and study populations would need to be operationally defined. Consider what problems might occur if this were not done.
- Select a broad subject area of interest to you and 'dissect' it into subareas.

Now, as you have gone through the chapter, try answering the following questions:

- Broadly outline the differences in formulating a research problem in quantitative and qualitative research;
- Select a subject area of interest to you and dissect it into subareas as suggested in Figure 4.1.
- What considerations should you bear in mind in the wording of objectives?
- Select an area of interest to you and map the process of formulating a research problem.

Want to learn more? Visit
http://www.uk.sagepub.com/kumar4e
or scan this QR code to gain access to a range of online resources to support your study including practice quizzes, videos, weblinks, flashcards, and journal articles.

5

IDENTIFYING VARIABLES

In this chapter you will learn about

- What variables and concepts are and how they are different
- How to turn concepts into operational variables
- Types of variables from the viewpoint of causation, the study design and unit of measurement
- Types of measurement scales: nominal or classificatory, ordinal or ranking, interval and ratio

At the end of this chapter, you should have an understanding of

- Different types of variables from various perspectives
- Place of variables in research
- How to convert concepts into variables
- Different types of measurement scale

If it exists, it can be measured. (Babbie 1989: 105)

In the process of formulating a research problem in quantitative research, there are two important considerations that you should keep in mind: whether or not you are researching a concept(s) in the process of undertaking your study; and whether or not you are testing a hypothesis. Both concepts and hypotheses place additional responsibility on you in terms of their operationalisation. Concepts need to be operationalised in behavioural terms, and hypotheses need to be constructed and their outcome communicated in a specific manner. In the previous chapter, we established that concepts are highly subjective as their understanding may vary from person to person. It follows, therefore, that as such they may not be uniformly (and thus accurately) measurable. In a research study it is important that the concepts used should be operationalised in measurable terms so that the extent of variation in respondents' understanding is reduced if not eliminated. Using techniques to operationalise concepts, and knowledge about variables and their measurement, play an important role in reducing this variability and 'fine-tuning' your research problem.

What is a variable?

Whether we accept it or not, we all make value judgements constantly in our daily lives: 'This food is *excellent*'; 'I did not sleep *well* last night'; 'I do not *like* this'; and 'I think this is *wonderful*'. These are all judgements based upon our *own* preferences, indicators or assessment. Because they explain feelings or preferences, the basis on which they are made may vary markedly from person to person. There is no uniform yardstick with which to measure them. A particular food may be judged 'excellent' by one person but 'awful' by another, and something else could be wonderful to one person but ugly to another. When people express these feelings or preferences, they do so on the basis of certain criteria in their minds, or in relation to their expectations. If you were to question them you would discover that their judgement is based upon indicators and/or expectations that lead them to conclude and express a particular opinion.

Let us consider this in a professional context:

- 'This programme is *effective*.'
- 'This programme is *not effective*.'
- 'We are providing a *quality* service to our clients.'
- 'This is a *waste of time*.'
- 'In this institution women are *discriminated* against.'
- 'There is no *accountability* in this office.'
- 'This product is not doing *well*.'

These are not preferences per se; they are judgements that require a sound basis on which to proclaim. For example, if you want to find out if a programme is effective, if a service is of quality or if there is discrimination, you need to be careful that such judgements have a rational and sound basis. This warrants the use of a measuring mechanism and it is in the process of measurement that knowledge about variables plays an important role.

An image, perception or concept that is capable of measurement – hence capable of taking on different values – is called a variable. According to Kerlinger (1986: 27), 'A variable is a property that takes on different values. Putting it redundantly, a variable is something that varies … A variable is a symbol to which numerals or values are attached.' Black and Champion (1976: 34) define variables as 'rational units of analysis that can assume any one of a number of designated sets of values'. A variable, then, is a concept that can be measured on any one of the four types of measurement scale, which have varying degrees of precision in measurement (measurement scales are discussed later in this chapter).

However, there are some who believe that scientific methods are incapable of measuring feelings, preferences, values and sentiments. In the author's opinion most of these things can be measured, though there are situations where they must be measured indirectly through appropriate indicators rather than directly. These feelings and judgements are based upon observable behaviours in real life, though the extent to which the behaviours reflect their judgements may vary from person to person. In the words of Cohen and Nagel (1966: 352):

> There are, indeed, a great many writers who believe that scientific method is inherently inapplicable to such judgements as estimation or value, as 'This is beautiful', 'This is good' or 'This ought to be done' … all judgements of the latter type express nothing but feelings, tastes or individual preferences, such judgements cannot be said to be true or false (except as descriptions of the personal feelings of the one who utters them) … Almost all human discourse would become meaningless if we took the view that every moral or aesthetic judgement is no more true or false than any other.

The difference between a concept and a variable

The main difference between a concept and a variable is measurability. Concepts are mental images or perceptions and therefore their meanings vary markedly from

Table 5.1 Examples of concepts and variables

Concepts	Variables
• Effectiveness	• Gender (male/female)
• Satisfaction	• Attitude
• Impact	• Age (*x* years, *y* months)
• Excellent	• Income ($ −− per year)
• High achiever	• Weight (−− kg)
• Self-esteem	• Height (−− cm)
• Rich	• Religion (Catholic, Protestant, Jewish, Muslim)
• Domestic violence	• etc.
• Extent and pattern of alcohol consumption	
• etc.	
− Subjective impression	− Measurable, though the degree of precision
− No uniformity as to its understanding among different people	varies from scale to scale and from variable to variable (e.g. attitude − subjective, income −
− As such cannot be measured	objective)

individual to individual, whereas variables are measurable, though, of course, with varying degrees of accuracy depending upon the measurement scale used. A concept as such cannot be measured, whereas a variable can be subjected to measurement by crude/refined or subjective/objective units of measurement. Concepts are subjective impressions which, if measured as such, would cause problems in comparing responses obtained from different respondents. According to Young (1966: 18):

> Each collaborator must have the same understanding of the concepts if the collaborative data are to be similarly classified and the findings pooled and tested, or reproduced. Classification and comparison demand uniform and precise definitions of categories expressed in concepts.

It is therefore important for the concepts to be converted into variables (either directly or through a set of indicators) as they can be subjected to measurement, even though the degree of precision with which they can be measured markedly varies from one measurement scale (*nominal, ordinal, interval* and *ratio*) to another. Table 5.1 gives examples of concepts and variables to illustrate the differences between them.

Converting concepts into variables

If you are using a concept in your study, you need to consider its operationalisation – that is, how it will be measured. In most cases, to operationalise a concept you first need to go through the process of identifying indicators – a set of criteria reflective of the concept – which can then be converted into variables. The choice of indicators for a concept might vary with the researcher, but those selected must have a logical link with the concept.

Some concepts, such as 'rich' (in terms of wealth), can easily be converted into indicators and then variables. For example, to decide objectively if a person is 'rich', one first needs to decide upon the indicators of wealth. Assume that we decide upon income and assets as the indicators. Income is already a variable since it can be measured in some unit of currency, say dollars; therefore, you do not need to convert this into a variable. Although the assets owned by an individual are indicators of his/her 'richness', they still belong to the category of concepts. You need to look further at the indicators of assets. For example, house, boat, car and investments are indicators of assets. Converting the value of each one into dollars will give the total value of the assets owned by a person. Next, fix a level, based upon available information on income distribution and an average level of assets owned by members of a community, which acts as the basis for classification. Then analyse the information on income and the total value of the assets to make a decision about whether the person should be classified as 'rich'. The operationalisation of other concepts, such as the 'effectiveness' or 'impact' of a programme, may prove more difficult. Table 5.2 shows some examples that will help you to understand the process of converting concepts into variables. Note that in these examples only some of the indicators have been picked up. Also, the values set for decision levels are arbitrary and have no empirical validity.

One of the main differences between quantitative and qualitative research studies is in the area of variables. In qualitative research, as it usually involves studying perceptions, beliefs, or feelings, you do not make any attempt to establish uniformity in them across respondents and hence measurements and variables do not carry much significance. On the other hand, in quantitative studies, as the emphasis is on exploring commonalities in the study population, measurements and variables play an important role.

Types of variable

A variable can be classified in a number of ways. The classification developed here results from looking at variables in three different ways (see Figure 5.1):

- the causal relationship;
- the study design;
- the unit of measurement.

From the viewpoint of causal relationship

In studies that attempt to investigate a causal relationship or association, four sets of variables may operate (see Figure 5.2):

- variables that are responsible for *bringing about change* in a phenomenon, situation or circumstance;
- *outcome* variables, which are the effects, impacts or consequences of a change variable;
- variables which *affect or influence* the link between cause-and-effect variables; and
- *connecting* or *linking* variables, which in certain situations are necessary to complete the relationship between cause-and-effect variables.

Table 5.2 Converting concepts into variables

Concepts → Indicators → Variables

Concepts	Indicators	Variables	
		Variables	Decision level (working definitions)
Rich/poor	1 Income 2 Value of all assets	1 Total income per year 2 Total value of: home(s); car(s); boat; investments	Considered rich: 1 if income is > 200,000 p.a. 2 if total value of assets is > 2,000,000
High academic achievement	1 Performance in examinations 2 Performance in practical work/field placements 3 Performance in tutorial presentations 4 Overall performance etc.	1 Marks in examinations 2 Marks in practical work/field placements 3 Marks in tutorial presentations 4 Overall marks	Considered high achiever: 1 if > 85% 2 if > 85% 3 if > 85% 4 if > 85%
Effectiveness (of a health programme)	1 Changes in the utilisation pattern of services 2 Changes in the morbidity pattern of the community 3 Changes in the illness episodes in a specific period 4 Changes in child mortality rates 5 Changes in the nutritional status of children (weight, height, illness episodes etc.)	1 Increase or decrease in the number of patients per month 2 (a) Changes in the morbidity pattern (b) Changes in morbidity typology 3 Increase or decrease in the number of illness episodes in a month 4 Changes in age-specific death rate 5 Increase or decrease in the crude death rate in the community 6 Changes in the weight, height and illness episodes among children up to 5 years of age in the community	Considered effective if: 1 after a year, the number of patients increases by 25% 2 changes in the morbidity pattern are significant, as judged by a group of experts 3 after a year, the number of illness episodes falls by 30% 4 the crude death rate falls by 0.05 by the end of the year, or any change considered significant by a group of experts 5 there is a significant increase in weight and height and significant reduction in the illness episodes among children under 5 as judged by a group of experts

In research terminology, change variables are called independent variables, outcome/effect variables are called dependent variables, the unmeasured variables affecting the cause-and-effect relationship are called extraneous variables, and the variables that link a cause-and-effect relationship are called intervening variables. To give a little more detail:

VARIABLES

1. Independent variable – the cause supposed to be responsible for bringing about change(s) in a phenomenon or situation.
2. Dependent variable – the outcome or change(s) brought about by introduction of an independent variable.
3. Extraneous variable – several other factors operating in a real-life situation may affect or effect changes in the dependent variable. These factors, not measured in the study, may increase or decrease the magnitude or strength of the relationship between independent and dependent variables.
4. Intervening variable – sometimes called the confounding variable (Grinnell 1988: 203), it links the independent and dependent variables. In certain situations the relationship between an independent and a dependent variable cannot be established without the intervention of another variable. The cause, or independent, variable will have the assumed effect only in the presence of an intervening variable.

To explain this typology, let us consider some examples. Suppose you want to study the relationship between smoking and cancer. You assume that smoking is a cause of cancer. Studies have shown that there are many factors affecting this relationship, such as the number of cigarettes or the amount of tobacco smoked every day; the duration of smoking; the age of the smoker; dietary habits; and the amount of exercise taken by the individual. All of these factors may affect the extent to which smoking might cause cancer. These variables may either increase or decrease the magnitude of the relationship.

In this example the extent of smoking is the independent variable, incidence of cancer is the dependent variable, and all the variables that might affect this relationship, either positively or negatively, are extraneous variables. See Figure 5.3.

Let us take another example. Suppose you want to study the effects of a marriage counselling service on marital problems among clients of an agency providing such a service. Figure 5.4 shows the sets of variables that may operate in studying the relationship between counselling and marriage problems.

In studying this relationship, it is assumed that the counselling service will influence the extent of marital problems. Thus, the type of counselling service is the independent variable and the extent of marriage problems is the dependent variable. The magnitude or strength of this relationship can be affected, positively or negatively, by a number of other factors that are not the focus of the study. These extraneous variables might be the birth of a child; improvement in a couple's economic situation; the couple's motivation to change the situation; the involvement of another person; self-realisation; and pressure from relatives and friends. Extraneous variables that work both ways can increase or decrease the strength of the relationship.

The example in Figure 5.5 should help you to understand intervening variables. Suppose you want to study the relationship between fertility and mortality. Your aim is to explore what happens to fertility when mortality declines. The history of demographic transition has shown that a reduction in the fertility level follows a decline in the mortality

IDENTIFYING VARIABLES 85

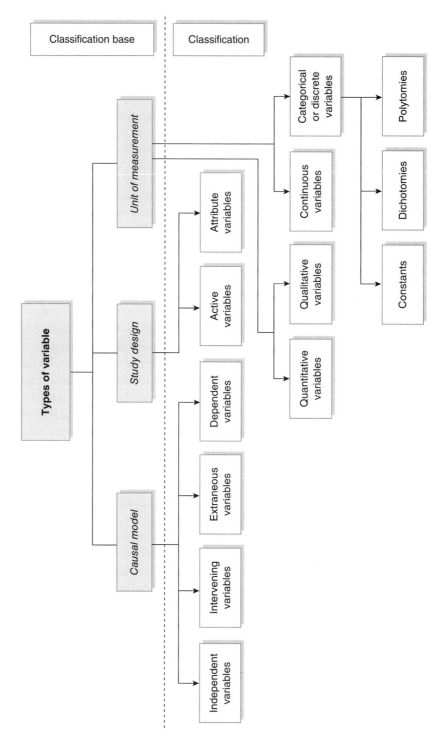

Figure 5.1 Types of variable

Note: Classification across a classification base is not mutually exclusive but classification within a classification base is. Within a study an independent variable can be an active variable, or a quantitative or a qualitative variable, and it can also be a continuous or a categorical variable, but it cannot be a dependent, an extraneous or an intervening variable.

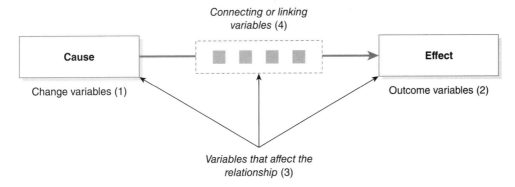

Figure 5.2 Types of variable in a causal relationship

level, though the time taken to attain the same level of reduction in fertility varies markedly from country to country. As such, there is no direct relationship between fertility and mortality. With the reduction in mortality, fertility will decline only if people attempt to limit their family size. History has shown that for a multiplicity of reasons (the discussion of which is beyond the scope of this book) people have used one method or another to control their fertility, resulting in lower fertility levels. It is thus the intervention of contraceptive methods that completes the relationship: the greater the use of contraceptives, the greater the decline in the fertility level, and the sooner the adoption of contraceptive methods by people, the sooner the decline. The extent of the use of contraceptives

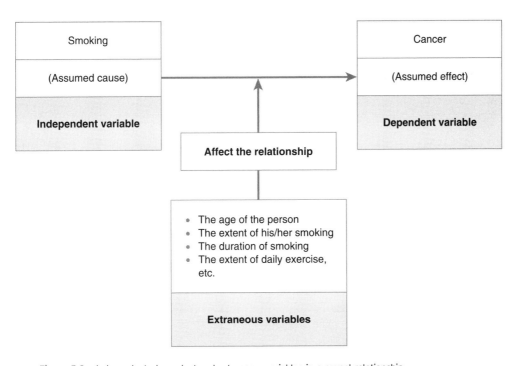

Figure 5.3 Independent, dependent and extraneous variables in a causal relationship

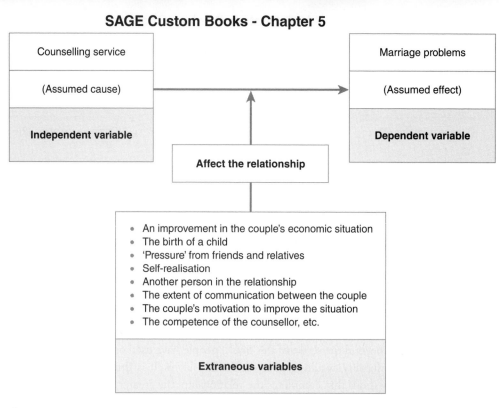

Figure 5.4   Sets of variables in counselling and marriage problems

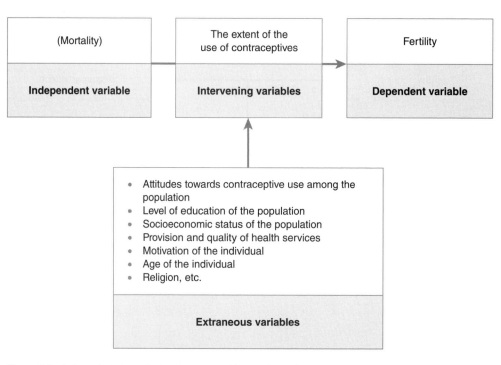

Figure 5.5   Independent, dependent, extraneous and intervening variables

is also affected by a number of other factors, for example attitudes towards contraception, level of education, socioeconomic status and age, religion, and provision and quality of health services. These are classified as extraneous variables.

In this example, decline in mortality is assumed to be the cause of a reduction in fertility, hence the mortality level is the independent variable and fertility is the dependent variable. But this relationship will be completed only if another variable intervenes – that is, the use of contraceptives. A reduction in mortality (especially child mortality) increases family size, and an increase in family size creates a number of social, economic and psychological pressures on families, which in turn create attitudes favourable to a smaller family size. This change in attitudes is eventually operationalised in behaviour through the adoption of contraceptives. If people do not adopt methods of contraception, a change in mortality levels will not be reflected in fertility levels. The population explosion in developing countries is primarily due to lack of acceptance of contraceptives. The extent of the use of contraceptives determines the level of the decline in fertility. The extent of contraceptive adoption by a population is dependent upon a number of factors. As mentioned earlier, in this causal model, the fertility level is the dependent variable, the extent of contraceptive use is the intervening variable, the mortality level is the independent variable, and the unmeasured variables such as attitudes, education, age, religion and the quality of services are all extraneous variables. Without the intervening variable the relationship between the independent and dependent variables will not be complete.

From the viewpoint of the study design

A study that examines association or causation may be a controlled/contrived experiment, a quasi-experiment or an *ex post facto* or non-experimental study. In controlled experiments the independent (cause) variable may be introduced or manipulated either by the researcher or by someone else who is providing the service. In these situations there are two sets of variables (see Figure 5.6):

- Active variables – those variables that can be manipulated, changed or controlled.
- Attribute variables – those variables that cannot be manipulated, changed or controlled, and that reflect the characteristics of the study population, for example age, gender, education and income.

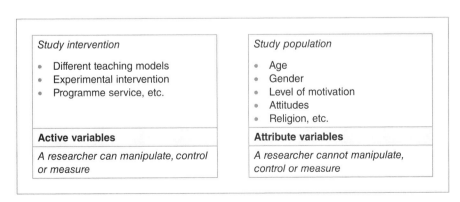

Study intervention	Study population
• Different teaching models • Experimental intervention • Programme service, etc.	• Age • Gender • Level of motivation • Attitudes • Religion, etc.
Active variables	**Attribute variables**
A researcher can manipulate, control or measure	*A researcher cannot manipulate, control or measure*

Figure 5.6   Active and attribute variables

Suppose a study is designed to measure the relative effectiveness of three teaching models (A, B and C). The structure and contents of these models could vary and any model might be tested on any population group. The contents, structure and testability of a model on a population group may also vary from researcher to researcher. On the other hand, a researcher has no control over characteristics of the student population such as their age, gender or motivation to study. These characteristics of the study population are called attribute variables. However, a researcher does have the ability to control and/or change the teaching models. S/he can decide what constitutes a teaching model and on which group of the student population it should be tested (if randomisation is not used).

From the viewpoint of the unit of measurement

From the viewpoint of the unit of measurement, there are two ways of categorising variables:

- whether the unit of measurement is categorical (as in nominal and ordinal scales) or continuous in nature (as in interval and ratio scales);
- whether it is qualitative (as in nominal and ordinal scales) or quantitative in nature (as in interval and ratio scales).

On the whole there is very little difference between categorical and qualitative, and between continuous and quantitative, variables. The slight difference between them is explained below.

Categorical variables are measured on nominal or ordinal measurement scales, whereas for continuous variables the measurements are made on either an interval or a ratio scale. There are three types of categorical variables:

- constant variable – has only one category or value, for example taxi, tree and water;
- dichotomous variable – has only two categories, as in male/female, yes/no, good/bad, heads/tails, up/down and rich/poor;
- polytomous variable – can be divided into more than two categories, for example religion (Christian, Muslim, Hindu); political parties (Labour, Liberal, Conservative); and attitudes (strongly favourable, favourable, uncertain, unfavourable, strongly unfavourable).

Continuous variables, on the other hand, have continuity in their measurement, for example age, income and attitude score. They can take any value on the scale on which they are measured. Age can be measured in years, months and days. Similarly, income can be measured in dollars and cents.

In many ways qualitative variables are similar to categorical variables as both use either nominal or ordinal measurement scales. However, there are some differences. For example, it is possible to develop categories on the basis of measurements made on a continuous scale, such as measuring the income of a population in dollars and cents and then developing categories such as 'low', 'middle' and 'high' income. The measurement of income in dollars and cents is classified as the measurement of a continuous variable, whereas its subjective measurement in categories such as 'low', middle' and 'high' groups is a qualitative variable.

Table 5.3 Categorical/continuous and quantitative/qualitative variables

	Categorical				
Constant	**Dichotomous**	**Polytomous**	**Continuous**	**Qualitative**	**Quantitative**

• water
• tree
• taxi
	• yes/no
	• good/bad
	• rich/poor
	• day/night
	• male/female
	• hot/cold
		Attitudes
		  • strongly agree
		  • agree
		  • uncertain
		  • disagree
		  • strongly disagree
		
		Political parties
		  • Labour
		  • Liberal
		  • Conservative
		
		Age[a]
		  • old
		  • child
		  • young
		
		Income[b]
		  • high
		  • middle
		  • low
			Income ($)
			Age (years)
			Weight (kg)
				Gender
				  • female
				  • male
				
				Educational level
				  • high
				  • average
				  • low
				
				Age[a]
				  • old
				  • young
				  • child
				
				Income
				  • high
				  • middle
				  • low
				
				Temperature[c]
				  • hot
				  • cold
					Educational level:
					____ no. of years completed
					Age:[a]
					____ years/months
					Income:[b]
					____ $ per year
					Temperature:[c]
					____ °C or °F

[a] Can be classified in qualitative categories, e.g. old, young, child; or quantitatively on a continuous scale, e.g. in years, months and days.

[b] Can be measured quantitatively in dollars and cents as well as qualitatively in categories such as high, middle and low.

[c] Can be measured quantitatively in degrees on different scales (Celsius, Fahrenheit) or in qualitative categories such as hot and cold.

Although this distinction exists, for most practical purposes there is no real difference between categorical and qualitative variables or between continuous and quantitative variables. Table 5.3 shows similarities and differences among the various types of variable.

For a beginner it is important to understand that the way a variable is measured determines the type of analysis that can be performed, the statistical procedures that can be applied to the data, the way the data can be interpreted and the findings that can be communicated. You may not realise at the beginning that the style of your report is entirely dependent upon the way the different variables have been measured – that is, the way a question has been asked and its response recorded. The way you measure the variables in your study determines whether a study is 'qualitative' or 'quantitative' in nature. It is therefore important to know about the measurement scales for variables.

Types of measurement scale

The frame into which we wish to make everything fit is one of our own construction; but we do not construct it at random, we construct it by measurement so to speak; and that is why we can fit the facts into it without altering their essential qualities. (Poincaré 1952: xxv)

Measurement is central to any enquiry. In addition to the ideology and philosophy that underpin each mode of enquiry, the most significant difference between qualitative and quantitative research studies is in the types of measurement used in collecting information from the respondents. Qualitative research mostly uses descriptive statements to seek answers to the research questions, whereas in quantitative research these answers are usually sought on one of the measurement scales (nominal, ordinal, interval or ratio). If information is not collected using one of the scales at the time of data collection, it is transformed into variables by using these measurement scales at the time of analysis. Measurement on these scales could be either in the form of qualitative categories or through a precise unit of measurement. Those scales which have a unit of measurement (interval and ratio) are considered to be more refined, objective and accurate. On the other hand, nominal and ordinal scales are considered subjective and hence not as accurate as they do not have a unit of measurement per se. The greater the refinement in the unit of measurement of a variable, the greater the confidence placed in the findings by others, other things being equal. One of the main differences between the physical and the social sciences is the units of measurement used and the degree of importance attached to them. In the physical sciences measurements have to be absolutely accurate and precise, whereas in the social sciences they may vary from the very subjective to the very quantifiable. Within the social sciences the emphasis on precision in measurement varies markedly from one discipline to another. An anthropologist normally uses very 'subjective' units of measurement, whereas an economist or an epidemiologist emphasises 'objective' measurement.

There are two main classification systems in the social sciences for measuring different types of variable. One was developed by S. S. Stevens (in 1946; see Stevens 1951) and the other by Duncan (1984). According to Smith (1991: 72), 'Duncan (1984) has enumerated, in increasing order of interest to scientists, five types of measurement: nominal classification, ordinal scaling, cardinal scaling, ratio scaling, and probability scaling'. Duncan (1984: viii) writes about Stevens's classification as follows:

MEASUREMENT
SCALES

> The theory of scale types proposed in 1946 by S. S. Stevens focused on nominal, ordinal, interval, and ratio scales of measurement. Some of his examples of these types − notably those concerning psychological test scores − are misleading.

However, Bailey (1978: 52) considers that 'S. S. Stevens constructed a widely adopted classification of levels of measurement'. As this book is written for the beginner and as Stevens's classification is simpler, this is what is used for discussion in this chapter. Stevens classified the different types of measurement scale into four categories:

- nominal or classificatory scale;
- ordinal or ranking scale;
- interval scale;
- ratio scale.

Table 5.4 summarises the characteristics of the four scales.

Table 5.4   Characteristics and examples of the four measurement scales

Measurement scale	Examples	Characteristics of the scale
Nominal or classificatory	Tree, house, taxi, etc. Gender: male/female Attitude: agree/disagree Political parties • Labour • Liberal • Democrats • Greens Psychiatric disorders • Schizophrenic • Paranoid • Manic-depressive, etc. Religions • Christian • Islam • Hindu, etc.	Each subgroup has a characteristic/property which is common to all classified within that subgroup
Ordinal or ranking	Income • above average • average • below average Socioeconomic status • upper • middle • lower Attitudes • strongly agree • agree • uncertain • disagree • disagree Likert attitudinal scale (see Chapter 10)	This has the characteristics of a nominal scale, e.g. individuals, groups, characteristics classified under a subgroup have a common characteristic PLUS • Subgroups have a relationship with one another • They are arranged in relation to their respective magnitude either in ascending or descending order
Interval	Temperature • Celsius • Fahrenheit Thurstone attitudinal scale (see Chapter 10):	This has all the characteristics of an ordinal scale (which also includes a nominal scale) PLUS • It has a unit of measurement with an arbitrary starting and terminating point
Ratio	Height: cm Income: $ Age: years/months Weight: kg Attitudinal score: Guttman scale (see Chapter 10)	This has all the properties of an interval scale PLUS • It has a fixed starting point at zero

The nominal or classificatory scale

A nominal scale enables the classification of individuals, objects or responses based on a common/shared property or characteristic. Such individuals, objects or responses are divided into a number of subgroups in such a way that each member of the subgroup shares a common characteristic or a property. A variable measured on a nominal scale may have one, two or more subcategories depending upon the extent of variation. For example, 'water' and 'taxi' have only one subgroup, whereas the variable 'gender' can be classified into two subcategories: male and female. Political parties in Australia can similarly be classified into four main subcategories: Labour, Liberal, Democrats and Greens. Those who identify themselves, either by membership or belief, as belonging to the Labour Party are classified as 'Labour', those identifying with the Liberals are classified as 'Liberal', and so on. The name chosen for a subcategory is notional, but for effective communication it is best to choose something that describes the characteristic of the subcategory.

> Classification by means of a nominal scale ensures that individuals, objects or responses within the same subgroup have a common characteristic or property as the basis of classification. The sequence in which subgroups are listed makes no difference as there is no order relationship among subgroups.

The ordinal or ranking scale

An ordinal scale has all the properties of a nominal scale – categorising individuals, objects, responses or a property into subgroups on the basis of a common characteristic – but also ranks the subgroups in a certain order. They are arranged in either ascending or descending order according to the extent to which a subcategory reflects the magnitude of variation in the variable. For example, income can be measured either quantitatively (in dollars and cents) or qualitatively, using subcategories: 'above average', 'average' and 'below average'. (These categories can also be developed on the basis of quantitative measures, for example below $10 000 is defined as below average, $10 000–$25 000 as average, and above $25 000 as above average.) The subcategory 'above average' indicates that people so grouped have more income than people in the 'average' category, and people in the 'average' category have more income than those in the 'below average' category. These subcategories of income are related to one another in terms of the magnitude of people's income, but the magnitude itself is not quantifiable, and hence the difference between 'above average' and 'average' or between 'average' and 'below average' subcategories cannot be ascertained. The same is true for other variables such as socioeconomic status and attitudes measured on an ordinal scale.

To summarise, an ordinal scale has all the properties/characteristics of a nominal scale, in addition to its own. Subcategories are arranged in order of the magnitude of the property/characteristic. Also, the 'distance' between the subcategories is not equal as there is no quantitative unit of measurement.

The interval scale

An interval scale has all the characteristics of an ordinal scale; that is, individuals or responses belonging to a subcategory have a common characteristic and the subcategories are arranged in an ascending or descending order. In addition, an interval scale uses a unit of measurement that enables the individuals or responses to be placed at equally spaced intervals in relation to the spread of the variable. This scale has a starting and a terminating point and is divided into equally spaced units/intervals. The starting and terminating points and the number of units/intervals between them are arbitrary and vary from scale to scale.

Celsius and Fahrenheit scales are examples of an interval scale. In the Celsius system the starting point (considered as the freezing point) is 0°C and the terminating point (considered as the boiling point) is 100°C. The gap between the freezing and boiling points is divided into 100 equally spaced intervals, known as degrees. In the Fahrenheit system the freezing point is 32°F and the boiling point is 212°F, and the gap between the two points is divided into 180 equally spaced intervals. Each degree or interval is a measurement of temperature – the higher the degree, the higher the temperature. As the starting and terminating points are arbitrary, they are not absolute; that is, you cannot say that 60°C is twice as hot as 30°C or 30°F is three times hotter than 10°F. This means that while no mathematical operation can be performed on the readings, it can be performed on the differences between readings. For example, if the difference in temperature between two objects, A and B, is 15°C and the difference in temperature between two other objects, C and D, is 45°C, you can say that the difference in temperature between C and D is three times as great as that between A and B. An attitude towards an issue measured on the Thurstone scale is similar. However, the Likert scale does not measure the absolute intensity of the attitude but simply measures it in relation to another person.

To summarise, the interval scale is relative; that is, it plots the position of individuals or responses in relation to one another with respect to the magnitude of the measurement variable. Hence, an interval scale has all the properties of an ordinal scale, and it has a unit of measurement with an arbitrary starting and terminating point.

The ratio scale

A ratio scale has all the properties of nominal, ordinal and interval scales and it also has a starting point fixed at zero. Therefore, it is an absolute scale – the difference between the intervals is always measured from a zero point. This means the ratio scale can be used for mathematical operations. The measurement of income, age, height and weight are examples of this scale. A person who is 40 years of age is twice as old as a 20-year-old. A person earning $60 000 per year earns three times the salary of a person earning $20 000.

Summary

The understanding and interpretation of a concept or a perception may vary from respondent to respondent, hence its measurement may not be consistent. A variable has some basis of classification and hence there is far less inconsistency in its meaning and understanding. Concepts are mental perceptions, whereas variables are measurable either subjectively or objectively on one of the measurement scales. When you convert a concept into a variable you classify it on the basis of measurement into categories, thereby minimising the inherent variability in understanding. When you are unable to measure a concept directly, you need first to convert it into indicators and then into variables.

The way the required information is collected in quantitative and qualitative research is the most significant difference between them. Qualitative research mostly uses descriptive or narrative statements as the 'units of measurement', whereas quantitative research places greater emphasis of measuring responses on one of the four measurement scales. Though qualitative research places emphasis on descriptive statements in data collection, in some cases these statements are classified at the time of analysis into categories on the basis of the main themes they communicate. However, there are times when you will prefer to use verbatim descriptions and narrations to build your logic and arguments.

Knowledge of the different types of variables and the way they are measured plays a crucial role in quantitative research. Variables are important in bringing clarity and specificity to the conceptualisation of a research problem, to the formulation of hypotheses and to the development of a research instrument. They affect how the data can be analysed, what statistical tests can be applied to the data, what interpretations can be made, how the data can be presented and what conclusions can be drawn. The way you ask a question determines its categorisation on a measurement scale, which in turn affects how the data can be analysed, what statistical tests can be applied to the data, what interpretations can be made, how the data can be presented and what conclusions can be drawn. Also, the way variables are measured at the data collection stage to a great extent determines whether a study is considered to be predominantly 'qualitative' or 'quantitative' in nature.

It is important for a beginner to understand the different ways in which a variable can be measured and the implications of this for the study. A variable can be classified from three perspectives that are not mutually exclusive: causal relationship, design of the study and unit of measurement. From the perspective of causality a variable can be classified into one of four categories: independent, dependent, extraneous and intervening. From the viewpoint of study design, there are two categories of variable: active and attribute. If we examine a variable from the perspective of the unit of measurement, it can be classified into categorical and continuous or qualitative and quantitative.

There are four measurement scales used in the social sciences: nominal, ordinal, interval and ratio. Any concept that can be measured on these scales is called a variable. Measurement scales enable highly subjective responses, as well as responses that can be measured with extreme precision, to be categorised. The choice of measuring a variable on a measurement scale is dependent upon the purpose of your study and the way you want to communicate the findings to readers.

FOR YOU TO THINK ABOUT

- Refamiliarise yourself with the keywords listed at the beginning of this chapter, and if you are uncertain about the meaning or application of any of them revisit them in the chapter before moving on.
- Imagine that you have been asked to evaluate your lecturer. Determine which aspects of teaching you would consider important and develop a set of indicators that might reflect these.
- Self-esteem is a difficult concept to operationalise. Think about how you might go about developing a set of indicators to determine variation in the level of self-esteem in a group of individuals.
- Critically examine the typology of variables developed in this chapter. What changes would you like to propose?

Now, as you have gone through the chapter, try answering the following questions:

- Explain the differences between a concept and a variable.
- Develop the typology of variables from different perspectives.
- What is the difference between extraneous and intervening variables?
- What are the different types of measurement scale? What purpose do they serve in a research study?

Want to learn more? Visit
http://www.uk.sagepub.com/kumar4e
or scan this QR code to gain access to a range of online resources to support your study including practice quizzes, videos, weblinks, flashcards, and journal articles.

6

CONSTRUCTING HYPOTHESES

In this chapter you will learn about

- The definition of a hypothesis
- The functions of a hypothesis in your research
- How hypotheses are tested
- How to formulate a hypothesis
- Different types of hypotheses and their applications
- How errors in the testing of a hypothesis can occur
- The use of hypotheses in qualitative research

> **Keywords**
>
> alternative hypotheses, hunch, hypothesis, hypothesis of point
>
> prevalence, null hypothesis, operationalisable,
>
> research hypothesis, Type I error, Type II error, unidimensional, valid.

At the end of this chapter, you should have an understanding of

- The place of hypotheses in research
- Testing of a hypothesis
- Types of hypothesis
- Errors in the testing of a hypothesis

Almost every great step [in the history of science] has been made by the 'anticipation of nature', that is, by the invention of hypotheses which, though verifiable, often had very little foundation to start with. (T.H. Huxley, cited in Cohen & Nagel 1966: 197)

The definition of a hypothesis

The second important consideration in the formulation of a research problem in quantitative research is the construction of a hypothesis. Hypotheses bring clarity, specificity and focus to a research problem, but are not essential for a study. You can conduct a valid investigation without constructing a single formal hypothesis. On the other hand, within the context of a research study, you can construct as many hypotheses as you consider to be appropriate. Some believe that one must formulate a hypothesis to undertake an investigation; however, the author does not hold this opinion. Hypotheses primarily arise from a set of 'hunches' that are tested through a study, and one can conduct a perfectly valid study without having these hunches or speculations. However, in epidemiological studies, to narrow the field of investigation, it is important to formulate hypotheses. The importance of hypotheses lies in their ability to bring direction, specificity and focus to a research study. They tell a researcher what specific information to collect, and thereby provide greater focus.

RESEARCH
QUESTIONS AND
HYPOTHESES

Let us imagine you are at the races and you place a bet. You bet on a hunch that a particular horse will win. Only after the race will you know if your hunch was right. To take another example, suppose you have a hunch that there are more smokers than non-smokers in your class. To test your hunch, you ask either all or just some of the class if they are smokers. You can then conclude whether your hunch was right or wrong.

Now let us take a slightly different example. Suppose you work in the area of public health. Your clinical impression is that a higher rate of a particular condition prevails among people coming from a specific population subgroup. You want to find out first whether or not your hunch is right, and second what are the probable causes of this condition. There could be many causes. To explore every conceivable possibility would require an enormous amount of time and resources. Hence, to narrow the choice, based on your knowledge of the field, you could identify what you assume to be the most probable cause. You could then design a study to collect the information needed to verify your hunch. If on verification you were able to conclude that there is a prevalence of the assumed condition in the population subgroup and that the assumed cause really is the reason, your assumptions would be proved right.

In these examples, you started with a superficial hunch or assumption. In one case (horse racing) you waited for the event to take place, and in the other two instances you designed a study to assess the validity of your assumption, and only after careful investigation did you arrive at a conclusion about the validity of your assumptions.

Hypotheses are based upon similar logic. As a researcher you *do not know* about a phenomenon, a situation, the prevalence of a condition in a population or the outcome of a programme, but you do have a hunch to form the basis of certain *assumptions* or guesses. You test these by collecting the information that will enable you to conclude whether or not your hunch was right. The verification process can have one of three outcomes. Your hunch may prove to be right, partially right or wrong. Without this process of verification, you cannot conclude anything about the validity of your assumption.

Hence, a hypothesis is a hunch, assumption, suspicion, assertion or an idea about a phenomenon, relationship or situation, the reality or truth of which you do not know. A researcher refers to these assumptions, assertions, statements or hunches as hypotheses, and they become the basis of an enquiry. In most studies the hypothesis will be based upon either previous studies or your own or someone else's observations.

There are many definitions of a hypothesis. According to Kerlinger (1986: 17), 'A hypothesis is a conjectural statement of the relationship between two or more variables'. *Webster's Third New International Dictionary* (1976) defines a hypothesis as:

> a proposition, condition, or principle which is assumed, perhaps without belief, in order to draw out its logical consequences and by this method to test its accord with facts which are known or may be determined.

Black and Champion (1976: 126) define a hypothesis as 'a tentative statement about something, the validity of which is usually unknown'. In another definition, Bailey (1978: 35) defines a hypothesis as:

> a proposition that is stated in a testable form and that predicts a particular relationship between two (or more) variables. In other words, if we think that a relationship exists, we first state it as a hypothesis and then test the hypothesis in the field.

According to Grinnell (1988: 200):

> A hypothesis is written in such a way that it can be proven or disproven by valid and reliable data – it is in order to obtain these data that we perform our study.

From the above definitions it is apparent that a hypothesis has certain characteristics:

1. It is a tentative proposition.
2. Its validity is unknown.
3. In most cases, it specifies a relationship between two or more variables.

The functions of a hypothesis

While some researchers believe that to conduct a study requires a hypothesis, having a hypothesis is not essential, as already mentioned. However, a hypothesis is important in terms of bringing clarity to the research problem. Specifically, a hypothesis serves the following functions:

- The formulation of a hypothesis forces you to precisely specify what you want to find out about, thus bringing specificity and clarity to your study.
- The specificity and clarity needed to construct a hypothesis ensure you only collect the information you need, thereby providing focus to the study. This also enhances the validity of your study as it ensures you are measuring what you set out to measure.
- As it provides a focus, the construction of a hypothesis enhances objectivity in a study.
- The testing of a hypothesis enables you to specifically conclude what is true or what is false, thus enabling you to contribute towards theory formulation.

The testing of a hypothesis

To test a hypothesis you need to go through a process that comprises three phases: (1) constructing the hypothesis; (2) gathering appropriate evidence; and (3) analysing evidence to draw conclusions as to the validity of the hypothesis. Figure 6.1 shows this process diagrammatically. It is only after analysing the evidence that you can conclude whether your hunch or hypothesis was true or false. Conventionally, when drawing your conclusion about a hypothesis, you specifically make a statement about the correctness or otherwise of a hypothesis in the form of 'the hypothesis is true' or 'the hypothesis is false'. It is therefore imperative that you formulate your hypotheses clearly, precisely and in a form that is testable. In arriving at a conclusion about the validity of your hypothesis, the way you collect your evidence is of central importance and it is therefore essential that your study design, sample, data collection method(s), data analysis and conclusions, and communication of the conclusions be valid, appropriate and free from any bias. Testing and drawing conclusions about the validity of a hypothesis become meaningless if the study design, sampling, methods of data collection etc. used in testing the hypothesis are inappropriate. You need to be certain about the appropriateness of the whole research process when testing a hypothesis.

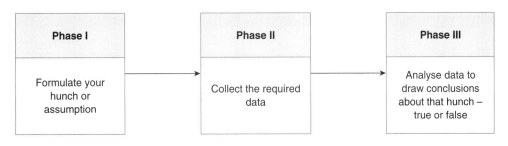

Figure 6.1   The process of testing a hypothesis

The characteristics of a hypothesis

There are a number of considerations to keep in mind when constructing a hypothesis, as they are important for valid verification. The wording of a hypothesis therefore must have certain attributes that make it easier for you to ascertain its validity.

First, a hypothesis should be *simple, specific* and *conceptually clear*. There is no place for ambiguity in the construction of a hypothesis, as ambiguity will make the verification of your hypothesis almost impossible. It should be 'unidimensional' – that is, it should test only one relationship or hunch at a time. To be able to develop a good hypothesis you must be familiar with the subject area (the literature review is of immense help). The more insight you have into a problem, the easier it is to construct a hypothesis. For example:

The average age of the male students in this class is higher than that of the female students.

The above hypothesis is clear, specific and easy to test. It tells you what you are attempting to compare (average age of this class), which population groups are being compared (female and male students), and what you want to explore (whether male students have higher average age).

Let us take another example:

Suicide rates vary inversely with social cohesion. (Black & Champion 1976: 126)

This hypothesis is clear and specific, but a lot more difficult to test. There are three aspects of this hypothesis: 'suicide rates'; 'vary inversely', which stipulates the direction of the relationship; and 'social cohesion'. To find out the suicide rates and to establish whether the relationship is inverse or otherwise are comparatively easy, but to ascertain social cohesion is a lot more difficult. What determines social cohesion? How can it be measured? This problem makes it more difficult to test this hypothesis.

Second, a hypothesis should be *capable of verification*. Methods and techniques must be available for data collection and analysis. There is no point in formulating a hypothesis if it cannot be subjected to verification because there are no techniques to verify it. However, this does not necessarily mean that you should not formulate a hypothesis for which there are no methods of verification. You might, in the process of doing your research, develop new techniques to verify it.

Third, a hypothesis should be *related to the existing body of knowledge*. It is important that your hypothesis emerges from the existing body of knowledge, and that it adds to it, as this is an important function of research. This can only be achieved if the hypothesis has its roots in the existing body of knowledge.

Finally, a hypothesis should be *operationalisable*. This means that it can be expressed in terms that can be measured. If it cannot be measured, it cannot be tested, and hence no conclusions can be drawn.

Types of hypothesis

Theoretically there should be only one type of hypothesis, that is the research hypothesis – the basis of your investigation. However, because of the conventions in scientific enquiry and because of the wording used in the construction of a hypothesis, hypotheses can be classified into several types. Broadly, there are two categories of hypothesis:

1. research hypotheses;
2. alternative hypotheses.

The formulation of an alternative hypothesis is a convention in scientific circles. Its main function is to explicitly specify the relationship that will be considered as true in case the research hypothesis proves to be wrong. In a way, an alternate hypothesis is the opposite of the research hypothesis. Conventionally, a null hypothesis, or hypothesis of no difference, is formulated as an alternate hypothesis.

Let us take an example. Suppose you want to test the effect that different combinations of maternal and child health services (MCH) and nutritional supplements (NS) have on the infant mortality rate. To test this, you adopt a two-by-two factorial experimental design (see Figure 6.2). Within the framework of this study you can formulate a hypothesis in several ways. For example:

1. There will be no difference in the level of infant mortality among the different treatment modalities (Null hypothesis usually written as H_0).
2. The MCH and NS treatment groups will register a greater decline in infant mortality than the MCH-only treatment group, the NS-only treatment group or the control group.
3. Infant mortality in the MCH treatment group will reach a level of 30 per 1000 over 5 years.
4. Decline in the infant mortality rate will be three times greater in the MCH treatment group than in the NS group only over 5 years.

RESEARCH METHODOLOGY

		Maternal and child health services (MCH)	
		Yes	No
Nutritional supplements (NS)	Yes	MCH + NS	NS
	No	MCH	Control

Figure 6.2   Two-by-two factorial experiment to study the relationship between MCH, NS and infant mortality

CONSTRUCTING HYPOTHESES   103

Let us take another example. Suppose you want to study the smoking pattern in a community in relation to gender differentials. The following hypotheses could be constructed:

1. There is no significant difference in the proportion of male and female smokers in the study population.
2. A greater proportion of females than males are smokers in the study population.
3. A total of 60 per cent of females and 30 per cent of males in the study population are smokers.
4. There are twice as many female smokers as male smokers in the study population.

NULL HYPOTHESIS

In both sets of examples, the way the first hypothesis has been formulated indicates that there is no difference either in the extent of the impact of different treatment modalities on the infant mortality rate or in the proportion of male and female smokers. When you construct a hypothesis stipulating that there is no difference between two situations, groups, outcomes, or the prevalence of a condition or phenomenon, this is called a null hypothesis and is usually written as H_0.

The second hypothesis in each example implies that there is a difference either in the extent of the impact of different treatment modalities on infant mortality or in the proportion of male and female smokers among the population, though the extent of the difference is not specified. A hypothesis in which a researcher stipulates that there will be a difference but does not specify its magnitude is called a hypothesis of difference.

A researcher may have enough knowledge about the smoking behaviour of the community or the treatment programme and its likely outcomes to speculate about the exact prevalence of the situation or the outcome of a treatment programme in quantitative units. Examine the third hypothesis in both sets of examples: the level of infant mortality is 30 per 1000 and the proportion of female and male smokers is 60 and 30 per cent, respectively. This type of hypothesis is known as a hypothesis of point-prevalence.

The fourth hypothesis in both sets of examples posits a relationship between the impact of different combinations of MCH and NS programmes on the dependent variable (infant mortality) or the relationship between the prevalence of a phenomenon

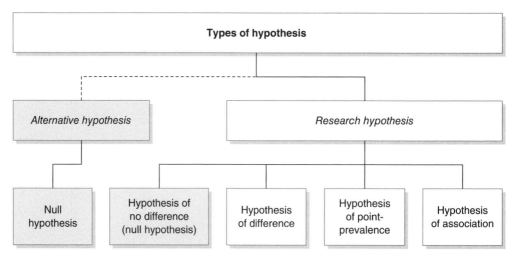

Figure 6.3   Types of hypothesis

(smoking) among different populations (male and female).This type of hypothesis stipulates the extent of the relationship in terms of the effect of different treatment groups on the dependent variable ('three times greater in the MCH treatment group than in the NS group over 5 years') or the prevalence of a phenomenon in different population groups ('twice as many female as male smokers'). This type of hypothesis is called a hypothesis of association.

Note that in Figure 6.3 the null hypothesis is also classified as a hypothesis of no difference under 'research hypothesis'. Any type of hypothesis, including a null hypothesis, can become the basis of an enquiry. When a null hypothesis becomes the basis of an investigation, it becomes a research hypothesis.

Errors in testing a hypothesis

As already mentioned, a hypothesis is an assumption that may prove to be either correct or incorrect. It is possible to arrive at an incorrect conclusion about a hypothesis for a variety of reasons. Incorrect conclusions about the validity of a hypothesis may be drawn if:

- the study design selected is faulty;
- the sampling procedure adopted is faulty;
- the method of data collection is inaccurate;
- the analysis is wrong;
- the statistical procedures applied are inappropriate; or
- the conclusions drawn are incorrect.

Any, some or all of these aspects of the research process could be responsible for the inadvertent introduction of error in your study, making conclusions misleading. Hence, in the testing of a hypothesis there is always the possibility of errors attributable to the reasons identified above. Figure 6.4 shows the types of error that can result in the testing of a hypothesis.

When a null hypothesis is actually:

	True	False
Accept	Correct decision	Type II error
Reject	Type I error	Correct decision

When your decision is to:

Figure 6.4   Type I and Type II errors in testing a hypothesis

Hence, in drawing conclusions about a hypothesis, two types of error can occur:

- *Rejection* of a null hypothesis when it is true. This is known as a Type I error.
- *Acceptance* of a null hypothesis when it is false. This is known as a Type II error.

Hypotheses in qualitative research

One of the differences between qualitative and quantitative research is around the importance attached to and the extent of use of hypotheses when undertaking a study. As qualitative studies are characterised by an emphasis on describing, understanding and exploring phenomena using categorical and subjective measurement procedures, construction of hypotheses is neither greatly advocated nor significantly practised. In addition, as the degree of specificity needed to test a hypothesis is deliberately not adhered to in qualitative research, the testing of a hypothesis becomes difficult. This does not mean that you cannot construct hypotheses in qualitative research; however non-specificity of the problem as well as methods and procedures make the convention of hypothesis formulation far less practicable and advisable. Even within quantitative studies the importance attached to and the practice of formulating hypotheses vary markedly from one academic discipline to another. For example, hypotheses are most prevalent in epidemiological research and research relating to the establishment of causality of a phenomenon, where it becomes important to narrow the list of probable causes so that a specific cause-and-effect relationship can be studied. In the social sciences formulation of hypotheses is mostly dependent on the researcher and the academic discipline, whereas within an academic discipline it varies markedly between the quantitative and qualitative research paradigms.

Summary

Hypotheses, though important, are not essential for a study. A perfectly valid study can be conducted without constructing a single hypothesis. Hypotheses are important for bringing clarity, specificity and focus to a research study.

A hypothesis is a speculative statement that is subjected to verification through a research study. In formulating a hypothesis it is important to ensure that it is simple, specific and conceptually clear; can be verified; is rooted in an existing body of knowledge; and can be operationalised.

There are two broad categories of hypothesis: a research hypothesis and an alternative hypothesis. A research hypothesis can be further classified, based upon the way it is formulated, as a null hypothesis, a hypothesis of difference, a hypothesis of point-prevalence and a hypothesis of association.

One of the main differences in qualitative and quantitative research is the extent to which hypotheses are used and the importance attached to them. In qualitative research, because of the purpose of an investigation and methods used to obtain information, hypotheses are not used and almost no importance is given to them. However, in quantitative research, their use is far more prevalent though it varies markedly from one academic discipline to another and from researcher to researcher. On the whole it can be said that if the aim of a study is to explore where very little is known, hypotheses are usually not formulated; however, if a study aims to test an assertion by way of causality or association, validate the prevalence of something or establish its existence, hypotheses can be constructed.

The testing of a hypothesis becomes meaningless if any one of the aspects of your study – design, sampling procedure, method of data collection, analysis of data, statistical procedures applied or conclusions drawn – is faulty or inappropriate. This can result in erroneous verification of a hypothesis: Type I error occurs where you reject a null hypothesis when it is true and should not have been rejected; and Type II error is introduced where you accept a null hypothesis when it is false and should not have been accepted.

FOR YOU TO THINK ABOUT

- Refamiliarise yourself with the keywords listed at the beginning of this chapter, and if you are uncertain about the meaning or application of any of them revisit them in the chapter before moving on.
- To what extent do you think that the use of hypotheses is relevant to social research?
- Formulate two or three hypotheses that relate to your own areas of interest and consider the factors that might affect their validity.

Now, as you have gone through the chapter, try answering the following questions:

- What is a hypothesis and what functions does it serve in a research study?
- The validity of a hypothesis test is dependent on a number of prerequisites. What are these requisites?
- What are the different types of hypothesis? What is the main function of a null hypothesis?
- What are the two types of error in testing of a hypothesis? Explain them.

Want to learn more? Visit
http://www.uk.sagepub.com/kumar4e
or scan this QR code to gain access to a range of online resources to support your study including practice quizzes, videos, weblinks, flashcards, and journal articles.

DEVELOPING A RESEARCH PROJECT: A SET OF EXERCISES FOR BEGINNERS

Application is the essence of knowledge. However, there always remains a gap between theoretical knowledge and its application. It is only with practice that this gap can be narrowed. A beginner attempting to apply theoretical knowledge needs direction and guidance. This set of exercises, each one of which is attached to an operational step, has been developed with this belief in mind. Working through them will help you to develop a research project.

The main aim of these exercises is to provide you with a broad framework that is central to the operationalisation of each step of the research process. In most cases, a separate exercise is provided for quantitative and qualitative studies, so it is important that you know before you start which approach you are going to take. Within each exercise, there are brief reminders of some of the key issues relating to the process and a series of questions to help you to think through procedures and provide a framework for the development of your study.

Answers to these questions and awareness of the issues that the exercises outline will put you in a position to complete the framework suggested for writing a research proposal (Chapter 13), and therefore these will also constitute the core of your research proposal.

It is important for a beginner to work through these exercises with considerable thought and care.

Congratulations!

Now you have learnt how to take the first step towards your research journey. By this time you should have a reasonably good understanding about how to formulate a research problem. You should be ready to put your knowledge and skills into practice by actually working through the process of formulating a research problem. This exercise is designed to help you to formulate a research problem of interest to you. Good luck!

Exercise I: Formulation of a research problem
Quantitative studies

Now that you have gone through all the chapters that constitute Step I of the research process, this exercise provides you with an opportunity to apply that knowledge to formulate a research problem that is of interest to you. As you know, selecting a research problem is one of the most important aspects of social research, so this exercise will help you in formulating your research problem by raising questions and issues that will guide you to examine critically various facets and implications of what you are proposing to study. The exercise is designed to provide a directional framework that guides you through the problem formulation path. Keep in mind that the questions and issues raised in this exercise are not prescriptive but indicative and directional, hence you need to be critical and innovative while working through them. Thinking through a research problem with care can prevent a tremendous waste of human and financial resources.

TEMPLATE OF
EXERCISE I

A research problem should be clearly stated and be specific in nature. The feasibility of the study in terms of the availability of technical expertise, finances and time, and in terms of its relevance, should be considered thoroughly at this stage. In studies that attempt to establish a causal relationship or an association, the accuracy of the measurement of independent (cause) and dependent (effect) variables is of crucial importance and, hence, should be given serious consideration. If you have already selected a problem, you need not go through this process.

Start by identifying a *broad subject area* of interest to you. For example, health, education, crime, immigration, public health, tourism, recreation, parenting, crime, social justice. This exercise is designed to help you to dissect and then select the subarea(s) of interest to you to become the basis of your study. Chapter 4 of this book will help you to work through this exercise.

Step I: Select a broad area of study that interests you from within your academic discipline.

Having selected an area, the next step is to 'dissect' it in order to identify its various aspects and subareas. For example, suppose your broad area of interest is migration. Some aspects or subareas of migration are:

- a socioeconomic-demographic profile of immigrants;
- reasons for immigration;
- problems of immigrants;
- services provided to immigrants;
- attitudes of immigrants towards migration;
- attitudes of host communities towards immigrants;
- the extent of acculturation and assimilation;
- racial discrimination in the host country.

Or perhaps you are interested in studying a public health programme. Dissect it as finely as possible in order to identify the aspects that could be studied. List them as they come to you. For example:

- a socioeconomic-demographic profile of the target group;
- the morbidity and mortality patterns in a community;
- the extent and nature of programme utilisation;
- the effects of a programme on a community;
- the effectiveness of a particular health promotion strategy.

Or your interest may be in studying delinquents. Some aspects of delinquency are:

- delinquency as related to unemployment, broken homes or urbanisation;
- a profile of delinquents;
- reasons for delinquency;
- various therapeutic strategies.

Step II: 'Dissect' the broad area that you selected in Step I into subareas as discretely and finely as possible. Have a one-person (with yourself) brainstorming session.

1. _____
2. _____
3. _____
4. _____
5. _____

To investigate all these subareas is neither advisable nor feasible. Select only those subareas that would be possible for you to study within the constraints of time, finance and expertise at your disposal. One way to select your subarea is to start with a process of elimination: delete those areas you are not very interested in. Towards the end it may become difficult but you need to keep eliminating until you have selected a subarea(s) that can be managed within your constraints. Even one subarea can provide you with a valid and exhaustive study.

Step III: From the above subareas, select a subarea or subareas in which you would like to conduct your study.

1. _____
2. _____
3. _____

Step IV: Within each chosen subarea, what research questions do you hope to answer? (Be as specific as possible. You can select one or as many subareas as you want.)

Subarea	Specific research questions to be answered
1a	1 _____
	2 _____
	3 _____
1b	1 _____
	2 _____

1 (a) _____
   (b) _____
   (c) _____
   (d) _____
   (e) _____

2 (a) _____
   (b) _____
   (c) _____
   (d) _____
   (e) _____

3 (a) _____
   (b) _____
   (c) _____
   (d) _____
   (e) _____

The research questions to be answered through the study become the basis of your objectives. Now you need to formulate your study objectives. In so doing, use action-oriented words. The main difference between research questions and objectives is the way they are written. Questions are worded in question form and objectives are statements referring to the achievement of a task.

> Your main objective should indicate the overall focus of your study and the subobjectives, its specific aspects. Subobjectives should be listed numerically. They should be worded clearly and unambiguously. Make sure each objective contains only one aspect of the study.

Step V: On the basis of your research questions, formulate the main objective and the subobjectives of your study.

Main objective (the main focus of your study):

_____

_____

_____

Subobjectives (specific aspects of your study):

1. _____
2. _____
3. _____
4. _____
5. _____

Step VI: Carefully consider the following aspects of your study.

Task	What is involved	Time needed	Approx. cost	Technical expertise needed	Gaps in knowledge and skills
Literature review					
Instrument construction					
Data collection					
Data analysis					
Draft report					
Final report					

> Now you have developed the objectives of your study. Take some time to think about them. Be clear about what tasks are involved, what time is realistically required and what skills you need to develop in order to conduct your study. Consider these areas carefully again.

Step VII: Double-check:

• Are you really interested in the study?

Yes ☐   No ☐   Uncertain ☐

- Do you agree with the objectives of the study?

  Yes ☐   No ☐   Uncertain ☐

- Are you certain you want to pursue the study?

  Yes ☐   No ☐   Uncertain ☐

- Do you have adequate resources?

  Yes ☐   No ☐   Uncertain ☐

- Do you have access to an appropriate study population?

  Yes ☐   No ☐   Uncertain ☐

If your answer to any of these questions is either 'no' or 'uncertain', re-examine the selected aspects carefully and make the appropriate changes in your objectives.

What, in your opinion, is the relevance of this study to theory and practice? How will your study contribute to the existing body of knowledge, help the practitioners in your profession and assist in programme development and policy formulation?

Relevance to theory:

_____

_____

_____

_____

Relevance to practice:

_____

_____

_____

_____

Now that you have formulated your research problem, it is important to examine your objective, research questions and hypotheses to identify if you have used any concepts in their formulation. When you convert concepts into variables an understanding about variables plays a very important role. Concepts are highly subjective as their understanding varies from person to person and, as such, they may not be measurable. Any concept, perception or imagination that can be measured on any one of the four measurement scales (nominal, ordinal, interval or ratio) is called a variable. It is important for concepts used in a study to be operationalised in measurable terms so that the extent of variation in a study population's understanding of them is reduced, if not eliminated.

At this stage, when you have formulated your objectives, it is important for you to think how you will operationalise any concepts used in the objectives, research questions or hypotheses formulated: what are their indicators and how will they be measured?

The following table suggests how you might operationalise the concept of 'effectiveness', in relation to a health education programme on AIDS. It lists the indicators of effectiveness (you can have other indicators), sets out the variables that measure the indicators and describes the unit of measurement for the variables.

EXERCISE I   113

Concept $\longrightarrow$	Indicator $\longrightarrow$	Variable(s) $\longrightarrow$	Unit of measurement
Effectiveness	*Awareness* of AIDS	Extent of change in:	Change in the proportion of the population, before and after the health education programme, with respect to:
	Knowledge about AIDS	Awareness Knowledge practice	Awareness of, and knowledge about, different aspects of AIDS
	Use of contraceptives (practice)		Use of contraceptives for safe sex

This part of the exercise is designed to help you operationalise the major concepts used in your study. Refer to Chapter 5 for additional information on variables.

Step VIII: Operationalise your concepts.

Objectives/research questions/hypotheses	Major concepts	Indicators	Variables	Unit of measurement

It is essential to develop a working or operational definition of your study population. For example, who would you consider to be a patient, an immigrant, a youth, a psychologist, a teacher, a delinquent or a Christian? Working definitions play a crucial role in avoiding ambiguities in the selection of a sample and help you to narrow your study population.

Step IX: Operationally define your study population.

_____

_____

_____

_____

_____

114   **RESEARCH METHODOLOGY**

Skip this section if you are *not* constructing a hypothesis.

As discussed, some believe that one must have a hypothesis to undertake an investigation; however, in the author's opinion, hypotheses, although they bring clarity, specificity and focus to a research problem, are not essential for a study. You can conduct a valid investigation without constructing a single formal hypothesis. On the other hand, you can construct as many hypotheses as you think appropriate. In epidemiological studies, to narrow the field of investigation, one must construct a hypothesis as to the probable cause of the condition to be investigated.

A hypothesis is a hunch, assumption, suspicion, assertion or idea about a phenomenon, relationship or situation, which you intend to investigate in order to find out if you are right. If it proves to be right, your assumption was correct; hence, you prove that your hypothesis was true. Otherwise, you conclude your hypothesis to be false.

Disproving a hypothesis is as important as, or more important than, proving it. As a hypothesis is usually constructed on the basis of what is commonly believed to be right, your disproving it might lead to something new that has been ignored by previous researchers.

A hypothesis should be conceptually simple, clear and specific, and be capable of verification and being expressed operationally.

There is a specific way of writing a hypothesis, with which you need to be familiar (refer to Chapter 6).

Step X: Construct your hypothesis or hypotheses for each subobjective/research question.

Objectives/research questions	Hypotheses to be tested
	1
	2
	3
	1
	2
	3
	1
	2
	3

Qualitative studies

As mentioned earlier, the difference in qualitative and quantitative research studies starts with the way you think about and formulate your research problem. In qualitative studies, it is preferred that the research problem is broad, flexible and continuously formulated as the information is collected. In the process of data collection, if you find something interesting relating to your broad area of study, you add the aspect(s) and change the focus to accommodate the new vision.

This flexibility is an important strength of qualitative research but it is also important that you develop a conceptual framework of issues and questions for your study, as non-specificity about what you want to find out can often create problems for your respondents. Many do not feel comfortable or are not in a position to articulate the multiple aspects of an area without being prompted. For situations like this it is important that you are fully prepared with a framework in mind for your enquiry. No doubt you can develop this framework during data collection, while talking to your respondents, but this may create a problem in terms of completeness and comparability with the information obtained during the early phase of the study. You can minimise some of these problems by developing a conceptual framework in advance. It is also important that you communicate with respondents in specific terms without bias or influencing their thinking.

Remember, these are not the questions that you will ask of your respondents. These are just reminders for raising issues or questions if nothing much is forthcoming from a respondent.

In qualitative research the following would be considered as broad areas of interest:

- What does it mean to have a child with ADHD in the family?
- How resilient is this community?
- What is community responsiveness?
- Living with HIV/AIDS.
- How has a community coped after a major bush fire or tsunami?

Step I: Select a broad area of study that interests you or a question that you want to find answers to through the research study.

_____

_____

Step II: Having selected your main research question or broad area of study, list all questions to which you want to find answers. Also list all issues that you want to discuss with your respondents. Your literature review, discussions with others and consultation with potential respondents will be of immense help at this stage.

Questions:_____

_____

_____

_____

_____

_____

_____

_____

_____

Issues: _____

_____

_____

STEP II

CONCEPTUALISING A RESEARCH DESIGN

This operational step includes two chapters:

- Chapter 7: The Research Design
- Chapter 8: Selecting a Study Design

7

THE RESEARCH DESIGN

In this chapter you will learn about

- What research design means
- The important functions of research design
- Issues to consider when designing your own research
- The theory of causality and the research design

Keywords

chance variables,	independent variable,	randomisation,
control group,	matching, 'maxmincon'	research design,
experimental group,	principle of variance,	study design,
extraneous variables,	random error,	treatment group

At the end of this chapter, you should have an understanding of

- Research design and its functions in social research
- The relationship between the theory of causality and experimental designs
- Factors responsible for bringing about change in a phenomenon
- Quantification of the impact of extraneous variables in impact assessment studies

If you are clear about your research problem, your achievement is worth praising. You have crossed one of the most important and difficult sections of your research journey. Having decided *what* you want to study, you now need to determine *how* you are going to conduct your study. There are a number of questions that need to be answered before you can proceed with your journey. What procedures will you adopt to obtain answers to research questions? How will you carry out the tasks needed to complete the different components of the research process? What should you do and what should you not do in the process of undertaking the study? Basically, answers to these questions constitute the core of a research design.

RESEARCH DESIGN

What is a research design?

A research design is the road map that you decide to follow during your research journey to find answers to your research questions as validly, objectively, accurately and economically as possible. It is a procedural-cum-operational plan that details what and how different methods and procedures to be applied during the research process. According to Kerlinger (1986: 279):

> A research design is a plan, structure and strategy of investigation so conceived as to obtain answers to research questions or problems. The plan is the complete scheme or programme of the research. It includes an outline of what the investigator will do from writing the hypotheses and their operational implications to the final analysis of data.

According to Thyer (1993: 94):

> A traditional research design is a blueprint or detailed plan for how a research study is to be completed — operationalizing variables so they can be measured, selecting a sample of interest to study, collecting data to be used as a basis for testing hypotheses, and analysing the results.

According to Selltiz et al. (1962: 50):

122   **RESEARCH METHODOLOGY**

A research design is the arrangement of conditions for collection and analysis of data in a manner that aims to combine relevance to the research purpose with economy in procedure.

A research design is a plan through which you decide for yourself and communicate to others your decisions regarding what study design you propose to use, how you will collect information from your respondents, how you will select your respondents, how the information you will collect is to be analysed and how you will communicate your findings. In addition, you detail your rationale and justification for each decision that shapes your answers to the 'how' of the research journey. In presenting your rationale and justification you need to support them critically from the literature reviewed. You also need to assure yourself and others that the path you have proposed will yield valid and reliable results.

The functions of a research design

The above definitions suggest that a research design has two main functions. The first relates to the identification and/or development of procedures and logistical arrangements required to undertake a study, and the second emphasises the importance of quality in these procedures to ensure their validity, objectivity and accuracy. Hence, through a research design you:

- conceptualise an operational plan to undertake the various procedures and tasks required to complete your study;
- ensure that these procedures are adequate to obtain valid, objective and accurate answers to the research questions. Kerlinger (1986: 280) calls this function the control of variance.

Let us take the first of these functions. The research design should detail for you, your supervisor and other readers all the procedures you plan to use and the tasks you will perform to obtain answers to your research questions. One of the most important requirements of a research design is to specify everything clearly so that a reader will understand what procedures to follow and how to follow them. These should be written in such detail and clarity that if someone else wants to conduct the study, he/she should be able to follow exactly the way you would have done. A research design, therefore, should include the following:

- Name the study design per se – that is, 'cross-sectional', 'before-and-after', 'comparative', 'control experiment' or 'random control' (Chapter 8 describes some of the commonly used study designs).
- Provide detailed information about the following aspects of the study (details of these are covered in the subsequent chapters of the book):
  - Who will constitute the study population?
  - How will the study population be identified?
  - Will a sample or the whole population be selected?
  - If a sample is selected, how will it be contacted?
  - How will consent be sought?
  - What method of data collection will be used and why?
  - In the case of a questionnaire, where will the responses be returned?

- ○ How should respondents contact you if they have queries?
- ○ In the case of interviews, where will they be conducted?
- ○ How will ethical issues be taken care of?

The theory of causality and the research design

Now let us turn to the second function of the research design – ensuring that the procedures undertaken are adequate to obtain valid, objective and accurate answers to the research questions. In the social sciences there are many causes that are responsible for changing a phenomenon as we are exposed to so many factors on which we do not have any control. These factors can affect the phenomenon in a number of ways. However, in most studies you examine one cause (independent variable) and occasionally two. As you add more independent variables, the design becomes more and more complicated, expensive and difficult to manage. All these variables which have a link with the dependent variable but are not the focus of your study, are considered extraneous variables. The theory of causality helps you to understand the different sets of variables that cause the change in the dependent variable. It also helps you to determine and isolate the impact of different categories of variables so that you validly, objectively and accurately ascertain the impact of independent variables. To explain this, let us examine a few examples.

Suppose you want to examine the effectiveness of a marriage counselling service provided by an agency – that is, the extent to which the service has been able to help its clients to resolve their marital problems. In studying such relationships you must understand that in real life there are many outside factors that can influence the outcome of your intervention. For example, during visits to your agency for counselling, your client may get a better job. If some of the marital problems came about because of economic hardship, and if the problem of money is now solved, it may be a factor in reducing the marital problems. On the other hand, if a client loses his/her job, the worsening of the economic problems may either intensify or lessen the marital problems; that is, for some couples a perceived financial threat may increase marital problems, whereas for others it may create more closeness between partners. In some situations, an improvement in a marriage may have very little to do with the counselling received, coming about almost entirely because of a change in economic circumstances. Other events such as the birth of a child to a couple or a couple's 'self-realisation', independently arrived at, may also affect the extent and nature of marital problems. Figure 7.1 lists other possible factors under the category of extraneous variables. This list is by no means exhaustive.

CORRELATION AND
CAUSALITY

Continuing the example of marriage and counselling, there are sets of factors that can affect the relationship between counselling and marriage problems. These are:

1. Counselling per se (the independent variable).
2. Any reason, other than counselling, that can produce change, positive or negative, in the extent of marital problems (the extraneous variables).
3. The change or otherwise in the extent of the marital problems (the dependent variable).
4. Sometimes, the variation in response to questions about marital problems can be accounted for by either the mood of respondents or ambiguity in the questions. Some respondents may either overestimate or

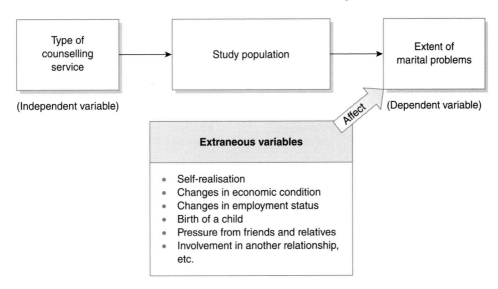

Figure 7.1 Factors affecting the relationship between a counselling service and the extent of marital problems

underestimate their marital problems because of their state of mind at the time. Some respondents, in spite of being in exactly the same situation, may respond to non-specific or ambiguous questions differently, according to how they interpret the question (the chance or random variables).

As already explained in Chapter 5, any variable that is responsible for bringing about a change is called an *independent variable*. In this example, the counselling is an independent variable. When you study a cause-and-effect relationship, usually you study the impact of only one independent variable. Occasionally you may study the impact of two independent variables, or (very rarely) more than two, but these study designs are more complex.

For this example *counselling* was the assumed cause of change in the *extent of marital problems*; hence, the extent of marital problems is the *dependent variable*, as the change in the degree of marital problems was dependent upon counselling.

All other factors that affect the relationship between marital problems and counselling are called *extraneous variables*. In the social sciences, extraneous variables operate in every study and cannot be eliminated. However, they can be controlled to some extent. (Some of the methods for controlling them are described later in this chapter.) Nevertheless, it is possible to examine the impact attributable to extraneous variables. This is done with the introduction of a control group in the study design. The sole function of a control group is to quantify the impact of extraneous variables on the dependent variable(s).

Changes in the dependent variable, because of the respondent's state of mood or ambiguity in the research instrument, are called random variables or chance variables. The error thus introduced is called the *chance* or *random error*. In most cases the net effect of chance variables is considered to be negligible as respondents who overreport tend to cancel out those who underreport. The same applies to responses to ambiguous questions in a research instrument.

THE RESEARCH DESIGN   125

Hence in any causal relationship, changes in the dependent variable may be attributed to three types of variable:

Change in the dependent variable	=	Change attributable to independent variable	±	Change attributable to extraneous variables	±	Change attributable to chance or random variables

Let us take another example. Suppose you want to study the impact of different teaching models on the level of comprehension of students, and you adopt a comparative study design. In this study, the change in the level of comprehension can be attributed not only to the teaching models but also to a number of other factors, some of which are shown in Figure 7.2:

[change in level of comprehension]

    = [change attributable to the teaching model]
      ± [change attributable to extraneous variables]
      ± [change attributable to chance variables]

In fact, in any study that attempts to establish a causal relationship, you will discover that there are three sets of variables operating to bring about a change in the dependent variable. This can be expressed as an equation:

[change in the outcome variable]

    = [change because of the change variable]
      ± [change because of extraneous variables]
      ± [change because of chance or random variables]

This can also be expressed (in research terminology) as:

[change in the dependent variable]

    = [change attributable to the independent variable]
      ± [change attributable to extraneous variables]
        ± [change attributable to chance variables]

or in statistical/technical terms:

[total variance]

    = [variance attributable to the independent variable]
      ± [variance attributable to extraneous variables]
      ± [random or chance variance]

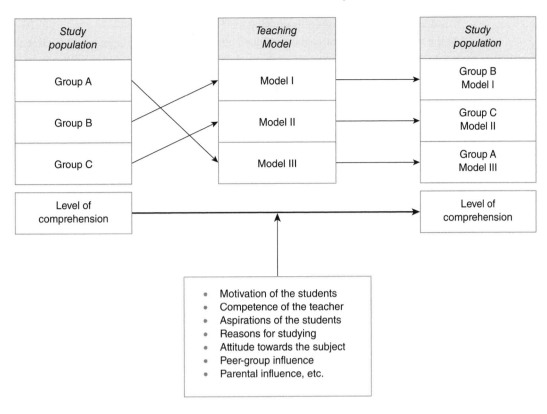

Figure 7.2   The relationship between teaching models and comprehension

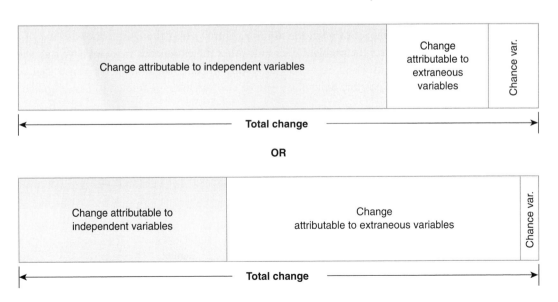

Figure 7.3   The components of total change: independent, extraneous and chance

It can also be expressed graphically (Figure 7.3).

As the total change measures the combined effects of all three components it is difficult to isolate the individual impact of each of them (see Figure 7.3). Since your aim as a researcher is to determine the change that can be attributed to the independent variable, you need to design your study to ensure that the independent variable has the *maximum* opportunity to have its full effect on the dependent variable, while the effects that are attributed to extraneous and chance variables are minimised (if possible) or quantified or eliminated. This is what Kerlinger (1986: 286) calls the maxmincon principle of variance.

One of the most important questions is: how do we minimise the effects attributable to extraneous and chance variables? The simple answer is that in most situations we cannot; however, it can be quantified. The sole purpose of having a control group, as mentioned earlier, is to measure the change that is a result of extraneous variables. The effect of chance variables is often assumed to be none or negligible because of the neutralising effect. As discussed, chance variation comes primarily from two sources: respondents and the research instrument. It is assumed that if some respondents affect the dependent variable positively, others will affect it negatively. For example, if some respondents are extremely positive in their attitude towards an issue, being very liberal or positively biased, there are bound to be others who are extremely negative (being very conservative or negatively biased). Hence, they tend to cancel each other out so the net effect is assumed to be zero. However, if in a study population most individuals are either negatively or positively biased, a systematic error in the findings will be introduced. Similarly, if a research instrument is not reliable (i.e. it is not measuring correctly what it is supposed to measure), a systematic bias may be introduced into the study.

EXPERIMENTAL
DESIGN

In the physical sciences a researcher can control extraneous variables as experiments are usually done in a laboratory. By contrast, in the social sciences, the laboratory is society, over which the researcher lacks control. Since no researcher has control over extraneous variables, their effect, as mentioned, in most situations cannot be minimised. The best option is to quantify their impact through the use of a control group, though the introduction of a control group creates the problem of ensuring that the extraneous variables have a similar effect on both control and experimental groups. In some situations their impact can be eliminated (this is possible only where one or two variables are known to have a marked

Figure 7.4   Building into the design

impact on the dependent variable). There are two methods used to ensure that extraneous variables have a similar effect on control and experimental groups and two methods for eliminating extraneous variables:

1. Ensure that extraneous variables have a similar impact on control and experimental groups. It is assumed that if two groups are comparable, the extent to which the extraneous variables will affect the dependent variable will be similar in both groups. There are two methods that ensure that the control and experimental groups are comparable with one another: randomisation and matching (discussed in Chapter 8).

2. Eliminate or isolate extraneous variable(s). Sometimes it is possible to eliminate an extraneous variable or to build it into the study design. This is usually done when there is strong evidence that the extraneous variable has a high correlation with the dependent variable. There are two methods used to achieve this:

   (a) Build the extraneous variable into the design of the study. To explain this concept let us take an example. Suppose you want to study the impact of maternal health services on the infant mortality of a population. It can be assumed that the nutritional status of children also has a marked effect on infant mortality. To study the impact of maternal health services per se, you adopt a two-by-two factorial design as explained in Figure 7.4. In this way you can study the impact of the extraneous variable separately as well as interactively with the independent variable.

   (b) Eliminate the variable. To understand this, let us take another example. Suppose you want to study the impact of a health education programme on the attitudes towards, and beliefs about, the causation and treatment of a certain illness among non-indigenous Australians and indigenous Australians living in a particular community. As attitudes and beliefs vary markedly from culture to culture, studying non-indigenous Australians and indigenous Australians as one group will not provide an accurate picture. In such studies it is appropriate to eliminate the cultural variation in the study population by selecting and studying the populations separately or by constructing culture-specific cohorts at the time of analysis.

Summary

In this chapter you have learnt about the functions of a research design. A research design serves two important functions: (1) to detail the procedures for undertaking a study; and (2) to ensure that, in the case of causality, the independent variable has the maximum opportunity to have its effect on the dependent variable while the effect of extraneous and chance variables is minimised or quantified. In terms of the first function, a research design should outline the logistical details of the whole process of the research journey. You need to spell out in detail what type of study design you are proposing to use and why, who will be your respondents and how they will be selected, from how many you propose to get the required information, how you will collect the information and how you will analyse it. For each aspect you need to provide your rationale and justification and as far as possible support them from the literature reviewed.

Through the second function, 'control of variance', when establishing association or causality, you assure your supervisor and readers that you have set up your study in such a way that your independent variable has the maximum chance of affecting the dependent variable and that the effects of extraneous and chance variables are minimised, quantified and/or controlled (the 'maxmincon' principle of variance).

A study without a control group measures the total change (change attributable to independent variable ± change attributable to extraneous variables ± change attributable to chance variables) in a phenomenon or situation. The purpose of introducing a control group is to quantify the impact of extraneous and chance variables.

The study design is a part of the research design. The research design also includes other logistical details which are proposed to complete the study.

FOR YOU TO THINK ABOUT

- Refamiliarise yourself with the keywords listed at the beginning of this chapter, and if you are uncertain about the meaning or application of any of them revisit them in the chapter before moving on.
- Provide examples from your own area of study to illustrate the main variables in terms of causality (you may find it useful to refer back to Chapter 5).
- Identify one or two examples from an area that interests you to demonstrate how the 'maxmincon' principle of variance can be applied.

Now, as you have gone through the chapter, try answering the following questions:

- Explain, by providing an example, the three sets of variables that affect the dependent variable when studying association or causality.
- What are the main functions of a research design? Why is it important to have a research design before undertaking a study?
- How might you quantify the impact of extraneous variables when studying the impact of a programme?
- Identify the aspects of a study that need to be described in a research design.
- Can you eliminate the impact of extraneous variables when undertaking impact assessment studies? If yes, how?
- Visit the companion website and read some of the materials provided on causality and qualitative research. What issues do you think choosing a qualitative method of data collection might raise when thinking about causality?

CAUSALITY IN QUALITATIVE RESEARCH

Want to learn more? Visit
http://www.uk.sagepub.com/kumar4e
or scan this QR code to gain access to a range of online resources to support your study including practice quizzes, videos, weblinks, flashcards, and journal articles.

8

SELECTING A STUDY DESIGN

In this chapter you will learn about

- The differences between quantitative and qualitative study designs
- Common study designs in quantitative research and when to use them
- Common study designs in qualitative research and when to use them
- The strengths and weaknesses of different study designs

Keywords

action research, after-only design, attrition, before-and-after study design, blind studies, case studies, cohort studies, conditioning effect, control studies, cross-sectional study design,

double-blind studies, experimental mortality, experimental study design, feminist research, focus studies, longitudinal studies, maturation effect, non-experimental studies, panel studies, power gap,

prospective study design, quasi-experimental studies, reactive effect, reflective journal, regression effect, retrospective studies, semi-experimental studies, trend studies.

At the end of this chapter, you should have an understanding of

- What differentiates quantitative and qualitative research designs
- What the common study designs in quantitative and qualitative research are
- What the strengths and weaknesses of each study design are
- Considerations that you should have in mind when selecting a study design

Differences between quantitative and qualitative study designs

In this chapter we will discuss some of the most commonly used study designs in both quantitative and qualitative research. Overall, there are many more study designs in quantitative research than in qualitative research. Quantitative study designs are specific, well structured, have been tested for their validity and reliability, and can be explicitly defined and recognised. Study designs in qualitative research either do not have these attributes or have them to a lesser degree. They are less specific and precise, and do not have the same structural depth. Qualitative designs are described in the following words by Maxwell (2013: 3):

> To design a qualitative study, you can't just develop (or borrow) a logical strategy in advance and implement it faithfully. You need, to a substantial extent, to *construct* and *reconstruct* your research design, and this is a major rationale for my design model. Qualitative research design, to a much greater extent than quantitative research, is a 'do-it-yourself' rather than an 'off-the-shelf' process, one that involves 'tacking' back and forth between the different components of the design, assessing their implications for one another. It does not begin from a predetermined starting point or proceed through a fixed sequence of steps, but involves interconnection and interaction among the different design components.

Differences in philosophical perspectives in each paradigm, combined with the aims of a study, to a large extent determine the focus, approach and mode of enquiry, which in turn determine the structural aspects of a study design. The main focus in qualitative research is to understand, explain, explore, discover and clarify situations, feelings, perceptions, attitudes, values, beliefs and experiences of a group of people. The study designs are therefore often based on deductive rather than inductive logic, are flexible and emergent in nature, and are often non-linear and non-sequential in their operationalisation. The study designs mainly entail the selection of people from whom the information, through an open frame of enquiry, is gathered and explored. The parameters of the scope of a study, and information gathering methods and processes, are often flexible and evolving; hence, most qualitative designs are not as structured and sequential as quantitative ones. On the other hand, in quantitative research, the measurement and classification requirements of the information that is to be gathered demand that study designs are more structured, rigid, fixed and predetermined to ensure validity and reliability of the information and its classification.

In qualitative studies the distinction between study designs and methods of data collection is far less clear. Quantitative study designs have more clarity and distinction between designs and methods of data collection. In qualitative research there is an overlap between the two. Some designs are basically methods of data collection. For example, in-depth interviewing is a design as well as a method of data collection, and so are oral history and participant observation.

One of the most distinguishing features of qualitative research is the adherence to the concept of respondent concordance, whereby you as a researcher make every effort to seek agreement of your respondents with your interpretation, presentation of the situations, experiences, perceptions and conclusions. In quantitative research respondent concordance does not occupy an important place. Sometimes it is assumed to be achieved by circulating or sharing the findings with those who participated in the study.

The 'power gap' between the researcher and the study population in qualitative research is far smaller than in quantitative research because of the informality in structure and situation in which data is collected.

In quantitative research enough detail about a study design is provided for it to be replicated for verification and reassurance. In qualitative research little attention is paid to study designs or the other structural aspects of a study, hence the replication of a study design and its findings becomes almost impossible.

Another difference in the designs in qualitative and quantitative studies is the possibility of introducing researcher bias. Because of flexibility and lack of control it is more difficult to check for researcher bias in qualitative studies.

Study designs in each paradigm are appropriate for finding different things. Study designs in qualitative research are more appropriate for exploring the variation and diversity in any aspect of social life, whereas in quantitative research they are more suited to finding out the extent of this variation and diversity. If your interest is in studying values, beliefs, understandings, perceptions, meanings, etc., qualitative study designs are more appropriate as they provide immense flexibility. On the other hand, if your focus is to measure the magnitude of that variation – how many people have a particular value, belief, etc. – the quantitative designs are more appropriate. For good quantitative research it is important that you combine quantitative skills with qualitative ones when ascertaining the nature and extent of diversity and variation in a phenomenon. In the author's opinion, the qualitative–quantitative–qualitative approach to research is comprehensive and worth consideration. This involves starting with qualitative methods to determine the spread of diversity, using quantitative methods to quantify the spread, and then going back to qualitative to explain the observed patterns. As already stated, the author does not recommend your locking yourself into either the qualitative or quantitative paradigm and, though you may have your preference, it is the purpose that should determine the choice between quantitative and qualitative study designs. If you already know (from previous studies or practice knowledge) the nature of diversity in the area of interest to you, knowledge about its extent can be determined only by using quantitative methods. In most cases where you want to explore both, you need to use methods that fall in the domain of both paradigms.

Study designs in quantitative research

All study designs used in quantitative studies can be classified by examining them from three different perspectives:

1. the number of contacts with the study population;
2. the reference period of the study;
3. the nature of the investigation.

These perspectives are arbitrary bases of classification; hence, the terminology used to describe them is not universal. However, the names of the designs within each classification base are universally used. Note that the designs *within* each category are mutually exclusive; that is, if a particular study is cross-sectional in nature it cannot at the same time be a before-and-after or a longitudinal study, but it can be a non-experimental or experimental study, as well as a retrospective study or a prospective study. See Figure 8.1.

The chapter concludes with a section on commonly used designs which are based on a certain philosophy or methodology, and which have acquired their own names.

Study designs based on the number of contacts

Based on the number of contacts with the study population, designs can be classified into three groups:

1. cross-sectional studies;
2. before-and-after studies;
3. longitudinal studies.

CROSS-SECTIONAL
STUDY

The cross-sectional study design

Cross-sectional studies, also known as *one-shot* or *status studies*, are the most commonly used design in the social sciences. This design is best suited to studies aimed at finding out the prevalence of a phenomenon, situation, problem, attitude or issue, by taking a cross-section of the population. They are useful in obtaining an overall 'picture' as it stands at the time of the study. They are 'designed to study some phenomenon by taking a cross-section of it at one time' (Babbie 1989: 89). Such studies are cross-sectional with regard to both the study population and the time of investigation.

134   **RESEARCH METHODOLOGY**

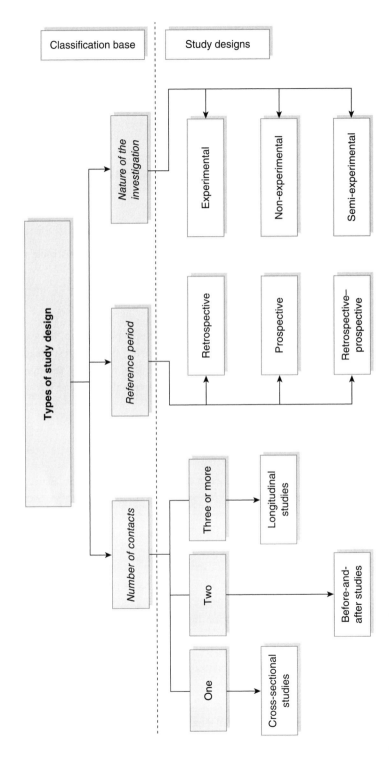

Figure 8.1 Types of study design

A cross-sectional study is extremely simple in design. You decide what you want to find out about, identify the study population, select a sample (if you need to) and contact your respondents to find out the required information. For example, a cross-sectional design would be the most appropriate for a study of the following topics:

- The attitude of the study population towards uranium mining in Australia.
- The socioeconomic-demographic characteristics of immigrants in Western Australia.
- The incidence of HIV-positive cases in Australia.
- The reasons for homelessness among young people.
- The quality assurance of a service provided by an organisation.
- The impact of unemployment on street crime (this could also be a before-and-after study).
- The relationship between the home environment and the academic performance of a child at school.
- The attitude of the community towards equity issues.
- The extent of unemployment in a city.
- Consumer satisfaction with a product.
- The effectiveness of random breath testing in preventing road accidents (this could also be a before-and-after study).
- The health needs of a community.
- The attitudes of students towards the facilities available in their library.

As these studies involve only one contact with the study population, they are comparatively cheap to undertake and easy to analyse. However, their biggest disadvantage is that they cannot measure change. To measure change it is necessary to have at least two data collection points – that is, at least two cross-sectional studies, at two points in time, on the same population.

The before-and-after study design

The main advantage of the before-and-after design (also known as the *pre-test/post-test* design) is that it can measure change in a situation, phenomenon, issue, problem or attitude. It is the most appropriate design for measuring the impact or effectiveness of a programme. A before-and-after design can be described as two sets of cross-sectional data collection points on the same population to find out the change in the phenomenon or variable(s) between two points in time. The change is measured by comparing the difference in the phenomenon or variable(s) before and after the intervention (sees Figure 8.2).

PRE-TEST/
POST-TEST

A before-and-after study is carried out by adopting the same process as a cross-sectional study, except that it comprises two cross-sectional data sets, the second being undertaken after a certain period. Depending upon how it is set up, a before-and-after study may be either an experiment or a non-experiment. It is one of the most commonly used designs in evaluation studies. The difference between the two sets of data collection points with respect to the dependent variable is considered to be the impact of the programme. The following are examples of topics that can be studied using this design:

- The impact of administrative restructuring on the quality of services provided by an organisation.
- The effectiveness of a marriage counselling service.
- The impact of sex education on sexual behaviour among schoolchildren.

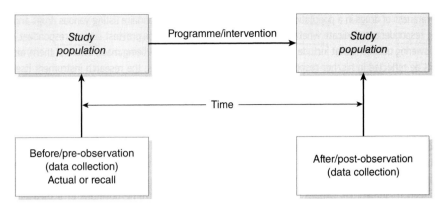

Figure 8.2   Before-and-after (pre-test/post-test) study design

- The effect of a drug awareness programme on the knowledge about, and use of, drugs among young people.
- The impact of incentives on the productivity of employees in an organisation.
- The impact of increased funding on the quality of teaching in universities.
- The impact of maternal and child health services on the infant mortality rate.
- The effect of random breath testing on road accidents.
- The effect of an advertisement on the sale of a product.

The main advantage of before-and-after design is its ability to measure change in a phenomenon or to assess the impact of an intervention. However, there can be disadvantages which may not occur, individually or collectively, in every study. The prevalence of a particular disadvantage(s) is dependent upon the nature of the investigation, the study population and the method of data collection. These disadvantages include the following:

- As two sets of data must be collected, involving two contacts with the study population, the study is more expensive and more difficult to implement. It also requires a longer time to complete, particularly if you are using an experimental design, as you will need to wait until your intervention is completed before you collect the second set of data.
- In some cases the time lapse between the two contacts may result in *attrition in the study population*. It is possible that some of those who participated in the pre-test may move out of the area or withdraw from the experiment for other reasons.
- One of the main limitations of this design, in its simplest form, is that as it measures *total change* you cannot ascertain whether independent or extraneous variables are responsible for producing change in the dependent variable. Also, it is not possible to quantify the contribution of independent and extraneous variables separately.
- Depending on the age of the study population and if there is a significant time lapse between the before-and-after sets of data collection, changes in the study population may be because it is maturing. This is particularly true when you are studying young children. The effect of this maturation, if it is significantly correlated with the dependent variable, is reflected in the 'after' observation and is known as the maturation effect.
- Sometimes the instrument itself educates the respondents. This is known as the reactive effect of the instrument. For example, suppose you want to ascertain the impact of a programme designed to create

- The relationship between levels of unemployment and street crime (can be retrospective as well as prospective depending upon the way data is collected. If the data is collected from secondary sources pertaining to the past, it is a retrospective study. If it is collected on an ongoing basis to become the basis of exploring the relationship, it becomes a prospective study.)

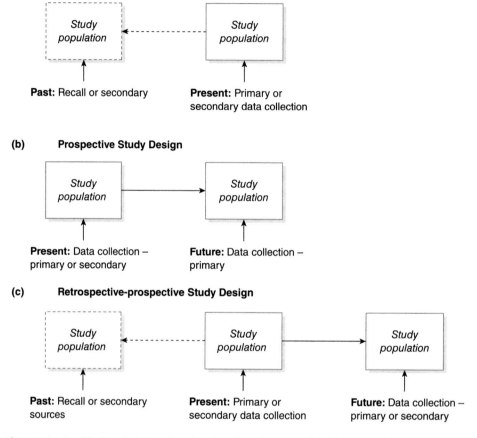

Figure 8.5   Classification of study designs based on the reference period: (a) retrospective; (b) prospective; (c) retrospective–prospective

The prospective study design

Prospective studies refer to the likely prevalence of a phenomenon, situation, problem, attitude or outcome in the future (Figure 8.5b). Such studies attempt to establish the outcome of an event or what is likely to happen. Experiments are usually classified as prospective studies as the researcher must wait for an intervention to register its effect on the study population. The following are classified as prospective studies:

- To determine, under field conditions, the impact of maternal and child health services on the level of infant mortality.

- To establish the effects of a counselling service on the extent of marital problems.
- To determine the impact of random breath testing on the prevention of road accidents.
- To find out the effect of parental involvement on the level of academic achievement of their children.
- To measure the effects of a change in migration policy on the extent of immigration in Australia.

The retrospective–prospective study design

Retrospective–prospective studies focus on past trends in a phenomenon and study it into the future. Part of the data is collected retrospectively from the existing records before the intervention is introduced and then the study population is followed to ascertain the impact of the intervention (Figure 8.5c).

A study is classified under this category when you measure the impact of an intervention without having a control group. In fact, most before-and-after studies, if carried out without having a control – where the baseline is constructed from the same population before introducing the intervention – will be classified as retrospective–prospective studies. Trend studies, which become the basis of projections, fall into this category too. Some examples of retrospective–prospective studies are:

- The effect of random breath testing on road accidents.
- The impact of incentives on the productivity of the employees of an organisation.
- The impact of maternal and child health services on the infant mortality rate.
- The effect of an advertisement on the sale of a product.

Study designs based on the nature of the investigation

On the basis of the nature of the investigation, study designs in quantitative research can be classified as:

- experimental;
- non-experimental;
- quasi- or semi-experimental.

To understand the differences, let us consider some examples. Suppose you want to test the following: the impact of a particular teaching method on the level of comprehension of students; the effectiveness of a programme such as random breath testing on the level of road accidents; or the usefulness of a drug such as azidothymidine (AZT) in treating people who are HIV-positive. In such situations there is assumed to be a cause-and-effect relationship. There are two ways of studying these relationships. The first involves the researcher (or someone else) introducing the intervention that is assumed to be the 'cause' of change, and waiting until it has produced – or has been given sufficient time to produce – the change. The second consists of the researcher observing a phenomenon and attempting to establish what caused it. In this instance the researcher starts from the effect(s) or outcome(s) and attempts to determine the causes. If a relationship is studied in the first way, starting from the cause to establish the effects, it is classified as an experimental study. If the second path is followed – that is, starting from the effects to trace the cause – it is classified as a non-experimental study (see Figure 8.6).

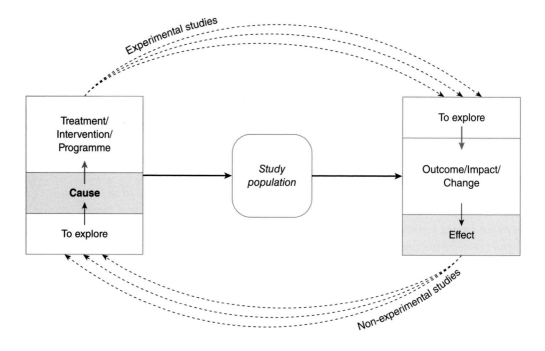

Figure 8.6   Experimental and non-experimental studies

In the former case the independent variable can be 'observed', introduced, controlled or manipulated by the researcher or someone else, whereas in the latter this cannot happen as the assumed cause has already occurred. Instead, the researcher retrospectively links the cause(s) to the outcome(s). A semi-experimental study or quasi-experimental study has the properties of both experimental and non-experimental studies; part of the study may be non-experimental and the other part experimental.

An experimental study can be carried out in either a 'controlled' or a 'natural' environment. For an experiment in a controlled environment, the researcher (or someone else) introduces the intervention or stimulus to study its effects. The study population is in a 'controlled' situation such as a room and such experiments are called controlled experiments. For an experiment in a 'natural' environment, the study population is exposed to an intervention in its own environment.

Experimental studies can be further classified on the basis of whether or not the study population is randomly assigned to different treatment groups. One of the biggest problems in comparative designs (those in which you compare two or more groups) is a lack of certainty that the different groups are in fact comparable in every respect except the treatment. The process of randomisation is designed to ensure that the groups are comparable. In a random design, the study population, the experimental treatments or both are not predetermined but randomly assigned (see Figure 8.7). Random assignment in experiments means that any individual or unit of a study population group has an *equal* and *independent* chance of becoming part of an experimental or control group or, in the case of multiple treatment

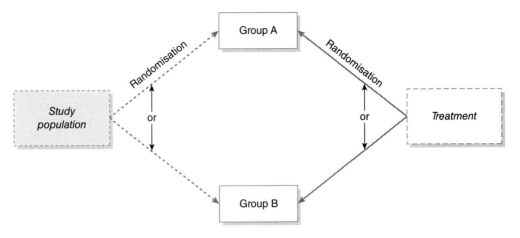

Figure 8.7   Randomisation in experiments

modalities, any treatment has an equal and independent chance of being assigned to any of the population groups. It is important to note that the concept of randomisation can be applied to any of the experimental designs we discuss.

Experimental study designs

There are so many types of experimental design that not all of them can be considered within the scope of this book. This section, therefore, is confined to describing those most commonly used in the social sciences, the humanities, public health, marketing, education, epidemiology, social work, and so on:

- the after-only experimental design;
- the before-and-after experimental design;
- the control group design;
- the double-control design;
- the comparative design;
- the matched control experimental design;
- the placebo design.

The after-only experimental design

In an after-only design the researcher knows that a population is being, or has been, exposed to an intervention and wishes to study its impact on the population. In this design, baseline information (pre-test or before observation) is usually 'constructed' on the basis of respondents' recall of the situation before the intervention, or from information available in existing records – secondary sources (Figure 8.8). The change in the dependent variable is measured by the difference between the 'before'(baseline) and 'after' data sets. Technically, this is a faulty design for measuring the impact of an intervention as there are no proper baseline data to compare the 'after' observation with. One of the major problems is that the two data sets are not strictly comparable. For example, some of the changes in the dependent variable may be attributable to the difference in the way the two sets of data were compiled. Another

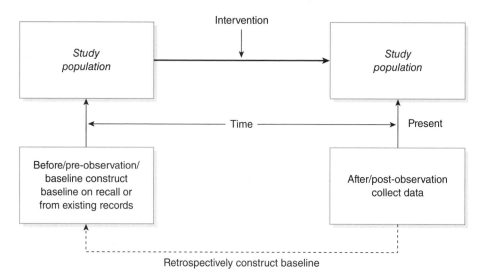

Figure 8.8   The after-only design

problem with this design is that it measures total change, including change attributable to extraneous variables; hence, it cannot identify the net effect of an intervention. However, this design is widely used in impact assessment studies, as in real life many programmes operate without the benefit of a planned evaluation at the programme planning stage (though this is rapidly changing) in which case it is just not possible to follow the sequence strictly – collection of baseline information, implementation of the programme and then programme evaluation. An evaluator therefore has no choice but to adopt this design.

In practice, the adequacy of this design depends on having reasonably accurate data available about the prevalence of a phenomenon before the intervention is introduced. This might be the case for situations such as the impact of random breath testing on road accidents, the impact of a health programme on the mortality of a population, the impact of an advertisement on the sale of a product, the impact of a decline in mortality on the fertility of a population, or the impact of a change in immigration policy on the extent of immigration. In these situations it is expected that accurate records are kept about the phenomenon under study and so it may be easier to determine whether any change in trends is primarily because of the introduction of the intervention or change in the policy.

The before-and-after experimental design

The before-and-after design overcomes the problem of retrospectively constructing the 'before' observation by establishing it before the intervention is introduced to the study population (see Figure 8.2). Then, when the programme has been completely implemented or is assumed to have had its effect on the population, the 'after' observation is carried out to ascertain the impact attributable to the intervention (see Figure 8.9).

The before-and-after design takes care of only one problem of the after-only design – that is, the comparability of the before-and-after observations. It still does not enable one to conclude

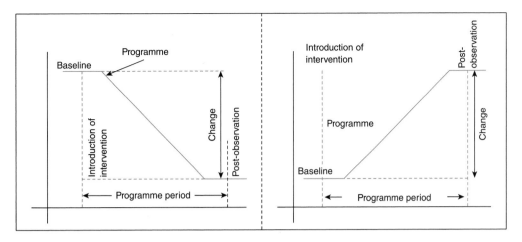

Figure 8.9   Measurement of change through a before-and-after design

that any change – in whole or in part – can be attributed to the programme intervention. To overcome this, a *control group* is used. Before-and-after designs may also suffer from the problems identified earlier in this chapter in the discussion of before-and-after study designs. The impact of the intervention in before-and-after design is calculated as follows:

[change in dependent variable]

= [status of the dependent variable at the 'after' observation]
– [status of the dependent variable at the 'before' observation]

The control group design

In a study utilising the control design the researcher selects two population groups instead of one: a control group and an experimental group (Figure 8.10). These groups are expected to be comparable as far as possible in every respect except for the intervention (which is assumed to be the cause responsible for bringing about the change). The experimental group receives or is exposed to the intervention, while the control group is not. First, the 'before' observations are made on both groups at the same time. The experimental group is then exposed to the intervention. When it is assumed that the intervention has had an impact, an 'after' observation is made on both groups. Any difference in the 'before' and 'after' observations between the groups regarding the dependent variable(s) is attributed to the intervention.

In the experimental group, the total change in the dependent variable (Y_e) can be calculated as follows:

$$Y_e = E_a - E_b$$

where E_a is the 'after' observation on the experimental group and E_b is the 'before' observation on the experimental group. In other words,

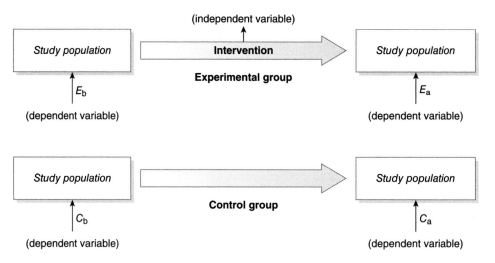

Figure 8.10 The control experimental design

$$E_a - E_b = \text{(impact of programme intervention)} \pm \text{(impact of extraneous variables)}$$
$$\pm \text{(impact of chance variables)}$$

In the control group, the total change in the dependent variable (Y_c) can be calculated as follows:

$$Y_c = C_a - C_b$$

where C_a is the 'after' observation on the control group and C_b is the 'before' observation on the control group. In other words,

$$C_a - C_b = \text{(impact of extraneous variables)} \pm \text{(impact of chance variables)}$$

The difference between the control and experimental groups can be calculated as

$$Y_e - Y_c = (E_a - E_b) - (C_a - C_b)$$

which is

{(impact of programme intervention) ± (impact of extraneous variables in experimental groups) ± (impact of chance variables in experimental groups)} – {(impact of extraneous variables in control group) ± (impact of chance variables in control group)}

Using simple arithmetic operations, this equals the impact of the intervention. Therefore, the impact of any intervention is equal to the difference in the 'before' and 'after' observations in the dependent variable between the experimental and control groups.

It is important to remember that the chief objective of the control group is to quantify the impact of extraneous variables. This helps you to ascertain the impact of the intervention only.

The double-control design

Although the control design helps you to quantify the impact that can be attributed to extraneous variables, it does not separate out other effects that may be due to the research instrument (such as the reactive effect) or respondents (such as the maturation or regression effects, or placebo effect). When you need to identify and separate out these effects, a double-control design is required.

In double-control studies, you have two control groups instead of one. To quantify, say, the reactive effect of an instrument, you exclude one of the control groups from the 'before' observation (Figure 8.11).

You can calculate the different effects as follows:

$Y''_e - Y'_e =$ (impact of programme intervention) ± (impact of extraneous variables) ±
(reactive effect) ± (random effect)

$Y''_{c1} - Y'_{c1} =$ (impact of extraneous variables) ± (reactive effect) ± (random effect)

$Y''_{c2} - Y'_{c1} =$ (impact of extraneous variables) ± (random effect)

(Note that the latter expression is $Y''_{c2} - Y'_{c1}$ and not $Y''_{c2} - Y'_{c2}$ as there is no 'before' observation for the second control group.) The differences are:

$Y''_e - Y'_e - (Y''_{c1} - Y'_{c1}) =$ impact of programme intervention

$Y''_{c1} - Y'_{c1} - (Y'_{c2} - Y'_{c1}) =$ reactive effect

The net effect of the programme intervention can be calculated in the same manner as for the control group designs as explained earlier.

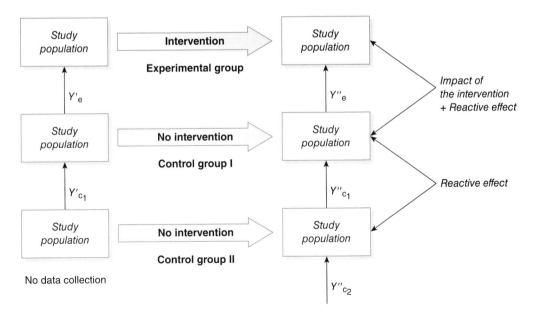

Figure 8.11   Double-control designs

The comparative design

Sometimes you seek to compare the effectiveness of different treatment modalities, and in such situations a comparative design is appropriate.

With a comparative study design, as with most other designs, a study can be carried out either as an experiment or as a non-experiment. In the comparative experimental design, the study population is divided into the same number of groups as the number of treatments to be tested. For each group the baseline with respect to the dependent variable is established. The different treatment models are then introduced to the different groups. After a certain period, when it is assumed that the treatment models have had their effect, the 'after' observation is carried out to ascertain any change in the dependent variable. The degree of change in the dependent variable in the different population groups receiving various treatment modalities is then compared to establish the relative effectiveness of the various interventions.

In the non-experimental form of comparative design, groups already receiving different interventions are identified, and only the post-observation with respect to the dependent variable is conducted. The pre-test data set is constructed either by asking the study population in each group to recall the required information relating to the period before the introduction of the treatment, or by extracting such information from existing records. Sometimes a pre-test observation is not constructed at all, on the assumption that if the groups are comparable the baseline must be identical. As each group is assumed to have the same baseline, the difference in the post-test observation is assumed to be because of the intervention.

To illustrate this, imagine you want to compare the effectiveness of three teaching models (A, B and C) on the level of comprehension of students in a class (Figure 8.12). To undertake the study, you divide the class into three groups (X, Y and Z), through randomisation, to ensure their comparability. Before exposing these groups to the teaching

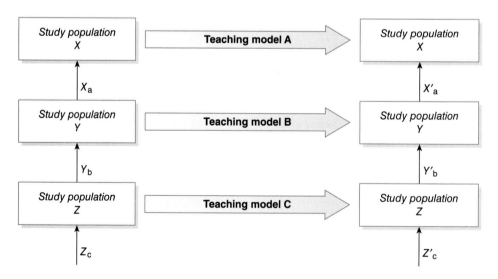

Figure 8.12 Comparative experimental design

models, you first establish the baseline for each group's level of comprehension of the chosen subject. You then expose each group to a different teaching model to teach the chosen subject. Afterwards, you again measure the groups' levels of comprehension of the material. Suppose X_a is the average level of comprehension of group X before the material is taught, and X'_a is this group's average level of comprehension after the material is taught. The change in the level of comprehension, $X'_a - X_a$, is therefore attributed to model A. Similarly, changes in groups Y and Z, $Y'_b - Y_b$ and $Z'_c - Z_c$, are attributed to teaching models B and C, respectively. The changes in the average level of comprehension for the three groups are then compared to establish which teaching model is the most effective. (Note that extraneous variables will affect the level of comprehension in all groups equally, as they have been formed randomly.)

It is also possible to set up this study as a non-experimental one, simply by exposing each group to one of the three teaching models, following up with an 'after' observation. The difference in the levels of comprehension is attributed to the difference in the teaching models as it is assumed that the three groups are comparable with respect to their original level of comprehension of the topic.

The matched control experimental design

Comparative groups are usually formed on the basis of their overall comparability with respect to a relevant characteristic in the study population, such as socioeconomic status, the prevalence of a certain condition or the extent of a problem in the study population. In matched studies, comparability is determined on an individual-by-individual basis. Two individuals from the study population who are almost identical with respect to a selected characteristic and/or condition, such as age, gender or type of illness, are matched and then each is allocated to a separate group (the matching is usually done on an easily identifiable characteristic). In the case of a matched control experiment, once the two groups are formed, the researcher decides through randomisation or otherwise which group is to be considered control, and which experimental. The matched design can pose a number of challenges:

- Matching increases in difficulty when carried out on more than one variable.
- Matching on variables that are hard to measure, such as attitude or opinion, is extremely difficult.
- Sometimes it is hard to know which variable to choose as a basis for matching. You may be able to base your decision upon previous findings, or you may have to undertake a preliminary study to determine your choice of variable.

Matched controlled designs are most commonly used in the testing of new drugs.

The placebo design

A patient's belief that s/he is receiving treatment can play an important role in his/her recovery from an illness even if treatment is ineffective. This psychological effect is known as the placebo effect. A placebo design attempts to determine the extent of this effect. A placebo study involves two or three groups, depending on whether or not the researcher wants to have a control group (Figure 8.13). If the researcher decides to have

BEN GOLDACRE ON
PLACEBO EFFECT

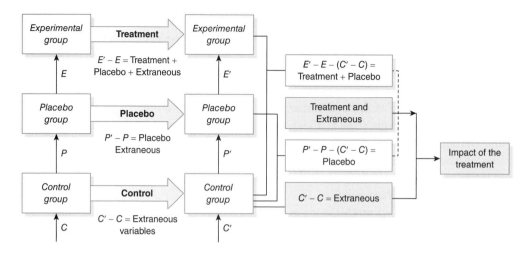

Figure 8.13   The placebo design

a control group, the first group receives the treatment, the second receives the placebo treatment, and the third – the control group – receives nothing. The decision as to which group will be the treatment, the placebo or the control group can also be made through randomisation.

Other designs commonly used in quantitative research

There are some study designs that may be classified in the typology described above but, because of their uniqueness and prevalence, they have acquired their own names. They are therefore described separately below.

Online surveys

Advancements in and increased use of digital technology, in particular for communication, have created a unique opportunity for it to be used for social research. The last few years have witnessed a substantial increase in the use of online surveys for researching social issues. 'Like all research methods, online surveys research has benefits and drawbacks; the method works for some research projects but is by no means appropriate for all research objectives' (Sue & Ritter 2012: 1).

ONLINE SURVEYS

There are three common options for online surveys: e-mail, websites and mobile phones. Data collection through these follows the same developmental process as for a normal questionnaire. You develop a questionnaire through the use of software and store it on an Internet server for retrieval by a potential respondent via an Internet link. As a potential respondent, you retrieve the questionnaire via the link and answer the questions in the same way as you would have done for a normal questionnaire. The only difference is that in a normal questionnaire you complete the questionnaire by hand and in an online questionnaire you use a computer keyboard.

Sue and Ritter (2012: Chapter 1) have identified many situations in which online surveys are desirable to conduct. Online surveys are extremely useful when you have a large and geographically diverse sample. They are quicker and cheaper. However, there are a number of constraints on their use. First and foremost, not everyone has Internet or mobile phone access, so online surveys cannot be used for all population groups. In addition, the population with Internet and mobile phone access may have very different characteristics as compared to the general population so may not truly represent the general population. It is also impossible to select a random sample as there is no sampling frame for Internet users. Use of the Internet also requires the researcher to have adequate technical knowledge and skills in the development of a digital survey. But if you have the requisite technical expertise and there are no other constraints, the use of the Internet for social research could be fast, efficient and low cost.

According to Sue and Ritter (2012: 14), 'When we refer to e-mail surveys, we mean surveys created by using survey software and accessed by respondents through a link in an e-mail invitation. These are among the most common online surveys because anyone who has access to online survey software, such as SurveyMonkey, Zoomerang, or InstantSurvey, can create an e-mail survey.'

The main difference between an e-mail and an Internet survey is the way a respondent accesses the survey questionnaire. In an e-mail survey the access is through a link provided in the e-mail, whereas in an Internet survey the questionnaire 'appears on a webpage, either as a link posted somewhere on the page or as a pop-up or crawl-in link' (Sue & Ritter 2012: 17–18).

With the development of smartphones and computer tablets the scope of mobile surveys has changed. Formerly, mobile surveys 'referred primarily to a series of text messages sent to respondents' mobile phones' (Sue & Ritter 2012: 19). Nowadays, with the advancement in technology, there are programs that enable you to do full online surveys on smartphones and tablets.

'To conduct an e-mail, website, or mobile survey, you will need software and the service of a web-based survey host' (Sue & Ritter 2012: 20). There are many web-based survey hosts in the market providing different types of survey software, and you need to do some research to determine their suitability for your situation. In addition, you also need to thoroughly consider their terms and conditions of use as set out by the application service provider that you intend to use. You should thoroughly consider all technical and logistical aspects before undertaking an online study. There is much to think about, and you are advised to read references specifically dealing with online surveys before venturing into one.

The cross-over comparative experimental design

The denial of treatment to the control group is considered unethical by some professionals. In addition, it may be unacceptable to some individuals in the control group, which could result in them dropping out of the experiment and/or going elsewhere to receive treatment. The former increases experimental mortality, and the latter may contaminate the study. The cross-over comparative experimental design makes it possible to measure the impact of a treatment without denying treatment to any group, though this design has its own problems.

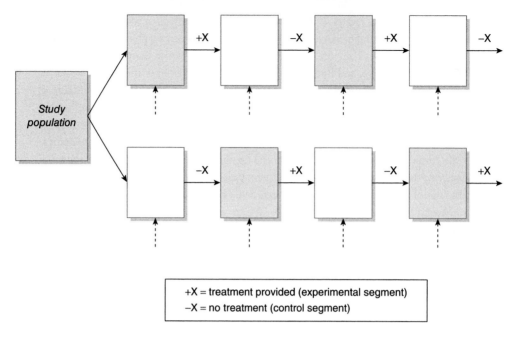

+X = treatment provided (experimental segment)
−X = no treatment (control segment)

Figure 8.14   The cross-over experimental design

In the cross-over design, also called the ABAB design (Grinnell 1993: 104), two groups are formed, the intervention is introduced to one of them and, after a certain period, the impact of this intervention is measured. Then the interventions are 'crossed over'; that is, the experimental group becomes the control and vice versa, sometimes repeatedly over the period of the study (Figure 8.14). However, in this design, population groups do not constitute experimental or control groups but only segments upon which experimental and control observations are conducted.

One of the major issues is in relation to the discontinuity in treatment. The main question is: what impact would intervention have produced had it not been withdrawn from the experimental segments, that is, how would the discontinuity in the treatment have affected the overall impact of the treatment?

The replicated cross-sectional design

In practice one usually examines programmes already in existence and ones in which clients are at different stages of an intervention. Evaluating the effectiveness of such programmes within a conventional experimental design is impossible because a baseline cannot be established as the intervention has already been introduced. This means that the usual method of selecting a group of people recently recruited to the programme and following them through until the intervention has been completed may take a long time. In such situations, it is possible to choose clients who are at different stages of the programme to form the basis of your study (Figure 8.15).

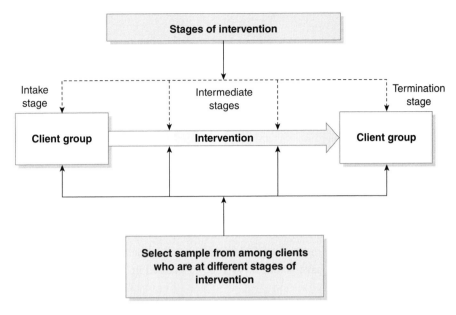

Figure 8.15   The replicated cross-sectional design

The replicated cross-sectional design is based upon the assumption that participants at different stages of a programme are similar in terms of their socioeconomic-demographic characteristics and the problem for which they are seeking intervention. Assessment of the effectiveness of an intervention is done by taking a sample of clients at different stages of the intervention. The difference in the dependent variable among clients at intake and termination stage is considered to be the impact of the intervention.

Trend studies

If you want to map changes in a phenomenon, situation, attitudes or facts relating to an area of interest to you over a period, a trend study is the most appropriate method of investigation. Trend analysis enables you to find out what has happened in the past, what is happening now and what is likely to happen in the future in a population group. This design involves selecting a number of data observation points in the past, together with a picture of the present or immediate past with respect to the phenomenon under study, and then making certain assumptions as to the future trends. In a way you are collecting cross-sectional observations about the trend being observed at different points in time in the past, present and future. From these cross-sectional observations you draw conclusions about the pattern of change.

Trend studies are useful in making forecasts by extrapolating present and past trends, thus making a valuable contribution to planning. Trends regarding the phenomenon under study can be correlated with other characteristics of the study population. For example, you may want to examine the changes in political preference of a study population in relation to age, gender, income or ethnicity. This design can also be classified as a retrospective–prospective design.

Cohort studies

Cohort studies are based upon the existence of a common characteristic, such as year of birth, graduation or marriage, within a subgroup of a population. Suppose you want to study the employment pattern of a batch of accountants who graduated from a university in 1985, or study the fertility behaviour of women who were married in 1970. To study the accountants' career paths you would contact all the accountants who graduated from the university in 1985 to find out their employment histories. Similarly, you would investigate the fertility history of those women who married in 1970. Both of these studies could be carried out either as cross-sectional or longitudinal designs. If you adopt a cross-sectional design you gather the required information in one go, but if you choose the longitudinal design you collect the required information at different points in time over the study period. Both these designs have their strengths and weaknesses. In the case of a longitudinal design, it is not important for the required information to be collected from the same respondents, though it is important that all the respondents belong to the cohort being studied; that is, in the above examples they must have graduated in 1985 or married in 1970.

COHORT STUDIES

Panel studies

Panel studies are similar to trend and cohort studies except that, in addition to being longitudinal, they are prospective in nature and the information is always collected from the same respondents. (In trend and cohort studies the information can be collected in a cross-sectional manner and the observation points can be retrospectively constructed.) Suppose you want to study the changes in the pattern of expenditure on household items in a community. To do this, you would select a few families to find out how much they spend (say) every fortnight on household items. You would keep collecting the same information from the same families over a period of time to ascertain the changes in the expenditure pattern. Similarly, a panel study design could be used to study the morbidity pattern in a community.

Blind studies

The concept of a blind study is used in relation to comparable and placebo designs and is applicable to studies that are designed to measure the effectiveness of a drug or an intervention. In a blind study, the study population does not know whether or not it is getting real or fake treatment or, in the case of comparative testing, which treatment. The main objective of using a blind study design is to isolate the placebo effect by not letting the participants know about the treatment.

Double-blind studies

Double-blind studies are very similar to blind studies but also try to eliminate researcher bias by concealing the identity of the experimental and placebo groups from the researcher. In other words, in a double-blind study neither the researcher nor the study participants know who is receiving real and who is receiving fake treatment or which treatment they are receiving.

Study designs in qualitative research

This section provides a brief description of some of the designs commonly used in qualitative research. The author does not like to segregate quantitative and qualitative designs, but has done so to enable the newcomer to research to gain a better understanding. Keep in mind, as has been repeated a number of times, that many qualitative study designs are quite prevalent in quantitative research studies. For an in-depth understanding you are advised to consult books on qualitative research.

Case study

The **case study**, though predominantly a qualitative study design, is also prevalent in quantitative research. A case could be an individual, a group, a community, an instance, an episode, an event, a subgroup of a population, a town or a city. To be called a case study it is important to treat the total study population as one entity.

CASE STUDY

In a case study design the case you select becomes the basis of a thorough, holistic and in-depth exploration of the aspect(s) that you want to find out about. It is an approach 'in which a particular instance or a few carefully selected cases are studied intensively' (Gilbert 2008: 36). According to Burns (1997: 364), 'to qualify as a case study, *it must be a bounded system*, an entity in itself. A case study should focus on a bounded subject/unit that is either very representative or extremely atypical.' A case study, according to Grinnell (1981: 302), 'is characterized by a very flexible and open-ended technique of data collection and analysis'.

The case study design is based upon the assumption that the case being studied is typical of cases of a certain type and therefore a single case can provide insight into the events and situations prevalent in a group from where the case has been drawn. According to Burns (1997: 365), 'In a case study the focus of attention is the case in its idiosyncratic complexity, not on the whole population of cases'. In selecting a case therefore you usually use purposive, judgemental or information-oriented sampling techniques.

It is a very useful design when exploring an area where little is known or where you want to have a holistic understanding of the situation, phenomenon, episode, site, group or community. According to Gilbert (2008: 36), 'The advantage of the case study design is that the research can be much more detailed than would be possible if one is studying a large sample, but the corresponding disadvantage is that it is much more difficult and often impossible to generalise the findings'. This design is of immense relevance when the focus of a study is on extensively exploring and understanding rather than confirming and quantifying. It provides an overview and in-depth understanding of a case(s), process and interactional dynamics within a unit of study but cannot claim to make any generalisations to a population beyond cases similar to the one studied.

In this design you are attempting not to select a random sample but a case that can provide you with as much information as possible to understand the case in its totality. When studying an episode or an instance, you attempt to gather information from all available sources so as to understand it in its entirety. If the focus of your study is a group or community you should spend sufficient time building a good rapport with its members before collecting any information about them.

Though you can use a single method, in-depth interviewing, the use of multiple methods to collect data, such as obtaining information from secondary records, gathering data through observations, and collecting information through focus groups and group interviews, is an important aspect of a case study. However, it is important that at the time of analysis you continue to consider the case as a single entity.

Oral history

ORAL HISTORY

Oral history is more a method of data collection than a study design; however, in qualitative research, it has become an approach to the study of perceptions, experiences and accounts of an event or gathering historical knowledge as viewed by individuals. It is a picture of something in someone's own words. Oral history is a process of obtaining, recording, presenting and interpreting historical or current information, based upon personal experiences and opinions of some members of a study group or unit. These opinions or experiences could be based upon eyewitness evidence or information passed on from other sources such as older people, ancestors, folklore and stories. According to Ritchie (2003:19), 'Memory is the core of oral history, from which meaning can be extracted and preserved. Simply put, oral history collects memories and personal commentaries of historical significance through recorded interviews.' According to Burns (1997: 368), 'these are usually first person narratives that the researcher collects using extensive interviewing of a single individual'.

In terms of design it is quite simple. You first decide what types of account, experience, perception or historical event you want to find out about. Then you need to identify the individuals or sources (which could be difficult and time-consuming) that can best provide you with the required information. You then collect information from them to be analysed and interpreted.

Focus groups/group interviews

FOCUS GROUPS

Focus groups are a form of strategy in qualitative research in which attitudes, opinions or perceptions towards an issue, product, service or programme are explored through a free and open discussion between members of a group and the researcher. Both focus groups and group interviews are facilitated group discussions in which a researcher raises issues or asks questions that stimulate discussion among members of the group. Because of its low cost, it is a popular method for finding information in almost every professional area and academic field. Social, political and behavioural scientists, market research and product testing agencies, and urban and town planning experts often use this design for a variety of situations. For example, in marketing research this design is widely used to obtain consumers' opinion of and feedback on a product, their opinions on the quality of the product, its acceptance and appeal, price and packaging, how to improve the quality and increase the sale of the product, etc. Focus groups are also prevalent in formative and summative evaluations and for developing social programmes and services. It is a useful tool in social and urban planning for identifying issues, options, development strategies, and future planning and development directions.

In its design it is very simple. As a researcher, you select a group of people who you think are best equipped to discuss what you want to explore. The group could comprise individuals drawn from a group of highly trained professionals or average residents of a community, depending upon the objectives of the focus group. In the formation of a focus group the size of the group is an important consideration. It should be neither too large nor too small as this can impede upon the extent and quality of the discussion; about eight to ten people is usually considered optimal. You need to identify carefully the issues for discussion, providing every opportunity for additional relevant ones to emerge. You need to decide, in consultation with the group, the process of recording the discussion. This may include very simple things such as fixing the times that the group can meet, and more complex matters such as how to arrive at agreement if disagreement emerges in the group.

Your records of the discussions then become the basis of analysis for findings and conclusions. The main difference between a focus group and a group interview is in the degree of specificity with respect to the issues to be discussed. The issues discussed in focus groups are more specific and focused than in group interviews and they are largely predetermined by the researcher. In a group interview you let the group members discuss whatever they want. However, your role as a researcher is to bring them back to the issues of interest as identified by the group.

Compared with other designs this is less expensive and needs far less time to complete. The information generated can be detailed and rich and can be used to explore a vast variety of issues. However, the disadvantage is that if the discussion is not carefully directed it may reflect the opinion of those who have a tendency to dominate a group. This design is very useful for exploring the diversity in opinions on different issues, but will not help you if you want to find out the extent or magnitude of this diversity.

Participant observation

Participant observation is another strategy for gathering information about a social interaction or a phenomenon in qualitative studies. This is usually done by developing a close interaction with members of a group or 'living' in the situation which is being studied. Though predominantly a qualitative research design, it is also used in quantitative research, depending upon how the information has been generated and recorded. In qualitative research, an observation is always recorded in a descriptive format, whereas in quantitative research it is recorded either in categories or on a scale. It can also be a combination of both – some categorisation and some description or categorisation accompanied by a descriptive explanation. You can also change a descriptive recording into a categorical one through analysis and classification. In addition to the observation itself, where you as an observer generate information, the information can also be collected through other methods such as informal interviewing, in-depth interviewing, group discussions, previous documents, and oral histories. Use of multiple methods will enhance the richness of the information collected by participant observation.

PARTICIPANT
OBSERVATION

In its design it is simple. You as a researcher get involved in the activities of the group, create a rapport with group members and then, having sought their consent, keenly observe the situation, interaction, site or phenomenon. You make detailed notes of what you observe in a format that best suits you as well as the situation. You can also collect information using other methods of data collection, if need be. You analyse records of your observations and data collected by other means to draw inferences and conclusions.

The main advantage of participant observation is that as you spend sufficient time with the group or in the situation, you gain much deeper, richer and more accurate information, but the main disadvantage is that, if you are not very careful, you can introduce your own bias.

Holistic research

The holistic approach to research is once again more a philosophy than a study design. The 'design' is based upon the philosophy that as a multiplicity of factors interact in our lives, we cannot understand a phenomenon from just one or two perspectives. To understand a situation or phenomenon you need to look at it in its totality – that is, holistically from every perspective. You can use any design when exploring a situation from different perspectives and the use of multiple methods is prevalent and desirable.

Community discussion forums

WHAT IS
NETNOGRAPHY?

Community discussion forums are designed to find the opinions, attitudes and/or ideas of a community with regard to community issues and problems. They are a very popular way to seek a community's participation in deciding about issues of concern to its members. Such forums are used in developing town planning options and community health programmes for a community, seeking the participation of its members in resolving issues relating to traffic management, infrastructure development and determining future directions for the area, and informing communities of new initiatives.

Community forums are very similar to group discussions but are on a bigger scale in terms of the number of participants. Also, in group discussions you may select the participants, but community forums involve self-selection of the participants as they are open to everyone with an interest in the issues or concerns. You as a researcher usually use local media to inform the residents of a local community about such forums.

This is a useful design for finding out about the spread of issues, concerns, etc., at a community level. It is economical and quick, but there are some disadvantages. For example, it is possible that a few people with a vested interest can dominate the discussion in a forum, and it is equally possible that on occasions there may be very low attendance. Such situations may result in the discussion not reflecting the community's attitudes.

Reflective journal log

Basically, this design entails keeping a reflective journal log of your thoughts as a researcher whenever you notice anything, talk to someone, participate in an activity or observe something that helps you understand or add to whatever you are trying to find out about. These reflective records then become the basis of your findings and conclusions. You can have a reflective journal as the only method of data collection, or it can be used in combination with other methods such as interviewing, group interviews, or secondary sources.

Other commonly used philosophy-guided designs

There are a number of other approaches to research that have acquired recognition in the research literature. While not designs per se, they do advance a particular philosophical perspective in social research. These are: action research, feminist research, participatory research and collaborative enquiry. Strictly speaking, a piece of research within each of these could be either quantitative or qualitative, though they are considered predominantly as qualitative designs. The need to place them in a separate category stems from their prominence and possible use in each paradigm. These designs are more philosophy guided than methods based. For example, action research is guided by the philosophy that a piece of research should be followed by some form of appropriate action to achieve betterment in life or service; feminist research is influenced by the philosophy that opposes and challenges the predominant male bias in social science research, and seems to believe that issues relating to women are best understood and researched by women alone. For participatory research and collaborative enquiry, the involvement of research participants or the community in the research process is the underlying philosophy. One of the important aspects of all these 'designs' is that they attempt to involve research participants in the research process. The research findings are then used to depict the current situation with respect to certain issues or problems and help to form a sound basis for strategy development to deal with them.

Action research

As the name suggests, action research comprises two components: *action* and *research* (see Figure 8.16). Research is a means to action, either to improve your practice or to take action to deal with a problem or an issue. Since action research is guided by the desire to take action, strictly speaking it is not a design per se. Most action research is concerned with

ACTION
RESEARCH

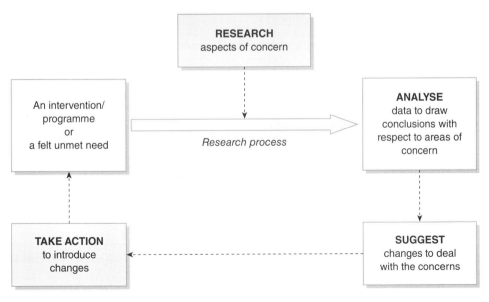

Figure 8.16   Action research design

improving the quality of service. It is carried out to identify areas of concern, develop and test alternatives, and experiment with new approaches.

Action research seems to follow two traditions. The British tradition tends to view action research as a means of improvement and advancement of practice (Carr & Kemmis 1986), whereas in the US tradition it is aimed at systematic collection of data that provides the basis for social change (Bogdan & Biklen 1992).

Action research, in common with participatory research and collaborative enquiry, is based upon a philosophy of community development that seeks the involvement of community members. The two salient features of all three approaches are the involvement and participation of a community in the total process from problem identification to implementation of solutions. Data is collected through a research process that can be either quantitative, qualitative or mixed, and changes are achieved through action. This action is taken either by officials of an institution or the community itself in the case of action research, or by members of a community in the case of collaborative or participatory research.

There are two focuses of action research:

1. An existing programme or intervention is studied in order to identify possible areas of improvement in terms of enhanced efficacy and/or efficiency. The findings become the basis of bringing about changes.
2. A professional identifies an unattended problem or unexplained issue in the community or among a client group, and research evidence is gathered to justify the introduction of a new service or intervention. Research techniques establish the prevalence of the problem or the importance of an issue so that appropriate action can be taken to deal with it.

Feminist research

Feminist research is characterised by a feminist theory philosophical base that underpins all enquiries and feminist concerns act as the guiding framework. Feminist research differs from traditional research in three ways:

FEMINIST
RESEARCH

1. Its main focus is the experiences and viewpoints of women. It uses research methods aimed at exploring these.
2. It actively tries to remove or reduce the power imbalance between the researcher and respondents.
3. The goal of feminist research is to change the social inequality between men and women. In fact, feminist research may be classified as action research in the area of gender inequality, using research techniques to create awareness of women's issues and concerns, and to foster action promoting equality between sexes.

Any study design could be used in feminist research.

Participatory research and collaborative enquiry

WHAT IS
PARTICIPATORY
RESEARCH?

As already mentioned, to the author's mind, these are not designs per se but signify a philosophical perspective that advocates the active involvement of research participants in the research process. Both participatory research and collaborative enquiry are based upon the principle of minimising the 'gap' between the researcher and the research participants and emphasis on increased community involvement and participation to enhance

160   **RESEARCH METHODOLOGY**

the relevance of the research findings to their needs. It is assumed that such involvement will increase the possibility of the community accepting the research findings and, if need be, its willingness and involvement in solving the problems and issues that confront it. You can undertake a quantitative or qualitative study in these perspectives but the main emphasis is on people's engagement, collaboration and participation in the research process. In a way these designs are based on the community development model where engagement of a community by way of consultation and participation in planning and execution of research tasks is imperative. You are not merely a researcher but also a community organiser seeking active participation of the community.

As a researcher you work at two different levels: (1) community organisation and (2) research. As community organiser you seek a community's involvement and participation in identifying community demands and needs, prioritising them, developing solutions, planning strategies and executing tasks to meet them. In terms of research, your main responsibility is to develop, in consultation with the community, the research tasks and procedures and share research findings with its members. Consultation with research participants at both these levels is a continuous and integral part of these designs.

Summary

In this chapter various study designs in both quantitative and qualitative research have been examined. For each study design, details have been provided on the situations in which the design is appropriate to use, its strengths and weaknesses, and the process adopted in its operationalisation.

In quantitative research the various study designs have been examined from three perspectives. The terminology used to describe these perspectives is that of the author, but the names of the study designs are universally used. The different study designs across each category are mutually exclusive, but not so within a category.

The three perspectives are the number of contacts, the reference period and the nature of the investigation. The first includes cross-sectional studies, before-and-after studies and longitudinal studies. The second categorises the studies as retrospective, prospective and retrospective–prospective. The third classifies studies as experimental, non-experimental and semi-experimental studies. Designs such as after-only experimental designs, before-and-after experimental designs, control designs, comparative designs, matched control, the placebo design have been described in detail. The chapter also details some of the commonly used designs in quantitative research. These are online surveys, cross-over comparative design, trend studies, cohort studies, panel studies, and blind and double-blind studies.

Qualitative study designs are not as specific, precise and well defined as designs in quantitative research. Also, there is a degree of overlap between study designs and methods of data collection. Some designs can easily be considered as methods of data collection. Some of the commonly used designs in qualitative research are: case study design, oral history, focus group studies, participant observation, community discussion forums and the reflective journal log.

Four additional approaches to research have been described: action research, feminist research, participatory research and collaborative enquiry. Though these cannot really be considered designs in themselves, they have acquired their own identity. Both action and feminist research can be carried out either quantitatively or qualitatively, but participatory and collaborative enquiries are usually qualitative in nature.

FOR YOU TO THINK ABOUT

- Refamiliarise yourself with the keywords listed at the beginning of this chapter, and if you are uncertain about the meaning or application of any of them revisit them in the chapter before moving on.
- Identify two or three situations relating to your own area of interest where you think qualitative study designs might be more beneficial, and consider why this might be the case.
- Take an example from your own academic field or professional area where an experimental control or placebo group might be used and explore the ethical issues relating to this.

Now, as you have gone through the chapter, try answering the following questions:

- What are the differences between quantitative and qualitative study designs?
- In this book the typology of study designs is developed from three perspectives. Critically examine the validity of these perspectives.
- Define the following:
  - ☐ Regression effect
  - ☐ Maturation effect
  - ☐ Reactive effect
- In an experimental study, what purpose does a control group serve?
- What is the difference between an experimental and non-experimental study?
- What is randomisation and what purpose does it serve in a study?

Want to learn more? Visit
http://www.uk.sagepub.com/kumar4e
or scan this QR code to gain access to a range of online resources to support your study including practice quizzes, videos, weblinks, flashcards, and journal articles.

Exercise II: Conceptualising a study design
For quantitative studies

Exercise I helped you to develop your research problem, providing you with a clear idea about *what* you want to find out about. Now the next step is to decide *how* to go about it. Exercise II is designed to help you to take this step. This includes deciding on an overall plan and selecting procedures and methods that you propose to use during your research journey. The details of your plan and procedures become the core of your study design.

A study design describes the design per se, that is, the type of study design you propose to adopt; for example, whether the proposed study is cross-sectional, correlational or experimental. It should also provide details of the logistical procedures required for gathering information from the study population. This exercise helps you to put forward your arguments to justify the selection of the design you are proposing for your study, critically examining its strengths and weaknesses, and thus enabling you to select the best and workable study design. The exercise also challenges you to think through other logistical procedures such as outlining the process of identifying and contacting your study population and your plan to obtain the required information from your potential respondents, thus helping you to develop the roadmap for your journey.

For qualitative studies the process is the same though it varies in content.

The issues raised in this exercise will help you to conceptualise your study design. Chapter 8 details the various types of study design in both quantitative and qualitative research for you to refer to while working through this exercise.

A: Answers to the following questions will help you to develop your study design (Step II).

1 Is the design that you propose to adopt to conduct your study cross-sectional, longitudinal, experimental or comparative in nature? If possible draw a diagram depicting the design.

_____

_____

_____

2 Why did you select this design?

_____

_____

_____

3 What, in your opinion, are the strengths of this design?

_____

_____

_____

4 What are the weaknesses and limitations of this design?

Weaknesses:

_____

_____

_____

Limitations:

_____

_____

_____

5 Who constitutes your study population?

_____

_____

_____

6 Will you be able to identify each respondent in your study population?
   Yes ☐   No ☐

   (a)   If yes, how will they be identified?

   _____

   _____

   _____

   (b)   If no, how do you plan to get in touch with them?

   _____

   _____

   _____

7 Do you plan to select a sample?
   Yes ☐   No ☐

In either case, explain the reasons for your decision.

_____

_____

_____

8 How will you collect data from your respondents (e.g. interview, questionnaire)?

_____

_____

_____

   (a)   Why did you select this method of data collection?

   _____

   _____

   _____

   (b)   What, in your opinion, are its strengths and weaknesses?

   Strengths:

   _____

   _____

   _____

Weaknesses:

_____

_____

_____

(c)   If you are interviewing, where will the interviews be held?

_____

_____

_____

(d)   If you are using mailed questionnaires:

    (i)   From where will you obtain the addresses of potential respondents?

_____

_____

_____

    (ii)   Are you planning to enclose a self-addressed stamped envelope with the questionnaires?

    Yes ☐   No ☐

    (iii)   In the case of a low response rate, will you send a reminder?

    Yes ☐   No ☐

    (iv)   If there are queries, how should respondents get in touch with you?

_____

_____

_____

B: On the basis of the above information, describe your study design. (For further guidance, consult Chapter 8.)

For qualitative studies

A: Answers to the following questions will help you in developing a roadmap for your research journey.

1   In which geographical area, community, group or population group would you like to undertake your study?

_____

_____

_____

_____

2 How do you plan to get entry into the area, community or group? Which network, if any, are you planning to use?

_____

_____

_____

_____

3 Why did you select this group?

_____

_____

_____

_____

4 From whom will you gather the required information? (Who will be your respondents?)

_____

_____

_____

_____

5 If you are gathering information from secondary sources, have you checked their availability?

Yes ☐   No ☐   Not Applicable ☐

6 Have you checked the availability of the required information in them?

Yes ☐   No ☐   Not Applicable ☐

7 If you are gathering information from individuals, how many will you contact?

_____

_____

8 What will be the basis of selection of these individuals?

_____

_____

_____

_____

9 How will you collect the required information? List all methods that you plan to use.

_____

_____

_____

_____

STEP III

CONSTRUCTING AN INSTRUMENT FOR DATA COLLECTION

This operational step includes three chapters:

- Chapter 9: Selecting a Method of Data Collection
- Chapter 10: Collecting Data Using Attitudinal Scales
- Chapter 11: Establishing the Validity and Reliability of a Research Instrument

9

SELECTING A METHOD OF DATA COLLECTION

In this chapter you will learn about

- ■ Differences in methods of data collection in quantitative, qualitative and mixed methods research
- ■ Major approaches to information gathering
- ■ Collecting data using primary sources
    - □ Observation
    - □ The interview
    - □ The questionnaire
- ■ Methods of data collection in qualitative research
- ■ Collecting data using secondary sources

Keywords

closed questions, content analysis, covering letter, double-barrelled questions, elevation effect, error of central tendency, focus group, halo effect, Hawthorne effect, in-depth

interviews, interview schedule, leading questions, narratives, non-participant observation, observer bias, open-ended questions, oral history, participant observation,

response rate, primary data, primary sources, questionnaire, secondary data, secondary sources, self-selecting bias, structured interview, unstructured interview.

At the end of this chapter, you should have an understanding of

- The difference between primary and secondary data
- Different methods of data gathering and their respective advantages and disadvantages
- Advantages and disadvantages of open-ended and closed questions
- How to develop a questionnaire or an interview schedule
- Gathering data through qualitative, quantitative or mixed approaches

Differences in the methods of data collection in quantitative, qualitative and mixed methods research

RESEARCH
METHODS VIDEOS

Most methods of data collection can be used across studies that are classified as qualitative, quantitative or mixed methods. As a matter of fact the way a specific method is employed for data collection determines the classification of a study to a large extent. The distinction is mainly determined by the restrictions imposed on the philosophy underpinning the enquiry, freedom and flexibility in the structure and approach in gathering data, and the depth and freedom given to you as a researcher in probing to obtain answers to your research questions. Quantitative studies favour these restrictions, whereas qualitative ones advocate against them. The respective restrictions or flexibilities in mixed methods studies are dependent upon what and how the specific methods are employed. The classification of a method as quantitative, qualitative or mixed depends upon your answers to the following questions:

- What philosophical epistemology is underpinning your approach to research enquiry?
- How was the information collected? Was it through a structured or unstructured/flexible format of data collection or a combination of both?
- Were the questions or issues discussed during data collection predetermined or developed during data collection?
- How was the information you gathered recorded? Was it in a descriptive, narrative, categorical, quantitative form or on a scale?

170   **RESEARCH METHODOLOGY**

- How was the information analysed? Was it a descriptive, categorical or numerical analysis?
- How do you propose to communicate the findings? Do you want to write in a descriptive or analytical manner?
- How many different methods were used in undertaking the study?

If your answers to the above questions are that you adopted the philosophical epistemology that is embedded in empiricism, you collected the information through an unstructured and flexible format, you indentified issues for discussion during the data collection process, you recorded the information in a descriptive and narrative format and subjected it to categorical and descriptive analysis, and you communicated the findings in a non-analytical style, the research process is labelled as qualitative; otherwise it is quantitative. If you used more than one method, quantitative or qualitative or both, then it is a mixed methods study. For example, if an observation is recorded in a narrative or descriptive format, it becomes qualitative information, but if it is recorded in categorical form or on a scale, it will be classified as quantitative information, and use of both the methods would mean a mixed methods classification. Similarly for data collected through interviews. An unstructured interview, recorded in a descriptive or narrative form, becomes a qualitative method, but in a structured interview, if the information is recorded in response categories or if the categories are developed and quantified out of descriptive responses, it is a quantitative method. Descriptive responses obtained in reply to open-ended questions are all qualitative, but if the responses are numerical they will be considered quantitative. If you develop categories and quantify the categorisations as a part of the analysis of descriptive responses to an open-ended question, it becomes a quantitative analysis. Data generated by focus groups, oral histories, narratives, group interviews is always qualitative in nature; however, you can subject the data to categorical analysis which then becomes quantitative analysis. The differences between quantitative and qualitative approaches, in brief, depend upon three things: how the data was collected; how it was analysed; and how the findings were communicated.

Major approaches to information gathering

There are two major approaches to gathering information about a situation, person, problem or phenomenon. When you undertake a research study, in most situations, you need to collect the required information; however, sometimes the information required is already available and need only be extracted. Based upon these broad approaches to information gathering, data can be categorised as:

- primary data;
- secondary data.

Information gathered using the first approach is said to be collected from primary sources, whereas the sources used in the second approach are called secondary sources. Examples of primary sources include finding out first-hand the attitudes of a community towards health services, ascertaining the health needs of a community, evaluating a social programme, determining the job satisfaction of the employees of an organisation, and ascertaining the quality of service provided by a worker. On the other hand, extracting data from

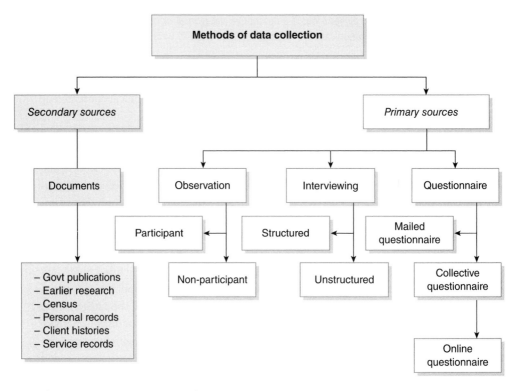

Figure 9.1   Methods of data collection

a census to obtain information on the age–sex structure of a population, the use of hospital records to find out the morbidity and mortality patterns in a community, the use of an organisation's records to ascertain its activities, and the collection of data from sources such as articles, journals, magazines, books and periodicals to obtain historical and other types of information, are all classified as information obtained from secondary sources. In summary, primary sources provide first-hand information and secondary sources provide second-hand data. Figure 9.1 shows the various methods of data collection.

None of the methods of data collection provides 100 per cent accurate and reliable information. The quality of the data gathered is dependent upon a number of other factors, which we will identify as we discuss each method. Your skill as a researcher lies in your ability to take care of the factors that could affect the quality of your data. One of the main differences between experienced and amateur researchers lies in their understanding of, and ability to control, these factors. It is therefore important for a beginner to be aware of them.

Collecting data using primary sources

Several methods can be used to collect primary data. The choice of a method depends upon the purpose of the study, the resources available and the skills of the researcher. There are times when the method most appropriate to achieve the objectives of a study cannot be used because of constraints such as a lack of resources and/or required skills.

In such situations you should be aware of the problems that these limitations impose on the quality of the data.

In selecting a method of data collection, the socioeconomic-demographic characteristics of the study population play an important role. You should know as much as possible about characteristics such as educational level, age structure, socioeconomic status and ethnic background. If possible, it is helpful to know the study population's interest in, and attitude towards, participation in the study. Some populations, for a number of reasons, may not feel at ease with a particular method of data collection (such as being interviewed) or comfortable with expressing opinions in a questionnaire. Furthermore, people with little education may respond differently to certain methods of data collection compared to people with more education.

Another important determinant of the quality of your data is the way the purpose and relevance of the study are explained to potential respondents. Whatever method of data collection is used, make sure that respondents clearly understand the purpose and relevance of the study. This is particularly important when you use a questionnaire to collect data, because in an interview situation you can answer a respondent's questions but in a questionnaire you will not have this opportunity.

In the following sections each method of data collection is discussed from the point of view of its applicability and suitability to a situation, and the problems and limitations associated with it.

Observation

Observation is one way to collect primary data. It is a purposeful, systematic and selective way of watching and listening to an interaction or phenomenon as it takes place. There are many situations in which observation is the most appropriate method of data collection; for example, when you want to learn about the interaction in a group, study the dietary patterns of a population, ascertain the functions performed by a worker, or study the behaviour or personality traits of an individual. It is also appropriate in situations where full and/or accurate information cannot be elicited by questioning, because respondents either are not co-operative or are unaware of the answers because it is difficult for them to detach themselves from the interaction. In summary, when you are more interested in the behaviour than in the perceptions of individuals, or when subjects are so involved in the interaction that they are unable to provide objective information about it, observation is the best approach to collecting the required information.

Types of observation

There are two types of observation:

1. participant observation;
2. non-participant observation.

Participant observation is when you, as a researcher, participate in the activities of the group being observed, in the same manner as its members, with or without their knowing that they are being observed. For example, as a student of occupational therapy, you are interested in studying reactions of the general population towards people in wheelchairs. To do so, you pretend to have a handicap that requires you to use a wheelchair. As you use the wheelchair in a public area you observe the reactions of people you encounter. You make appropriate observational notes for your study when appropriate. Or suppose you want to study what it means to be prisoner and to do so, one way or another, you become a prisoner to achieve your aim. You live exactly the way other prisoners live and collect the information required to achieve the objectives of your study. Or suppose you want to study a tribe in some remote area and to do so you go and live with them and collect the data you need. Many anthropological studies have been conducted by using this approach.

Non-participant observation, on the other hand, is when you, as a researcher, do not get involved in the activities of the group but remain a passive observer, watching and listening to its activities and drawing conclusions from this. For example, you might want to study the functions carried out by nurses in a hospital. As an observer, you could watch, follow and record the activities as they are performed. After making a number of observations, you could draw conclusions about the functions nurses carry out in the hospital. Any occupational group in any setting can be observed in the same manner.

Problems with using observation as a method of data collection

The use of observation as a method of data collection may suffer from a number of problems, which is not to suggest that all or any of these necessarily prevail in every situation. But as a beginner you should be aware of these potential problems:

- When individuals or groups become aware that they are being observed, they may change their behaviour. Depending upon the situation, this change could be positive or negative – it may increase or decrease, for example, their productivity – and may occur for a number of reasons. When a change in the behaviour of persons or groups is attributed to their being observed it is known as the Hawthorne effect. The use of observation in such a situation may introduce distortion: what is observed may not represent their normal behaviour.
- There is always the possibility of observer bias. If an observer is not impartial, s/he can easily introduce bias and there is no easy way to verify the observations and the inferences drawn from them.
- The interpretations drawn from observations may vary from observer to observer.
- There is the possibility of incomplete observation and/or recording, which varies with the method of recording. An observer may watch keenly but at the expense of detailed recording. The opposite problem may occur when the observer takes detailed notes but in doing so misses some of the interaction.

Situations in which observations can be made

Observations can be made under two conditions:

1. natural;
2. controlled.

Observing a group without interfering in its normal activities, is referred to as observation under natural conditions. Introducing a stimulus to the group for it to react to and observing the reaction is referred to as observation under controlled conditions.

Recording of observations

There are many ways of recording observations. The selection of a method of recording depends upon the purpose of the observation. The way an observation is recorded also determines whether it is a quantitative or qualitative study. Narrative and descriptive recording is mainly used in qualitative research, but if you are doing a quantitative study you would record an observation in categorical form or on a numerical scale. Keep in mind that each method of recording an observation has its advantages and disadvantages.

In *narrative* recording the researcher records a description of the interaction in his/her own words. Such recording clearly falls in the domain of qualitative research. Usually, the researcher makes brief notes while observing the interaction and then, soon after completing the observation, makes detailed notes in narrative form. In addition, some researchers may interpret the interaction and draw conclusions from it. The biggest advantage of narrative recording is that it provides a deeper insight into the interaction. However, a disadvantage is that an observer may be biased in his/her observation and, therefore, the interpretations and conclusions drawn from the observation may also be biased. In addition, interpretations and conclusions drawn are bound to be subjective, reflecting the researcher's perspectives. Also, if a researcher's attention is on observing, s/he might forget to record an important piece of interaction. Furthermore, in the process of recording, part of the interaction may be missed. Hence, there is always the possibility of incomplete recording and/or observation. In addition, when there are different observers the comparability of narrative recording can be a problem.

Some observers may sometimes prefer to develop a *scale* in order to rate various aspects of the interaction or phenomenon. The recording is done on a scale developed by the observer/researcher. A scale may be one-, two- or three-directional, depending upon the purpose of the observation. For example, in the scale in Figure 9.2 – designed to record the nature of the interaction within a group – there are three directions: positive, negative and neutral.

The main advantage of using scales in recording an observation is that you do not need to spend time on taking detailed notes and can thus concentrate on observation. On the other hand, one problem with using a scale is that it does not provide specific and in-depth information about the interaction. In addition, it may suffer from any of the following errors:

- Unless the observer is extremely confident of his/her ability to assess an interaction, s/he may tend to avoid the extreme positions on the scale, using mostly the central part. The error that this tendency creates is called the error of central tendency.
- Some observers may prefer certain sections of the scale in the same way that some teachers are strict markers and others are not. When observers have a tendency to use a particular part of the scale in recording an interaction, this phenomenon is known as the elevation effect.
- Another type of error that may be introduced is when the way an observer rates an individual on one aspect of the interaction influences the way s/he rates that individual on another aspect of the interaction. Again something similar to this can happen in teaching when a teacher's assessment of the performance of a student in one subject may influence his/her rating of that student's performance in another. This type of effect is known as the halo effect.

SELECTING A METHOD OF DATA COLLECTION   175

Sometimes an observer may decide to set down his/her observations using *categorical recording*. The type and number of categories depend upon the type of interaction and the observer's choice about how to classify the observation. Examples are passive/active (two categories); introvert/extrovert (two categories); always/sometimes/never (three categories); or strongly agree/agree/uncertain/disagree/strongly disagree (five categories). The use of categories to record an observation may suffer from the same problems as those associated with scales.

Observations can also be recorded using a video camera or other *electronic devices* and then analysed. The advantage of recording an interaction in this way is that the observer can see it a number of times before interpreting an interaction or drawing any conclusions from it and can also invite other professionals to view the interaction in order to arrive at more objective conclusions. However, one of the disadvantages is that some people may feel uncomfortable or may behave differently before a camera. Therefore the interaction may not be a true reflection of the situation.

The choice of a particular method for recording your observation is dependent upon the purpose of the observation, the complexity of the interaction and the type of population being observed. It is important to consider these factors before deciding upon the method for recording your observation.

The interview

INTERVIEWING

Interviewing is a commonly used method of collecting information from people. There are many definitions of interviews, but it is essentially a person-to-person interaction, either face to face or otherwise, between two or more individuals with a specific purpose in mind. According to Monette et al. (1986: 156), 'an interview involves an interviewer

A study of the nature of interaction in a group

Aspects of interaction	Positive				Neutral		Negative			
Participation	5	4	3	2	1	0	1	2	3	4	5
Rapport	5	4	3	2	1	0	1	2	3	4	5
Confidence	5	4	3	2	1	0	1	2	3	4	5
Aggressiveness	5	4	3	2	1	0	1	2	3	4	5
Withdrawnness	5	4	3	2	1	0	1	2	3	4	5
Friendliness	5	4	3	2	1	0	1	2	3	4	5
Aloofness	5	4	3	2	1	0	1	2	3	4	5

Figure 9.2 Observing/recording group interactions on a three-directional rating scale

reading questions to respondents and recording their answers'. According to Burns (1997: 329), 'an interview is a verbal interchange, often face to face, though the telephone may be used, in which an interviewer tries to elicit information, beliefs or opinions from another person'.

When interviewing a respondent, as a researcher, you have the freedom to decide the format and content of your questions, choose how to word them, decide how you want to ask them and in what order. The process of asking questions can be either very flexible, where you as the interviewer have the freedom to think about and formulate questions as they come to your mind around the issue being investigated, or inflexible, where you have to keep strictly to questions decided on beforehand – including their wording, sequence and the manner in which they are asked. Interviews are classified into different categories according to this degree of flexibility as in Figure 9.3.

Unstructured interviews

The main strength of an unstructured interview lies in having almost complete freedom in terms of its structure, contents, question wording and order. You are free to ask whatever you want, and in a format that is relevant to the situation. You also have complete freedom in terms of the wording you use and the way you explain questions to your respondents. You may formulate questions and raise issues on the spur of the moment, depending upon what occurs to you in the context of the discussion.

Unstructured interviews are extremely useful in exploring intensively and extensively and digging deeper into a situation, phenomenon, issue or problem. They provide varied and in-depth information and are best suited to identifying diversity and variety. However, their disadvantage lies in the high level of skills they require in conducting them.

Unstructured interviews are prevalent in both quantitative and qualitative research. The difference is in how information obtained through them in response to your questions

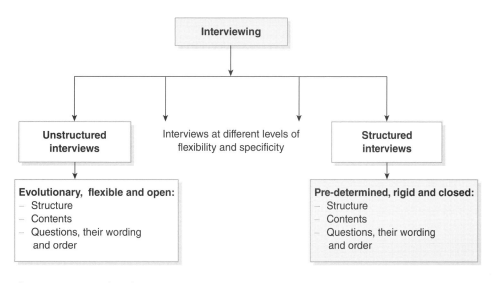

Figure 9.3 Types of interview

is likely to be used. In quantitative research you develop response categorisations from responses which are then coded and quantified. In qualitative research the responses are used as descriptors, often verbatim, and can be integrated with your arguments, flow of writing and sequence of logic. As unstructured interviews are predominantly used in qualitative research, they are described in greater detail under 'Methods of data collection in qualitative research' later in this chapter.

Structured interviews

In a structured interview the researcher asks a predetermined set of questions, using the same wording and order of questions as specified in the interview schedule. An interview schedule is a written list of questions, open-ended or closed, thoroughly pre-tested for standardised wording, meaning and interpretation, prepared for use by an interviewer in a person-to-person interaction (this may be face to face, by telephone or by other electronic media). Note that an interview schedule is a research tool/instrument for collecting data, whereas interviewing is a method of data collection.

One of the main advantages of the structured interview is that it provides uniform information, which assures the comparability of data. Structured interviewing requires fewer interviewing skills than does unstructured interviewing.

The questionnaire

QUESTIONNAIRES

A questionnaire is a written list of questions, the answers to which are recorded by respondents. Thus, respondents read the questions, interpret what is expected and then write down the answers. The only difference between an interview schedule and a questionnaire is that in the former it is the interviewer who asks the questions (and if necessary, explains them) and records the respondent's replies on an interview schedule, and in the latter the replies are recorded by the respondents themselves. This distinction is important in accounting for the respective strengths and weaknesses of the two methods and their respective use in gathering data.

In a questionnaire, as there is no one to explain the meaning of questions to respondents, it is important that the questions are clear and easy to understand. Also, the layout of a questionnaire should be such that it is easy to read and pleasant to the eyes, and the sequence of questions should be easy to follow. A questionnaire should be developed in an interactive style. This means respondents should feel as if someone is talking to them. In a questionnaire, a sensitive question or a question that respondents may feel hesitant about answering should be prefaced by an interactive statement explaining the relevance of the question. It is a good idea to use a different font for these statements to distinguish them from the actual questions. Examples in Figures 9.4 and 9.5, taken from two surveys recently carried out by the author with the help of two students, explain some of the above points.

Ways of administering a questionnaire

A questionnaire can be administered in a number of ways. Your selection of a particular method of administration depends upon the ease in assessing your respondent population

---

Where to go? A study of occupational mobility among immigrants

The questionnaire developed for this study opened with the following interactive statement:

Personal circumstances, and educational and occupational background, to a great extent determine the occupational mobility of an individual. This is especially true for immigrants. We would therefore like to ask you some questions about you and your family background. Knowledge of these factors is also important for assessing the representativeness of those who participated in the study and to understand the extent, nature and reasons of occupational mobility in relation to your background. We would appreciate your answering these questions as the information you provide will be very useful to us. We would like to emphasise that your responses are extremely valuable to us and we would greatly appreciate your answering all questions. However, if you feel that you do not want to answer a particular question, we will gladly accept your decision. We can assure you that your responses will be completely anonymous and will not be used for any other purpose.

Before asking questions about family background, the following interactive statement was inserted in the questionnaire:

Now, we would like to ask some questions about your family. Your family circumstances can affect your choice of an occupation after immigration. Again, we assure you of the complete anonymity of your responses.

Before ascertaining respondents' experiences with respect to recognition of their qualifications in Australia, the following interactive statement prepared them to be at ease with the area of enquiry:

Recognition of educational and professional qualifications, in addition to other factors, plays a major role in determining an individual's occupational mobility in a new country. In this section we would like to ask your opinion about the process of getting your qualifications recognised. We would also like to know how satisfied or dissatisfied you are with the outcome. If you are dissatisfied, we would like to know your reasons as this information may help decision makers to improve the process. Again, we assure you that your answers will be completely confidential. However, if you still feel that you do not want to answer a particular question, please feel free to omit it.

Figure 9.4   Where to go? A study of occupational mobility among immigrants

and your impressions about how they would prefer to participate in your study. The various ways in which you can administer a questionnaire are as follows:

- The mailed questionnaire. The most common approach to collecting information is to send the questionnaire to prospective respondents by mail. Obviously this approach presupposes that you have access to their addresses. It may not be easy to get addresses, so before you decide to collect your data through this method, make sure of the availability of addresses of your potential respondents. Usually it is a good idea to send a prepaid, self-addressed envelope with the questionnaire as this might increase the response rate. A mailed questionnaire must be accompanied by a *covering letter* (see below). One of the major problems with this method is the low response rate. In the case of an extremely low response rate, the findings have very limited applicability to the population studied.
- Collective administration. One of the best ways of administering a questionnaire is to obtain a captive audience such as students in a classroom, people attending a function, participants in a programme or people assembled in one place. This ensures a very high response rate as you will find few people refuse to participate in your study. Also, as you have personal contact with the study population, you can explain the purpose, relevance and importance of the study and can clarify any questions that respondents may have. The author's advice is that if you have a captive audience for your study, don't miss the opportunity – it is the quickest way of collecting data, ensures a very high response rate and saves you money on postage.

SELECTING A METHOD OF DATA COLLECTION   179

Ways of administering a questionnaire

Occupational redeployment: a study of occupational redeployment among state government employees

The following interactive statement was inserted in the questionnaire before asking questions about the socioeconomic-demographic background of respondents:

In order to gain an understanding of the situation of employees who have experienced occupational redeployment in state government departments during the last three years, we would like to ask some questions about your background. Your answers will help us to determine the types of occupation where redeployment has occurred and the backgrounds of the employees who have been affected by it. Please do not feel obliged to answer a question if you do not wish to, though we assure you your answers to these questions are extremely important to us to ascertain the nature and extent of the shift in your career path. We again assure you that any information you provide will be treated with strict confidentiality.

Questions about occupational history were prefaced by the following statement:

We would like to ask some questions about your work history. The answers to these questions will enable us to compare the type of work you have been doing since entering the workforce with the job you have been assigned after redeployment. This will help us to establish the nature and extent of change in your job before and after redeployment. Again, there is no obligation to answer a question if you do not want to. However, answers to these questions are extremely important to us. We assure you of the anonymity of the information you provide.

Before asking questions about the impact of redeployment, the following interactive statement was incorporated into the questionnaire:

The following questions ask you to express your opinion about different aspects of your job after and before redeployment. Your answers will help us to gauge the impact of redeployment on different aspects of your work and family situation. We would appreciate your honest opinions. Be assured that your responses will be completely anonymous.

Figure 9.5   Occupational redeployment: a study among state government employees

WEB SURVEY
METHODOLOGY

- **Online questionnaire.** With the advancement in communication technology, the use of the online questionnaire to collect information to answer your research questions has become quite common. You develop a questionnaire in the same way as you normally do using a program that is designed for the purpose (see Chapter 8). The main difference is that instead of personally delivering, collectively distributing or individually mailing, you post it either on a website or provide a link in your email for potential respondents to access it and respond. In the same way you could send the questionnaire to mobile phones. You can also analyse the data collected through online questionnaires using an appropriate program. There are many such programs and you need to identify the one most appropriate for your situation. Before you use this method of data collection, it is important for you to familiarise yourself with the process and program that you intend to use. In case of emailing or sending it to mobile phones you need to collect respondents' email addresses or phone numbers.
- **Administration in a public place.** Sometimes you can administer a questionnaire in a public place such as a shopping centre, health centre, hospital, school or pub. Of course this depends upon the type of study population you are looking for and where it is likely to be found. Usually the purpose of the study is explained to potential respondents as they approach and their participation in the study is requested. Apart from being slightly more time-consuming, this method has all the advantages of administering a questionnaire collectively.

180   **RESEARCH METHODOLOGY**

Choosing between an interview schedule and a questionnaire

The choice between a questionnaire and an interview schedule is important and should be considered thoroughly as the strengths and weaknesses of the two methods can affect the validity of the findings. The nature of the investigation and the socioeconomic-demographic characteristics of the study population are central in this choice. The selection between an interview schedule and a questionnaire should be based upon the following criteria:

- The nature of the investigation. If the study is about issues that respondents may feel reluctant to discuss with an investigator, a questionnaire may be the better choice as it ensures anonymity. This may be the case with studies on drug use, sexuality, indulgence in criminal activities and personal finances. However, there are situations where better information about sensitive issues can be obtained by interviewing respondents. It depends on the type of study population and the skills of the interviewer. You need to explore and decide what would be better suited for your study and respondents.
- The geographical distribution of the study population. If potential respondents are scattered over a wide geographical area, you have no choice but to use a questionnaire, as interviewing in these circumstances would be extremely expensive.
- The type of study population. If the study population is illiterate, very young or very old, or handicapped, there may be no option but to interview respondents.

Advantages of a questionnaire

A questionnaire has the following advantages:

- It is less expensive. As you do not interview respondents, you save time, and human and financial resources. The use of a questionnaire, therefore, is comparatively convenient and inexpensive, especially when it is administered collectively to a study population.
- It offers greater anonymity. As there is no face-to-face interaction between respondents and interviewer, this method provides greater anonymity. In some situations where sensitive questions are asked it helps to increase the likelihood of obtaining accurate information.

Disadvantages of a questionnaire

Although a questionnaire has several disadvantages, it is important to note that not all data collection using this method has these disadvantages. The prevalence of a particular disadvantage depends on a number of other factors. However, you need to be aware of these disadvantages to understand their possible bearing on the quality of the data. Some of these disadvantages are as follows:

- Limited application. One main disadvantage is that application is limited to a study population that can read and write. It also cannot be used on a population that is very young, very old or handicapped.
- Low response rate. Questionnaires are notorious for their low response rates; that is, people fail to return them. If you plan to use a questionnaire, keep in mind that because not everyone will return their questionnaire, your sample size will in effect be reduced. The response rate depends upon a number of factors: the interest of the sample in the topic of the study; the layout and length of the questionnaire; the quality of the letter explaining the purpose and relevance of the study; and the

methodology used to deliver the questionnaire. You should consider yourself lucky to obtain a 50 per cent response rate, and sometimes it may be as low as 20 per cent. However, as mentioned, the response rate is not a problem when a questionnaire is administered in a collective situation.

- **Self-selecting bias.** Since not everyone who receives a questionnaire returns it, there is a self-selecting bias. Those who return their questionnaire may have attitudes, attributes or motivations that are different from those who do not. Hence, if the response rate is very low, the findings may not be representative of the total study population.
- **Lack of opportunity to clarify issues.** If, for any reason, respondents do not understand some questions, there is almost no opportunity for them to have the meaning clarified unless they get in touch with the researcher (which does not happen often). If different respondents interpret questions differently, this will affect the quality of the information provided.
- **No opportunity for spontaneous responses.** Mailed questionnaires are inappropriate when spontaneous responses are required, as most respondents will glance though the whole questionnaire before answering. This gives them time to reflect before answering, which may make them change their answers to some questions.
- **The response to a question may be influenced by the response to other questions.** As respondents can read all the questions before answering (which usually happens), the way they answer a particular question may be affected by their knowledge of other questions.
- **Others can influence the answers.** With mailed questionnaires respondents may consult other people before responding. In situations where an investigator wants to find out only the study population's opinions, this method may be inappropriate, though requesting respondents to express their own opinion may help.
- **A response cannot be supplemented with other information.** The information gathered by interviewing can sometimes be supplemented with information from other methods of data collection such as observation. However, a questionnaire lacks this advantage.

Advantages of the interview

- **More appropriate for complex situations.** It is the most appropriate approach for studying complex and sensitive areas as the interviewer has the opportunity to prepare a respondent before asking sensitive questions and to explain complex ones to respondents in person.
- **Useful for collecting in-depth information.** In an interview situation it is possible for an investigator to obtain in-depth information by probing. Hence, in situations where in-depth information is required, interviewing is the preferred method of data collection.
- **Information can be supplemented.** An interviewer is able to supplement information obtained from responses with those gained from observation of non-verbal reactions.
- **Questions can be explained.** It is less likely that a question will be misunderstood as the interviewer can either repeat a question or put it in a form that is understood by the respondent.
- **Has a wider application.** An interview can be used with almost any type of population: children, the handicapped, illiterate or very old.

Disadvantages of the interview

- **Time-consuming and expensive.** This is especially so when potential respondents are scattered over a wide geographical area. However, if you have a situation such as an office, a hospital or an agency where potential respondents come to obtain a service, interviewing them in that setting may be less expensive and less time-consuming.

- **The quality of data depends upon the quality of the interaction.** In an interview the quality of interaction between an interviewer and interviewee is likely to affect the quality of the information obtained. Also, because the interaction in each interview is unique, the quality of the responses obtained from different interviews may vary significantly.
- **The quality of data depends upon the quality of the interviewer.** In an interview situation the quality of the data generated is affected by the experience, skills and commitment of the interviewer.
- **The quality of data may vary when multiple interviewers are used.** Use of multiple interviewers may magnify the problems identified in the previous two points.
- **Possibility of researcher bias.** In an interview situation a researcher's bias either in the framing of questions and/or in the interpretation of responses obtained is always possible. If the interviews are conducted by a person or persons, paid or voluntary, other than the researcher, it is also possible that they may exhibit bias in the way they interpret responses, select response categories or choose words to summarise respondents' expressed opinions.

Contents of the covering letter

It is essential that you write a covering letter with your mailed questionnaire. In it you should very briefly:

- introduce yourself and the institution you represent;
- describe in two or three sentences the main objectives of the study;
- explain the relevance of the study;
- convey any general instructions;
- indicate that participation in the study is voluntary – if recipients do not want to respond to the questionnaire, they have the right not to;
- assure respondents of the anonymity of the information provided by them;
- provide a contact number in case they have any questions;
- give a return address for the questionnaire and a deadline for its return;
- thank them for their participation in the study.

Types of question

The way you formulate a question (open-ended or closed) and the wording you use in its framing in an interview schedule or a questionnaire are extremely important as they influence the type and quality of information you obtain from your respondents. The wording and structure of questions should therefore be clear, succinct, appropriate, relevant, and free from any of the problems discussed in the section on 'Formulating effective questions' later in this chapter. It is therefore important for you to know the types of questions commonly used in social research with their respective strengths and weaknesses. You also need to know the attributes of the wording used in their construction. This section deals with their types, characteristics, the process of formulation, and some of the common problems associated with the way they are worded.

WRITING SURVEY
QUESTIONS

There are two types of question commonly used in social research:

- open-ended questions; and
- closed questions.

In an open-ended question the possible response categories are *not* provided in the research instrument. In the case of a questionnaire, the respondent writes down the answers in his/her own words, but in the case of an interview schedule the investigator records the answers either verbatim or in a summary. In a closed question the possible answers are set out in the questionnaire or schedule and the respondent or investigator ticks the category that best describes the respondent's answer. It is usually wise to provide a category 'Other/please explain' to accommodate any response not listed. The questions in Figure 9.6 are examples of closed questions. The same questions could be asked as open-ended questions, as shown in Figure 9.7.

When deciding whether to use open-ended or closed questions to obtain information about a variable, visualise how you plan to use the information generated. This is important because the way you frame your questions determines the unit of measurement which could be used to classify the responses. The unit of measurement in turn dictates what statistical procedures can be applied to the data and the way the information can be analysed and displayed.

A. Please indicate your age by placing a tick in the appropriate category.

Under 15 ☐
15–19 years ☐
20–24 years ☐

B. How would you describe your current marital status?

Married ☐
Single ☐
De facto ☐
Divorced ☐
Separated ☐

C. What is your average annual income?

Under $10 000 ☐
$10 000–$19 999 ☐
$20 000–$29 999 ☐
$30 000–$39 999 ☐
$40 000+ ☐

OR

C(a). How would you categorise your average annual income?

Above average ☐
Average ☐
Below average ☐

D. What, in your opinion, are the qualities of a good administrator?

Able to make decisions ☐
Fast decision maker ☐
Able to listen ☐
Impartial ☐
Skilled in interpersonal communication ☐
Other, please specify

_____
_____

Figure 9.6 Examples of closed questions

A. What is your current age? ——————— years

B. How would you describe your current marital status? ———————

C. What is your average annual income? $ ———————

D. What, in your opinion, are the qualities of a good administrator?

1 ———————————

2 ———————————

3 ———————————

4 ———————————

5 ———————————

Figure 9.7 Examples of open-ended questions

Let us take, as an example, the question about the variable 'income'. In closed questions income can be qualitatively recorded in categories such as 'above average/average/below average', or quantitatively in categories such as 'under $10 000/$10 000–$19 999/...'. Your choice of qualitative and quantitative categories affects the unit of measurement for income (qualitative uses the ordinal scale and quantitative the ratio scale of measurement), which in turn will affect the application of statistical procedures. For example, you cannot calculate the average income of a person from the responses to question C(a) in Figure 9.6; nor can you calculate the median or modal category of income. From the responses to question C, you can accurately calculate the modal category of income, but not the mean or the median income (such calculations are usually made under certain assumptions). From the responses to question C in Figure 9.7, where the income for a respondent is recorded in exact dollars, the different descriptors of income can be calculated very accurately. In addition, information on income can be displayed in any form. You can precisely calculate the mean, median or mode of income for a given study group. The same is true for any other information obtained in response to an open-ended question.

In closed questions, having developed categories, you cannot change them; therefore, you should be very certain about your categories when developing them. If you ask an open-ended question, you can develop any number of categories in any form at the time of analysis.

Advantages and disadvantages of open-ended and closed questions

Both open-ended and closed questions have their advantages and disadvantages in different situations. To some extent, their advantages and disadvantages depend upon whether they are being used in an interview or in a questionnaire and on whether they are being used to seek information about facts or opinions. As a rule, closed questions are extremely useful for eliciting factual information and open-ended questions for seeking opinions, attitudes and perceptions. The choice of open-ended or closed questions should be made according to the purpose for which a piece of information is to be used, the type of study population from which information is going to be obtained, the proposed format for communicating the findings and the socioeconomic background of the readership.

Open-ended questions have the following advantages and disadvantages:

- Open-ended questions provide in-depth information if used in an interview by an experienced interviewer. In a questionnaire, open-ended questions can provide a wealth of information provided respondents feel comfortable about expressing their opinions and are fluent in the language used. On the other hand, analysis of open-ended questions is more difficult. The researcher usually needs to go through another process – content analysis – in order to classify the data.
- In a questionnaire, open-ended questions provide respondents with the opportunity to express themselves freely, resulting in a greater variety of information. Thus respondents are not 'conditioned' by having to select answers from a list. The disadvantage of free choice is that, in a questionnaire, some respondents may not be able to express themselves, and so information can be lost.
- As open-ended questions allow respondents to express themselves freely, they virtually eliminate the possibility of investigator bias (investigator bias is introduced through the response pattern presented to respondents). On the other hand, there is a greater chance of interviewer bias in open-ended questions.

Closed questions have the following advantages and disadvantages:

- One of the main disadvantages of closed questions is that the information obtained through them lacks depth and variety.
- There is a greater possibility of investigator bias because the researcher may list only the response patterns that s/he is interested in or those that come to mind at the time of developing the research instrument. Even if the category of 'other' is offered, most people will usually select from the list of given responses, and so the findings may still reflect researcher bias.
- In a questionnaire, the given response pattern for a question could condition the thinking of respondents, and so the answers provided may not truly reflect respondents' opinions. Rather, they may reflect the extent of agreement or disagreement with the researcher's opinion or analysis of a situation.
- The ease of answering a ready-made list of responses may create a tendency among some respondents and interviewers to tick a category or categories without thinking through the issue.
- Closed questions, because they provide 'ready-made' categories within which respondents reply to the questions asked by the researcher, help to ensure that the information needed by the researcher is obtained and the responses are also easier to analyse.

Formulating effective questions

The way you ask a question, to a great extent, determines the response that you are likely to get from your respondents. Your output in terms of the responses and their quality depends upon your input in terms of questions you ask of your respondents. The wording and tone of your questions are therefore extremely important. You should be very careful about the way you formulate questions. The following are some suggestions and considerations to keep in mind when formulating questions:

- Always use simple and everyday language. Your respondents may not be highly educated, and even if they are they still may not know some of the 'simple' technical jargon that you are used to. Particularly in a questionnaire, take extra care to use words that your respondents will understand as you will have no opportunity to explain questions to them. A pre-test should show you what is and what is not understood by your respondents. For example:

Is anyone in your family a *dipsomaniac*? (Bailey 1978: 100)

In this question many respondents, even some who are well educated, will not understand 'dipsomaniac' and, hence, they either do not answer or answer the question without understanding.

- **Do not use ambiguous questions.** An ambiguous question is one that contains more than one meaning and that can be interpreted differently by different respondents. This will result in different answers, making it difficult, if not impossible, to draw any valid conclusions from the information. The following questions highlight the problem:

  Is your work made difficult because you are expecting a baby? (Moser & Kalton 1989: 323)
  Yes ☐ No ☐

In the survey all women were asked this question. Those women who were not pregnant ticked 'No', meaning no they were not pregnant, and those who were pregnant and who ticked 'No' meant pregnancy had not made their work difficult. The question has other ambiguities as well: it does not specify the type of work and the stage of pregnancy.

  Are you satisfied with your canteen? (Moser & Kalton 1989: 319)

This question is also ambiguous as it does not ask respondents to indicate the aspects of the canteen with which they may be satisfied or dissatisfied. Is it with the service, the prices, the physical facilities, the attitude of the staff or the quality of the meals? Respondents may have any one of these aspects in mind when they answer the question. Or the question should have been worded differently – for example, 'Overall, are you satisfied with your canteen?'

- **Do not ask double-barrelled questions.** A double-barrelled question is a question within a question. The main problem with this type of question is that one does not know which particular question a respondent has answered. Some respondents may answer both parts of the question and others may answer only one of them.

  How often and how much time do you spend on each visit?

This question was asked in a survey in Western Australia to ascertain the need for child-minding services in one of the hospitals. The question has two parts: how often do you visit, and how much time is spent on each visit? In this type of question some respondents may answer the first part, whereas others may answer the second part and some may answer both parts. Incidentally, this question is also ambiguous in that it does not specify 'how often' in terms of a period of time. Is it in a week, a fortnight, a month or a year?

  Does your department have a special recruitment policy for racial minorities and women? (Bailey 1978: 97)

This question is double-barrelled in that it asks respondents to indicate whether their office has a special recruitment policy for two population groups: racial minorities and women. A 'yes' response does not necessarily mean that the office has a special recruitment policy for both groups.

SELECTING A METHOD OF DATA COLLECTION   187

- **Do not ask leading questions.** A leading question is one which, by its contents, structure or wording, leads a respondent to answer in a certain direction. Such questions are judgemental and lead respondents to answer either positively or negatively.

Unemployment is increasing, isn't it?

Smoking is bad, isn't it?

The first problem is that these are not questions but statements. Because the statements suggest that 'unemployment is increasing' and 'smoking is bad', respondents may feel that to disagree with them is to be in the wrong, especially if they feel that the researcher is an authority and that if s/he is saying that 'unemployment is increasing' or 'smoking is bad', it must be so. The feeling that there is a 'right' answer can 'force' people to respond in a way that is contrary to their true position.

- **Do not ask questions that are based on presumptions.** In such questions the researcher assumes that respondents fit into a particular category and seeks information based upon that assumption.

How many cigarettes do you smoke in a day? (Moser & Kalton 1989: 325)

What contraceptives do you use?

Both these questions were asked without ascertaining whether or not respondents were smokers or sexually active. In situations like this it is important to ascertain first whether or not a respondent fits into the category about which you are enquiring.

Constructing a research instrument in quantitative research

The construction of a research instrument or tool is an extremely important aspect of a research project because anything you say by way of findings or conclusions is based upon the type of information you collect, and the data you collect is entirely dependent upon the questions that you ask of your respondents. The famous saying about computers – 'garbage in, garbage out'– is also applicable to data collection. The research tool provides the input to a study and therefore the quality and validity of the output, the findings, are solely dependent upon it.

In spite of its immense importance, to the author's knowledge, no specific guidelines for beginners on how to construct a research tool exist. Students are left to learn for themselves under the guidance of their research supervisor. The guidelines suggested below outline a broad approach, especially for beginners. The underlying principle is to ensure the validity of your instrument by making sure that *the questions you ask of your respondents directly relate to the objectives of your study*. Therefore, clearly stated objectives, research questions and hypotheses play an extremely important role in ensuring the validity of your research instrument as, in the suggested approach, each question in the instrument stems from them. It is suggested that a beginner should adopt the following approach in the development of a research instrument:

Step I	If you have not already done so, clearly define and individually list all the specific objectives, research questions or hypotheses, if any, to be tested.
Step II	For each objective, research question or hypothesis, list all the associated questions that you want to answer through your study.
Step III	Take each question that you identified in Step II and list the information required to answer it.
Step IV	Formulate question(s) that you want to ask of your respondents to obtain the required information.

In the above process you may find that the same piece of information is required for a number of questions. In such a situation the question should be asked once only. To understand this process, study Table 9.1 for which we have already developed a set of objectives in Figure 4.4 in Chapter 4. Note that each research objective, question or hypothesis is linked to some of the questions that you ask of your respondents. In other words, each question that you ask of your respondents can be linked to one of the objectives, research questions or hypotheses, thus enhancing the validity of your research instrument. Most of the time you might need to ask more than one question to fully achieve the total intentions of an objective or research questions.

Asking personal and sensitive questions

In the social sciences, sometimes one needs to ask questions that are of a personal nature. Some respondents may find this offensive. It is important to be aware of this as it may affect the quality of information or even result in an interview being terminated or questionnaires not being returned. Researchers have used a number of approaches to deal with this problem, but it is difficult to say which approach is best. According to Bradburn and Sudman (1979: 12–13), 'no data collection method is superior to other methods for all types of threatening questions. If one accepts the results at face value, each of the data gathering methods is best under certain conditions.'

In terms of the best technique for asking sensitive or threatening questions, there appear to be two opposite opinions, based on the manner in which the question is asked: direct or indirect. The advantage of the direct approach is that one can be sure that an affirmative answer is accurate. Those who advocate the indirect approach believe that direct questioning is likely to offend respondents and hence they are unlikely to answer even non-sensitive questions. Some ways of asking personal questions in an indirect manner are as follows:

* by showing drawings or cartoons;
* by asking the respondent to complete a sentence;
* by asking the respondent to sort cards containing statements;
* by using random devices.

A detailed description of these methods is beyond the scope of this book.

Table 9.1   Guidelines for constructing a research instrument (quantitative research): a study to evaluate community responsiveness in a health programme

Objectives/research questions/hypotheses → Step I	Main and associated research questions → Step II	Information required → Step III	Questions Step IV
1 To find out the understanding of the concept 'community responsiveness' among health administrators, planners, service providers and consumers of health services	What is community responsiveness? What does it mean when people use the term 'community responsiveness'?	1 Perception of community responsiveness	Q1.1 When you use the term 'community responsiveness', what do you mean by it? Q1.2 What comes to your mind when you use the term 'community responsiveness' in the delivery of health services? Q1.3 What, in your opinion, are the characteristics of 'community responsiveness'? Q1.4 What, in your opinion, is the difference between 'community development' and 'community responsiveness'?
2 To identify the strategies needed to foster community responsiveness in the delivery of health services	What are the differences in the perception of community responsiveness among health administrators, planners, service providers and consumers of health services?	2 Occupational status, i.e. health administrator, planner, service provider or consumer	Q2.1 What would you categorise your job as? • Health administrator/planner • Service provider • Health consumer
3 To develop a set of indicators to evaluate the effectiveness of strategies to foster community responsiveness		3 Age, gender, education	Q3.1 How old are you? ____ Q3.2 Are you ____ female ____ male? Q3.3 What is the highest level of educational achievement you have attained?

The order of questions

The order of questions in a questionnaire or in an interview schedule is important as it affects the quality of information, and the interest and even willingness of a respondent to participate in a study. Again, there are two categories of opinion as to the best way to order questions. The first is that questions should be asked in a random order, and the second is that they should follow a logical progression based upon the objectives of the study. The author believes that the latter procedure is better as it gradually leads respondents into the themes of the study, starting with simple themes and progressing to complex ones. This approach sustains the interest of respondents and gradually stimulates them to answer the questions. However, the random approach is useful in situations where the researcher wants respondents to express their agreement or disagreement with different aspects of an issue. In this case a logical listing of statements or questions may 'condition' a respondent to the opinions expressed by the researcher through the statements.

Pre-testing a research instrument

Having constructed your research instrument, whether an interview schedule or a questionnaire, it is important that you test it out before using it for actual data collection. Pre-testing a research instrument entails a critical examination of the understanding of each question by respondents. A pre-test should be carried out under actual field conditions on a group of people similar to your study population. The purpose is not to collect data but to identify problems that the potential respondents might have in understanding or interpreting a question. Your aim is to identify if there are problems in understanding the way a question has been worded, the appropriateness of the meaning it communicates, whether different respondents interpret a question differently, and to establish whether their interpretation is different from what you were trying to convey. If there are problems you need to re-examine the wording to make it clearer and unambiguous.

Prerequisites for data collection

Before you start obtaining information from potential respondents it is imperative that you make sure of their:

- motivation to share the required information – It is essential for respondents to be willing to share information with you. You should make every effort to motivate them by explaining clearly and in simple terms the objectives and relevance of the study, either at the time of the interview or in the covering letter accompanying the questionnaire and/or through interactive statements in the questionnaire.
- clear understanding of the questions – Respondents must understand what is expected of them in the questions. If respondents do not understand a question clearly, the response given may be either wrong or irrelevant, or make no sense.
- possession of the required information – It is a prerequisite that respondents must have the information sought. This is of particular importance when you are seeking factual or technical information. If respondents do not have the required information, they cannot provide it.

SELECTING A METHOD OF DATA COLLECTION   191

Methods of data collection in qualitative research

To draw a clear distinction between quantitative and qualitative methods of data collection is both difficult and inappropriate because of the overlap between them. The difference between them mainly lies in the manner in which a method is applied in an actual data collection situation. Use of these methods in quantitative research demands standardisation of questions to be asked of the respondents, a rigid adherence to their structure and order, an adoption of a process that is tested and predetermined, and making sure of the validity and reliability of the process as well as the questions. However, the methods of data collection in qualitative research follow a convention which is almost opposite to quantitative research. The wording, order and format of these questions are neither predetermined nor standardised. Qualitative methods are characterised by flexibility and freedom in terms of structure and order on the part of the researcher.

As mentioned in the previous chapter, most qualitative study designs are method based: that is, the method of data collection seems to determine the design. In some situations it becomes difficult to separate a study design from the method of data collection. For example, in-depth interviewing, narratives and oral history are both designs and methods of data collection. This may confuse some, but in this chapter they are detailed as methods and not designs.

The various methods of data collection in qualitative research can be classified into three categories. These are:

1. unstructured interviews;
2. observations; and
3. secondary sources.

Unstructured interviews

RESEARCH
INTERVIEWS

Unstructured interviewing is a very common method of data collection in qualitative research. Unstructured interviews are based upon most of the characteristics that underpin the philosophy of qualitative research. They are flexible in structure, in-depth in their search, free from rigid boundaries, and at liberty to deviate from their predetermined course if need be. In addition, they differ from structured interviews in the manner the raw data is generated and analysed and the style in which the findings are communicated.

Flexibility, freedom and spontaneity in content and structure underpin an interaction in all types of unstructured interview. This interaction can be at a one-to-one (researcher and respondent) or a group (researcher and a group of respondents) level. There are several types of unstructured interview that are prevalent in qualitative research: *in-depth interviewing, focus group interviewing, narratives* and *oral histories*. Below is a brief description of each of these. For a detailed understanding readers should consult the relevant references listed in the Bibliography.

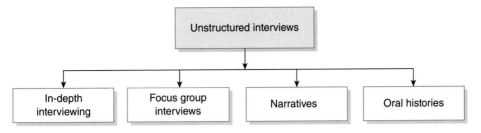

Figure 9.8   Types of unstructured interviews

In-depth interviews

The theoretical roots of in-depth interviewing are in what is known as the interpretive tradition. According to Taylor and Bogdan (1998: 77), in-depth interviewing is 'repeated face-to-face encounters between the researcher and informants directed towards under-standing informants' perspectives on their lives, experiences, or situations as expressed in their own words'. This definition underlines two essential characteristics of in-depth inter-viewing: it involves face-to-face, repeated interaction between the researcher and his/her informant(s); and it aims to understand the perspectives of the latter. Because this method involves repeated contacts and hence an extended length of time spent with an informant, it is assumed that the rapport between researcher and informant will be enhanced, and that the corresponding understanding and confidence between the two will lead to in-depth and accurate information.

In its design, the in-depth interviewing is very simple. You select individuals who you think can provide you with the best information, and make contact with them to detail dif-ferent aspects of the study, to seek their informed consent to their participation, to explain their expected involvement, and to decide where and when to carry out the interviews.

Recording the details of your discussions with your respondents is extremely important. You need to decide how and when you are going to record these details, and how the recorded material is to be given to your respondent(s) for confirmation and verification.

Focus group interviews

The only difference between a focus group interview and an in-depth interview is that the former is undertaken with a group and the latter with an individual. In a focus group interview you explore the perceptions, experiences and understandings of a group of people who have some experience in common with regard to a situation or event. For example, you may explore with relevant groups such issues as domestic violence, physi-cal disability or asylum seeking in Australia. The purpose is to find out the experiences and opinions of those who have collectively experienced an event or situation.

In focus group interviews, broad areas of discussion topics are developed beforehand, either by the researcher or by the group. These only provide a broad frame for discussions which are followed by the specific discussion points that emerge as a part of the discussion. Members of a focus group express their opinions while discussing these issues.

SELECTING A METHOD OF DATA COLLECTION   193

As a researcher, you need to ensure that whatever is expressed or discussed is recorded accurately. Use the method of recording that suits you best. You may audiotape discussions, employ someone else to record them or record them yourself immediately after each session. If you are taking your own notes during discussions, you need to be careful not to lose something of importance because of your involvement in discussions. You can and should take your write-up of discussions back to your focus group for correction, verification and confirmation.

Narratives

WHAT IS NARRATIVE RESEARCH?

The narrative technique of gathering information has even less structure than the focus group. Narratives have almost no predetermined content except that the researcher seeks to hear a person's retelling of an incident or happening in his/her life. Essentially, the person tells his/ her story about an incident or situation and you, as the researcher, listen passively. Occasionally, you encourage the individual by using active listening techniques; that is, you say words such as 'uh huh', 'mmmm', 'yeah', 'right' and nod as appropriate. Basically, you let the person talk freely and without interrupting.

Narratives are a very powerful method of data collection for situations which are sensitive in nature. For example, you may want to find out about the impact of child sexual abuse on people who have gone through such an experience. As a researcher, you ask these people to narrate their experiences and how they have been affected. Narratives may have a therapeutic impact; that is, sometimes simply telling their story may help a person to feel more at ease with the event. Some therapists specialise in narrative therapy. But here, we are concerned with narratives as a method of data collection.

As with focus group interviews, you need to choose the recording system that suits you best. Having completed narrative sessions you need to write up your detailed notes and give them back to the respondent to check for accuracy.

Oral histories

Oral histories, like narratives, involve the use of both passive and active listening. Oral histories, however, are more commonly used for learning about a historical event or episode or for gaining information about a culture, custom or story that has been passed from generation to generation. Narratives are more about a person's personal experiences, whereas oral histories are about historical, social or cultural events.

Suppose you want to find out about the experiences of people who were displaced after the Second World War in Europe. Talking to some of them and eliciting their stories will become the basis of your conclusions about life experiences after the War. Or suppose you want to find out about the living conditions of Aboriginal and Torres Strait Island people in the 1960s. To do so you would talk to persons who were alive during that period and ask them about life at that time.

Data collection through unstructured interviewing is extremely useful in situations where either in-depth information is needed or little is known about the area. The flexibility allowed to the interviewer in what s/he asks of a respondent is an asset as it can elicit extremely rich information. As it provides in-depth information, this technique is used by many researchers to construct a structured research instrument. On the other hand, since an unstructured interview does not list specific questions to be asked of respondents, the comparability of questions asked and responses obtained may become a problem. As the researcher gains experience during the interviews, the questions asked of respondents change; hence, the type of information obtained from those who are interviewed at the beginning may be markedly different from that obtained from those interviewed towards the end. Also, this freedom can introduce investigator bias into the study. Using an interview guide as a means of data collection requires much more skill on the part of the researcher than does using a structured interview.

Observation

Observation is another method used for data collection in qualitative research. The difference between the use of observation in quantitative and qualitative research lies in the degree of flexibility and freedom in what and how to observe, and in recording and analysing the data generated through it. In qualitative research you have almost no framework for observation, and the recording is done in descriptive and narrative form. Use of observation in quantitative studies follows a predetermined framework and the recording is either categorical or on a scale. You can have both types of observation, participant and non-participant, as a method of data collection in qualitative research. Observation as a method of data collection has been adequately covered earlier in this chapter.

ETHNOGRAPHY

Secondary sources

There are many sources that can provide data for your qualitative research study. These sources are covered later in this chapter. The only difference in their use in quantitative and qualitative research is the way the information is extracted, analysed and communicated.

Constructing a research instrument in qualitative research

Data in qualitative research is not collected through a set of predetermined questions but by raising issues around different areas of enquiry. Hence, as such, there are no predetermined set of questions that you ask of your respondents. However, many people develop a loose list of issues and discussion points that they want to discuss with respondents or to have ready in case what they want to discuss does not surface during the discussions. This loosely developed list of issues is called an interview guide. It is a research tool that is used only as a back-up in qualitative designs. In the author's opinion, particularly for a beginner, it is important to develop an interview guide to ensure desired coverage of the areas of enquiry and comparability of information across respondents. Note that in-depth interviewing is both a method of data collection and a study design in qualitative research, and the interview guide is a research tool that is used to collect data in this design.

Recently the author conducted a study using in-depth interviewing and focus group methodologies to construct a conceptual service delivery model for providing child protection services through family consultation, involvement and engagement. The project was designed to develop a model that can be used by the field workers when dealing with a family in matters relating to child protection. To start with, the author conducted a number of in-depth interviews with some staff members working at different levels and the client group to gather ideas about the issues and discussion points that they thought important to raise with the staff and clients. On the basis of these in-depth interviews, a list of likely topics/issues was prepared. This list, the interview guide, became the basis for collecting the required information from individuals and focus groups in order to construct the conceptual model. Nevertheless, the focus groups were encouraged to raise any issue relating to the service delivery. And in situations where nothing much came out of the discussions, the discussion was directed around the following topics, which formed the core of the interview guide for focus groups and in-depth interviews:

- What do you understand by the concept of family engagement and involvement when deciding about a child?
- What should be the extent and nature of the involvement?
- How can it be achieved?
- What do you think are the advantages of involving families in the decision making?
- What in your opinion are its disadvantages?
- What is your opinion about this concept?
- What can a field worker do to involve a family?
- How can the success or failure of this model be measured?
- How will this model affect current services to children?
- What additional training is needed for the staff to effectively work within the framework of the model?
- What indicators can be used to measure the effectiveness of the model?

Note that these topics only served as starting points for discussions, in the absence of issues raised by the group members. The group members were encouraged to discuss whatever they wanted to in relation to the perceived model. All one-to-one in-depth interviews and focus group discussions were recorded on audiotape and were analysed to identify major themes that emerged from these discussions.

Collecting data using secondary sources

So far we have discussed primary sources of data collection, where the required data is collected either by you or by someone else for the specific purpose you have in mind. There are occasions when your data has already been collected by someone else or already exists as a part of the routine record keeping by an organisation and what you need to do is to extract the required information for the purpose of your study. The following list gives some idea of possible secondary sources, grouped into categories:

- Government or quasi-government publications – There are many government and quasi-government organisations that collect data on a regular basis in a variety of areas and publish it for use by members of the public and interest groups. Some common examples are the census, vital statistics registration, labour force surveys, health reports, economic forecasts and demographic information.

- Earlier research – For some topics, a vast array of research studies that have already been done by others can provide you with the required information.
- Personal records – Some people write historical and personal records (e.g. diaries) that may provide the information you need.
- Mass media – Reports published in newspapers, in magazines, on the Internet, and so on, may be another good source of data.

All qualitative, quantitative and mixed methods research studies can use secondary sources as a method of data collection. In qualitative research you usually extract descriptive and narrative information (such as information from historical accounts of an event, descriptions of a situation, stories about beliefs and superstitions, or descriptions of a site). In quantitative studies the information is usually extracted in numerical or categorical form. In mixed methods approaches it depends upon the methods that are being used. In all situations where you are using secondary sources, you first need to decide what information you need, where it is available and how to extract it. It might be a good idea to develop a form to record the required information in the format that is best suited to your needs.

Problems with data from secondary sources

When using data from secondary sources you need to be careful as there may be problems with the availability, format and quality of data. The extent of these problems varies from source to source. While using such data some of the issues you should keep in mind are as follows:

- Validity and reliability – The validity of information may vary markedly from source to source. For example, information obtained from a census is likely to be more valid and reliable than that obtained from most personal diaries.
- Personal bias – Information from personal diaries, newspapers and magazines may have the problem of personal bias as these writers are likely to exhibit less rigour and objectivity than one would expect in research reports.
- Availability of data – It is common for beginning researchers to assume that the required data will be available, but you cannot and should not make this assumption. Therefore, it is important to make sure that the required data is available before you proceed further with your study.
- Format – Before deciding to use data from secondary sources it is equally important to ascertain that the data is available in the required format. For example, you might need to analyse age in the categories 23–33, 34–48, and so on, but, in your source, age may be categorised as 21–24, 25–29, and so on.

Summary

In this chapter you have learnt about the various methods of data collection. Information collected about a situation, phenomenon, issue or group of people can come from either primary sources or secondary sources.

Primary sources are those where you or others collect information from respondents for the specific purpose for which a study is undertaken. These include interviewing, observation and the use of questionnaires. All other sources, where the information required is already available, such as government publications, reports and previous research, are called secondary sources.

There is a considerable overlap in the methods of data collection between quantitative and qualitative research studies. The difference lies in the way the information is generated, recorded and analysed. In quantitative research the information, in most cases, is generated through a set of predetermined questions and either the responses are recorded in categorical format or the categories are developed out of the descriptive responses at the time of analysis through the process called content analysis. The information obtained then goes through data processing and is subjected to a number of statistical procedures. In qualitative research the required information is generated through a series of questions which are not predetermined and pre-worded. In addition, the recording of information is in descriptive format and the main mode of analysis is content analysis to identify the main themes. Structured interviews, use of questionnaires and structured observations are the most common methods of data collection in quantitative research, whereas in qualitative research unstructured interviews (oral histories, in-depth interviews and narratives) and participant observation are the main methods of data collection from primary sources.

The choice of a particular method of collecting data depends upon the purpose of collecting information, the type of information being collected, the resources available, your skills in the use of a particular method of data collection and the socioeconomic-demographic characteristics of your study population. Each method has its own advantages and disadvantages and each is appropriate for certain situations. The choice of a particular method for collecting data is important in itself for ensuring the quality of the information, but no method of data collection will guarantee 100 per cent accurate information. The quality of your information is dependent upon several methodological, situational and respondent-related factors and your ability as a researcher lies in either controlling or minimising the effect of these factors in the process of data collection.

The use of open-ended and closed questions is appropriate for different situations. Both have strengths and weaknesses and you should be aware of these so that you can use them appropriately.

The construction of a research instrument is the most important aspect of any research endeavour as it determines the nature and quality of the information you gather. This is the input of your study and the output, the relevance and accuracy of your conclusions, is entirely dependent upon it. A research instrument in quantitative research must be developed in light of the objectives of your study. The method suggested in this chapter ensures that questions in an instrument have a direct link to your objectives. The wording of questions can pose several problems and you should keep them in mind while formulating your questions.

In qualitative research you do not develop a research instrument as such, but it is advisable that you develop a conceptual framework of the likely areas you plan to cover, providing sufficient allowance for new ones to emerge when collecting data from your respondents.

FOR YOU TO THINK ABOUT

- Refamiliarise yourself with the keywords listed at the beginning of this chapter, and if you are uncertain about the meaning or application of any of them revisit them in the chapter before moving on.
- Identify two or three examples from your own academic field where it may be better to use a questionnaire rather than interviewing, and vice versa.
- Identify three situations where it would be better to use open-ended questions and three where closed questions might be more useful.
- There is a considerable overlap in the methods of data collection between quantitative and qualitative research. In spite of this they are different. List a few of the factors that differentiate them.

Now, as you have gone through the chapter, try answering the following questions:

- List the different methods of data collection in quantitative research.
- Describe the problems that can affect the quality of data when collecting through observation.
- Compare the advantages and disadvantages of using questionnaire versus interviewing for data collection.
- What are the different forms of questions and what are their respective advantages and disadvantages?
- What considerations would you keep in mind when constructing a questionnaire?
- Detail the various methods commonly used in qualitative research to collect information from respondents.
- Discuss the quantitative and qualitative methods of data collection that you can use in a mixed methods approach.

Want to learn more? Visit
http://www.uk.sagepub.com/kumar4e
or scan this QR code to gain access to a range of online resources to support your study including practice quizzes, videos, weblinks, flashcards, and journal articles.

10

COLLECTING DATA USING ATTITUDINAL SCALES

In this chapter you will learn about

- What attitudinal scales are and how to use them
- The functions of attitudinal scales in quantitative research
- Difficulties in developing an attitudinal scale and how to overcome them
- Different types of attitudinal scales and when to use them
- The relationship between attitudinal and measurement scales
- Methods for exploring attitudes in qualitative research

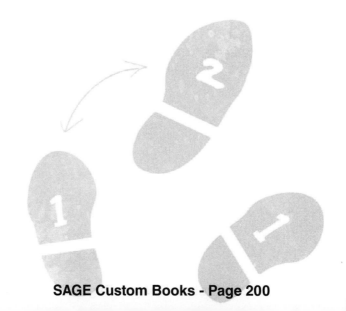

At the end of this chapter, you should have an understanding of

- Types of attitudinal scales in social research and how to construct them
- Strengths and weaknesses of each scale
- Attitudinal scales and their relationship with measurement scales
- Measuring attitudes through qualitative methods

Measurement of attitudes in quantitative and qualitative research

A common practice in social research is to explore the attitudes of people towards various conditions, issues, situations, policies, problems or anything that is of interest and/or concern to us in our daily lives. The importance of attitudinal scales lies in their ability to help us to find out how people feel towards these situations and issues. Knowledge about how people feel towards them plays an important role in formulating new policies and programmes to achieve improvement and betterment. For example: How do people feel towards recreational facilities in their community? What are the needs of the members of the community and how important are these needs to them? What is the attitude of people towards an urban development plan for their area? How do students feel about their lecturer's teaching? What are the attitudes of people towards a programme? How satisfied are they with the services provided by an institution? What are the problems encountered by tourists vising this town? What do consumers think of this product? These are some of the situations that are better explored by finding out attitudes towards them. The exploration of attitudes can be done in a descriptive form where you ask people to describe, discuss and explore with them their attitudes towards an issue. This description becomes the basis for ascertaining their attitudes or you can explore them through the use of the attitudinal scales.

There are a number of differences in the way attitudes are measured in quantitative and qualitative research. In quantitative research you are able to explore, measure, determine the intensity and combine attitudes to different aspects of an issue to arrive at a single indicator that is reflective of the overall attitude. In qualitative research, you can only explore the spread of attitudes and establish the types of attitudes prevalent. In quantitative research you can ascertain the types of attitudes people have in a community, how many people have a particular attitude and the intensity of those attitudes. A number of techniques have been developed to measure attitudes and their intensity in quantitative research, but such techniques are lacking in qualitative research. This is mainly because in qualitative research you do not make an attempt to measure or quantify. The concept of attitudinal scales, therefore, is more prevalent in quantitative than in qualitative research.

Attitudinal scales in quantitative research

In quantitative research there are three scales which have been developed to 'measure' attitudes. Each of these scales is based upon different assumptions and follows different procedures in its construction. As a beginner in research methods it is important for you to understand these procedures and the assumptions behind them so that you can make an appropriate and accurate interpretation of the findings. As you will see, it is not very easy to construct an attitudinal scale. Of the three scales, the Likert scale is the easiest to construct and therefore the most frequently used. The Thurstone scale is more difficult to construct than the Likert scale. The Guttman scale is much more complex than the Thurstone scale and therefore far less used in social research, hence, its relevance for beginners is marginal and it is not included in this book.

Functions of attitudinal scales

If you want to find out the attitude of respondents towards an issue, you can ask either a closed or an open-ended question. For example, suppose that you want to ascertain the attitude of students in a class towards their lecturer and that you have asked them to respond to the following question: 'What is your attitude towards your lecturer?' If your question is open-ended, it invites each respondent to describe the attitude that s/he holds towards the lecturer. If you have framed a closed question, with categories such as 'extremely positive', 'positive', 'uncertain', 'negative' and 'extremely negative', this guides the respondents to select a category that best describes their attitude. This type of questioning, whether framed descriptively or in a categorical form, elicits an overall attitude towards the lecturer. While ascertaining the overall attitude may be sufficient in some situations, in many others, where the purpose of attitudinal questioning is to develop strategies for improving a service or intervention, or to formulate policy, eliciting attitudes on various aspects of the issue under study is required.

But as you know, every issue, including that of the attitude of students towards their lecturers, has many aspects. For example, the attitude of the members of a community towards the provision of a particular service comprises their attitude towards the need for the service, its manner of delivery, its location, the physical facilities provided to users, the behaviour of the staff, the competence of the staff, the effectiveness and efficiency of the service, and so on. Other examples – such as the attitude of employees towards the management of their organisation, the attitude of employees towards occupational redeployment and redundancy, the attitude of nurses towards death and dying, the attitude of consumers towards a particular product, the attitude of students towards a lecturer, or the attitude of staff towards the strategic plan for their organisation – can be broken down in the same manner.

Respondents usually have different attitudes towards different aspects. Only when you ascertain the attitude of respondents to an issue by formulating a question for each aspect, using either open-ended or closed questions, do you find out their attitude towards each aspect. The main limitation of this method is that it is difficult to draw any conclusion about the overall attitude of a respondent from these responses. Take the earlier example, where you want to find out the attitude of students towards a lecturer. There are different aspects of teaching: the content of lectures; the organisation of material; the lecturer's ability to communicate material; the presentation and style; knowledge of the subject; responsiveness; punctuality; and so on. Students may rate the lecturer differently on different aspects. That is, the lecturer might be considered extremely competent and knowledgeable in his/her subject but may not be considered a good communicator by a majority of students. Further, students may differ markedly in their opinion regarding any one aspect of a lecturer's teaching. Some might consider the lecturer to be a good communicator and others might not. The main problem is: how do we find out the 'overall' attitude of the students towards the lecturer? In other words, how do we combine the responses to different aspects of any issue to come up with one indicator that is reflective of an overall attitude? Attitudinal scales play an important role in overcoming this problem.

Attitudinal scales serve two main functions: they measure the intensity of respondents' attitudes towards the various aspects of a situation or issue; and they provide techniques to combine the attitudes towards different aspects into one overall indicator. This reduces the risk of an expression of opinion by respondents being influenced by their opinion on only one or two aspects of that situation or issue.

Difficulties in developing an attitudinal scale

In the development of an attitudinal scale you are likely to face three problems:

1. Which aspects of a situation or issue should be included when seeking to measure an attitude towards an issue or problem? For instance, in the example cited above, what aspects of teaching should be included in a scale to find out the attitude of students towards their lecturer?
2. What procedure should be adopted for combining the different aspects to obtain an overall picture?
3. How can one ensure that a scale really is measuring what it is supposed to measure?

The first problem is extremely important as it largely determines the third problem: the extent to which the statements on different aspects are reflective of the main issue largely determines the validity of the scale. You can solve the third problem by ensuring that your statements on the various aspects have a logical link with the main issue under study – the greater the link, the higher the validity. The different types of attitudinal scale (Likert, Thurstone or Guttman) provide an answer to the second problem. They guide you as to the procedure for combining the attitudes towards various aspects of an issue, though the degree of difficulty in following the procedure for these scales varies from scale to scale.

Types of attitudinal scale

There are three major types of attitudinal scale:

1 the summated rating scale, also known as the Likert scale;
2 the equal-appearing interval scale or differential scale, also known as the Thurstone scale;
3 the cumulative scale, also known as the Guttman scale.

The summated rating or Likert scale

SURVEY MONKEY:
LIKERT SCALE

The summated rating scale, more commonly known as the Likert scale, is based upon the assumption that each statement/item on the scale has equal attitudinal value, importance or weight in terms of reflecting an attitude towards the issue in question. This assumption is also the main limitation of this scale, as statements on a scale seldom have equal attitudinal value. For instance, in the examples in Figures 10.1 and 10.2, 'knowledge of subject' is not as important in terms of the degree to which it reflects the attitude of the students towards the lecturer as 'has published a great deal' or 'some students like, some do not', but, on the Likert scale, each is treated as having the same attitudinal weight. A student may not bother much about whether a lecturer has published a great deal, but may be more concerned about 'knowledge of the subject',' communicates well' and 'knows how to teach'.

It is important to remember that the Likert scale does not measure attitude per se. It does help to place different respondents in relation to each other in terms of the intensity of their attitude towards an issue: it shows the strength of one respondent's view in relation to that of another and not the absolute attitude.

Considerations in constructing a Likert scale

In developing a Likert scale, there are a number of things to consider. Firstly, decide whether the attitude to be measured is to be classified into one-, two- or three-directional categories

The lecturer:	Strongly agree	Agree	Uncertain	Disagree	Strongly Disagree
1 Knows the subject well	☐	☐	☐	☐	☐
2 Is unenthusiastic about teaching	☐	☐	☐	☐	☐
3 Shows concern for students	☐	☐	☐	☐	☐
4 Makes unreasonable demands	☐	☐	☐	☐	☐
5 Has poor communication skills	☐	☐	☐	☐	☐
6 Knows how to teach	☐	☐	☐	☐	☐
7 Can explain difficult concepts in simple terms	☐	☐	☐	☐	☐
8 Is hard to approach	☐	☐	☐	☐	☐
9 Is liked by some students and not by others	☐	☐	☐	☐	☐
10 Is difficult to get along with	☐	☐	☐	☐	☐

Figure 10.1   An example of a categorical scale

204   **RESEARCH METHODOLOGY**

The lecturer:

		7	6	5	4	3	2	1
1	Knows the subject well	7	6	5	4	3	2	1
2	Is enthusiastic about teaching	7	6	5	4	3	2	1
3	Shows no concern for students	7	6	5	4	3	2	1
4	Demands too much	7	6	5	4	3	2	1
5	Communicates well	7	6	5	4	3	2	1
6	Knows how to teach	7	6	5	4	3	2	1
7	Can explain difficult concepts in simple terms	7	6	5	4	3	2	1
8	Is seldom available to the students	7	6	5	4	3	2	1
9	Is liked by some students and not by others	7	6	5	4	3	2	1
10	Has published a great deal	7	6	5	4	3	2	1

Figure 10.2 An example of a seven-point numerical scale

1:   The lecturer

(a) knows the subject *extremely well*
(b) knows the subject *well*
(c) has an *average* knowledge of the subject
(d) *does not know* the subject
(e) has an *extremely poor knowledge* of the subject

Figure 10.3 An example of a scale with statements reflecting varying degrees of an attitude

(i.e. whether you want to determine positive, negative and neutral positions in the study population) with respect to their attitude towards the issue under study. Next, consider whether you want to use categories or a numerical scale. This should depend upon whether you think that your study population can express itself better on a numerical scale or in categories. The decision about the number of points or the number of categories on a categorical scale depends upon how finely you want to measure the intensity of the attitude in question and on the capacity of the population to make fine distinctions. Figure 10.1 shows a five-point categorical scale that is three-directional and Figure 10.2 illustrates a seven-point numerical scale that is one-directional. Sometimes you can also develop statements reflecting opinion about an issue in varying degrees (Figure 10.3). In this instance the respondent is asked to select the statement which best describes his/her opinion.

Figure 10.4 shows the procedure used in constructing a Likert scale.

Calculating attitudinal scores

Suppose you have developed a questionnaire/interview schedule to measure the attitudes of a class of students towards their lecturer using a scale with five categories.

Procedure

Step 1 Assemble or construct statements that are reflective of the attitudes towards the main issue in question. Statements should be worded to reflect both positive and negative attitudes towards the issue; that is, they should be for, as well as against, the issue. (If your scale is one-directional, you need only positive statements.) Make sure that all the statements have a logical link with the main issue. You also need to decide whether you want respondents to answer in categories or on a numerical scale.

Step 2 Administer the statements to a small group of people to test them for clarity.

Step 3 Analyse the responses by assigning a weighting – a numerical value – to the responses. Numerical values are assigned differently to positive and negative statements. For a positive statement the response indicating the most favourable attitude is to be given the highest score. For example, on a five-category or five-point scale, 5 is assigned to the response that indicates the most favourable attitude and 1 to the response which indicates the least favourable attitude. By contrast, a person who agrees strongly with a negative statement indicates that s/he does not have a favourable attitude; hence, the scoring is reversed, i.e. 1 is assigned to the response where a respondent strongly agrees with a negative statement and 5 to the response where s/he strongly disagrees with it.

Step 4 Calculate each respondent's attitudinal score by adding the numerical values assigned in Step 3 to the responses s/he gave to each statement.

Step 5 Compare all respondents' scores for each item to identify non-discriminative items. A non-discriminative item is where respondents with high attitudinal score have responded in a similar manner to respondents with low attitudinal scale, that is, both groups have responded to the statement in the same manner. Non-discriminative statements do not help you to distinguish respondents with respect to attitude as almost everyone responds to them in the same way.

Step 6 Eliminate non-discriminative items.

Step 7 Construct a questionnaire/interview schedule comprising the selected statements/items.

Figure 10.4   The procedure for constructing a Likert scale

In Figure 10.5, statement 1 is a positive statement; hence, if a respondent ticks 'strongly agree', s/he is assumed to have a more positive attitude on this item than a person who ticks 'agree'. The person who ticks 'agree' has a more positive attitude than a person who ticks 'uncertain', and so on. Therefore, a person who ticks 'strongly agree' is given the highest score, 5, as there are five response categories. If there were four categories you would assign a score of 4. As a matter of fact, any score can be assigned as long as the intensity of the response pattern is reflected in the score and the highest score is assigned to the response with the highest positive intensity.

Statement 2 is a negative statement. In this case a person who ticks 'strongly disagree' has comparatively the most positive attitude on the aspect that is reflected by this item; hence, the highest score is assigned, 5. On the other hand, a respondent who ticks 'strongly agree' has the least positive attitude on the item and therefore is assigned the lowest score, 1. The same scoring system is followed for the other statements.

Note statement 9. There will always be some people who like a lecturer and some who do not; hence, this type of statement is neutral. There is no point in including such items in the scale; we have done so here purely for illustrative purposes.

The lecturer:	SA	A	U	D	SD
1 Knows the subject well (+)	5	4	3	2	1
2 Is unenthusiastic about teaching (−)	1	2	3	4	5
3 Shows concern for students (+)	5	4	3	2	1
4 Makes unreasonable demands (−)	1	2	3	4	5
5 Has poor communication skills (−)					
6 Knows how to teach (+)					
7 Can explain difficult concepts in simple terms (+)					
8 Is hard to approach (−)					
9 Is liked by some students and not by others (+/−)					
10 Is difficult to get along with (−)					

SA = strongly agree, A = agree, U = uncertain, D = disagree, SD = strongly disagree

Figure 10.5   Scoring positive and negative statements

The lecturer:	SA	A	U	D	SD
1 Knows the subject well (+)	@				#
2 Is unenthusiastic about teaching (−)		#			@
3 Shows concern for students (+)			@		#
4 Makes unreasonable demands (−)		#			@
5 Communicates poorly (−)		#			@
6 Knows how to teach (+)			@	#	
7 Can explain difficult concepts in simple terms (+)	@	#			
8 Is hard to approach (−)			@#		
9 Is liked by some students and not by others (+/−)				@#	
10 Is difficult to get along with (−)			#		@

SA = strongly agree, A = agree, U = uncertain, D = disagree, SD = strongly disagree

Figure 10.6   Calculating an attitudinal score

To illustrate how to calculate an individual's attitudinal score, let us take the example of two respondents who have ticked the different statements marked in our example by # and @ (see Figure 10.6). Let us work out their attitudinal scores:

Statement no.	1	2	3	4	5	6	7	8	9	10	
Respondent @ =	5 +	5 +	3 +	5 +	5 +	4 +	5 +	3 +	2 +	5	= 42
Respondent # =	1 +	2 +	1 +	2 +	2 +	2 +	4 +	3 +	2 +	3	= 22

The analysis shows that, overall, respondent @ has a 'more' positive attitude towards the lecturer than respondent #. You cannot say that the attitude of respondent @ is twice (42/22 = 1.91) as positive as that of respondent #. The attitudinal score only places respondents in a position relative to one another. Remember that the Likert scale does not measure the attitude per se, but helps you to rate a group of individuals in descending or ascending order with respect to their attitudes towards the issues in question.

The equal-appearing interval or Thurstone scale

THURSTONE SCALE

Unlike the Likert scale, the Thurstone scale calculates a weight or attitudinal value for each statement. The weight (equivalent to the median value) for each statement is calculated on the basis of ratings assigned to a statement by a group of judges. Each statement with which respondents express agreement (or to which they respond in the affirmative) is given an attitudinal score equivalent to the attitudinal value of the statement. The procedure for constructing the Thurstone scale is as given in Figure 10.7.

The main advantage of this scale is that, as the importance of each statement is determined by judges, it reflects the absolute rather than relative attitudes of respondents. The scale is thus able to indicate the intensity of people's attitudes and any change in this intensity should the study be replicated. On the other hand, the scale is difficult to construct, and a major criticism is that judges and respondents may assess the importance of a particular statement differently and, therefore, the respondents' attitudes might not be reflected.

Step 1   Assemble or construct statements reflective of attitudes towards the issue in question.

Step 2   Select a panel of judges who are experts in the field of the attitudes being explored.

Step 3   Send the statements to these judges with a request to rate each statement's importance in reflecting an attitude towards the issue being studied. Ask them to rate each statement on an 11-point scale.

Step 4   Calculate the median value of these judges' ratings for each item.

Step 5   If the judges' ratings of any item are scattered over the scale, this indicates that, even among the experts, there is no agreement as to the degree to which that statement reflects an attitude towards the issue in question. Discard such statements.

Step 6   From the remaining statements select items that best reflect attitudes towards various aspects of the issue.

Step 7   Construct a questionnaire/interview schedule comprising the selected items.

Figure 10.7   The procedure for constructing the Thurstone scale

The cumulative or Guttman scale

GUTTMAN SCALE

The Guttman scale is one of the most difficult scales to construct and therefore is rarely used. This scale does not have much relevance for beginners in research and so is not discussed in this book.

Attitudinal scales and measurement scales

Different attitudinal scales use different measurement scales. It is important to know which attitudinal scale belongs to which measurement scale as this will help you in the interpretation of respondents' scores. Table 10.1 shows attitudinal scales in relation to measurement scales.

Table 10.1 The relationship between attitudinal and measurement scales

Attitudinal scales	Measurement scales
Likert scale	Ordinal scale
Thurstone scale	Interval scale
Guttman scale	Ratio scale

Attitudes and qualitative research

As mentioned at the beginning of this chapter, in qualitative research you can only explore the spread of the attitudes. Whatever methods of data collection you use – in-depth interviewing, focus group, observation – you can explore the diversity in the attitudes but cannot find other aspects such as how many people have a particular attitude, the intensity of a particular attitude, or overall what the attitude of a person is. Qualitative methods are therefore best suited to explore the diversity of attitudes rather than their intensity.

Summary

One of the significant differences between quantitative and qualitative research is in the availability of methods and procedures to measure attitudes. In quantitative research there are a number of methods that can be used to measure attitudes, but qualitative research lacks methodology in this aspect primarily because its aim is to explain rather than to measure and quantify. Through qualitative research methodology you can find the diversity or spread of attitudes towards an issue but not their intensity and a combined overall indicator.

Attitudinal scales are used in quantitative research to measure attitudes towards an issue. Their strength lies in their ability to combine attitudes towards different aspects of an issue and to provide an indicator that is reflective of an overall attitude. However, there are problems in developing an attitudinal scale. You must decide which aspects should be included when measuring attitudes towards an issue, how the responses given by a respondent should be combined to ascertain the overall attitude, and how you can ensure that the scale developed really measures attitude towards the issue in question.

There are three types of scale that measure attitude: the Likert, Thurstone and Guttman scales. The Likert scale is most commonly used because it is easy to construct. The main assumption of the scale is that each statement is equally important. The importance of each item for the Thurstone scale is determined by a panel of judges.

FOR YOU TO THINK ABOUT

- Refamiliarise yourself with the keywords listed at the beginning of this chapter, and if you are uncertain about the meaning or application of any of them revisit them in the chapter before moving on.
- Identify examples of how the Likert and Thurstone scales can be applied to research in your own academic field.
- Consider how you would go about developing a five-point Likert scale to measure the self-esteem of a group of university students, and the difficulties you might face in trying to do so.

Now, as you have gone through the chapter, try answering the following questions:

- What are the main advantages of attitudinal sales in social research?
- Name the different types of attitudinal scales and the assumptions made in their construction.
- Identify different situations which are appropriate for measuring attitudes by Likert and Thurstone scales in the social sciences.
- What aspects of self-esteem would you include in a five-point Likert scale to measure the self-esteem of group of unemployed youth?

Want to learn more? Visit
http://www.uk.sagepub.com/kumar4e
or scan this QR code to gain access to a range of online resources to support your study including practice quizzes, videos, weblinks, flashcards, and journal articles.

11

ESTABLISHING THE VALIDITY AND RELIABILITY OF A RESEARCH INSTRUMENT

In this chapter you will learn about

- The concept of validity
- Different types of validity in quantitative research
- The concept of reliability
- Factors affecting the reliability of a research instrument
- Methods of determining the reliability of an instrument in quantitative research
- Validity and reliability in qualitative research

Keywords

concurrent validity, confirmability, construct validity, content

validity, credibility, dependability, external consistency,

face validity, internal consistency, reliability, transferability, validity.

At the end of this chapter, you should have an understanding of

- Validity and reliability as applied in social research
- Validity and reliability in quantitative and qualitative research
- How to ascertain validity and reliability in social research
- Ensuring validity and reliability in a research study

In the previous two chapters we discussed various methods of data collection in quantitative, qualitative and mixed methods research. The questions asked of your respondents are the basis of your findings and conclusions. These questions constitute the 'input' for your conclusions (the 'output'). This input passes through a series of steps – the selection of a sample, the collection of information, the processing of data, the application of statistical procedures and the writing of a report – and the manner in which all of these are done can affect the accuracy and quality of your conclusions. Hence, it is important for you to attempt to establish the quality of your results. As a researcher you can also be asked by others to establish the appropriateness, quality and accuracy of the procedures you adopted for finding answers to your research questions. Broadly, this concept of appropriateness and accuracy as applied to a research process is called validity. As inaccuracies can be introduced into a study at any stage, the concept of validity can be applied to the research process as a whole or to any of its steps: study design, sampling strategy, conclusions drawn, the statistical procedures applied or the measurement procedures used. Broadly, there are two perspectives on validity:

1. Is the research investigation providing answers to the research questions for which it was undertaken?
2. If so, is it providing these answers using appropriate methods and procedures?

In this chapter we will discuss the concept of validity as applied to measurement procedures or the research tools used to collect the required information from your respondents.

There are prominent differences between quantitative and qualitative research in relation to the concepts of validity and reliability. Because of the defined and established structures and methods of data collection in quantitative research, the concepts of validity and reliability and the methods to determine them are well developed. However, in qualitative research it would be appropriate to say that these concepts cannot be rigorously applied in the same way as they are in quantitative research because of the flexibility, freedom and spontaneity given to a researcher in the methods and procedures of data collection. It becomes difficult to establish standardisation in the method(s) of data collection in qualitative research and, hence, their validity and reliability. Despite these difficulties, methods have been proposed to establish validity and reliability in qualitative research which are detailed in this chapter.

The concept of validity

To examine the concept of validity, let us take a very simple example. Suppose you have designed a study to ascertain the health needs of a community. In doing so, you have developed an interview schedule. Further suppose that most of the questions in the interview schedule relate to the attitude of the study population towards the health services being provided to them. Note that your aim was to *find out about health needs* but the interview schedule is finding out what *attitudes respondents have to the health services*; thus, the instrument is not measuring what it was designed to measure. The author has come across many similar examples among students and less skilled researchers.

In terms of measurement procedures, therefore, validity is the ability of an instrument to measure what it is designed to measure: 'Validity is defined as the degree to which the researcher has measured what he has set out to measure' (Smith 1991: 106). According to Kerlinger (1973: 457), 'The commonest definition of validity is epitomised by the question: Are we measuring what we think we are measuring?'. Babbie (1989: 133) writes, 'validity refers to the extent to which an empirical measure adequately reflects the real meaning of the concept under consideration'. These definitions raise two key questions:

- Who decides whether an instrument is measuring what it is supposed to measure?
- How can it be established that an instrument is measuring what it is supposed to measure?

Obviously the answer to the first question is the person who designed the study, the readership of the report and experts in the field. The second question is extremely important. On what basis do you (as a researcher), a reader or an expert make this judgement? In the social sciences there appear to be two approaches to establishing the validity of a research instrument. These approaches are based upon either logic that underpins the construction of the research tool or statistical evidence that is gathered using information generated through the use of the instrument. Establishing validity through logic implies justification of each question in relation to the objectives of the study, whereas the statistical procedures provide hard evidence by way of calculating the correlations between the questions and the outcome variables.

Establishing a logical link between the questions and the objectives is both simple and difficult. It is simple in the sense that you may find it easy to see a link for yourself, and difficult because your justification may lack the backing of experts and the statistical evidence to convince others. Establishing a logical link between questions and objectives is easier when the questions relate to tangible matters. For example, if you want to find out about age, income, height or weight, it is relatively easy to establish the validity of the questions, but to establish whether a set of questions is measuring, say, the effectiveness of a programme, the attitudes of a group of people towards an issue, or the extent of satisfaction

THE VALIDITY AND RELIABILITY OF A RESEARCH INSTRUMENT   213

of a group of consumers with the service provided by an organisation is more difficult. When a less tangible concept is involved, such as effectiveness, attitude or satisfaction, you need to ask several questions in order to cover different aspects of the concept and demonstrate that the questions asked are actually measuring it. Validity in such situations becomes more difficult to establish, especially in qualitative research where you are mostly exploring feelings, experiences, perceptions, motivations or stories.

It is important to remember that the concept of validity is pertinent only to a particular instrument and it is an ideal state that you as a researcher aim to achieve.

Types of validity in quantitative research

RELIABILITY AND
VALIDITY

There are three types of validity in quantitative research:

1. face and content validity;
2. concurrent and predictive validity;
3. construct validity.

Face and content validity

The judgement that an instrument is measuring what it is supposed to is primarily based upon the logical link between the questions and the objectives of the study. Hence, one of the main advantages of face and content validity is that it is easy to apply. Each question or item on the research instrument must have a logical link with an objective. Establishment of this link is an indication of the validity of the instrument. Greater the link, higher the face validity of the instrument. It is equally important that the items and questions cover all the aspects of the issue or attitude being measured. Establishing that the different items of a research instrument cover various aspects of the issue is an indication of the content validity of the instrument. Greater the coverage, higher the validity. In addition, the coverage of the issue or attitude should be balanced; that is, each aspect should have similar and adequate representation in the questions or items. Content validity is also judged on the basis of the extent to which statements or questions represent the issue they are supposed to measure, as judged by you as a researcher, your readership and experts in the field. Although it is easy to present logical arguments to establish validity, there are certain problems:

- The judgement is based upon subjective logic; hence, no definite conclusions can be drawn. Different people may have different opinions about the face and content validity of an instrument.
- The extent to which questions reflect the objectives of a study may differ. If the researcher substitutes one question for another, the magnitude of the link may be altered. Hence, the validity or its extent may vary with the questions selected for an instrument.

Concurrent and predictive validity

'In situations where a scale is developed as an indicator of some observable criterion, the scale's validity can be investigated by seeing how good an indicator it is' (Moser & Kalton 1989: 356) by comparing the findings with the observable criterion. The greater the comparability, the greater the validity. Suppose you develop an instrument to determine the suitability of applicants for a profession. The instrument's validity might be determined by comparing it with another assessment, for example by a psychologist, or with a future observation of how well these applicants have done in the job. If both assessments are similar, the instrument used to make the assessment at the time of selection is assumed to have higher validity. These types of comparisons establish two types of validity: predictive validity and concurrent validity. Predictive validity is judged by the degree to which an instrument can forecast an outcome. Concurrent validity is judged by how well an instrument compares with a second assessment concurrently done: 'It is usually possible to express predictive validity in terms of the correlation coefficient between the predicted status and the criterion. Such a coefficient is called a validity coefficient' (Burns 1997: 220).

Construct validity

Construct validity is an indication of the quality of a research instrument to measure what it is supposed to. It is based upon statistical procedures. It is determined by ascertaining the contribution of each construct to the total variance observed in a phenomenon.

Suppose you are interested in carrying out a study to find the degree of job satisfaction among the employees of an organisation. You consider status, the nature of the job and remuneration as the three most important factors indicative of job satisfaction, and construct questions to ascertain the degree to which people consider each factor important for job satisfaction. After the pre-test or data analysis you use statistical procedures to establish the contribution of each construct (status, the nature of the job and remuneration) to the total variance (job satisfaction). The contribution of these factors to the overall job satisfaction (total variance) is an indication of the degree of validity of the instrument. The greater the variance attributable to the constructs, the higher the validity of the instrument.

One of the main disadvantages of construct validity is that you need to know about the required statistical procedures.

The concept of reliability

We use the word 'reliable' very often in our lives. When we say that a person is reliable, what do we mean? We mean that s/he is dependable, consistent, predictable, stable and honest.

The concept of reliability in relation to a research instrument has a similar meaning: if a research tool is consistent and stable, hence predictable and accurate, it is said to be reliable. The greater the degree of consistency and stability in an instrument, the greater its reliability. Therefore, 'a scale or test is reliable to the extent that repeat measurements made by it under constant conditions will give the same result' (Moser & Kalton 1989: 353).

The concept of reliability can, therefore, be looked at from two sides:

1. How reliable is an instrument?
2. How unreliable is it?

The first question focuses on the ability of an instrument to produce consistent measurements. When you collect the same set of information more than once using the same instrument and get the same or similar results under the same or similar conditions, an instrument is considered to be reliable. The second question focuses on the degree of inconsistency in the measurements made by an instrument – that is, the extent of difference in the measurements when you collect the same set of information more than once, using the same instrument under the same or similar conditions. Hence, the degree of inconsistency in the different measurements is an indication of the extent of its inaccuracy. This 'error' is a reflection of an instrument's unreliability. Therefore, reliability is the degree of accuracy or precision in the measurements made by a research instrument. The lower the degree of 'error' in an instrument, the higher the reliability.

Let us take an example. Suppose you develop a questionnaire to ascertain the prevalence of domestic violence in a community. You administer this questionnaire and find that domestic violence is prevalent in, say, 5 per cent of households. If you follow this, without any time lag, with another survey using the same questionnaire on the same population under the same conditions, and discover that the prevalence of domestic violence is, say, 15 per cent, the questionnaire has not given a comparable result, which may mean it is unreliable. The less the difference between the two sets of results, the higher the reliability of the instrument.

Factors affecting the reliability of a research instrument

In the social sciences it is impossible to have a research tool which is 100 per cent accurate, not only because a research instrument cannot be so, but also because it is impossible to control the factors affecting reliability. Some of these factors are as follows:

- The wording of questions – A slight ambiguity in the wording of questions or statements can affect the reliability of a research instrument as respondents may interpret the questions differently at different times, resulting in different responses.
- The physical setting – In the case of an instrument being used in an interview, any change in the physical setting at the time of the repeat interview may affect the responses given during the initial interview by a respondent, which may affect reliability.
- The respondent's mood – A change in a respondent's mood when responding to questions or writing answers in a questionnaire can change and may affect the reliability of that instrument.
- The interviewer's mood – As the mood of a respondent could change from one interview to another so could the mood, motivation and interaction of the interviewer, which could affect the responses given by respondents, thereby affecting the reliability of the research instrument.
- The nature of the interaction – In an interview situation, the interaction between the interviewer and the interviewee can affect responses significantly. During the repeat interview the responses given may be different due to a change in interaction, which could affect reliability.
- The regression effect of an instrument – When a research instrument is used to measure attitudes towards an issue, some respondents, after having expressed their opinion, may feel that, as compared to their normal attitude, they have been either too negative or too positive towards the issue. The second time they may express their opinion differently, thereby affecting reliability.

Methods of determining the reliability of an instrument in quantitative research

There are a number of ways of determining the reliability of an instrument, and these can be classified as either external or internal consistency procedures.

External consistency procedures

External consistency procedures compare findings from two independent processes of data collection with each other as a means of verifying the reliability of the measure. The two methods are test/retest and parallel forms of the same test.

Test/retest is a commonly used method for establishing the reliability of a research tool. An instrument is administered once (test), and then again (retest), under the same or similar conditions. The ratio or difference between the test and retest scores (these may be findings such as the prevalence of domestic violence or incidence of an illness) is an indication of the reliability of the instrument – the greater the ratio or the smaller the difference, the higher the reliability of the instrument. A test/retest ratio of 1 or a test/retest difference of 0 shows 100 per cent reliability (no difference between test and retest) and any deviation from this indicates less reliability – the smaller the ratio or the larger the difference, the less the reliability of the instrument.

The main advantage of the test/retest procedure is that it permits the instrument to be compared with itself, thus avoiding the sort of problems that could arise with the use of another instrument.

The main disadvantage of the procedure is that a respondent may recall the responses that s/he gave in the first round, which in turn may affect the reliability of the instrument. Where an instrument is reactive in nature (when an instrument educates the respondent with respect to what the researcher is trying to find out) this method will not provide an accurate assessment of its reliability. One of the ways of overcoming this problem is to increase the time span between the two tests, but this may affect reliability for other reasons, such as the maturation of respondents and the impossibility of achieving conditions similar to those under which the questionnaire or interview schedule was first administered.

In the *parallel forms of the same test* procedure you construct two instruments that are intended to measure the same phenomenon. The two instruments are then administered either to the same population or two similar populations. The results obtained from one test are compared with those obtained from the other. If they are similar, it is assumed that the instrument is reliable.

The main advantage of this procedure is that it does not suffer from the problem of recall found in the test/retest procedure. Also, a time lapse between the two tests is not required. A disadvantage is that you need to construct two instruments instead of one. Moreover, it is extremely difficult to construct two instruments that are comparable in their measurement of a phenomenon. It is equally difficult to achieve comparability in the two population groups and in the two conditions under which the tests are administered.

THE VALIDITY AND RELIABILITY OF A RESEARCH INSTRUMENT   217

Internal consistency procedures

The idea behind internal consistency procedures is that items or questions measuring the same phenomenon, if they are reliable indicators, should produce similar results irrespective of their number, that is, how many questions in an instrument. Even if you randomly select a few items or questions from the total pool to test the reliability of an instrument, each segment of questions thus constructed should reflect reliability more or less to the same extent. It is based upon the logic that if each item or question is an indicator of some aspect of a phenomenon, each segment constructed will still reflect different aspects of the phenomenon even though it is based upon fewer items/questions. Hence, even if we reduce the number of items or questions, as long as they reflect some aspect of a phenomenon, a lesser number of items can provide an indication of the reliability of an instrument. The internal consistency procedure is based upon this logic.

The *split-half technique* is commonly used for measuring the reliability of an instrument in this way. It is designed to correlate half of the items with the other half and is appropriate for instruments that are designed to measure attitudes towards an issue or phenomenon. The questions or statements are divided in half in such a way that any two questions or statements intended to measure the same aspect fall into different halves. The scores obtained by administering the two halves are correlated. Reliability is calculated by using the product moment correlation (a statistical procedure) between scores obtained from the two halves. Because the product moment correlation is calculated on the basis of only half the instrument, it needs to be corrected to assess reliability for the whole. This is known as *stepped-up reliability*. The stepped-up reliability for the whole instrument is calculated by a statistical procedure known as the Spearman–Brown formula.

Validity and reliability in qualitative research

QUALITY OF
QUALITATIVE
RESEARCH

One of the areas of difference between quantitative and qualitative research is in the use of and importance given to the concepts of validity and reliability. The debate centres on whether or not, given the framework of qualitative research, these concepts can or even should be applied in qualitative research. As you know, validity in the broader sense refers to the ability of a research instrument to demonstrate that it is finding out what you designed it to and reliability refers to consistency in its findings when used repeatedly. In qualitative research, as answers to research questions are explored through multiple methods and procedures which are both flexible and evolving, to ensure standardisation of research tools as well as processes becomes difficult. As a newcomer to research you may wonder how these concepts can be applied in qualitative research when it does not use standardised and structured methods and procedures which are the bases of testing validity and reliability as defined in quantitative research. You may ask how you can ascertain the ability of an instrument to measure what it is expected to and how consistent it is when the data collection questions are neither fixed nor structured?

However, there are some attempts to define and establish validity and reliability in qualitative research. In a chapter entitled 'Competing paradigms in qualitative research' (pp. 105–117) in the *Handbook of Qualitative Research*, edited by Denzin and Lincoln (1994), Guba and Lincoln have suggested a framework of four criteria as a part of the constructivism paradigm paralleling validity and reliability in quantitative research. According to them, the goodness or quality of an inquiry in this paradigm can be judged by its *trustworthiness* and *authenticity*. According to Guba and Lincoln, trustworthiness in a qualitative study is determined by four indicators closely related to validity and reliability: credibility (paralleling internal validity), transferability (paralleling external validity), dependability (paralleling reliability) and confirmability (paralleling objectivity).

Trochim and Donnelly (2007) compare the four criteria proposed by Guba and Lincoln with validity and reliability as defined in quantitative research:

Table 11.1 Criteria for judging research

Traditional criteria for judging quantitative research	Alternative criteria for judging qualitative research
Internal Validity	Credibility
External Validity	Transferability
Reliability	Dependability
Objectivity	Confirmability

(Trochim and Donnelly 2007: 149)

- Credibility – According to Trochim and Donnelly (2007: 149), 'credibility involves establishing that the results of qualitative research are credible or believable from the perspective of the participant in the research'. As qualitative research studies explore people's perceptions, experiences, feelings and beliefs, it is believed that the respondents are the best judge of whether or not the research findings have been able to reflect their opinions and feelings accurately. Hence, credibility, which is synonymous with validity in quantitative research, is judged by the extent of respondent concordance when you take your findings to those who participated in your research for confirmation, congruence, validation and approval. The higher the agreement of the respondents with the findings, the higher the validity of the study.
- Transferability – This 'refers to the degree to which the results of qualitative research can be generalised or transferred to other contexts or settings' (Trochim & Donnelly 2007: 149). Though it is very difficult to establish transferability primarily because of the approach you adopt in qualitative research, to some extent this can be achieved if you extensively and thoroughly describe the process you adopted for others to follow and replicate.
- Dependability – In the framework suggested by Guba and Lincoln this is very similar to the concept of reliability in quantitative research: 'It is concerned with whether we would obtain the same results if we could observe the same thing twice' (Trochim & Donnelly 2007: 149). Again, as qualitative research advocates flexibility and freedom, it may be difficult to establish unless you keep an extensive and detailed record of the process for others to replicate to ascertain the level of dependability.
- Confirmability – This 'refers to the degree to which the results could be confirmed or corroborated by others' (Trochim & Donnelly 2007: 149). Confirmability is also similar to reliability in quantitative research. It is only possible if researchers follow the process in an identical manner for the results to be compared.

To the author's mind, it is to some extent possible to establish the 'validity' and 'reliability' of findings in qualitative research in the form of the model suggested by Guba and Lincoln, but its success is mostly dependent upon the identical replication of the process and methods for data collection, which may not be easy to achieve in qualitative research.

THE VALIDITY AND RELIABILITY OF A RESEARCH INSTRUMENT   219

Summary

One of the differences in quantitative and qualitative research is in the use of and importance attached to the concepts of validity and reliability. These concepts, their use and methods of determination are more accepted and developed in quantitative than qualitative research. The concept of validity refers to a situation where the findings of your study are in accordance with what you designed it to find out. The notion of validity can be applied to any aspect of the research process. With respect to measurement procedures, it relates to whether a research instrument is measuring what it set out to measure. In quantitative research, there are two approaches used to establish the validity of an instrument: the establishment of a logical link between the objectives of a study and the questions used in an instrument, and the use of statistical analysis to demonstrate these links. There are three types of validity in quantitative research: face and content, concurrent and predictive, and construct validity. However, the use of the concept of validity in qualitative research is debatable and controversial. In qualitative research 'credibility' as described by Guba and Lincoln (1994) seems to be the only indicator of internal validity and is judged by the degree of respondent concordance with the findings. The methods used to establish 'validity' are different in quantitative and qualitative research.

The reliability of an instrument refers to its ability to produce consistent measurements each time. When we administer an instrument under the same or similar conditions to the same or a similar population and obtain similar results, we say that the instrument is 'reliable' – the more similar the results, the greater the reliability. You can look at reliability from two sides: reliability (the extent of accuracy) and unreliability (the extent of inaccuracy). Ambiguity in the wording of questions, a change in the physical setting for data collection, a respondent's mood when providing information, the nature of the interaction between interviewer and interviewee, and the regressive effect of an instrument are factors that can affect the reliability of a research instrument. In qualitative research 'reliability' is measured by 'dependability' and 'confirmability' as suggested by Guba and Lincoln (1994).

There are external and internal consistency procedures for determining reliability in quantitative research. Test/retest and parallel forms of the same test are the two procedures that determine the external reliability of a research instrument, whereas the split-half technique is classified under internal consistency procedures. There seem to be no set procedures for determining the various indicators of validity and reliability in qualitative research.

FOR YOU TO THINK ABOUT

- Refamiliarise yourself with the keywords listed at the beginning of this chapter, and if you are uncertain about the meaning or application of any of them revisit them in the chapter before moving on.
- Explore how the concepts of reliability and validity are applicable to research in your academic field or profession.

- Consider what strategies or procedures you could put in place to limit the affect on reliability of the following factors:

    □ wording of questions;
    □ physical setting;
    □ respondent's mood;
    □ interviewer's mood;
    □ nature of interaction;
    □ regression effect of an instrument.

Now, as you have gone through the chapter, try answering the following questions:

- What do you see as the relevance of validity and reliability in research?
- What are the different types of validity? Explain the logic behind each of them.
- Explain the concept of reliability and factors affecting it.
- Critically examine the application of the concepts of validity and reliability in qualitative studies.
- Compare criteria used in quantitative and qualitative research for judging validity and reliability.

Want to learn more? Visit
http://www.uk.sagepub.com/kumar4e
or scan this QR code to gain access to a range of online resources to support your study including practice quizzes, videos, weblinks, flashcards, and journal articles.

Exercise III: Developing a research instrument

TEMPLATE OF
EXERCISE III

> Congratulations once again! You are about to take the most important step of your research journey. Everything that follows after this depends upon how well you take this step, so you need to be extra careful about it. You need to be very wary in developing your research instrument to ensure its relevance and quality as the quality of your research outcome is entirely dependent on it.

The construction of a research instrument is the first practical step in operationalising your study. It is an important aspect of your research as it constitutes the input; the quality of your output (the findings and conclusions) is entirely dependent upon the quality and appropriateness of this input. Items in a research instrument are questions asked of respondents. Responses to these questions become the raw data that is processed to find answers to your research questions. The famous saying about computers, 'garbage in, garbage out', also equally applies to the research instrument. To a large extent, the validity of the findings depends upon the quality of the raw data which, in turn, depends upon the research instrument you have used or developed. If the latter is valid and reliable, the findings should also be valid and reliable.

The quality of a research instrument largely depends upon your experience in research. It is important for a beginner to follow the suggested steps outlined in Chapter 9.

For quantitative studies

Quantitative research is structured and predetermined in terms of what you want to find out about and how. As a part of this operational step, you need to decide what questions to ask of your respondents, the wording you are going to use and the order in which the questions will be asked. This exercise is designed to help to develop skills in constructing an instrument.

One of the ways to formulate the questions that are going to constitute your research instrument is by examining each subobjective, research question and hypothesis you have developed for your study, specifying for each the information you require, identifying the variables that are needed, and then formulating questions to be asked of your respondents to get information about those variables.

The wording of your questions should be simple and unambiguous. Do not ask leading questions or questions based upon presumptions. Avoid double-barrelled questions.

The pre-test of a research instrument is an integral part of instrument construction. As a rule, the pre-test should not be carried out on your sample but on a similar population.

Step I   On a separate piece of paper, draw a table as shown below, then list all your subobjectives, research questions and hypotheses in the first column and work through the other columns listing the required information.

222   **RESEARCH METHODOLOGY**

Specific objectives/ research questions/ hypotheses	Specifically, what information do you require?	Identify the required variables	Formulate questions (on a separate piece of paper)

Step II   Formulate the questions, preferably on a separate piece of paper, giving particular attention to their wording and order. In your own mind you must examine the relevance and justification of each question in relation to the objectives of your study. If you cannot relate the relevance and justification of a question to the objectives of your study, it should be discarded.

Step III   If you are developing a questionnaire, incorporate interactive statements at appropriate places (see Chapter 9).

Step IV   After developing the first draft of your research instrument, answer the questions yourself; that is, interview yourself or complete the questionnaire. You need to imagine that you are a member of the study population who will be asked these questions or requested to complete the questionnaire. If you find it difficult to answer a question, re-examine it.

Step V   Once you are satisfied with the research instrument, pre-test it with a few respondents from a population similar to the one you are going to study. The purpose of the pre-test/field test is not to obtain information but to uncover problems with the instrument. If the instrument is an interview schedule, interview the pre-test respondents to find out if they understood the questions. If a question is not understood, find out what the respondent did not understand. If the same problem is identified by a number of respondents, change the wording. If your instrument is a questionnaire, ask the pre-test respondents to go through the questions with the aim of identifying any questions that are difficult to understand. Discuss the problems that they had in understanding or interpreting a question. In light of these discussions, if necessary, change the wording of questions with which pre-test respondents have difficulties.

Step VI   Having pre-tested and, if necessary, amended the instrument, take a piece of paper and draw a table with two columns. In the first column write each subobjective, research question and hypothesis separately, and in the other, write the question number(s) that provide information for these objectives, research questions or hypotheses. In other words, make each question match the objective for which it provides information. If a question cannot be linked to a specific objective, research question or hypothesis, examine why it was included.

StepVII   Prepare the final draft of your research instrument. If you plan to use a computer for data analysis, you may provide space on the research instrument for coding the data.

For qualitative studies

If you are doing a qualitative study, you do not need to develop a list of specific questions that you want to discuss with your potential respondents. However, it is important that you construct a framework of the issues that you think you should cover to achieve the objectives of your study. This interview guide or conceptual framework of questions will help you to continue with your interviews if nothing much is forthcoming from your respondents. Your aim is to let a respondent bring out the issues, but this framework is ready in case that does not happen. See Chapter 9 on developing a conceptual framework.

As part of Exercise I you wrote a list of points to discuss with your respondents. Go back to that exercise and check that list, revising it necessary.

_____

_____

_____

_____

_____

_____

_____

_____

_____

_____

_____

STEP IV
SELECTING A SAMPLE

This operational step includes one chapter:

- Chapter 12: Selecting a Sample

12

SELECTING A SAMPLE

In this chapter you will learn about

- The differences between sampling in qualitative and quantitative research
- Definitions of sampling terminology
- The theoretical basis for sampling
- Factors affecting the inferences drawn from a sample
- Different types of sampling:

  - ☐ Random/probability sampling designs
  - ☐ Non-random/non-probability sampling designs
  - ☐ The 'mixed' sampling design

- The calculation of sample size
- The concept of saturation point

Keywords

accidental sampling, cluster sampling, data saturation point, disproportionate sampling, equal and independent, estimate, information-rich, judgemental sampling, multi-stage cluster

sampling, non-random sample, population mean, population parameters, quota sampling, random numbers, random sample, sample size, sample statistics, sampling, sampling design, sampling element,

sampling error, sampling frame, sampling population, sampling strategy, sampling unit, saturation point, snowball sampling, stratified sampling, study population, systematic sampling.

At the end of this chapter, you should have an understanding of

- The different sampling designs in quantitative and qualitative studies and their respective strengths and weaknesses
- Sampling designs in qualitative and quantitative research and how to use them in practice
- Principles that guide the sampling theory in quantitative studies.
- What it involves to work out sample size for a study in quantitative research
- The concept of saturation point in data collection in qualitative studies
- What determines the sample size in qualitative research

The differences between sampling in quantitative and qualitative research

SAMPLING: QUAL AND QUANT

The selection of a sample in quantitative and qualitative research is guided by two opposing philosophies. In quantitative research you attempt to select a sample in such a way that it is unbiased and represents the population from which it is selected. In qualitative research, a number of considerations may influence the selection of a sample, such as: the ease in accessing the potential respondents; your judgement that the person has extensive knowledge about an episode, event or situation of interest; how typical the case is of a category of individuals; or simply that it is totally different from the others. You make every effort to select either a case that is similar to the rest of the group or one which is totally different. Such considerations in the selection of a sample are not acceptable in quantitative research.

The purpose of sampling in quantitative research is to draw inferences, with respect to the focus of your enquiry, about the group from which you have selected the sample, whereas in qualitative research it is designed to gain in-depth knowledge either about a situation, event or episode or about different aspects of an individual on the assumption that the individual is typical of the group and hence will provide insight into the group.

Similarly, the determination of sample size in quantitative and qualitative research is based upon the two different philosophies. In quantitative research you are guided by a predetermined sample size that is based upon a number of other considerations in addition to the resources available. However, in qualitative research you do not have a predetermined sample size but during the data collection phase you wait to reach a point of data saturation. When you are not getting new information or it is negligible, it is assumed you have reached a data saturation point and you stop collecting additional information from other respondents.

Considerable importance is placed on the sample size in quantitative research, depending upon the type of study and the possible use of the findings. Studies which are designed to formulate policies, to test associations or relationships, or to establish impact assessments place a considerable emphasis on large sample size. This is based upon the principle that a larger sample size will ensure the inclusion of people with diverse backgrounds, thus making the sample representative of the study population. The sample size in qualitative research does not play any significant role as the purpose is to study only one or a few cases in order to identify the spread of diversity and not its magnitude. In such situations the data saturation stage during data collection determines the sample size.

In quantitative research, randomisation is used to ensure that a sample is selected in such a way that it represents the study population and to avoid bias. In qualitative research no such attempt is made in selecting a sample. You purposely select 'information-rich' respondents who will provide you with the information you need. In quantitative research, this is considered a biased sample.

Most of the sampling strategies, including some non-probability ones, described in this chapter can be used when undertaking a quantitative study provided it meets the requirements. However, when conducting a qualitative study only the non-probability sampling designs can be used.

Sampling in quantitative research
The concept of sampling

Let us take a very simple example to explain the concept of sampling. Suppose you are interested in the mean age of the students in your class. There are two ways of finding this out. The first method is to contact all students in the class, find out their ages, add them up and then divide this by the number of students (the procedure for calculating sample mean). The second method is to select a few students from the class, ask them their ages, add them up and then divide by the number of students you have asked. From this you make an *estimate* of the average age of the class. Similarly, suppose you want to find out the average income of families living in a city. Imagine the amount of effort and resources required to go to every family in the city to find out their income! You could instead select a few families as the basis of your enquiry and then, from what you have found out from the few families, make an estimate of the mean income of families in the city. A similar procedure is used in opinion polls. These are also based upon a very small group of people who are questioned about (say) their voting preferences and, on the basis of these results, a *prediction* is made about the probable outcome of an election.

Sampling, therefore, is the process of selecting a few (a sample) from a bigger group (the sampling population) as the basis for estimating or predicting the prevalence of an unknown piece of information, situation or outcome regarding the bigger group. A sample is a subgroup of the population that you are interested in. The focus of your study is to *find* answers to your research questions as they relate to the total study population and not the sample. However, through the process of sampling you attempt to *estimate* what is likely to be the situation in the total study population. (See Figure 12.1.)

This process of selecting a sample from the total population has advantages and disadvantages. The advantages are that it saves time as well as financial and human resources. However, the disadvantage is that you do not obtain information about the population's characteristics of interest to you but only *estimate* or *predict* them on the basis of what you found out in your sample. Hence, there is the possibility of an error in your estimation.

Sampling, therefore, is a trade-off between certain benefits and disadvantages. While on the one hand you save time and resources, on the other hand you may compromise the level of accuracy in your findings. Through sampling you only make an estimate about the actual situation prevalent in the total population from which the sample is drawn. If you ascertain a piece of information from the total sampling population, if your sample truly represents the study population and if your method of enquiry is correct, your findings should be reasonably accurate. But the possibility of an error is always there. Tolerance of this possibility of error is an important consideration in selecting a sample.

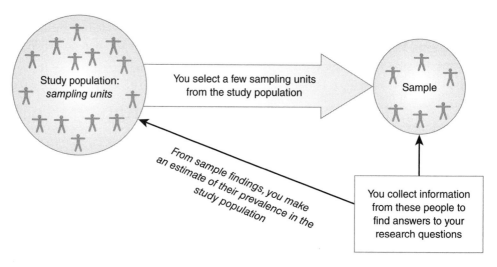

Figure 12.1   The concept of sampling

Sampling terminology

Let us again consider the examples used above where our main aims are to find out the mean age of the class, the average income of the families living in the city and the likely election outcome for a particular state or country. Let us assume that you adopt a sampling method – that is, you select a few students, families or voters to achieve these aims. In this process there are a number of aspects:

- The class, families living in the city or voters from which you select your sample are called the *population* or study population. The size of this population is usually denoted by the letter *N*.
- The small group of students, families or electors from whom you collect the required information to estimate the average age of the class, average income or the election outcome is called the sample.
- The number of students, families or electors from whom you obtain the required information is called the sample size and is usually denoted by the letter *n*.
- The way you select students, families or electors is called the sampling design or sampling strategy.
- Each student, family or elector that forms the basis for selecting your sample is called a sampling unit or sampling element.
- A list identifying each student, family or elector in the study population is called a sampling frame. If all the elements in a sampling population cannot be individually identified, you cannot have a sampling frame for that study population.
- Your findings based on the information obtained from your respondents (sample) are called sample statistics. Your sample statistics form the basis for estimating the prevalence of the characteristics of interest in the study population.
- Your main aim is to find answers to your research questions as they relate to the total study population, not to the sample you collected information from. From sample statistics we make an estimate of the possible answers to our research questions for the study population. The estimates arrived at from sample statistics are called *population parameters*. One example of a parameter is the population mean.

Principles of sampling

The theory of sampling is guided by three principles. To effectively explain these, we will take an extremely simple example. Suppose there are four individuals A, B, C and D. Further suppose that A is 18 years of age, B is 20, C is 23 and D is 25. As you know their ages, you can *find out* (calculate) their average age by simply adding $18 + 20 + 23 + 25 = 86$ and dividing by 4. This gives the average (mean) age of A, B, C and D as 21.5 years.

Now let us suppose that you want to select a sample of two individuals to make an *estimate* of the average age of the four individuals. To select an unbiased sample in the statistical sense, we need to make sure that each unit has an *equal* and *independent* chance of selection in the sample. Randomisation is a process that enables you to achieve this. In order to achieve randomisation we use the theory of probability in forming pairs which will provide us with six possible combinations of two: A and B; A and C; A and D; B and C; B and D; and C and D. Let us take each of these pairs to calculate the average age of the sample:

1 A + B = 18 + 20 = 38/2 = 19.0 years;
2 A + C = 18 + 23 = 41/2 = 20.5 years;
3 A + D = 18 + 25 = 43/2 = 21.5 years;
4 B + C = 20 + 23 = 43/2 = 21.5 years;
5 B + D = 20 + 25 = 45/2 = 22.5 years;
6 C + D = 23 + 25 = 48/2 = 24.0 years.

Notice that in most cases the average age calculated on the basis of these samples of two (sample statistics) is different. Now compare these sample statistics with the average of all four individuals – the population mean (population parameter) of 21.5 years. Out of a total

Table 12.1   The difference between sample statistics and the population mean

Sample	Sample mean (sample statistics) (1)	Population mean (population parameter) (2)	Difference between (1) and (2)
1	19.0	21.5	−2.5
2	20.5	21.5	−1.0
3	21.5	21.5	0.0
4	21.5	21.5	0.0
5	22.5	21.5	+1.0
6	24.0	21.5	+2.5

of six possible sample combinations, only in the case of two is there no difference between the sample statistic and the population mean. Where there is a difference, this is attributed to the sample and is known as sampling error. Again, the size of the sampling error varies markedly. Let us consider the difference in the sample statistics and the population mean for each of the six samples (Table 12.1).

This analysis suggests a very important principle of sampling:

> Principle 1. In a majority of cases where sampling is done, there will be a difference between the sample statistics and the true population mean, which is attributable to the selection of the units in the sample.

To understand the second principle, let us continue with the above example, but instead of a sample of two individuals we take a sample of three. There are four possible combinations of three that can be drawn:

1 A + B + C = 18 + 20 + 23 = 61/3 = 20.33 years;
2 A + B + D = 18 + 20 + 25 = 63/3 = 21.00 years;
3 A + C + D = 18 + 23 + 25 = 66/3 = 22.00 years;
4 B + C + D = 20 + 23 + 25 = 68/3 = 22.67 years.

Now, let us compare the difference between the sample statistics and the population mean (Table 12.2).

Compare the differences calculated in Table 12.1 and Table 12.2. In Table 12.1 the difference between the sample statistic and the population mean lies between –2.5 and

Table 12.2   The difference between sample statistics and population mean

Sample	Sample mean (1)	Population man (2)	Difference between (1) and (2)
1	20.33	21.5	−1.17
2	21.00	21.5	−0.5
3	22.00	21.5	+0.5
4	22.67	21.5	+1.17

+2.5 years, whereas in the second it is between –1.17 and +1.17 years. The gap between the sample statistic and the population mean is reduced in Table 12.2. This reduction is attributed to the increase in the sample size. This, therefore, leads to the second principle:

Principle 2. The greater the sample size, the more accurate the estimate of the true population mean.

The third principle of sampling is particularly important as a number of sampling strategies, such as stratified and cluster sampling, are based on it. To understand this principle, let us continue with the same example but use slightly different data. Suppose the ages of the four individuals are markedly different: A = 18, B = 26, C = 32 and D = 40. In other words, we are visualising a population where the individuals are markedly different with respect to age – the variable we are interested in.

Let us follow the same procedure, selecting samples of two individuals at a time and then three. If we work through the same procedures (described above) we will find that the difference in the average age in the case of samples of two ranges between –7.00 and + 7.00 years and in the case of the sample of three ranges between –3.67 and +3.67. In both cases the range of the difference is greater than previously calculated. This is attributable to the greater difference in the ages of the four individuals – the sampling population which in this instance is more heterogeneous (varied or diverse) in regard to age. In other words, if your study population is heterogeneous in terms of the variable under study, for a given level of accuracy, you need to select a larger sample as compared to if it was homogeneous.

Principle 3. The greater the difference in the variable under study in a population, for a given sample size, the greater the difference between the sample statistics and the true population mean.

These principles are crucial to keep in mind when you are determining the sample size needed for a particular level of accuracy, and in selecting the sampling strategy best suited to your study.

Factors affecting the inferences drawn from a sample

The above principles suggest that two factors may influence the degree of certainty about the inferences drawn from a sample:

1. The size of the sample – Findings based upon larger samples have more certainty than those based on smaller ones. As a rule, *the larger the sample size, the more accurate the findings.*
2. The extent of variation in the sampling population – The greater the variation in the study population with respect to the characteristics under study, for a given sample size, the greater the uncertainty. (In technical terms, the greater the standard deviation, the higher the standard error for a given sample size in your estimates.) If a population is homogeneous (uniform or similar) with respect to the characteristics under study, a small sample can provide a reasonably good estimate, but if it is heterogeneous (dissimilar or diversified), you need to select a larger sample to obtain the same level of accuracy. Of course, if all the elements in a population are identical, then the selection of even one will provide an absolutely accurate estimate. As a rule, *the higher the variation with respect to the characteristics under study in the study population, the greater the uncertainty for a given sample size.*

Aims in selecting a sample

When you select a sample in quantitative studies you are primarily aiming to achieve maximum precision in your estimates within a given sample size, and to avoid bias in the selection of your sample. Bias in the selection of a sample can occur if:

SAMPLING CHOICES

- sampling is done by a non-random method – that is, if the selection is consciously or unconsciously influenced by human choice;
- the sampling frame – list, index or other population records – which serves as the basis of selection, does not cover the sampling population accurately and completely;
- a section of a sampling population is impossible to find or refuses to co-operate.

Types of sampling

The various sampling strategies in quantitative research can be categorised as follows (Figure 12.2):

- random/probability sampling designs;
- non-random/non-probability sampling designs; and
- 'mixed' sampling design.

To understand these designs, we will discuss each type individually.

Random/probability sampling designs

PROBABILITY
SAMPLING

For a design to be called random sampling or probability sampling, it is imperative that each element in the study population has an *equal* and *independent* chance of selection in the sample. The concept of equality implies that the probability of selection of each element in the population is the same; that is, the choice of an element in the sample is not influenced by other considerations such as personal preference. The concept of independence means that the choice of one element is not dependent upon the choice of another element in the sampling; that is, the selection or rejection of one element does not affect the inclusion or exclusion of another. To explain these concepts let us return to our example of a class of students.

Suppose there are 80 students in the class. Assume 20 of these refuse to participate in your study. You want the entire population of 80 students in your study but, as 20 refuse to participate, you can only use a sample of 60 students. The 20 students who refuse to participate could have strong feelings about the issues you wish to explore, but your findings will not reflect their opinions. Their exclusion from your study means that each of the 80 students does not have an equal chance of selection. Therefore, your sample does not represent the total class.

The same could apply to a community. In a community, in addition to the refusal to participate, let us assume that you are unable to identify all the residents living in the community. If a significant proportion of people cannot be included in the sampling population because they either cannot be identified or refuse to participate, then any sample drawn will not give each element in the sampling population an equal chance of

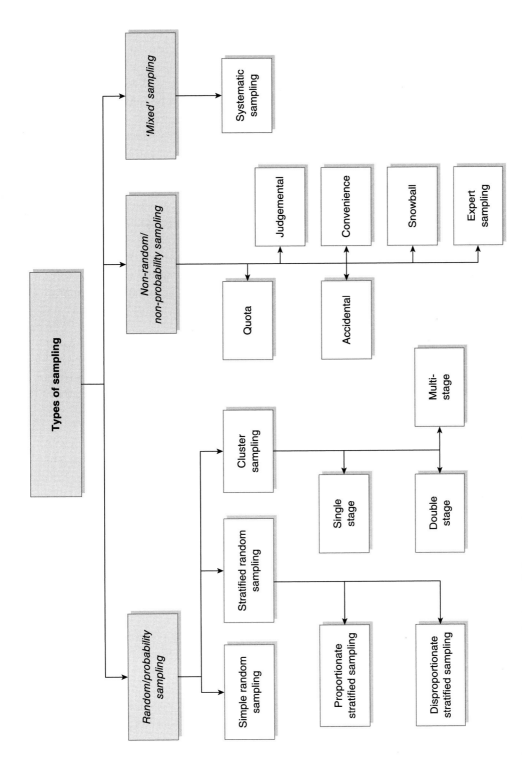

Figure 12.2   Types of sampling in quantitative research

being selected in the sample. Hence, the sample will not be representative of the total community.

To understand the concept of an independent chance of selection, let us assume that there are five students in the class who are extremely close friends. If one of them is selected but refuses to participate because the other four are not chosen, and you are therefore forced to select either the five or none, then your sample will not be considered an independent sample since the selection of one is dependent upon the selection of others. The same could happen in the community where a small group says that either all of them or none of them will participate in the study. In these situations where you are forced either to include or to exclude a part of the sampling population, the sample is not considered to be independent, and hence is not representative of the sampling population. However, if the number of refusals is fairly small, in practical terms, it should not make the sample non-representative. In practice there are always some people who do not want to participate in the study, but you only need to worry if the number is significantly large.

A sample can only be considered a random/probability sample (and therefore representative of the population under study) if both these conditions are met. Otherwise, bias can be introduced into the study. There are two main advantages of random/probability samples:

1. As they represent the total sampling population, the inferences drawn from such samples can be generalised to the total sampling population.
2. Some statistical tests based upon the theory of probability can be applied only to data collected from random samples. Some of these tests are important for establishing conclusive correlations.

Methods of drawing a random sample

Of the methods that you can adopt to select a random sample the three most common are:

1. The fishbowl draw – If your total population is small, an easy procedure is to number each element using separate slips of paper for each element, put all the slips into a bowl and then pick them out one by one without looking, until the number of slips selected equals the sample size you decided upon. This method is used in some lotteries.
2. A computer program – There are a number of programs that can help you to select a random sample.
3. A table of randomly generated numbers – Most books on research methodology and statistics include a table of randomly generated numbers in their appendices (see, for example, Table 12.3). You can select your sample using these tables according to the procedure described in Figure 12.3.

Let us take an example to illustrate the use of Table 12.3 for random numbers. Let us assume that your sampling population consists of 256 individuals. Number each individual from 1 to 256. Randomly select the starting page, in case of multiple pages. Then select the starting column (from 1 to 10 with five columns of digits) and identify three columns of digits (as the total number of potential respondents in your study population is comprised of three digits). Run down the selected three columns of digits and select all numbers less than 256. Respondents corresponding to the selected numbers become your sample. Having gone through the selected column, if needs to, go to the adjoining columns (1-10) on either

Step 1   Identify the total number of elements in the study population. Note the number of digits in this number (if your total sampling population is 9 or less, it is one digit; if it is 99 or less, it is two digits; etc.).

Step 2   Number each element starting from 1.

Step 3   If the table of random numbers is on more than one page, randomly choose the starting page. On the page thus chosen, randomly select a column or row as your starting point and proceed from there in a predetermined direction.

Step 4   Corresponding to the number of digits to which the total population runs, randomly select that number of digits within each column from the table.

Step 5   Decide on your sample size.

Step 6   Select the required number of elements for your sample from the table. If you happen to select the same number twice, discard it and go to the next. This can happen as the table for random numbers is generated by sampling with replacement.

Figure 12.3   The procedure for using a table of random numbers

side following the same process. Or you can randomly select another column for the purpose and continue to do so till you have selected the number of respondents equivalent to your sample size. You can select your sample using the rows in the same way.

Suppose you identify the ninth column of numbers and the last three digits of this column (underlined).Assume that you are selecting 10 per cent of the total population as your sample (25 elements). Let us go through the numbers underlined in the ninth column. The first number is 049, which is below 256 (the total population); hence, the 49th element becomes a part of your sample. The second number, 319, is more than the total elements in your population (256); hence, you cannot accept the 319th element in the sample. The same applies to the next element, 758, and indeed the next five elements, 589, 507, 483, 487 and 540. After 540 is 232, and as this number is within the sampling frame, it can be accepted as a part of the sample. Similarly, if you follow down the same three digits in the same column, you select 052, 029, 065, 246 and 161, before you come to the element 029 again. As the 29th element has already been selected, go to the next number, and so on until 25 elements have been chosen. Once you have reached the end of a column, you can either move to the next column or randomly select another one in order to continue the process of selection. For example, the 25 elements shown in Table 12.4 are selected from the ninth, tenth and second columns of Table 12.3.

Sampling with or without replacement

A random sample can be selected using two different systems:

1. sampling without replacement;
2. sampling with replacement.

Suppose you want to select a sample of 20 students out of a total of 80. The first student is selected from the entire class, so the probability of selection for the first student is 1/80. When you select the second student there are only 79 left in the class and the probability of selection for the second student is not 1/80 but 1/79. The probability of

SELECTING A SAMPLE   237

Table 12.3 Selecting a sample using a table of random numbers

	1	2	3	4	5	6	7	8	9	10
1	48461	14952	72619	73689	52059	37086	60050	86192	67049	64739
2	76534	38149	49692	31366	52093	15422	20498	33901	10319	43397
3	70437	25861	38504	14752	23757	29660	67844	78815	23758	86814
4	59584	03370	42806	11393	71722	93804	09095	07856	55589	46820
5	04285	58554	16085	51555	27501	73883	33427	33343	45507	50063
6	77340	10412	69189	85171	29802	44785	86368	02583	96483	76553
7	59183	62687	91778	80354	23512	97219	65921	02035	59487	91403
8	91800	04281	39979	03927	82564	28777	59049	97532	54540	79472
9	12066	24817	81099	48940	69554	55925	48379	12866	41232	21580
10	69907	91751	53512	23748	65906	91385	84983	27915	48491	91068
11	80467	04873	54053	25955	48518	13815	37707	68687	15570	08890
12	78057	67835	28302	45048	56761	97725	58438	91529	24645	18544
13	05648	39387	78191	88415	60269	94880	58812	42931	71898	61534
14	22304	39246	01350	99451	61862	78688	30339	60222	74052	25740
15	61346	50269	67005	40442	33100	16742	61640	21046	31909	72641
16	56793	37696	27965	30459	91011	51426	31006	77468	61029	57108
17	56411	48609	36698	42453	85061	43769	39948	87031	30767	13953
18	62098	12825	81744	28882	27369	88185	65846	92545	09065	22653
19	68775	06261	54265	16203	23340	84750	16317	88686	86842	00879
20	52679	19599	13687	74872	89181	01939	18447	10787	76246	80072
21	84096	87152	20719	25215	04349	54434	72344	93008	83282	31670
22	83964	55937	21417	49944	38356	98404	14850	17994	17161	98981
23	31191	75131	72386	11689	95727	05414	88727	45583	22568	77700
24	30545	68523	29850	67833	05622	89975	79042	27142	99257	32349
25	52573	91001	52315	26430	54175	30122	31796	98842	37600	26025
26	16586	81842	01076	99414	31574	94719	34656	80018	86988	79234
27	81841	88481	61191	25013	30272	23388	22463	65774	10029	58376
28	43563	66829	72838	08074	57080	15446	11034	98143	74989	26885
29	19945	84193	57581	77252	85604	45412	43556	27518	90572	00563
30	79374	23796	16919	99691	80276	32818	62953	78831	54395	30705
31	48503	26615	43980	09810	38289	66679	73799	48418	12647	40044
32	32049	65541	37937	41105	70106	89706	40829	40789	59547	00783
33	18547	71562	95493	34112	76895	46766	96395	31718	48302	45893
34	03180	96742	61486	43305	84183	99605	67803	13491	09243	29557
35	94822	24738	67749	83748	59799	25210	31093	62925	72061	69991
36	04330	60599	85828	19152	68499	27977	35611	96240	62747	89529
37	43770	81537	59527	95674	76692	86420	69930	10020	72881	12532
38	56908	77192	50623	41215	14311	42834	80651	93750	59957	31211
39	32787	07189	80539	75927	75475	73965	11796	72140	48944	74156
40	52441	78392	11733	57703	29133	71164	55355	31006	25526	55790

238   RESEARCH METHODOLOGY

	1	2	3	4	5	6	7	8	9	10
41	22377	54723	18227	28449	04570	18882	00023	67101	06895	08915
42	18376	73460	88841	39602	34049	20589	05701	08249	74213	25220
43	53201	28610	87957	21497	64729	64983	71551	99016	87903	63875
44	34919	78801	59710	27396	02593	05665	11964	44134	00273	76358
45	33617	92159	21971	16901	57383	34262	41744	60891	57624	06962
46	70010	40964	98780	72418	52571	18415	64362	90637	38034	04909
47	19282	68447	35665	31530	59838	49181	21914	65742	89815	39231
48	91429	73328	13266	54898	68795	40948	80808	63887	89939	47938
49	97637	78393	33021	05867	86520	45363	43066	00988	64040	09803
50	95150	07625	05255	83254	93943	52325	93230	62668	79529	66964

Source: Statistical Tables, 3rd edition, by F. James Rohlf and Robert R. Sokal. Copyright © 1969, 1981, 1994 by W.H. Freeman and Company. Used with permission.

Table 12.4   Elements selected using the table of random numbers

Column in Table 12.3	Elements selected
9	49, 232, 52, 29, 65, 246, 161, 243, 61, 213, 34, 40,
10	63, 68, 108, 72, 25, 234, 44, 211, 156, 220, 231,
2	149, 246

selecting the next student is 1/78. By the time you select the 20th student, the probability of his/her selection is 1/61. This type of sampling is called sampling without replacement. But this is contrary to our basic definition of randomisation; that is, each element has an equal and independent chance of selection. In the second system, called sampling with replacement, the selected element is replaced in the sampling population and if it is selected again, it is discarded and the next one is selected. If the sampling population is fairly large, the probability of selecting the same element twice is fairly remote.

Specific random/probability sampling designs

There are three commonly used types of random sampling design: simple random sampling (SRS), stratified random sampling and cluster sampling.

Simple random sampling

This is the most commonly used method of selecting a probability sample. In line with the definition of randomisation, whereby each element in the population is given an equal and independent chance of selection, a simple random sample is selected by the procedure presented in Figure 12.4.

To illustrate, let us again take our example of the class of students. There are 80 students in the class, and so the first step is to identify each student by a number from 1 to 80. Suppose you decide to select a sample of 20 using the simple random sampling

Step 1   Identify by a number all elements or sampling units in the population.

Step 2   Decide on the sample size *n*.

Step 3   Select *n* using the fishbowl draw, a table of random numbers or a computer program.

Figure 12.4   The procedure for selecting a simple random sample

technique. Use the fishbowl draw, a table for random numbers or a computer program to select the 20 students. These 20 students become the basis of your enquiry.

Stratified random sampling

As discussed, the accuracy of your estimate largely depends on the extent of variability or heterogeneity of the study population with respect to the characteristics that have a strong correlation with what you are trying to ascertain (Principle 3). It follows, therefore, that if the heterogeneity in the population can be reduced by some means, for a given sample size, you can achieve greater accuracy in your estimate. Stratified random sampling is based upon this logic.

In stratified random sampling the researcher attempts to stratify the population in such a way that the population within a stratum is homogeneous with respect to the characteristic on the basis of which it is being stratified. It is important that the characteristics chosen as the basis of stratification are clearly identifiable in the study population. For example, it is much easier to stratify a population on the basis of gender than on the basis of age, income or attitude. It is also important for the characteristic that becomes the basis of stratification to be related to the main variable that you are exploring. Once the sampling population has been separated into non-overlapping groups, you select the required number of elements from each stratum, using the simple random sampling technique. There are two types of stratified sampling: proportionate stratified sampling and disproportionate stratified sampling. In proportionate stratified sampling the number of elements from each stratum is selected in relation to its proportion in the total population, whereas in disproportionate stratified sampling consideration is not given to the size of the stratum. The procedure for selecting a stratified sample is schematically presented in Figure 12.5.

Cluster sampling

Simple random and stratified sampling are based on a researcher's ability to identify each element in a population. It is easy to do this if the total sampling population is small, but if the population is large, as in the case of a city, state or country, it becomes difficult and expensive to identify each sampling unit. In such cases the use of cluster sampling is more appropriate.

Cluster sampling is based on the ability of the researcher to divide the sampling population into groups (based upon visible or easily identifiable characteristics), called clusters, and then to select elements within each cluster, using the SRS technique. Clusters can be formed on the basis of geographical proximity or a common characteristic that has a correlation with the main variable of the study (as in stratified sampling). Depending on the level of clustering, sometimes sampling may be done at different

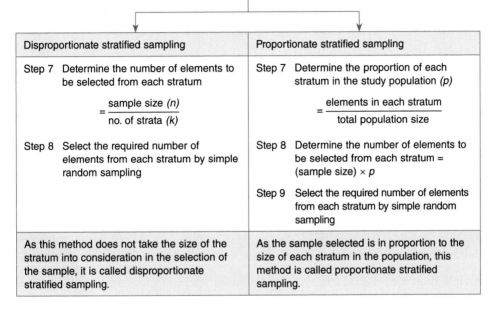

Step 1 Identify all elements or sampling units in the sampling population.
Step 2 Decide upon the different strata (*k*) into which you want to stratify the population.
Step 3 Place each element into the appropriate stratum.
Step 4 Number every element in each stratum separately.
Step 5 Decide the total sample size (*n*).
Step 6 Decide whether you want to select proportionate or disproportionate stratified sampling and follow the steps below.

Disproportionate stratified sampling	Proportionate stratified sampling
Step 7 Determine the number of elements to be selected from each stratum $$= \frac{\text{sample size } (n)}{\text{no. of strata } (k)}$$	Step 7 Determine the proportion of each stratum in the study population (*p*) $$= \frac{\text{elements in each stratum}}{\text{total population size}}$$
Step 8 Select the required number of elements from each stratum by simple random sampling	Step 8 Determine the number of elements to be selected from each stratum = (sample size) × *p*
	Step 9 Select the required number of elements from each stratum by simple random sampling
As this method does not take the size of the stratum into consideration in the selection of the sample, it is called disproportionate stratified sampling.	As the sample selected is in proportion to the size of each stratum in the population, this method is called proportionate stratified sampling.

Figure 12.5   The procedure for selecting a stratified sample

levels. These levels constitute the different stages (single, double or multiple) of clustering, which will be explained later.

Imagine you want to investigate the attitude of post-secondary students in Australia towards problems in higher education in the country. There are higher education institutions in every state and territory of Australia. In addition, there are different types of institutions (see Figure 12.6): universities, universities of technology, colleges of advanced education and colleges of technical and further education (TAFE). Within each institution various courses are offered at both undergraduate and postgraduate levels. Each academic course could take three to four years. You can imagine the magnitude of the task. In such situations cluster sampling is extremely useful in selecting a random sample.

The first level of cluster sampling could be at the state or territory level. Clusters could be grouped according to similar characteristics that ensure their comparability in terms of student population. For example, if you can establish that certain states are comparable in terms of student socioeconomic-demographic characteristics, instead of all, you randomly select only one or two states out of the cluster to become part of your study. If this is not easy, you may decide to select all the states and territories and then select a

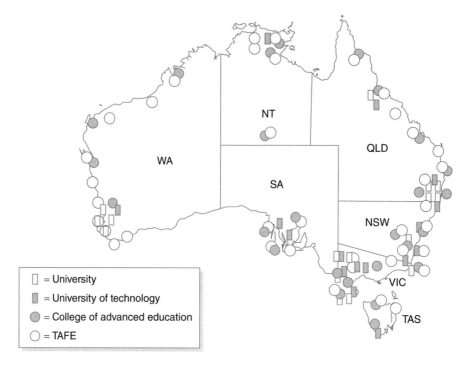

Figure 12.6 The concept of cluster sampling

sample at the institutional level. You can do similar selection with respect to educational institutions. If all the universities in a state are comparable in terms of student character-istics, you might randomly select only one or two for your study. Similarly, you select one or two institutions from other categories of institutions providing higher education. For example, with a simple random technique, one or two institutions from each category within each state could be selected (say, one university, one university of technology and one TAFE college). This is based upon the assumption that institutions within a category are fairly similar with regard to student profile. Then, within an institution, one or more academic programmes could be randomly selected, depending on resources. Within each study programme selected, students studying in a particular academic year could then be selected. Further, selection of a proportion of students studying in a particular academic year could then be made using the SRS technique. The process of selecting a sample in this manner is called *multi-stage cluster sampling*.

Non-random/non-probability sampling designs in quantitative research

Non-probability sampling designs do not follow the theory of probability in the choice of elements from the sampling population. These designs are used when either the num-ber of elements in a population is unknown or the elements cannot be individually identified. In such situations the selection of elements is dependent upon other consid-erations. There are six non-random designs, each based on different considerations, which are commonly used in both qualitative and quantitative research: quota sampling, accidental sampling, convenience sampling, judgemental or purposive sampling, expert sampling and snowball sampling.

What differentiates these designs being treated as quantitative or qualitative is the predetermined sample size. In quantitative research you use these designs to select a pre-determined number of cases (sample size), whereas in qualitative research you do not decide the number of respondents in advance but continue to select additional cases till you reach the data saturation point. In addition, in qualitative research, you will pre-dominantly use judgemental and accidental sampling strategies to select your respondents. Expert sampling is very similar to judgemental sampling except that in expert sampling the sampling population consists of experts in the field of enquiry. You can also use quota and snowball sampling in qualitative research but without having a predetermined num-ber of cases in mind (sample size).

Quota sampling

The main consideration behind quota sampling is the researcher's ease of access to the sam-ple population. In addition to convenience, you are guided by some visible characteristic, such as gender or race, of the study population that is of interest to you. You select the sample from a location convenient to you as a researcher; whenever you see a person with this visible relevant characteristic you ask that person to participate in the study. The process continues until you have been able to contact the required number of respondents (quota).

Let us suppose that you want to find out about the attitudes of Aboriginal and Torres Strait Islander students towards the facilities provided to them in your university. You might stand at a convenient location and, whenever you see such a student, collect the required information through whatever method of data collection (such as interviewing, questionnaire) you have adopted for the study.

The advantages of using this design are: it is the least expensive way of selecting a sample; you do not need any information, such as a sampling frame, the total number of elements, their location, or other information about the sampling population; and it guarantees the inclusion of the type of people you need. The disadvantages are: as the resulting sample is not a probability one, the findings cannot be generalised to the total sampling population; and the most accessible individuals selected from one location might have characteristics that are unique to them and hence might not be truly repre-sentative of the total sampling population. You can make your sample more representa-tive of your study population by selecting it from various locations where people of interest to you are likely to be available.

Accidental sampling

Accidental sampling is also based upon convenience in accessing the sampling popu-lation. Whereas quota sampling attempts to include people possessing an obvious/visible characteristic, accidental sampling makes no such attempt. You stop collecting data when you reach the required number of respondents you decided to have in your sample.

This method of sampling is common among market research and newspaper reporters. It has more or less the same advantages and disadvantages as quota sampling but, in addition, as you are not guided by any obvious characteristics, some people contacted may not have the required information.

Convenience sampling

Accidental and convenience sampling designs are extremely similar. Convenience sampling is primarily guided by the convenience to the researcher, whatever this might be – easy accessibility, geographical proximity, known contacts, ready approval for undertaking the study, or being a part of the group. Accidental sampling is primarily selecting a place where you are likely to find your potential respondents, which place may or may not be most convenient to you, and if a person of interest comes along, you collect the required information till either you have collected the information from a specific number of respondents or have reached the saturation point.

Judgemental or purposive sampling

The primary consideration in judgemental sampling or purposive sampling is your judgement as to who can provide the best information to achieve the objectives of your study. You only go to those people who in your opinion are likely to have the required information and be willing to share it with you.

This type of sampling is extremely useful when you want to construct a historical reality, describe a phenomenon or develop something about which only a little is known. This sampling strategy is more common in qualitative research, but when you use it in quantitative research you select a predetermined number of people who, in your judgement, are best positioned to provide you with the information needed for your study.

Expert sampling

The only difference between judgemental sampling and expert sampling is that in the case of the former it is entirely your judgement as to the ability of the respondents to contribute to the study. In the case of expert sampling, your respondents must be known experts in the field of interest to you. This is again used in both types of research, but more so in qualitative research studies. When you use it in qualitative research the number of people you talk to is dependent upon the data saturation point, whereas in quantitative research you decide on the number of experts to be contacted without considering the saturation point.

You first identify persons with demonstrated or known expertise in an area of interest to you, seek their consent for participation, and then collect the information either individually or collectively in the form of a group.

Snowball sampling

Snowball sampling is the process of selecting a sample using networks. To start with, a few individuals in a group or organisation are selected and the required information is collected from them. They are then asked to identify other people in the group or organisation, and the people selected by them become a part of the sample. Information is collected from

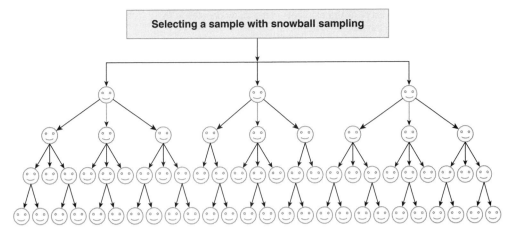

Figure 12.7   Snowball sampling

them, and then these people are asked to identify other members of the group and, in turn, those identified become the basis for further data collection (Figure 12.7). This process is continued until the required number or a saturation point has been reached, in terms of the information being sought.

This sampling technique is useful if you know little about the group or organisation you wish to study, as you need only to make contact with a few individuals, who can then direct you to the other members of the group. It is useful for studying communication patterns, decision making or diffusion of knowledge within a group. There are disadvantages to this technique, however. The choice of the entire sample rests upon the choice of individuals at the first stage. If they belong to a particular faction or have strong biases, the study may be biased. Also, it is difficult to use this technique when the sample becomes fairly large.

Systematic sampling design: a mixed design

Systematic sampling is treated in this book as a 'mixed' sampling design because it has the characteristics of both random and non-random sampling designs.

To use systematic sampling design it is imperative that you have a sampling frame for your study population; it is useful in situations where records for the study population are routinely maintained as a part of service delivery. In systematic sampling the sampling frame is first divided into a number of segments called *intervals*. Then, from the first interval, using the SRS technique, one element is selected. The selection of subsequent elements from other intervals is dependent upon the position of the element selected in the first interval. If it is the fifth element in the first interval, the fifth element of each subsequent interval is chosen. Notice that from the first interval the choice of an element is on a random basis, but the choice of the elements from subsequent intervals is dependent upon the choice from the first, so this method cannot be classified as a random sample. The procedure used in systematic sampling is presented in Figure 12.8.

SELECTING A SAMPLE   245

Step 1 Prepare a list of all the elements in the study population (*N*).
Step 2 Decide on the sample size (*n*).
Step 3 Determine the *width of the interval* (*k*)

$$k = \frac{\text{total population } (N)}{\text{sample size } (n)}$$

Step 4 Using SRS, select an element from the first interval (*i*th position).
Step 5 Select the *i*th element from each subsequent interval.

Figure 12.8 The procedure for selecting a systematic sample

You can deviate from the general procedure for selecting a sample by the systematic sampling technique by selecting a different element from each interval by the SRS technique. Systematic sampling done in this way can be classified under probability sampling designs.

To select a sample, as just mentioned, you must have a sampling frame (Figure 12.9). Sometimes this is impossible, or obtaining one may be too expensive. However, in real life there are situations where a kind of sampling frame exists, for example records of clients in an agency, enrolment lists of students in a school or university, electoral lists of people living in an area, or records of the staff employed in an organisation. All these can be used as a sampling frame to select a sample by systematic sampling. This convenience of having a 'ready-made' sampling frame may come at a price: in some cases it may not be a truly random listing. Mostly these lists are in alphabetical order, based upon a number assigned to a case, or arranged in a way that is convenient to the users of the records. If the 'width of an interval' is large, say, 1 in 30 cases, and if the cases are arranged in alphabetical order, you could exclude surnames starting with a letter that is not very common. It is also possible that some adjoining letter may not be included at all in the width of the interval.

Suppose there are 50 students in a class and you want to select 10 students using the systematic sampling technique. The first step is to determine the width of the interval (50/10 = 5). This means that from every five you need to select one student. Using the SRS technique, from the first interval (the first five students), select one of the students. Suppose you selected the third. From the rest of the intervals you would select every third student.

The calculation of sample size

What is the appropriate sample size in quantitative research? Basically, it depends on what you want to do with the findings and what type of relationships you want to establish. Your purpose in undertaking research is the main determinant of the level of accuracy required in the results, and this level of accuracy is an important determinant of sample size. However, in qualitative research, as the main focus is to explore or describe a situation, issue, process or phenomenon, the question of sample size is less important. You usually collect data till you think you have reached saturation point in terms of discovering new information. Once you think you are not getting much new data from your respondents, you stop collecting further information. Of course, the diversity or heterogeneity in what you are trying to find out about plays an important role in how fast you will reach saturation point. As a rule: *the*

246 **RESEARCH METHODOLOGY**

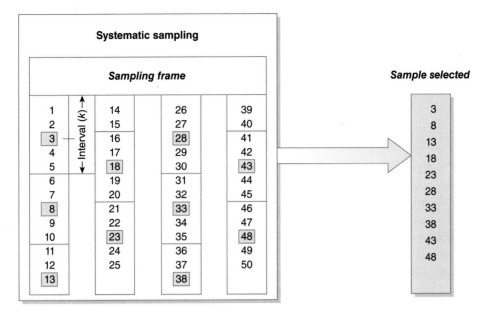

Figure 12.9   Systematic sampling

greater the heterogeneity or diversity in what you are trying to find out about, the greater the number of respondents you need to contact to reach saturation point.

In determining the size of your sample for quantitative studies and in particular for cause-and-effect studies, you need to consider the following:

- At what *level of confidence* do you want to test your results, findings or hypotheses?
- With what *degree of accuracy* do you wish to estimate the population parameters?
- What is the estimated *level of variation* (standard deviation), with respect to the main variable you are studying, in the study population?

Answering these questions is necessary regardless of whether you intend to determine the sample size yourself or have an expert do it for you. The size of the sample is important for testing a hypothesis or establishing an association, but for other studies the general rule is: *the larger the sample size, the more accurate your estimates.* In practice, your budget determines the size of your sample. Your skills in selecting a sample, within the constraints of your budget, lie in the way you select your elements so that they effectively and adequately represent your sampling population.

Sampling in qualitative research

As the main aim in qualitative enquiries is to explore diversity, sample size and sampling strategy do not play a significant role in the selection of a sample. If selected carefully, diversity can be extensively and accurately described on the basis of information obtained even from one individual. All non-probability sampling designs – purposive, judgemental, expert, accidental and snowball – can also be used in qualitative research, with two differences:

SELECTING A SAMPLE   247

1. In quantitative studies you collect information from a predetermined number of people, but in qualitative research you do not have a sample size in mind – instead you collect data until you feel you have reached the saturation point.
2. In quantitative research you are guided by your desire to select a random sample, whereas in qualitative research you are guided by your judgement as to who is likely to provide you with the 'best' information.

The concept of saturation point in qualitative research

As you already know, in qualitative research data is usually collected to a point where you are not getting new information or it is negligible – the data saturation point. This stage determines the sample size.

QUALITATIVE
SAMPLE SIZE

It is important for you to keep in mind that the concept of data saturation point is highly subjective. It is you who is collecting the data and decides when you have attained the saturation point in your data collection. How soon you reach the saturation point depends upon how diverse is the situation or phenomenon that you are studying. The greater the diversity, the greater the number of people from whom you need to collect the information to reach the saturation point.

The concept of saturation point is more applicable to situations where you are collecting information on a one-to-one basis. Where the information is collected in a collective format such as focus groups, community forums or panel discussions, you strive to gather as diverse and as much information as possible. When no new information is emerging it is assumed that you have reached the saturation point.

Summary

In this chapter you have learnt about sampling, the process of selecting a few elements from a sampling population. Sampling, in a way, is a trade-off between accuracy and resources. Through sampling you make an *estimate* of the information of interest. You do not find the true population mean.

Two opposing philosophies underpin the selection of sampling units in quantitative and qualitative research. In quantitative studies a sample is supposed to be selected in such a way that it represents the study population, which is achieved through randomisation. However, the selection of a sample in qualitative research is guided by your judgement as to who is likely to provide you with complete and diverse information. This is a non-random process.

Sample size does not occupy a significant place in qualitative research and it is determined by the data saturation point while collecting data instead of being fixed in advance.

In quantitative research, sampling is guided by three principles, one of which is that the greater the sample size, the more accurate the estimate of the true population mean, given that everything else remains the same. The inferences drawn from a sample can be affected by both the size of the sample and the extent of variation in the sampling population.

Sampling designs can be classified as random/probability sampling designs, non-random/non-probability sampling designs and 'mixed' sampling designs. For a sample to be called random, each element in the study population must have an equal and independent chance of selection. Three random designs were discussed: simple random sampling, stratified random sampling and cluster sampling. The procedures for selecting a sample using these designs are detailed step by step. The use of the fishbowl technique, a table of random numbers and specifically designed computer programs are three commonly used methods of selecting a probability sample.

There are six non-probability sampling designs: quota, accidental, convenience, judgemental, expert and snowball. Each is used for a different purpose and in different situations in both quantitative and qualitative studies. In quantitative studies their application is underpinned by the sample size, and in qualitative studies by the data saturation point.

Systematic sampling is a 'mixed' design as it has the properties of both probability and non-probability sampling designs.

The last section of the chapter described determinants of calculating sample size. At your level it is sufficient to be aware of the considerations rather than calculation of the actual sample size as it entails a reasonable degree of statistical knowledge. In qualitative research, the question of sample size is less important, as your aim is to explore, not quantify, the extent of variation and you would be guided by reaching saturation point in terms of new findings.

FOR YOU TO THINK ABOUT

- Refamiliarise yourself with the keywords listed at the beginning of this chapter, and if you are uncertain about the meaning or application of any of them revisit them in the chapter before moving on.
- Consider the implications of selecting a sample based upon your choice as a researcher and how you could make sure that you do not introduce bias.
- In the absence of a sampling frame for employees of a large organisation, which sampling design would you use to select a sample of 219 people? Explain why you would choose this design and the process you would undertake to ensure that the sample is representative.
- From your own area of interest, identify examples of where cluster sampling could be applied.

Now, as you have gone through the chapter, try answering the following questions:

- Describe the process of sampling, detailing its respective advantages and disadvantages.
- Explain what you understand by: study population, sample, sample size, sampling strategy, sampling unit, sampling element, sampling frame, sample statistics, and population parameters.
- What are the different types of sampling designs and what are their advantages and disadvantages?
- Describe the designs that are commonly used in qualitative research.
- Discuss the concept of saturation point in data collection, with its advantages and disadvantages.

Want to learn more? Visit
http://www.uk.sagepub.com/kumar4e
or scan this QR code to gain access to a range of online resources to support your study including practice quizzes, videos, weblinks, flashcards, and journal articles.

SELECTING A SAMPLE   249

Exercise IV: Selecting a sample

TEMPLATE OF
EXERCISE IV

The accuracy of what you find out through your research endeavour, among many other things, depends upon the way you select your sample, the people who are going to provide you with the information you need.

The underlying premise in sampling is that a small number of respondents, if selected correctly, can provide, to a sufficiently high degree of confidence, a reasonably accurate estimate of what you are trying to ascertain in the study population.

For details on sampling designs, refer to Chapter 12.

For quantitative studies

The basic objective of a sampling design in quantitative research is to minimise, within a given cost, any difference between the values obtained from your sample and those actually prevalent in the study population. Sampling theory in quantitative research is thus guided by two principles:

1 the avoidance of bias in the selection of a sample;
2 the attainment of maximum precision for a given outlay of resources.

In quantitative research you can select your sample with any of the probability or non-probability sampling designs. Both have advantages and disadvantages and both are appropriate for certain situations. But whatever sampling design you choose, make sure you take steps to avoid introducing your bias in the selection of sampling units. When selecting a sample in quantitative studies you need to decide on two things: the sample size you plan to select; and how to select the required sampling units. You also need to think about your reasons for deciding the size and choosing the sampling strategy.

This exercise is designed for you to think through the issues which are important in helping you to develop your sampling strategy.

Step I   Answer the following about your sampling design.

1   What is the total size of your study population?_____ ☐
    _____ Unknown ☐

2   Do you want to select a sample?
    Yes ☐   No ☐
    (a)   If yes, what will your sample size be? _____
    (b)   What are your reasons for choosing this sample size? _____
    _____
    _____
    _____
    _____

3   How will you select your sample? (What sampling design are you proposing?)

250   **RESEARCH METHODOLOGY**

4 Why did you select this sampling design? (What are its strengths?)

5 What are the limitations of this design?

Step II   On the basis of the answers to the above questions, write about your sampling design, detailing the process and your justification for using it (consult Chapter 12 for details).

_____
_____
_____
_____
_____
_____

For qualitative studies

In qualitative research your aim is not to select a random or unbiased sample but one which can provide you, as far as possible, with the detailed, accurate and complete information that you are looking for. Hence, you are predominantly guided by your convenience and judgement in the selection of your respondents.

In qualitative research you can only use non-probability designs. You can select your sample in two ways: (i) in the light of financial constraints decide from how many respondents you can collect data; or (ii) you decide to be guided by the saturation point in data collection. If you decide to be guided by the attainment of the saturation point, you do not specify your sample but the bases that will determine the saturation point.

You also need to decide who are going to be your respondents and how they are going to be identified. You need to think about the determinants on which you are going to base your judgement as to the suitability of your respondents for being your respondents.

Answers to the following questions will help you to think through the issues you are likely to face while developing a sampling strategy for your study.

A: What factors would you keep in mind when selecting a respondent?

_____
_____
_____
_____
_____
_____

B: How would you identify your potential respondents?

_____
_____
_____
_____
_____

EXERCISE IV   251

_____

_____

_____

C: How would you determine whether you have reached the saturation point in your data collection?

_____

_____

_____

_____

_____

STEP V
WRITING A RESEARCH PROPOSAL

This operational step includes one chapter:

13

WRITING A RESEARCH PROPOSAL

In this chapter you will learn about

- The purpose of the research proposal in quantitative and qualitative research
- The contents of a research proposal
- How to write a research proposal

Keywords

conceptual framework, data analysis, data processing, hypothesis,

limitations, literature review, research design, research problem,

sampling, study design, study objectives, theoretical framework, time-frame.

At the end of this chapter, you should have an understanding of

- What the differences are between quantitative and qualitative research proposals
- What to include in a research proposal

The research proposal in quantitative and qualitative research

All research endeavours, in both qualitative and quantitative research, in every academic and professional field are preceded by a research proposal. It informs your academic supervisor or potential research contract provider about your conceptualisation of the total research process that you propose to undertake so that they can examine its validity and appropriateness. In any academic field, your research proposal will go through a number of committees for approval. Unless it is approved by all of them, you will not be able to start your research. Hence, it is important for you to study closely what constitutes a research proposal.

You need to write a research proposal whether your research study is quantitative or qualitative, and in both cases you use a similar structure. The main difference is in the proposed procedures and methodologies for undertaking the research endeavour. When providing details for different parts of the research proposal, for quantitative studies you will detail quantitative methods, procedures and models, and for qualitative studies your proposed process will be based upon methods and procedures that form the qualitative research methodology. If you happen to use a mixed methods approach, you need to describe them as either qualitative or quantitative procedures under their respective headings.

A research proposal serves many functions. Specifically:

- It serves to remind you of what you are supposed to do at different steps of the research journey. It is the road map designed by you, and approved by your university, to guide you through your research journey. It is an overall plan designed to obtain answers to the research questions or problems that constitute your research project. It outlines the various tasks you plan to undertake to fulfil your research objectives, test hypotheses (if any) or obtain answers to your research questions. It should also state your reasons for undertaking the study. Broadly, a research proposal's main function is to detail the *operational plan for obtaining answers to your research questions*. In doing so it ensures and reassures the reader of the validity of the methodology for obtaining answers to your research questions accurately and objectively.

- It serves as a document for scientific scrutiny for others to judge the appropriateness of what you are proposing and provide their seal of approval. It serves to convince your research supervisor or a reviewer that your proposed methodology is meritorious, valid, appropriate and workable in terms of obtaining answers to your research questions or objective.

In order to achieve these functions, a research proposal must tell you, your research supervisor and reviewers:

- *what* you are proposing to do in your study;
- *how* you plan to find answers to *what* you are proposing;
- *why* you selected the proposed investigation strategies.

Contents of a research proposal

A research proposal should contain the following information about your study:

- an introduction, including a brief *literature review*;
- the *theoretical framework* that underpins your study;
- the *conceptual framework* that constitutes the basis of your study;
- the *objectives* or *research questions* of your study;
- the *hypotheses* to be tested, if applicable;
- the *study design* that you are proposing to adopt;
- the *setting* for your study;
- the *research instrument(s)* you are planning to use;
- the *sampling design* and *sample size*;
- the *ethical issues* involved and how you propose to deal with them;
- the *data processing procedures*;
- the *proposed chapters* of the report;
- the *problems* and *limitations* of the study;
- the proposed *time-frame* for the project.

A research proposal should communicate the above contents clearly and specifically in such a way that anyone going through it should be able to undertake all tasks in the same manner as you would have.

WRITING RESEARCH
PROPOSALS

Universities and other institutions may have differing requirements regarding the style and content of a research proposal. Requirements may also vary within an institution, from discipline to discipline or from supervisor to supervisor. There may be some additional specific requirements by some universities or supervisors, and you should acquaint yourself with these, but most of what is suggested here will be required by almost everyone. The framework suggested here can be easily adapted to suit your requirements and those of your university.

Your proposal should follow the suggested guidelines and be written in an academic style. It must contain appropriate references in the body of the text and a bibliography at the end. Your survey of the relevant literature should cover major publications on the topic. The theoretical framework for your study must emerge from this literature review and must have its grounding in empirical evidence. As a rule, the literature review includes:

WRITING A RESEARCH PROPOSAL   257

- a conceptual framework, and theoretical and empirical information about the main issues under study;
- some of the major research findings relating to your topic, research questions raised in the literature and gaps identified by previous researchers.

Your literature review should also raise issues relating to the methodology you are proposing. For example, it may examine how other studies operationalised the major variables of relevance to your study and may include a critique of methodology relevant to your study. The critiques of methods and procedures should be included under their respective headings. For example, a critique of the sampling design you adopt should be included under 'sampling' or a critique to the study design should be discussed under 'study design'.

Note that the suggested research proposal structure does not contain a section entitled 'survey of the literature' or 'literature review'. This is because references to the literature should be integrated with your arguments conceptually rather than chronologically and should become a part of all the aspects of your research report from problem conceptualisation to conclusions drawn from your findings. The literature should be reviewed under main themes that emerge from your reading of the literature and should be included in the introduction and 'research problem' section. Issues identified in the literature to do with research methodology and problems pertinent to the various aspects of research procedures should be discussed under their respective headings. For example, issues pertaining to the study design under 'study design', issues relating to sampling under 'sampling', and the literature pertaining to the research instrument under the 'measurement procedure'.

In suggesting this format it is assumed that you are reasonably well acquainted with research methodology and an academic style of writing. That is, you know how to write a set of objectives or construct a hypothesis, you are familiar with the various study designs and you can construct a research instrument and cite a reference.

The pages that follow outline a framework for a research proposal. The contents under each heading may vary markedly from discipline to discipline, according to the academic level of the student (BA, MA, PhD) and whether your study is predominantly quantitative or qualitative. For quantitative proposals you need to be very specific in proposing how you are going to undertake each step of the research journey, whereas for qualitative research proposals such details are not expected as your methodology is flexible and unstructured to accommodate in-depth search. However, you need to provide a broad approach to your enquiry as a part of your research proposal.

It is here that your exercises, after each operational step, will help you in writing your research proposal. All you need to do is to take the relevant information from these exercises and place it at the appropriate places in your research proposal. Each section of the proposed outline for a research proposal is divided into two parts:

1. a suggested title for the section and an outline of its contents;
2. examples outlining contents for the section – the same four examples of research projects, each taken from a different discipline, are used as illustrations in each section.

258   RESEARCH METHODOLOGY

Before we go into detail, note that the format of a research proposal for a qualitative study or mixed method study is very similar to that for a quantitative one, varying only in content and not structure.

Preamble/introduction

The proposal should start with an introduction to include some of the information listed below. Remember that some of the contents suggested in this section may not be relevant to certain studies, so use your discretion in selecting only what is pertinent to your study. In writing this section, the literature review (see Chapter 3 on reviewing the literature) is of central importance as it serves two main functions:

1. It acquaints you with the available literature in the area of your study, thereby broadening your knowledge base.
2. It provides you with information on the methods and procedures other people have used in similar situations and tells you what works and what does not.

The type, extent and quality of a literature review are mostly dependent upon the academic level for which you are writing the proposal. The contents of this section may also vary greatly according to the subject area under study.

Start with a very broad perspective of the main subject area, before gradually narrowing the focus to the central problem under investigation. In doing so, cover the following aspects of your study area:

- an overview of the main area under study;
- a historical perspective (development, growth, etc.) pertinent to the study area;
- philosophical or ideological issues relating to the topic;
- trends in terms of prevalence, if appropriate;
- major theories, if any;
- the main issues, problems and advances in the subject area under study;
- important theoretical and practical issues relating to the central problem under study;
- the main findings relating to the core issue(s).

Four examples of topics for the preamble/introduction for a research proposal follow.

Example A

Suppose that you are conducting a study to investigate the impact of immigration on family roles. The preamble/introduction should include a brief description of the following:

- The origins of migratory movements in the world.
- General theories developed to explain migratory behaviour.
- The reasons for migration.
- Current trends in migration (national and state).
- The impact of immigration on family roles and relationships (e.g. on husband and wife, on children and parents, on parental expectations of children, etc.).
- Occupational mobility.
- etc.

Example B

Suppose your research project is a study of the attitudes of foster carers towards foster payment in [name of the place/state/country]. The preamble/introduction would include a brief description of the following:

- The origins of foster placement, the philosophy of foster care, a historical overview of foster care and changes over the years.
- Reasons for foster care and changes over time.
- The origins of foster placement in [the country in which you are conducting your study].
- The effects of foster placement on children and parents.
- Policies with respect to foster care in [the region].
- The origins of foster care in [the region].
- Administrative procedures for foster care in [the region].
- The training of foster parents in [the region].
- The role and responsibility of foster parents.
- etc.

Example C

Suppose that you plan to study the relationship between academic achievement and social environment. The preamble/introduction would briefly include the following:

- The role of education in our society.
- Major changes in the philosophy of education over time.
- Factors affecting attitudes towards education.
- The development of education in [country].
- Trends in education participation rates in [country] with particular reference to the region in which the study is being carried out.
- Changing educational values.
- Role of parents and peers in academic achievement.
- Impact of social environment on academic achievement.
- etc.

Example D

Suppose you are undertaking a qualitative study to find out what it means to have a child with ADHD in the family. The preamble/introduction should include your thoughts and arguments, and what the literature says around the following aspects of ADHD.

- Definitions and symptoms of ADHD.
- Causes of ADHD.
- Medical perspective on ADHD.
- Effects of ADHD on family life.
- Treatment for ADHD.
- Implications for a child if untreated.
- Management of ADHD.
- etc.

260   **RESEARCH METHODOLOGY**

The research problem

Having provided a broad introduction to the area under study, now focus on issues relating to its central theme, identifying some of the gaps in the existing body of knowledge. Identify some of the main unanswered questions. Here some of the main research questions that you would like to answer through your study should also be raised, and a rationale and relevance for each should be provided. Knowledge gained from other studies and the literature about the issues you are proposing to investigate should be an integral part of this section. Specifically, this section should:

- identify the issues that are the basis of your study;
- specify the various aspects/perspectives on these issues;
- identify the main gaps in the existing body of knowledge;
- raise some of the main research questions that you want to answer through your study;
- identify what the literature says concerning your research questions, specifying the differences of opinion, if any, in the literature regarding these questions;
- develop a rationale for your study with particular reference to how your study will fill the identified gaps in the existing body of knowledge.

The following examples outline the topics on which the literature should be reviewed and included in the section entitled 'The problem'. Keep in mind that these are just suggestions and should serve only as examples for you to develop and change as you feel appropriate for your own study. (Use information developed in Exercise I in this section.)

Example A

- What settlement process does a family go through after immigration?
- What adjustments do immigrants have to make?
- What types of change can occur in family members' attitudes? (Theory of acculturation etc.)
- What is the possible impact of settlement on family roles and relationships?
- In terms of impact, what specific questions do you want to answer through the study? What does the literature say about these questions? What are the different viewpoints on these issues? What are your own ideas about these questions?
- What do you think will be the relevance of the findings of your study to the existing body of knowledge and to your profession?
- How will the findings add to the body of knowledge and be useful to professionals in your field?
- etc.

Example B

- What are the broad issues, debates, arguments and counter-arguments regarding foster-care payment?
- What are the attitudes of foster parents to the amount, mode and form of payment and what does the literature say about these issues?
- What are the different viewpoints/perspectives regarding payment for foster care?
- What main questions will your study answer?
- How will your findings help in policy formulation and programme development?
- etc.

Example C

- What theories have been developed to explain the relationship between academic achievement and social environment?
- What is the relationship between educational achievement and social environment: what theoretical model will be the basis of your study?
- What do previous theories and researches have to say regarding the components of the theoretical model and academic achievement? For example, the relationship between academic achievement and:

    - the self-esteem and aspirations/motivation of a student;
    - peer group influence;
    - parental involvement and its relationship with their socioeconomic status;
    - the motivation and interest of students in the subject;
    - employment prospects;
    - relationship with a teacher;
    - etc.

Example D

- What are the effects on the family of having a child with ADHD in the family, as identified in the literature?
- According to the literature, are there any differences between these effects and the type of family?
- What strategies have been used for the management of ADHD by a family?
- What effects, according to the literature, does ADHD have on sibling relationships?
- What are the perceptions of family members about the effects and management of ADHD?
- How do families cope when they have a child with ADHD in the family?
- etc.

Objectives of the study

In this section include a statement of both your study's main objective and subobjectives (see Chapter 4). Your main objective indicates the central thrust of your study, whereas the subobjectives identify the specific issues you propose to examine.

The objectives of the study should be clearly stated and specific in nature. Each subobjective should delineate only one issue. Use action-oriented verbs such as 'to determine', 'to find out' and 'to ascertain' in formulating subobjectives, which should be numerically listed. If the objective is to test a hypothesis, you must follow the conventions of hypothesis formulation in wording the specific objectives.

In qualitative studies the statement of objectives is not as precise as in quantitative studies. In qualitative studies you should simply mention an overall objective of the study, as your aim is to explore as much as possible as you go along. As you know, the strength of qualitative research is in flexibility of approach and the ability to incorporate new ideas while collecting data. Having structured statements that bind you to a predetermined framework of exploration is not a preferred convention in qualitative research. Statements that you intend to explore 'what it means to have a child with ADHD in the family', 'how it feels to be a victim of domestic violence', 'how people cope with racial discrimination', 'the relationship between resilience and yoga' or 'reconstructing life after a bushfire', are sufficient to communicate your intent of objectives in qualitative research. More detailed objectives, if need be, can be developed after a study is complete. (Use information developed in Exercise I in this section.)

Example A

Main objective:

To ascertain the impact of immigration on the family.

Subobjectives:

To determine the impact of immigration on husband/wife roles as perceived by immigrants.
To find out the impact of immigration on marital relations.
To ascertain perceived changes in parental expectations of children's academic and professional achievement.
To determine perceived changes of attitude towards marriage in the study population.

Example B

Main objective:

To determine the opinion of foster carers about the form and extent of foster payment they feel they should receive for taking care of a foster child.

Subobjectives:

To determine the form and mode of payment for taking care of a foster child.
To identify the factors that foster parents believe should be the basis for determining the rate of payment for fostering a child.
To determine the relationship, if any, between the socioeconomic-demographic characteristics of foster parents and their views on payment.

Example C

Main objective:

To examine the relationship between academic achievement and social environment.

Subobjectives:

To find out the relationship, if any, between self-esteem and a student's academic achievement at school.
To ascertain the association between parental involvement in a student's studies and his/her academic achievement at school.
To examine the links between a student's peer group and academic achievement.
To explore the relationship between academic achievement and the attitude of a student towards teachers.

Example D

Main objective:

To explore what it means to have a child with ADHD in the family.

Hypotheses to be tested

A hypothesis is a statement of your assumptions about the prevalence of a phenomenon or about a relationship between two variables that you plan to test within the framework of the study (sees Chapter 6). If you are going to test hypotheses, list them in this section. (Use the information developed in Exercise II in this section.)

When formulating a hypothesis you have an obligation to draw conclusions about it in the text of the report. Hypotheses have a particular style of formulation. You must be acquainted with the correct way of wording them. In a study you may have as many hypotheses as you want to test. However, it is *not* essential to have a hypothesis in order to undertake a study – you can conduct a perfectly satisfactory study without formulating a hypothesis.

Example A

H_1 = In most cases there will be a change in husband/wife roles after immigration.
H_2 = In a majority of cases there will be a change in parents' expectations of their children.
H_i = etc.

Example B

H_1 = Most people become foster parents because of their love of children.
H_2 = A majority of foster parents would like to be trained to care for foster children.
H_i = etc.

Example C

H_1 = A student's self-esteem and academic achievement at school are positively correlated.
H_2 = The greater the parental involvement in a student's studies, the higher the academic achievement.
H_3 = A student's attitude towards teachers is positively correlated with his/her academic achievement in that subject.
H_i = etc.

Example D

Hypotheses are usually not constructed in qualitative research.

Study design

Describe the study design (for details see Chapter 8) you plan to use to answer your research questions. (For example, say whether it is a case study, descriptive, cross-sectional, before-and-after, experimental or non-experimental design.) Identify the strengths and weaknesses of your study design.

Include details about the various logistical procedures you intend to follow while executing the study design. One characteristic of a good study design is that it explains the details with such clarity that, if someone else wants to follow the proposed procedure, s/he will be able to do exactly as you would have done. Your study design should include information about the following:

- Who makes up the study population?
- Can each element of the study population be identified? If yes, how?
- Will a sample or the total population be studied?
- How will you get in touch with the selected sample?
- How will the sample's consent to participate in the study be sought?
- How will the data be collected (e.g. by interview, questionnaire or observation)?
- In the case of a mailed questionnaire, to what address should the questionnaire be returned?
- Are you planning to send a reminder regarding the return of questionnaires?
- How will confidentiality be preserved?
- How and where can respondents contact you if they have queries?

(Use information developed in Exercise III in this section.)

Example A

The study is primarily designed to find out from a cross-section of immigrants from [names of countries] the perceived impact of immigration on family roles. Initial contact with the ethnic associations for these countries will be made through the elected office bearers to obtain a list of members. Five immigrants will be selected from the list at random, and will be contacted by phone to explain the purpose of the study and its relevance, and to seek their agreement to participate in the study. Those who give their consent will be interviewed at their homes or any other convenient place. To select a further sample, a snowball sampling technique will be used until the desired sample size is obtained.

Example B

The study design is cross-sectional in nature, being designed to find out from a cross-section of foster parents their opinions about foster payment. All foster parents currently registered with [department name] constitute the study population. From the existing records of this department it seems that there are 457 foster parents in [name of region]. As it is impossible for the researcher, within the constraints of time and money, to collect information from all the foster parents, it is proposed to select a sample of 50 per cent of the study population with the proposed sampling strategy. The questionnaire, with a supporting letter from the department, will be sent with a prepaid envelope. The respondents will be requested to return the questionnaire by [date]. The letter from the researcher attached to the questionnaire will explain the objectives and relevance of the study, assure the respondents of anonymity and give them the option of not participating in the study if they wish.

A contact number will be provided in case a respondent has any questions. In the case of a low response rate (less than 25 per cent), a reminder will be sent to respondents.

Example C

It is proposed that the study will be carried out in two government high schools in the metropolitan area. The principals of the schools most accessible to the researcher will be contacted to explain the purpose of the study and the help needed from the school, and to seek their permission for the students to participate in the study. As the constraints of time and resources do not permit the researcher to select more than two schools, negotiations with other schools will cease when two schools agree to participate in the study.

It is proposed to select year 9 students as the academic achievement of students in years 8 and 10 could be affected by factors unique to them. Year 8 students may be experiencing anxiety as a result of having just made the transition to a new system. The motivation of students in year 10 could be affected by their being at the stage in their education where they must decide if they will stay on at school.

In order to control the variance attributable to the gender of a student it is proposed to select only male students.

Once the principal of a school agrees to allow the study to be carried out, the researcher will brief the teacher in charge about the study and its relevance, and will arrange a date and time for administering the questionnaire.

When the students are assembled, ready to participate in the study, the researcher will explain its purpose and relevance, and then distribute the questionnaire. The researcher will remain with the class to answer any questions the students might have.

Example D

The researcher is known to a family that has a child with ADHD and that belongs to an ADHD support group which meets every month. The researcher proposes to make initial contact with the group through the known family. The researcher will attend one of the monthly meetings and brief the group on the purpose and relevance of the study, criteria for inclusion in the study, what it entails to be involved in the study, and other aspects of the study. The respondents will also be assured of the anonymity of the information shared by them and its ethical use. The members of the group will be encouraged to ask questions about any aspect of the study. Having sought their consent, the researcher will seek opinions of group members to decide who should participate in the study in light of the inclusion criteria.

It is proposed to select six families, three where both parents are involved in the treatment and management of an ADHD child and three from families where the mother is the sole carer. This is primarily to see if there are differences in looking after a child with ADHD among different types of family.

The potential respondents will be individually contacted by the researcher to seek their consent for participation in the study. Once consent has been obtained the place and timings for interviews will be fixed with each family. Depending upon the type of family, the issues will be discussed either collectively with the father and mother or with the mother only.

Before starting an interview, their permission to tape-record the interview will be sought. Having completed the interviews, the researcher will transcribe the responses and a copy will be given to the respondents for confirmation and validation.

The setting

Briefly describe the organisation, agency or community in which you will conduct your study. If the study is about a group of people, highlight some of the salient characteristics of the group (e.g. its history, size, composition and structure) and draw attention to any available relevant information.

If your research concerns an agency, office or organisation, include the following in your description:

- the main services provided by the agency, office or organisation;
- its administrative structure;
- the type of clients served;
- information about the issues that are central to your research.

If you are studying a community, briefly describe some of the main characteristics, such as:

- the size of the community;
- a brief social profile of the community (i.e. the composition of the various groups within it);
- issues of relevance to the central theme of your study.

Note that, due to the nature of the content, it would be difficult to provide examples.

Measurement procedures

This section should contain a discussion of your instrument (see Chapters 9 and 10) and the details of how you plan to operationalise your major variables (Chapter 5).

To start with, justify your choice of research tool, highlighting its strengths and pointing out its weaknesses. Then outline the major segments of your research tool and their relevance to the main objectives of the study. If you are using a standard instrument, briefly discuss the availability of evidence on its reliability and validity. If you adapt or modify it in any way, describe and explain the changes you have made.

You should also discuss how you are going to operationalise the major concepts. For example, if measuring effectiveness, specify how it will be measured. If you plan to measure the self-esteem of a group of people, mention the main indicators of self-esteem and the procedures for its measurement (e.g. the Likert or Thurstone scale, or any other procedure).

Ideally, for quantitative studies you should attach a copy of the research instrument to your proposal.

(Information developed in Exercise III should be incorporated here.)

Note that, due to the nature of the content, it would be difficult to provide examples for this section.

Ethical issues

All academic institutions are particular about any ethical implications of research. To deal with them, all institutions have some form of policy on ethics. You need to be acquainted with your institution's policy. It is imperative that in your proposal you identify any ethical issues and describe how you propose to deal with them. You need to look at the ethical issues particularly from the viewpoint of your respondents and, in case of any potential 'harm', psychological or otherwise, you need to detail the mechanism in place to deal with it. Further information on ethical issues

ETHICS GUIDEBOOK   is provided in Chapter 14. (Use information provide in Exercise III here.)

Sampling

Under this section of the proposal include the following:

- the size of the sampling population (if known) and from where and how this information will be obtained;
- the size of the sample you are planning to select and your reasons for choosing this size;
- an explanation of the sampling design you are proposing to use in the selection of the sample (simple random sampling, stratified random sampling, quota sampling, etc.).

(Your Exercise IV will provide you all the information you need to complete this section. Also consult Chapter 12 on sampling.)

Example A

Because the lack of information as to the exact location of migrant families makes it difficult to use a probability sampling design, it is proposed that the researcher will employ a snowball sampling technique. The researcher will make initial contact with five families who have emigrated from [name of country] during the past seven to ten years, who are either known to him/her or on the basis of information obtained from the office bearers of the formal associations representing the migrant groups. From each respondent the researcher will obtain names and addresses of other immigrants who have come from the same country during the same period. The respondents thus identified will then be interviewed and asked to identify other respondents for the researcher. This process will continue until the researcher has interviewed 70 respondents.

Example B

Because of the constraints of time and resources it is proposed to select 50 per cent of the foster parents currently registered (457) with the department using the systematic random sampling technique. Every other foster parent registered with the department will be selected, thus 229 individuals will constitute the sample for the study.

Example C

The selection of schools will be done primarily through quota sampling. Schools will be selected on the basis of their geographical proximity to the researcher. The researcher will prepare a list of schools, in rank order, of accessibility. Once two schools agree to participate in the study, negotiations with other schools will cease.

All year 9 male students will constitute the study population. It is expected that the sample will not exceed 100 students.

Example D

It is proposed to use the judgemental/purposive sampling technique to select six families from the group, three where both parents look after an ADHD child and three where only the mother has the main responsibility (single parent families). On the basis of informal discussions with the group members, those families who are expected to be information-rich in treating and managing a child with ADHD will be selected to be interviewed.

Analysis of data

Describe in general terms the strategy you intend to use for data analysis (Chapter 15). Specify whether the data will be analysed manually or by computer. For computer analysis, identify the program and where appropriate the statistical procedures you plan to perform on the data. For quantitative studies also identify the main variables for cross-tabulation.

For qualitative studies, describe how you plan to analyse your interviews or observation notes to draw meaning from what your respondents have said about issues discussed or observation notes made. One of the common techniques is to identify main themes by analysing the content of the information gathered in the field. You first need to decide whether you want to analyse this information manually or use a computer program for the purpose.

There are three ways to proceed with content analysis:

1. From your field notes develop a framework for your write-up and, as you go through your notes, directly integrate that information within the structure developed. If you adopt this method, you need to be reasonably clear about the structure. It does not mean that you cannot develop the structure as you go on analysing; still, a clear vision will be of immense help in slotting information gathered in the field by you into the write-up.
2. The second method is to transcribe your field notes so that you can read them over and over again to identify the main themes. These themes become the basis of your write-up.
3. There are computer programs such as NUD*IST, Ethnograph and NVivo specifically designed to handle descriptive data. You may prefer to use one of these programs. These programs are also based upon the principle of content analysis. The only difference is that instead of your searching manually, they identify where a particular text identifying the theme appears.

You need to specify which particular strategy you are proposing for data analysis for your study.

Example A

Frequency distributions in terms of:

- age;
- education;

- occupation;
- number of children;
- duration of immigration;
- etc.

Cross-tabulations of impact of husband/wife roles by:

- age;
- number of children;
- education;
- occupation;
- etc.

Example B

Frequency distributions in terms of:

- age;
- income;
- education;
- occupation;
- marital status;
- duration of foster care;
- number of foster children;
- etc.

Cross-tabulations of attitude towards foster payment by:

- age;
- number of children;
- education;
- occupation;
- etc.

Statistical tests to be applied:

- chi-square;
- regression analysis;
- etc.

Example C

Frequency distributions in terms of:

- age;
- parents' occupation;
- parents' educational levels;
- students' occupational aspirations;
- parental involvement in students' studies;
- self-esteem;

- peer group influence;
- number of hours spent on studies;
- etc.

Cross-tabulations of academic achievement by:

- peer group influence;
- parental involvement in students' studies;
- self-esteem;
- occupational aspirations;
- attitude towards teachers;
- etc.

Example D

The in-depth interviews carried out with the families will be transcribed using Microsoft Word. These transcribed interviews will be closely studied to identify the main themes they communicate. These themes will be sorted by issues relating to management and treatment of a child with ADHD. The themes will then become part of the write-up.

Structure of the report

As clearly as possible, state how you intend to organise the final report (see Chapter 17 and refer to your Exercise VII). In organising your material for the report, the specific objectives of your study are of immense help. Plan to develop your chapters around the main themes of your study. The title of each chapter should clearly communicate the main thrust of its contents.

The first chapter, possibly entitled 'Introduction', should be an overall introduction to your study, covering most of your project proposal and pointing out deviations, if any, from the original plan.

The second chapter should provide some information about the study population itself – that is, some of its socioeconomic-demographic characteristics. The main aim of this chapter is to give readers some background on the population from which you collected the information. The chapter may therefore be entitled 'Socioeconomic-demographic characteristics of the study population' or 'The study population' or any other title that communicates this theme to readers. Titles for the rest of the chapters will vary from study to study but, as mentioned, each chapter should be written around a main theme. Although the wording of chapter titles is an individual choice, each must communicate the main theme of the chapter. In developing these themes the specific objectives of the study should be kept in the front of your mind.

If your study is qualitative, the main issues identified during data collection and analysis stages should become the basis for developing the various chapters. Having developed significant issues, the next step is to organise the main themes under each issue and develop a structure that you will follow to communicate your findings to your readers.

Example A

It is proposed that the report will be divided into the following chapters:

Chapter 1: Introduction
Chapter 2: The socioeconomic-demographic characteristics of the study population
Chapter 3: The impact on husband/wife roles
Chapter 4: The impact on marital relations
Chapter 5: The impact on expectations of children
Chapter 6: The impact on attitudes towards marriage
Chapter 7: Summary, conclusions and recommendations

Example B

The study will be divided into the following chapters:

Chapter 1: Introduction
Chapter 2: A profile of the study population
Chapter 3: Foster carers' perceptions of their role
Chapter 4: Attitudes of foster carers towards foster-care payment
Chapter 5: The preferred method of payment
Chapter 6: General comments made by respondents about foster care
Chapter 7: Summary, conclusions and recommendations

Example C

It is proposed that the report will have the following chapters:

Chapter 1: Introduction
Chapter 2: The study population
Chapter 3: Occupational aspirations, self-esteem and academic achievement
Chapter 4: The extent of parental involvement and academic achievement
Chapter 5: Peer group influence and academic achievement
Chapter 6: Academic achievement and student attitudes towards teachers
Chapter 7: Summary, conclusions and recommendations

Example D

It is proposed that the report will have the following chapters:

Chapter 1: Introduction
Chapter 2: ADHD: A theoretical perspective
Chapter 3: Issues and difficulties faced by family members in bringing up a child with ADHD
Chapter 4: ADHD and its perceived effects on the child
Chapter 5: ADHD and its perceived impact on sibling relationships
Chapter 6: Managing ADHD treatment
Chapter 7: Perceived effects of ADHD on schooling of the child
Chapter 8: Perceived effects of ADHD on relationships with other children

Problems and limitations

This section should list any problems you think you might encounter concerning, for example, the availability of data, securing permission from the agency/organisation to carry out the study, obtaining the sample, or any other aspect of the study.

You will not have unlimited resources and, as this may be primarily an academic exercise, you may have to do less than an ideal job. However, it is important to be aware of – and communicate – any limitations that could affect the validity of your conclusions and generalisations.

Here, the word *problems* refers to difficulties relating to logistical details; *limitations*, on the other hand, are structural problems relating to methodological aspects of the study – for example, if in your opinion the study design you proposed may not be the best but you adopted it for a number of considerations. This is also true for sampling or measurement procedures. Such limitations should be communicated to readers.

Appendix

Your proposal must include a list of references as an appendix. For a quantitative study, also attach your research instrument.

Work schedule

PLANNING A
TIMELINE

You must set yourself deadlines to reflect the fact that you need to complete the research within a certain time-frame. List the various operational steps you need to undertake and indicate against each the date by which you aim to complete it, having carefully considered how long you will need. Remember to keep some time towards the end as a 'cushion' in case the research process does not go as smoothly as planned. Develop a chart as shown in Table 13.1.

Budget

FUNDING AND
BUDGETING

It is a good idea to have some estimate as to what the study is going to cost and ensure the availability of funds. Though most of the work that you will do is 'free', there are aspects of a study on which money will have to be spent. Think through and identify where you need to spend the money and how much. Where you need to spend, to a large extent, depends upon the type of study you are undertaking. The main difference in the cost is dependent upon two things: the method of data collection and the sample size. All other aspects of a study, irrespective of its design, would more or less entail similar expenses. Table 13.2 applies to most studies, but you can add others that are specific to yours.

WRITING A RESEARCH PROPOSAL   273

Table 13.1   Developing a time-frame for your study

Tasks (Any tasks which you consider important)	1	2	3	4	5	6	7	8	9	10	11	12	13	14	15
To be completed by (weeks or months)															
Proposal writing		→————→													
Instrument finalisation			→————→												
Data collection						→————→									
Coding								→————→							
Data analysis										→————→					
Report/first/second/third										→————————————→					
Report/final											→————————→				
Typing											→————————→				

Table 13.2   Estimated cost of the study

Aspects of the study	Approximate cost
Printing of the interview schedule or questionnaire	$ ...
Use of telephone	$ ...
Travel	$ ...
Preparation of the report	$ ...
Stationery	$ ....
etc.	
Total	
	$ ....

Summary

A research proposal details the operational plan for obtaining answers to research questions. It must tell your supervisor and others what you propose to do, how you plan to proceed and why the chosen strategy has been selected. It thus assures readers of the validity of the methodology used to obtain answers accurately and objectively.

The guidelines set out in this chapter provide only a framework within which a research proposal for both quantitative and qualitative studies should be written and assume that you are reasonably well acquainted with research methodology and an academic style of writing. The contents of your proposal are arranged under the following headings: preamble/introduction, the broad research problem or issue under study, objectives of the study, hypotheses to be tested, study design, setting, measurement procedures, sampling, analysis of data, structure of the report, and problems and limitations. The specifics, under each heading, will vary with the type of study you are proposing to undertake. The write-up for qualitative studies will be based upon qualitative methodology, and quantitative methodology will determine the contents of quantitative studies.

The 'preamble' or 'introduction' introduces the main area of the study. Start with a broad literature review, gradually narrowing it down to the specific problem you are investigating.

The theoretical framework should be a part of this section. The next section, 'the problem', details the specific problem under study. The research questions for which you are planning to find answers are raised in this section. 'Objectives of the study' contains your main objectives and your subobjectives. Hypotheses, if any, should be listed in the 'hypotheses to be tested' section. The logistical procedures you intend to follow are detailed under 'study design'. 'The setting' consists of a description of the organisation or community in which you plan to conduct your study. The procedure for obtaining information and the measurement of major variables are explained in the 'measurement procedures' section. You need to write about ethical issues that your study might have and how you propose to deal with them. How you will select your sample is described under 'sampling'. The procedure for data analysis is discussed under 'analysis of data'. The way you plan to structure your report is outlined under 'structure of the report'. Anticipated problems in conducting the study and limitations with its design are described under 'problems and limitations'. As an appendix to your proposal attach a copy of the research instrument and a list of the references. The differences in research proposals for quantitative and qualitative studies are mostly in content and not in structure. Their contents should be methodology-specific.

A work schedule provides a time-frame for your study.

FOR YOU TO THINK ABOUT

- Refamiliarise yourself with the keywords listed at the beginning of this chapter, and if you are uncertain about the meaning or application of any of them revisit them in the chapter before moving on.
- Compare the research proposal contents suggested in this chapter with those recommended by your university or department. If they are different, what are the differences?
- Find out the process that a research proposal goes through in your university before approval is granted.

Now, as you have gone through the chapter, try answering the following questions:

- What are the differences in a research proposal written for quantitative and qualitative studies?
- Critically examine the contents, as suggested in this chapter, of a research proposal.
- How has working through the exercises at the end of the each step helped you to complete your research proposal?

Want to learn more? Visit
http://www.uk.sagepub.com/kumar4e
or scan this QR code to gain access to a range of online resources to support your study including practice quizzes, videos, weblinks, flashcards, and journal articles.

Exercise V: Writing a research proposal

TEMPLATE OF
EXERCISE V

In your research journey, you have now reached a point where you can think of putting together your research proposal even though you have not yet covered everything that needs to be included in the proposal.

In this exercise you need, in the light of the contents proposed in Chapter 13, to decide on an outline specifically for your research proposal and start putting together the material already developed in other exercises.

As suggested, the outline for a research proposal for quantitative, qualitative or mixed methods studies is the same. The difference is only in the contents which are already described in this book. Look at Chapter 13 again and extract the relevant information from the various exercises you have already done to complete your research proposal.

Your proposal should be written in an academic style, incorporating appropriate references in the body of the text, integrating your literature review at relevant places in a thematic rather than chronological manner, raising your research questions, specifying the objectives of your study and detailing the whole procedure that you propose to go through in undertaking your research journey in a clear and succinct manner.

Follow the outline below in completing this exercise. Keep in mind that you have already completed most of the tasks when completing the exercises attached to each operational step.

The points given in the following outline are merely prompts. You need to work through them with a lot more depth and understanding. As mentioned, you have already done most of the work; here you only need to put it together.

Good luck, you are nearly there!!!

Introduction

_____

_____

_____

_____

Objectives of the study

_____

_____

_____

_____

Hypotheses to be tested (if applicable)

_____

_____

_____

_____

Study design

_____
_____
_____
_____
_____

Setting of the study

_____
_____
_____
_____

Research instrument

_____
_____
_____
_____

Sampling design

_____
_____
_____
_____
_____

Ethical issues

_____
_____
_____
_____

Data processing

_____
_____
_____
_____

Proposed chapters of the report

_____
_____
_____
_____

EXERCISE V   277

Problems and limitations of the study

_____
_____
_____
_____

Proposed time-frame

_____
_____
_____
_____

Proposed budget

_____
_____
_____
_____

STEP VI
COLLECTING DATA

This operational step includes one chapter to make you aware of the ethical issues in research:

- Chapter 14: Considering ethical issues in data collection

14

CONSIDERING ETHICAL ISSUES IN DATA COLLECTION

In this chapter you will learn about

- Ethics: the concept
- Stakeholders in research
- Ethical issues to consider concerning research participants
- Ethical issues to consider relating to the researcher
- Ethical issues to consider regarding the sponsoring organisation

Keywords		
bias, code of conduct, confidentiality, deprivation of treatment, ethos,	harm, informed consent, principles of conduct, research participants,	sensitive information, sponsoring organisations, stakeholders, subjectivity.

At the end of this chapter, you should have an understanding of

- The concept of ethics as used in social research
- The various stakeholders in social research
- Ethical issues from the viewpoints of various stakeholders

Ethics: the concept

All professions are guided by a code of ethics that has evolved over the years to accommodate the changing ethos, values, needs and expectations of those who hold a stake in the professions. Some professions are more advanced than others in terms of the level of development of their code of ethics. Some have very strict guidelines, monitor conduct effectively and take appropriate steps against those who do not abide by the guidelines.

Most professions have an overall code of conduct that also governs the way they carry out research. In addition, many research bodies have evolved a code of ethics separately for research. Medicine, epidemiology, business, law, education, psychology and other social sciences have well-established codes of ethics for research.

Let us first examine what we mean by 'ethics' or 'ethical behaviour'. According to the *Collins Dictionary* (1979: 502), ethical means 'in accordance with principles of conduct that are considered correct, especially those of a given profession or group'. The key phrases here, 'principles of conduct' and 'considered correct', raise certain questions:

- What are these principles of conduct?
- Who determines them?
- In whose judgement must they be considered correct?

Closely related questions are as follows:

- Are there universal principles of conduct that can be applied to all professions?
- Do these change with time and should they change?
- What happens when a professional does not abide by them?

The subject of ethics needs to be considered in light of these questions.

The way each profession serves society is continuously changing in accordance with society's needs and expectations and with the technology available for the delivery of a service. The ethical codes governing the manner in which a service is delivered also need to change. What has been considered ethical in the past may not be so judged at present, and what is ethical now may not remain so in the future. Any judgement about whether a particular practice is ethical is made on the basis of the code of conduct prevalent at that point in time.

As the service and its manner of delivery differ from profession to profession, no code of conduct can be uniformly applied across all professions. Each profession has its own code of ethics, though there are commonalities. If you want guidelines on ethical conduct for a particular profession, you need to consult the code of ethics adopted by that profession or discipline.

'What are these principles of conduct?' is the most important question as it addresses the issue of the contents of ethical practice in a profession. As the code of conduct varies from profession to profession, it is not possible to provide a universal answer to this question. However, in research, any dilemma stemming from a moral quandary is a basis of unethical conduct. There are certain behaviours in research – such as causing harm to individuals, breaching confidentiality, using information improperly and introducing bias – that are considered unethical in any profession.

The next question is: in whose judgement must a code of conduct be considered correct? Who decides whether a particular practice is wrong? If a procedure is carried out wrongly, what penalties should be imposed? It is the overall body of professionals or government organisations that collectively develops a professional code of conduct and forms a judgement as to whether or not it is being followed.

As mentioned, most professions have established an overall code of ethics and also a code of ethics for conducting research in their respective fields. As this book is designed for researchers in the social sciences, we will examine ethical issues relating to research in general and issues that are applicable to most social science disciplines.

Stakeholders in research

There are many stakeholders in research, whether it is quantitative, qualitative or mixed methods. It is important to look at ethical issues in relation to each of them. The various stakeholders in a research activity are:

1. the research participants or subjects;
2. the researcher;
3. the funding body.

Who should be considered as a research participant varies from profession to profession. Generally, all those with direct and indirect involvement in a research study are considered as research participants, hence stakeholders. In addition, those who are likely to be affected by the findings of a study are also considered as stakeholders. In the fields of medicine, public health, epidemiology and nursing, patients and non-patients who become part of a study and those who participate in an experiment to test the effectiveness of a drug or treatment are considered as research participants. Even the participants of a control group in an experiment are considered to be stakeholders. Service providers, service managers and planners who are involved in either providing the service or collecting information relating to the

ETHICAL ISSUES IN DATA COLLECTION   283

service are also stakeholders in the research. In the social sciences, the participants include individuals, groups and communities providing information to help a researcher to gain understanding of a phenomenon, situation, issue or interaction. In social work and psychology, participants include clients as well as non-clients of an agency from whom information is collected to find out the magnitude of a problem, the needs of a community or the effectiveness of an intervention; and service providers, social workers and psychologists, when they provide information for a study. In marketing, consumers as well as non-consumers of a product provide information about consumption patterns and behaviour. In education, subjects include students, teachers and perhaps the community at large who participate in educational research activities. Similarly, in any discipline in which a research activity is undertaken, those from whom information is collected or those who are studied by a researcher become participants of the study.

Researchers constitute the second category of stakeholders. Anyone who collects information for the specific purpose of understanding, consolidation, enhancement and development of professional knowledge, adhering to the accepted code of conduct, is a researcher. S/he may represent any academic discipline.

Funding organisations responsible for financing a research activity fall into the third category of stakeholders. Most research is carried out using funds provided by business organisations, pharmaceutical companies, service institutions (government, quasi-government or voluntary), research bodies and/or academic institutions. The funds are given for specific purposes.

Each category of stakeholders in a research activity may have different interests, perspectives, purposes, aims and motivations that could affect the way in which the research activity is carried out and the way results are communicated and used. Because of this, it is important to ensure that research is not affected by the self-interest of any party and is not carried out in a way that harms any party. It is therefore essential to examine ethical conduct in research concerning different stakeholders under separate categories.

Ethical issues to consider concerning research participants

There are many ethical issues to consider in relation to the participants in a research activity.

Collecting information

One might ask: why should a respondent give any information to a researcher? What right does a researcher have to knock on someone's door or to send out a questionnaire? Is it ethical to disturb an individual, even if you ask permission before asking questions? Why should a person give you his/her time? Your request for information may create anxiety or put pressure on a respondent. Is this ethical?

But these questions display a naive attitude. It is an attitude that prevents all progress in the world. Research is required in order to improve conditions. Provided any piece of research is likely to help society directly or indirectly, it is acceptable to ask questions, if you first obtain the respondents' informed consent. Before you begin collecting information, you must consider the relevance and usefulness of the research you are undertaking and also be able to convince others of this. If you cannot justify the relevance of the research you are conducting, you are wasting your respondents' time, which is unethical.

Seeking informed consent

SAMPLE CONSENT
FORMS

In every discipline it is considered unethical to collect information without the knowledge of participants, and their expressed willingness and informed consent. Seeking informed consent 'is probably the most common method in medical and social research' (Bailey 1978: 384). Informed consent implies that subjects are made adequately aware of the type of information you want from them, why the information is being sought, what purpose it will be put to, how they are expected to participate in the study, and how it will directly or indirectly affect them. It is important that the consent should also be voluntary and without pressure of any kind. Schinke and Gilchrist (1993: 83) write:

> Under standards set by the National Commission for the Protection of Human Subjects, all informed-consent procedures must meet three criteria: participants must be competent to give consent; sufficient information must be provided to allow for a reasoned decision; and consent must be voluntary and uncoerced.

Competency, according to Schinke and Gilchrist (1993: 83), 'is concerned with the legal and mental capacities of participants to give permission'. For example, some very old people, those suffering from conditions that exclude them from making informed decisions, people in crisis, people who cannot speak the language in which the research is being carried out, people who are dependent upon you for a service, and children are not considered to be in a position to give informed consent.

Providing incentives

Is it ethical to provide incentives to respondents for sharing information with you? Some researchers provide incentives to participants for their participation in a study, feeling this to be quite proper as participants are giving their time. Others think that the offering of inducements is unethical.

INCENTIVES

In the author's experience most people do not participate in a study because of incentives, but because they realise the importance of the study. Therefore, giving a small gift after having obtained your information, as a token of appreciation, is in the author's opinion not unethical. However, giving a present before data collection is unethical.

Seeking sensitive information

Information sought can pose an ethical dilemma in research. Certain types of information can be regarded as sensitive or confidential by some people, and thus seeking it constitutes an invasion of privacy. Asking for this information may upset or embarrass a respondent. However, if you do not ask for the information, it may not be possible to pursue your interest in the area and contribute to the existing body of knowledge.

ETHICAL ISSUES IN DATA COLLECTION   285

For most people, questions on sexual behaviour, drug use and shoplifting are intrusive. Even questions on marital status, income and age may be considered to be an invasion of privacy by some. In collecting data you need to be careful about the sensitivities of your respondents.

The dilemma you face as a researcher is whether you should ask sensitive and intrusive questions. In the author's opinion it is not unethical to ask such questions provided that you clearly and frankly tell your respondents the type of information you are going to ask, assure them of the confidentiality of the information, keep the information confidential and give them sufficient time to decide if they want to share the information with you, without any major inducement.

The possibility of causing harm to participants

FAMOUS UNETHICAL STUDIES

Is the research going to harm participants in any way? Harm includes 'not only hazardous medical experiments but also any social research that might involve such things as discomfort, anxiety, harassment, invasion of privacy, or demeaning or dehumanising procedures' (Bailey 1978: 384).

When you collect data from respondents or involve subjects in an experiment, you need to examine carefully whether their involvement is likely to harm them in any way. If it is, you must make sure that the risk is minimal. Minimum risk means that the extent of harm or discomfort in the research is not greater than that ordinarily encountered in daily life. It is unethical if the way you seek information creates anxiety or harassment, and if you think it may happen, you need to take steps to prevent it.

Maintaining confidentiality

CONFIDENTIALITY

Sharing information about a respondent with others for purposes other than research is unethical. Sometimes you need to identify your study population to put your findings into context. In such a situation you need to make sure that at least the information provided by respondents is kept anonymous. It is unethical to identify an individual respondent and the information provided by him/her. Therefore, you need to ensure that after the information has been collected, its source cannot be identified. In certain types of study you might need to visit respondents repeatedly, in which case you will have to identify them until the completion of your visits. In such situations you need to be extra careful that others do not have access to the information. It is unethical to be negligent in not protecting the confidentiality and anonymity of the information gathered from your respondents. If you are doing research for someone else, you need to make sure that confidentiality is maintained by this party as well.

Ethical issues to consider relating to the researcher

Avoiding bias

Bias on the part of the researcher is unethical. Bias is different from subjectivity. Subjectivity, as mentioned earlier, is a way of thinking that you develop due to such factors as your educational background, training, professional background, competence in research, overall intellectual capabilities, and philosophical perspective. Because of these you develop a way of looking at and interpreting things which could be different from that of others. You do not deliberately alter but interpret them differently, much as an economist will look at things differently than a psychologist or a doctor. Bias is a deliberate attempt either to hide what you have found in your study, or to highlight something disproportionately to its true existence. It is absolutely unethical to introduce bias into a research activity. If you are unable to control your bias, you should not be engaging in the research. Remember, it is the bias that is unethical and not the subjectivity.

Provision or deprivation of a treatment

Both the provision and deprivation of a treatment may pose an ethical dilemma for the researcher. When testing an intervention or a treatment, a researcher usually adopts a control experiment design. In such studies, is it ethical to provide a study population with an intervention or treatment that has not yet been conclusively proven effective or beneficial? But if you do not test a treatment/intervention, how can you prove or disprove its effectiveness or benefits? On the other hand, you are providing an intervention that may not be effective. Is this ethical? Is it ethical to deprive the control group of a treatment even if it may prove to be only slightly effective? And beyond the issue of control groups, is it ethical to deprive people who are struggling for life of the possible benefit, however small, which may be derived from a drug that is only under trial? As a researcher you need to be aware of these ethical issues. There are arguments and counter-arguments about these issues. However, it is usually accepted that deprivation of a trial treatment to a control group is not unethical as, in the absence of this, a study can never establish the effectiveness of a treatment which may deprive many others of its possible benefits. This deprivation of the possible benefits, on the other hand, is considered by some as unethical.

There are no simple answers to these dilemmas. Ensuring informed consent, 'minimum risk' and frank discussion as to the implications of participation in the study may help to resolve some of these ethical issues.

Using inappropriate research methodology

A researcher has an obligation to use appropriate methodology, within his/her knowledge base, in conducting a study. It is unethical to use deliberately a method or procedure you know to be inappropriate, such as by selecting a highly biased sample, using an invalid instrument or drawing wrong conclusions.

Incorrect reporting

To report the findings in a way that changes or slants them to serve your own or someone else's interest is unethical. Correct and unbiased reporting of the findings is an important characteristic of ethical research practice.

ETHICAL ISSUES IN DATA COLLECTION   287

Inappropriate use of information

How will the information obtained from respondents be used by the researcher? The use of information in a way that directly or indirectly affects respondents adversely is unethical. Can information be used adversely to affect the study population? If so, how can the study population be protected? As a researcher you need to consider and resolve these issues. Sometimes it is possible to harm individuals in the process of achieving benefits for organisations. An example would be a study to examine the feasibility of restructuring an organisation. Restructuring may be beneficial to the organisation as a whole but may be harmful to some individuals. Should you ask respondents for information that is likely to be used against them? If you do, the information may be used against them, and if you do not, the organisation may not be able to derive the benefits of restructuring. In the author's opinion, it is ethical to ask questions provided you tell respondents of the potential use of the information, including the possibility of its being used against some of them, and you let them decide if they want to participate. Some may participate for the betterment of the organisation even though it may harm them, and others may decide against it. However, to identify either of them is unethical in research.

Ethical issues regarding the sponsoring organisation

Restrictions imposed by the sponsoring organisation

Most research in the social sciences is carried out using funds provided by sponsoring organisations for a specific purpose. The funds may be given to develop a programme or evaluate it; to examine its effectiveness and efficiency; to study the impact of a policy; to test a product; to study the behaviour of a group or community; or to study a phenomenon, issue or attitude. Sometimes there may be direct or indirect controls exercised by sponsoring organisations. They may select the methodology, prohibit the publication of findings, or impose other restrictions on the research that may stand in the way of obtaining and disseminating accurate information. Both the imposition and acceptance of these controls and restrictions are unethical, as they constitute interference and could amount to the sponsoring organisation tailoring research findings to meet its vested interests.

The misuse of information

How will the sponsoring body use the information? How is this likely to affect the study population? Sometimes sponsoring organisations use research as a pretext for promoting management's agenda. It is unethical to let your research be used as a reason for justifying management decisions when the research findings do not support them. However, it is recognised that it may be extremely difficult or even impossible for a researcher to prevent this from happening.

Ethical issues in collecting data from secondary data

While it is important to consider ethical issues in collecting data from primary sources, it is equally important to consider them when collecting data from secondary sources. Some of the ethical considerations that you should keep in mind when collecting data from secondary sources are discussed in this section (see also http://www.lancs.ac.uk/researchethics).

Plagiarism is one of the important ethical issues in using data from secondary sources. It is the use of someone else's work, claiming it to be yours. It is absolutely unethical as well as illegal in research to plagiarise It could also have severe academic consequences. All borrowed ideas and citations should be properly acknowledged and cited.

It is also unethical to use a substantial piece of work by someone else without his/her informed consent. You must seek permission from the copyright holder and/or the author to use the data.

The mispresentation of data – changing its format, context, or content to suit your purpose – is both illegitimate and unethical. Any change, if it leads to a different interpretation of the original data, is unethical. The misinterpretation of data is another ethical issue in social research. The data must be presented in the same format and context. If these are changed make sure they do not communicate a different presentation.

You must take care to avoid disclosing data sources. Until expressed consent is given by the author or copyright holder, you must protect the identity of the participants, places and institutions. Make sure you anonymise the identifying information by using pseudonyms. Disclosing the anonymity and confidentiality of the source without permission is unethical.

Use of data collected by covert means – without the consent of participants, without adhering to the principle of client self-determination, or through any other unethical means – cannot be considered legitimate and hence its use is unethical.

Summary

This chapter is designed to make you aware of the ethical issues to be considered when conducting research. The ethical issues to be considered are the same in both quantitative and qualitative research. How you resolve them depends on you and the conditions under which you are working.

Being ethical means adhering to the code of conduct that has evolved over the years for an acceptable professional practice. Any deviation from this code of conduct is considered unethical and the greater the deviation, the more serious the breach. For most professions ethical codes in research are an integral part of their overall ethics, and some research bodies have evolved their own codes.

Ethical issues in research can be examined in relation to research participants, researchers and sponsoring organisations. With regard to research participants, the following areas could pose ethical issues if not dealt with properly: collecting information; seeking consent; providing incentives; seeking sensitive information; the possibility of causing harm to participants; and maintaining confidentiality. It is important to examine these areas thoroughly for any unethical practice. With regard to the researcher, areas of ethical concern include the following: introducing bias; providing and depriving individuals of treatment; using unacceptable research methodology; inaccurate reporting; and the inappropriate use of information. Ethical considerations in relation to sponsoring organisations concern restrictions imposed on research designs and the possible use of findings. There are unethical issues that you need to be aware of when collecting data from secondary sources. Some of them are: plagiarism, collection without formed consent, misinterpretation or misquotation of the information used, disclosing data sources and using data collected by covert means. As a newcomer to research you should be aware of what constitutes unethical practice and be able to put appropriate strategies in place to deal with any harm that may done to any stakeholder.

FOR YOU TO THINK ABOUT

- Refamiliarise yourself with the keywords listed at the beginning of this chapter, and if you are uncertain about the meaning or application of any of them revisit them in the chapter before moving on.
- Find a copy of your university's or department's code of ethics for research (or examples of codes of conduct for your chosen profession). Can you identify any areas of research or approaches that might come into conflict with these guidelines?
- Some might suggest that asking for any kind of information from an individual is unethical as it is an invasion of his/her privacy. Consider how you might argue for and against this suggestion.
- Ethical issues may arise at any point in the research process. Reflecting on the principles raised in this chapter, make a list of ethical issues that you think should be considered at each step in the eight-step model.
- Imagine you are planning to undertake a hypothetical research study in an area of interest to you. Identify the various stakeholder groups and list the possible ethical concerns you need to be aware of from the perspective of each one of the groups.

Now, as you have gone through the chapter, try answering the following questions:

- What specific practices in a research study would you consider as unethical? In the light of your own position, critically examine these practices.
- In this chapter ethical issues have been looked at from three perspectives. If you were asked to add another perspective, what would you add?
- What would you consider as unethical from the perspectives of research participants?
- How would you ensure that the research you undertake is ethical from your perspective as a researcher?
- What would be your position if your sponsoring organisation put pressure on you to change some of the findings you included in your study? Give reasons for your position.

Want to learn more? Visit
http://www.uk.sagepub.com/kumar4e
or scan this QR code to gain access to a range of online resources to support your study including practice quizzes, videos, weblinks, flashcards, and journal articles.

290   RESEARCH METHODOLOGY

STEP VII

PROCESSING AND DISPLAYING DATA

This operational step includes two chapters:

- Chapter 15: Processing Data
- Chapter 16: Displaying Data

15

PROCESSING DATA

In this chapter you will learn about

- Methods for processing data in quantitative studies
- How to edit data and prepare for coding
- How to code data
- How to code qualitative data in quantitative studies
- Methods for processing data in qualitative studies
- Analysing data in qualitative and quantitative studies
- The role of computers in data analysis
- The role of statistics in research

Keywords

analysis, closed questions, code book, coding, concepts, content analysis, cross-

tabulation, data display, data processing, editing, frame of analysis, frequency

distribution, multiple responses, open-ended questions, pre-test.

At the end of this chapter, you should have an understanding of

- What data processing in quantitative studies entails
- How to process data in qualitative studies
- How to develop a code book and the process of coding in quantitative studies
- Developing themes from open-ended responses, descriptions or narrations
- The role of computers and statistics in a research study

If you were actually doing a research study, you would by now have reached the stage of having either extracted or collected the required information for your study. But what to do with this information? What steps do you need to take beyond data collection to find answers to your research questions? How do you make sense of the information collected? How do you draw meaning from the data gathered? If you have a hypothesis, how do you accept or reject it? How should the information be analysed to achieve the objectives of your study? To answer these questions you need to subject your data to a number of procedures that constitute the core of data processing (Figure 15.1).

These procedures are the same whether your study is quantitative or qualitative, but what you do within each procedure is different. For both types of study you need to visualise how you are going to present your findings to your readership in the light of its background and the purpose of the study. You need to decide what type of analysis would be appropriate for the readers of your report. It is in the light of the purpose of your study and your impression about the level of understanding of your readership that you decide the type of analysis you should undertake. For example, there is no point in doing a sophisticated statistical analysis if your readers are not familiar with statistical procedures. In quantitative research the main emphasis in data analysis is to decide how you are going to analyse information obtained in response to each question that you asked of your respondents. In qualitative research the focus is on what should be the basis of analysis of the information obtained; that is, is it contents, discourse, narrative or event analysis? Because of the different techniques used in processing data in quantitative and qualitative research, this chapter deals separately with data processing in quantitative and qualitative studies.

Data processing in quantitative studies

Editing

Irrespective of the method of data collection, the information collected is called *raw data* or simply *data*. The first step in processing your data is to ensure that the data is

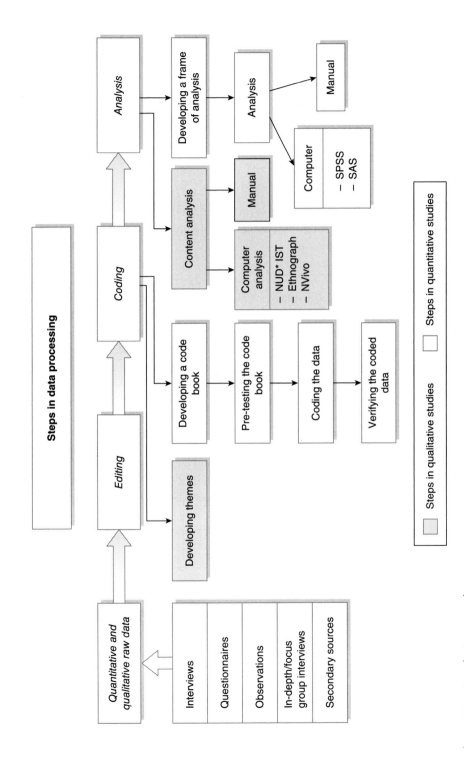

Figure 15.1   Steps in data processing

'clean' – that is, free from inconsistencies and incompleteness. This cleaning process is called editing.

Editing consists of scrutinising the completed research instruments to identify and minimise, as far as possible, errors, incompleteness, misclassification and gaps in the information obtained from the respondents. Sometimes even the best investigators can:

- forget to ask a question;
- forget to record a response;
- wrongly classify a response;
- write only half a response;
- write illegibly.

Similar problems can arise in questionnaires. These problems to a great extent can be reduced simply by (1) checking the contents for completeness, and (2) checking the responses for internal consistency.

The way you check the contents for completeness depends upon the way the data has been collected. In the case of an interview, just checking the interview schedule for the above problems may improve the quality of the data. It is good practice for an interviewer to take a few moments after completing an interview to peruse responses for possible incompleteness and inconsistencies. In the case of a questionnaire, again, just by carefully checking the responses some of the problems may be reduced. There are several ways of minimising such problems:

- By inference – Certain questions in a research instrument may be related to one another, and it might be possible to find the answer to one question from the answer to another. Of course, you must be careful about making such inferences or you may introduce new errors into the data.
- By recall – If the data is collected by means of interviews, sometimes it might be possible for the interviewer to recall a respondent's answers. Again, you must be extremely careful.
- By going back to the respondent – If the data has been collected by means of interviews or the questionnaires contain some identifying information, it is possible to visit or phone a respondent to confirm or ascertain an answer. This is, of course, expensive and time-consuming.

There are two ways of editing the data:

1. examine all the answers to one question or variable at a time;
2. examine all the responses given to all the questions by one respondent at a time.

The author prefers the second method as it provides a total picture of the responses, which also helps you to assess their internal consistency.

Coding

Having cleaned the data, the next step is to code it. The method of coding is largely dictated by two considerations:

1. the way a variable has been measured (measurement scale) in your research instrument (e.g. if a response to a question is descriptive, categorical or quantitative);
2. the way you want to communicate the findings about a variable to your readers.

For coding, the first level of distinction is whether a set of data is qualitative or quantitative in nature. For qualitative data a further distinction is whether the information is descriptive in nature (e.g. a description of a service to a community, a case history) or is generated through discrete qualitative categories. For example, the following information about a respondent is in discrete qualitative categories: income (above average, average, below average); gender (male, female); religion (Christian, Hindu, Muslim, Buddhist, etc.); and attitude towards an issue (strongly favourable, favourable, uncertain, unfavourable, strongly unfavourable). Each of these variables is measured either on a nominal scale or an ordinal scale. Some of them could also have been measured on a ratio scale or an interval scale. For example, income can be measured in dollars (ratio scale), or an attitude towards an issue can be measured on an interval or a ratio scale. The way you proceed with the coding depends upon the measurement scale used in the measurement of a variable at the time of collecting information and whether a question is open-ended or closed.

In addition, the types of statistical procedures that can be applied to a set of information to a large extent depend upon the measurement scale on which a variable was measured in the research instrument. For example, you can calculate different statistical descriptors such as mean, mode and median if income is measured on a ratio scale, but not if it is measured on an ordinal or a nominal scale. It is extremely important to understand that the way you are able to analyse a set of information is dependent upon the measurement scale used in the research instrument for measuring a variable. It is therefore important to visualise – particularly at the planning stage when constructing the research instrument – the way you are going to communicate your findings.

How you can analyse information obtained in response to a question depends upon how a question was asked, and how a respondent answered it. In other words, it depends upon the measurement scale on which a response can be measured or classified. If you study answers given by your respondents in reply to a question, you will realise that almost all responses can be classified into one of the following three categories:

1. quantitative responses;
2. categorical responses (which may be quantitative or qualitative);
3. descriptive responses (which are invariably qualitative – keep in mind that this is qualitative data collected as part of quantitative research and not qualitative research).

For the purpose of analysis, quantitative and categorical responses need to be dealt with differently from descriptive ones. Both quantitative and categorical information go through a process that is primarily aimed at transforming the information into numerical values, called codes, so that the information can be easily analysed, either manually or by computer. On the other hand, descriptive information first goes through a process called content analysis, whereby you identify the main themes that emerge from the descriptions given by respondents in answer to questions. Having identified the main themes, there are three ways that you can deal with them: (1) you can examine verbatim responses and integrate them into the text of your report to either support or contradict your argument; (2) you can assign a code to each theme and count how frequently each has occurred; and (3) you can combine both methods to communicate your findings. This is your choice, and it is based on your impression of the preference of your readers.

For coding quantitative and qualitative data in quantitative studies you need to go through the following steps:

Stage I   developing a code book;
Stage II   pre-testing the code book;
Stage III coding the data;
Stage IV   verifying the coded data.

Stage I: Developing a code book

A code book provides a set of rules for assigning numerical values to answers obtained from respondents. Let us take an example. Figure 15.2 lists some questions taken from a questionnaire used in a survey conducted by the author to ascertain the impact of occupational redeployment on an individual. The questions selected should be sufficient to serve as a prototype for developing a code book, as they cover the various issues involved in the process.

There are two formats for data entry: 'fixed' and 'free'. In this chapter we will be using the fixed format to illustrate how to develop a code book. The fixed format stipulates that a piece of information obtained from a respondent is entered in a specific column. Each column has a number and the 'Col. no.' in the code book refers to the column in which a specific type of information is to be entered. The information about an individual is thus entered in a row(s) comprising these columns.

For a beginner it is important to understand the structure of a code book. The example in Table 15.1 is based on the responses given to the questions listed in Figure 15.2.

In Table 15.1, *column 1* refers to the columns in which a particular piece of information is to be entered. Allocation of columns in a fixed format is extremely important because, when you write a program, you need to specify the column in which a particular piece of information is entered so that the computer can perform the required procedures.

Column 2 identifies the question number in the research instrument for which the information is being coded. This is primarily to identify coding with the question number in the instrument.

Column 3 refers to the name of the variable. Each variable in a program is given a unique name so that the program can carry out the requested statistical procedures. Usually there are restrictions on the way you can name a variable (e.g. the number of characters you can use to name a variable and whether you use the alphabet or numerals). You need to check the program you are using for this. It is advisable to name a variable in such a way that you can easily recognise it from its name.

Column 4 lists the possible responses to the various questions. Developing a response pattern for the questions is the most important, difficult and time-consuming part of developing a code book. The degree of difficulty in developing a response pattern differs with the types of questions in your research instrument (open-ended or closed). If a question is

1   Please indicate:

   (a) Your current age in completed years: _____
   (c) Your marital status: (Please tick)
      Currently married _____
      Living in a de facto relationship _____
      Separated _____
      Divorced _____
      Never married _____

2   (b)   If tertiary/university, please specify the level achieved and area of study. (Please specify all postgraduate qualifications.)

Level of achievement	Area of study: e.g. engineering, accounting
Associate diploma	
Diploma	
Bachelor	
Graduate diploma	
Masters	
PhD	

11 What, in your opinion, are the main differences between your jobs prior to and after redeployment?

_____

_____

12 We would like to know your perception of the two jobs *before* and *after* redeployment with respect to the following aspects of your job. Please rate them on a five-point scale using the following guide: 5 = extremely satisfied, 4 = very satisfied, 3 = satisfied, 2 = dissatisfied, 1 = extremely dissatisfied

Before redeployment					Areas	After redeployment				
1	2	3	4	5		1	2	3	4	5
					Job status					
					Job satisfaction					
					Motivation to work					
					Interest in the job					
					Self-esteem					
					Professional competence					
					Peer interaction					
					Morale					
					Work environment					
					Social interaction					

Figure 15.2   Example of questions from a survey

closed, the response pattern has already been developed as part of the instrument construction and all you need to do at this stage is to assign a numerical value to each response category. In terms of analysis, this is one of the main advantages of closed questions. If a closed question includes 'other' as one of the response categories, to accommodate any response that you may not have listed when developing the instrument, you should analyse the responses and assign them to non-overlapping categories in the same way as you would do for open-ended questions. Add these to the already developed response categories and assign each a numerical value.

If the number of responses to a question is less than nine, you need only one column to code the responses, and if it is more than nine but less than 99, you need two columns (column 1 in the code book). But if a question asks respondents to give more than one response, the number of columns assigned should be in accordance with the number of responses to be coded. If there are, say, eight possible responses to a particular question and a respondent is asked to give three responses, you need three columns to code the responses to the question. Such questions are called multiple response questions. Let us assume there are 12 possible responses to a question. To code each response you need two columns and, therefore, to code three responses you need six columns.

The coding of open-ended questions is more difficult. Coding of open-ended questions requires the response categories to be developed first through a process called content analysis. One of the easier ways of analysing open-ended questions is to select a number of interview schedules/questionnaires randomly from all the completed interview schedules/questionnaires received. Select an open-ended question from one of these schedules/questionnaires and write down the response(s) on a sheet of paper. If the person has given more than one response, write them separately on the same sheet. Similarly, from the same questionnaire/schedule select another open-ended question and write down the responses given on a separate sheet. In the same way you can select other open-ended questions and write down the response(s). Remember that the response to each question should be written on a separate sheet. Now select another questionnaire/interview schedule and go through the same process, adding response(s) given for the same question on the sheet for that question. Continue the process until you feel that the responses are being repeated and you are getting no or very few new ones – that is, when you have reached a saturation point.

Now, one by one, examine the responses to each question to ascertain the similarities and differences. If two or more responses are similar in meaning though not necessarily in language, try to combine them under one category. Give a name to the category that is descriptive of the responses. Remember, when you code the data you code categories, *not* responses per se. It is advisable to write down the different responses under each category in the code book so that, while coding, you know the type of responses you have grouped under a category. In developing these categories there are three important considerations:

1. The categories should be *mutually exclusive*. Develop non-overlapping categories. It should not be possible to place a response in two categories.
2. The categories should be *exhaustive*; that is, it should be possible to place almost every response in one of the categories. If too many responses cannot be so categorised, it is an indication of ineffective categorisation. In such a situation you should examine your categories again.
3. The use of the 'other' category, effectively a 'waste basket' for those odd responses that cannot be put into any category, must be kept to the absolute minimum because, as mentioned, it reflects the failure of the classification system. This category should not include more than 5 per cent of the total responses and should not contain more responses than any other category.

Column 5 lists the actual codes of the code book that you decide to assign to a response. You can assign any numerical value to any response so long as you do not repeat

Table 15.1 An example of a code book

Col. no.	Q. no.	Variable name	Response pattern	Code
1	2	3	4	5
1–3	S. no.	ID	Actual serial number	Code actual
4	Record no.	RNO	First record	1
			Second record	2
			Third record	3
5	1(a)	Age	20–24	1
			25–29	2
			30–34	3
			35–39	4
			40–44	5
			45–49	6
			No response	9
6	1(c)	MS	Currently married	1
			Living in a de facto relationship	2
			Separated	3
			Divorced	4
			Never married	5
			No response	9
	2(b)	TEDU	Assoc. Dip.	1
			Diploma	2
			Bachelors	3
			Grad. Dip.	4
			Masters	5
			PhD	6
			Not applicable	8
			No response	9
7		TEDU1	Same as in TEDU	Code
8		TEDU2	Same as in TEDU	as in
9		TEDU3	Same as in TEDU	TEDU
		STUDY	Behavioural Sciences	1
			Business	2
			Economics/Commerce	3
			Communication	4
			Engineering	5
			Geography	6
			History	7
			Graphics	8
			Librarianship	9
			Nursing	10
			Performing Arts	11

(Continued)

Table 15.1   (Continued)

Col. no.	Q. no.	Variable name	Response pattern	Code
			Secretarial	12
			Social Work	13
			Psychology	14
			Education	15
			Chartered Acct.	16
			Zoology	17
			Anthropology	18
			Social Sciences	19
			Public/Health Admin.	20
			English	21
			Audio-visual Aids Education	22
			Not applicable	88
			No response	99
10-11	2(b)	STUDY 1	Same as in STUDY	Code
12-13		STUDY 2	Same as in STUDY	as in
				STUDY
14-15		STUDY3	Same as in STUDY	
	11	DIFWK	Lack of job satisfaction	
			– current job	01
			– previous job	02
			Less responsibility	
			– current job	03
			– previous job	04
			Low morale	
			– current job	05
			– previous job	06
			Lack of recognition of hard work	
			– current job	07
			– previous job	08
			Skills irrelevant	
			– current job	09
			– previous job	10
			Repetitious nature	
			– current job	11
			– previous job	12
			Job more segmented	
			– current job	13
			– previous job	14
			Reduction in occup. status	15
			Greater involvement in total process	
			– current job	16

Col. no.	Q. no.	Variable name	Response pattern	Code
			– previous job	17
			More restricted duties	
			– current job	18
			– previous job	19
			Less flexibility	
			– current job	20
			– previous job	21
			More people contact	
			– current job	22
			– previous job	23
			Less people contact	
			– current job	24
			– previous job	25
			More responsibility	
			– current job	26
			– previous job	27
			Better work environment	
			– current job	28
			– previous job	29
			Better work morale	
			– current job	30
			– previous job	31
			Working in a team	
			– current job	32
			– previous job	33
			Work as an individual	
			– current job	34
			– previous job	35
			Lack of job security	
			– current job	36
			– previous job	37
			Current job full-time	38
			Better career prospects	
			– current job	39
			– previous job	40
			No commonality	41
			Different working conditions	42
			Change in occup. status (not specified)	43
			High occup. level	
			– current job	44
			– previous job	45

(Continued)

Table 15.1   (Continued)

Col. no.	Q. no.	Variable name	Response pattern	Code
			More job security in present job	46
			More professional environment in	
			− current job	47
			− previous job	48
			Different skills to learn in current job	49
			Higher workload	
			− current job	50
			− previous job	51
			Less supervision in	
			− current job	52
			− previous job	53
			Current job more relevant to my training	54
			Current job more rewarding	55
			Better morale in current job	56
			Greater variety of duties in	
			− current job	57
			− previous job	58
			Current job more	
			rewarding	59
			Better morale in	
			− current job	60
			Less variety of tasks	
			in current job	61
			Fewer skills required in	
			− current job	62
			− previous job	63
			Change in job title	64
			Previous job very demanding	65
			Opportunity to use initiative in previous job	66
			Current job does not require initiative	67
			Different skills required in current job	68
			No career prospects	
			− current job	69
			− previous job	70
			More professional environment in current job	71
			Different skills to learn in current job	72
			Different working conditions	73
			Change in occup. status (change not specified)	74
			Change in job resp. (change not specified)	75
			Current job is more structured	76
			Now part of the team	77

Col. no.	Q. no.	Variable name	Response pattern	Code
			No change	78
			Irrelevant response	79
			Other	80
			Not applicable	88
			No response	99
16–17	11	DIFWK1	Same as in DIFWK	Code as
18–19		DIFWK2	Same as in DIFWK	in
20–21		DIFWK3	Same as in DIFWK	DIFWK
22–23		DIFWK4		
24–25		DIFWK5		
			Extremely dissatisfied	1
			Dissatisfied	2
	12	BEAFTER	Satisfied	3
			Very satisfied	4
			Extremely satisfied	5
			Same as in BEAFTER	
26		JOBSTA	Same as in BEAFTER	Code as
27		JOBSTB	Same as in BEAFTER	in
				BEAFTER
28		JOBSTA	Same as in BEAFTER	Code as in
29		JOBSTA	Same as in BEAFTER	BEAFTER
			and so on	

it for another response within the same question. Two responses to questions are commonly repeated: 'not applicable' and 'no response'. You should select a number that can be used for these responses for all or most questions. For example, responses such as 'not applicable' and 'no response' could be given a code of 8 and 9 respectively, even though the responses to a question may be limited to only 2 or 3. In other words, suppose you want to code the gender of a respondent and you have decided to code female = 1 and male = 2. For 'no response', instead of assigning a code of 3, assign a code of 9. This suggestion helps in remembering codes, which will help to increase your speed in coding.

To explain how to code, let us take each of the questions listed in the example in Figure 15.2.

Question 1(a)

Your current age in completed years: _____

This is an open-ended quantitative question. In questions like this it is important to determine the range of responses – the respondent with the lowest and the respondent with the highest age. To do this, go through a number of questionnaires/interview schedules. Once the range is established, divide it into a number of categories. The categories developed are dependent upon a number of considerations such as the purpose of analysis, the way you want to communicate the findings of your study and whether the findings are going to be compared with those of another study. Let us assume that the range in the study is 23 to 49 years and assume that you decide on the following categories to suit your purpose: 20–24, 25–29, 30–34, 35–39, 40–44 and 45–49. If your range is correct you should need no other categories. Let us assume that you decide to code 20–24 = 1, 25–29 = 2, 30–34 = 3, and so on. To accommodate 'no response' you decide to assign a code of 9. Let us assume you decided to code the responses to this question in column 5 of the code sheet.

Question 1(c)

Your marital status: (Please tick)
Currently married_____
Living in a de facto relationship____
Separated_____
Divorced_____
Never married_____

This is a closed categorical question. That is, the response pattern is already provided. In these situations you just need to assign a numerical value to each category. For example, you may decide to code 'currently married' = 1, 'living in a de facto relationship' = 2, 'separated' = 3, 'divorced'= 4 and 'never married'= 5. You may add 'no response' as another category and assign it a code of 9. The response to this question is coded in column 6 of the code sheet.

Question 2(b)

If tertiary/university, please specify the level achieved and the area of study. (Please specify all postgraduate qualifications.)

In this question a respondent is asked about tertiary qualifications. The question asks for two aspects: (1) level of achievement, which is categorical; and (2) area of study, which is open-ended. Also, a person may have more than one qualification, which makes it a multiple response question. Both aspects of the question are to be coded – the level of achievement (e.g. associate diploma, diploma) and the area of study (e.g. engineering, accounting). When coding multiple responses, decide on the maximum possible number of responses to be coded. Let us assume you code a maximum number of three levels of tertiary education. (This would depend upon the maximum number of levels of achievement identified by the study population.) Firstly, code the levels of achievement TEDU (= *tertiary edu*cation) and then the area of study STUDY. In the above example, let us assume that you decided to code three levels of achievement. To distinguish them from each other we call the first level TEDU1, the second TEDU2 and the third TEDU3, and decide to code them in columns, 7, 8 and 9, respectively. Similarly, the names given to the three areas of study are STUDY1, STUDY2 and STUDY3 and we decide to code them in columns 10–11, 12–13 and 14–15. The codes (01 to 22) assigned to different qualifications are listed in the code book. If a respondent has only one qualification, the question of second and third qualifications is not applicable and you need to decide on a code for 'not applicable'. Assume you assigned a code of 88. 'No response' would then be assigned a code of 99 for this question.

Question 11

What, in your opinion, are the main differences between your jobs prior to and after redeployment?

_____

_____

_____

This is an open-ended question. To code this you need to go through the process of content analysis as explained earlier. Within the scope of this chapter it is not possible to explain the details, but response categories that have been listed are based upon the responses given by 109 respondents to the survey on occupational redeployment. In coding questions like this, on the one hand you need to keep the variation in the respondents' answers, and on the other you want to break them up into meaningful categories to identify the commonalities. Because this question is asking respondents to identify the differences between their jobs before and after redeployment, for easy identification let us assume this variable was named DIFWK (*diff*erence in *work*). Responses to this question are listed in Figure 15.3. These responses have been selected at random from the questionnaires returned.

A close examination of these responses reveals that a number of themes are common, for example: 'learning new skills in the new job'; 'challenging tasks are missing from the new position'; 'more secure in the present job'; 'more interaction in the present job'; 'less responsibility'; 'more variety'; 'no difference'; 'more satisfying'. There are many similar themes that hold for both the before and after jobs. Therefore, we developed these themes for 'current job' and 'previous job'.

One of the main differences between qualitative and quantitative research is the way responses are used in the report. In qualitative research the responses are normally used either verbatim or are organised under certain themes and the actual responses are provided to substantiate them.

In quantitative research the responses are examined, common themes are identified, the themes are named (or categories are developed) and the responses given by respondents are classified under these themes. The data then can also be analysed to determine the frequency of the themes if so desired. It is also possible to analyse the themes in relation to some other characteristics such as age, education and income of the study population.

The code book lists the themes developed on the basis of responses given. As you can see, many categories may result. The author's advice is not to worry about this as categories can always be combined later if required. The reverse is impossible unless you go back to the raw data.

Let us assume you want to code up to five responses to this question and that you have decided to name these five variables as DIFWK1, DIFWK2, DIFWK3, DIFWK4 and DIFWK5. Let us also assume that you have coded them in columns 16–17, 18–19, 20–21, 22–23 and 24–25, respectively.

Respondent 3
Hours now FT: totally different skills required; deal with public; busier, more structured day and duties; now a part of the team instead of an independent worker.

Respondent 20
That I am happy and made to feel as though I am a valuable part of a team.

Respondent 41
This one is great, other one was lousy due to mismanagement, poor morale and feelings that dedication and hard work counted for nothing. Department of ... is well managed and morale is good and the graphic design work is fun and I am supported by my supervisors and subordinates.

Respondent 48

Before	After
15 hours per week	*24 hours per week*
Monday to Friday	*Very satisfactory*
On the go the whole time	*Dealing with the public*
No sitting	*Dealing with severe psychiatric*
Dealings with the public	*patients can be very stressful.*

Respondent 52
No difference.

Respondent 54
My substantive position has been the same before and after the redeployment, but before the redeployment I was acting as Project Manager (level 5) and after being redeployed I was assigned to programming duties (level e).

Respondent 63
This position has more day-to-day administration (it includes corporate services, finance, PR, IT, etc.).

Respondent 69
Had to find my own job.

Respondent 72
The job I was doing I looked after the needs of a workshop where in this job I process files and deliver them.

Respondent 78
Challenging tasks are missing from the new position now that I am familiar with it. Many routine activities (that I have been glad to learn in terms of career development) but that I am becoming bored with. My previous job was much more difficult and interesting than this one.

Respondent 79
I am more secure in my present job and it is better paid as I work longer hours now. I only worked 6½ hours as a tea attendant.

Respondent 81
My previous job required me to be involved in the whole area of government/community and nongovernment requiring assistance in relation to settlement needs of migrants. My current position does not provide job satisfaction, particularly in relation to the offenders that I currently deal with.

Respondent 97
Less responsibility, more specific job, restricted job.

Respondent 105
More variety, more flexibility, more responsibility in the present job, but less confidence, more caution and some resentment.

Figure 15.3 Some selected responses to the open-ended question (no. 11) in Figure 15.2

Question 12

We would like to know your perception of the two jobs before and after redeployment with respect to the following aspects of your job. Please rate them on a five-point scale using the following guide:

5 = extremely satisfied, 4 = very satisfied, 3 = satisfied, 2 = dissatisfied, 1 = extremely dissatisfied

This is a highly structured question asking respondents to compare on a five-point ordinal scale their level of satisfaction with various areas of their job before and after redeployment. As we are gauging the level of satisfaction before and after redeployment, respondents are expected to give two responses to each area. In this example let us assume you have used the name JOBSTA for job status after redeployment (*job status after redeployment*) and JOBSTB for before redeployment (*job status before redeployment*). Similarly, for the second area, job satisfaction, you have decided that the variable name JOBSATA, will stand for the level of job satisfaction after redeployment (*job satisfaction after redeployment*) and JOBSATB for the level before redeployment (*job satisfaction before redeployment*). Other variable names have been similarly assigned. In this example the variable JOBSTA is entered in column 26, JOBSTB in column 27, and so on.

Stage II: Pre-testing the code book

Once a code book is designed, it is important to pre-test it for any problems before you code your data. A pre-test involves selecting a few questionnaires/interview schedules and actually coding the responses to ascertain any problems in coding. It is possible that you may not have provided for some responses and therefore will be unable to code them. Change your code book, if you need to, in light of the pre-test.

Stage III: Coding the data

Once your code book is finalised, the next stage is to code the raw data. There are three ways of doing this:

1. coding on the questionnaire/interview schedule itself, if space for coding was provided at the time of constructing the research instrument;
2. coding on separate code sheets that are available for purchase;
3. coding directly into the computer using a program such as SPSS or SAS.

To explain the process of coding let us take the same questions that were used in developing the code book. We select three questionnaires at random from a total of 109 respondents (Figures 15.4–15.6). Using the code book as a guide, we code the information from these sheets onto the coding sheet (Figure 15.7). Let us examine the coding process by taking respondent 3 (Figure 15.4).

Respondent 3

The total number of respondents is more than 99 and this is the third questionnaire, so the identification number 003 was entered in columns 1–3 (Figure 15.7). Because it is the first record for this respondent, 1 was entered in column 4. This respondent is 49 years of age and falls in the category 45–49, which was coded as 6. As the information on age belongs in column 5, 6 was entered in this column of the code sheet. The marital status of this person is 'divorced', hence 4 was entered in column 6. This person has a bachelor's degree in librarianship. The code chosen for a bachelor's degree is 3, which was entered in column 7. Three tertiary qualifications have been provided for, and as this person does not have any other qualifications, so TEDU2 and TEDU3 are "not applicable", and therefore a code of 8 is entered in columns 8 and 9. This person's bachelor's degree is in librarianship, for which code 09 was assigned and entered in columns 10–11. Since there is only one qualification, STUDY2 and STUDY3 are "not applicable"; therefore, a code of 88 was entered in columns 12–13 and 14–15. This person has given a number of responses to question no. 11 (DIFWK), which asks respondents to list the main differences between their jobs before and after redeployment. In coding such questions much caution is required.

Examine the responses named DIFWK1, DIFWK2, DIFWK3, DIFWK4 AND DIFWK5, to identify the codes that can be assigned. A code of 22 (now deal with public) was assigned to one of the responses, which we enter in columns 16–17. The second difference, DIFWK2, was assigned a code of 69 (totally different skill required), which is coded in columns 18–19. DIFWK3 was assigned a code of 77 (current job more structure) and coded in columns 20–21. Similarly, the fourth (DIFWK4) and the fifth (DIFWK5) difference in the jobs before and after redeployment are coded as 78 (now part of the team instead of independent worker) and 38 (hours – now full-time), which are entered in columns 22–23 and 24–25, respectively. Question 12 is extremely simple to code. Each area of a job has two columns, one for before and the other for after. Job status (JOBST) is divided into two variables, JOBSTA for a respondent's level of satisfaction after redeployment and JOBSTB for his/her level before redeployment. JOBSTA is entered in column 26 and JOBSTB in column 27. For JOBSTA the code 5 (as marked by the respondent) was entered in column 26 and for JOBSTB the code 4 is entered in column 27. Other areas of the job before and after redeployment are similarly coded.

The other two examples are coded in the same manner. The coded data is shown in Figure 15.7. In the process of coding you might find some responses that do not fit your predetermined categories. If so, assign them a code and add these to your code book.

Stage IV: Verifying the coded data

Once the data is coded, select a few research instruments at random and record the responses to identify any discrepancies in coding. Continue to verify coding until you are sure that there are no discrepancies. If there are discrepancies, re-examine the coding.

Developing a frame of analysis

Although a frame of analysis needs to evolve continuously while writing your report, it is desirable to broadly develop it before analysing the data. A frame of analysis should specify:

- which variables you are planning to analyse;
- what type of analysis they should be subjected to;

RESPONDENT = 3

1 Please indicate:
    (a) Your current age in completed years: __49__
    (c) Your marital status: (Please tick)
        Currently married _____
        Living in a de facto relationship _____
        Seperated _____
        Divorced __✓__
        Never married _____

2 (b) If teritiary/university, please specify the level achieved and area of study. (Please specify all postgraduate qualifications.)

Level of achievement	Area of study: e.g. engineering, accounting
Associate diploma	
Diploma	
Bachelor	Librarianship
Graduate diploma	
Masters	
PhD	

11 What, in your opinion, are the main differences between your jobs prior to and after redeployment?

Hours-now F.T, Totally different skills required, Now deal with public,
Busier, more structured day and duties, Now part of the team instead of independent worker

12 We would like to know your perception of the two jobs *before* and *after* redeployment with respect to the following aspects of your job. Please rate them on a five-point scale, using the following guide:
5 = extremely satisfied, 4 = very satisfied, 3 = satisfied, 2 = dissatisfied, 1 = extremely dissatisfied

Before redeployment					Areas	After redeployment				
1	2	3	4	5		1	2	3	4	5
			✓		Job status					✓
			✓		Job satisfaction					✓
			✓		Motivation to work					✓
			✓		Interest in the job					✓
			✓		Self-esteem					✓
			✓		Professional competence				✓	
			✓		Peer interaction					✓
			✓		Morale				✓	
			✓		Work environment				✓	
				✓	Social interaction			✓		

Figure 15.4   Some questions from a survey − respondent 3

- what cross-tabulations you are planning;
- which variables you need to combine to construct your major concepts or to develop indices (in formulating a research problem concepts are changed to variables – at this stage change them back to concepts);
- which variables are to be subjected to which statistical procedures.

To illustrate, let us take the example from the survey used in this chapter.

RESPONDENT = 59

1 Please indicate:
  (a) Your current age in completed years: __45__
  (c) Your marital status: (Please tick)
      Currently married __✓__
      Living in a de facto relationship _____
      Separated _____
      Divorced _____
      Never married _____

2 (b) If tertiary/university, please specify the level achieved and area of study. (Please specify all postgraduate qualifications.)

Level of achievement	Area of study: e.g. engineering, accounting
Associate diploma	
Diploma	
Bachelor	Behavioural Sciences
Graduate diploma	
Masters	
PhD	

11 What, in your opinion, are the main differences between your jobs prior to and after redeployment?

Less responsibility, More specific jobs, Restricted scope.

_____

_____

12 We would like to know your perception of the two jobs before and after redeployment with respect to the following aspects of your job. Please rate them on a five-point scale using the following guide:

5 = extremely satisfied, 4 = very satisfied, 3 = satisfied, 2 = dissatisfied, 1 = extremely dissatisfied

Before redeployment					Areas	After redeployment				
1	2	3	4	5		1	2	3	4	5
			✓		Job status		✓			
			✓✓		Job satisfaction			✓		
			✓✓		Motivation to work		✓			
				✓	Interest in the job			✓		
				✓	Self-esteem			✓		
				✓	Professional competence			✓		
				✓	peer interaction				✓	
				✓	Morale		✓			
				✓	Work environment			✓		
			✓		Social interaction				✓	

Figure 15.5   Some questions from a survey – respondent 59

RESPONDENT = 81
1 Please indicate:
   (a) Your current age in completed years: __42__
   (c) Your marital status: (Please tick)
      Currently married __✓__
      Living in a de facto relationship _____
      Separated _____
      Divorced _____
      Never married

2 (b) If tertiary/university, please specify the level achieved and area of study.
(Please specify all postgraduate qualifications.)

Level of achievement	Area of study: e.g. engineering, accounting
Associate diploma	
Diploma	
Bachelor	Social work
Graduate diploma	
Masters	
PhD	

11 What, in your opinion, are the main differences between your jobs prior to and after redeployment?
My previous job required me to be involved in the whole area of government/community and nongovernment requiring assistance in relation to settlement needs of migrants. My current position does not provide job satisfaction particularly in relation to the offenders that I currently deal with.

12 We would like to know your perception of the two jobs *before* and *after* redeployment with respect to the following aspects of your job. Please rate them on a five-point scale using the following guide:
5 = extremely satisfied, 4 = very satisfied, 3 = satisfied, 2 = dissatisfied, 1 = extremely dissatisfied

Before redeployment					Areas	After redeployment				
1	2	3	4	5		1	2	3	4	5
		✓			Job status		✓			
			✓		Job satisfaction		✓			
				✓	Motivation to work			✓		
			✓		Interest in the job		✓			
			✓		Self-esteem		✓			
		✓			Professional competence		✓			
		✓			Peer interaction					
			✓		Morale		✓			
			✓		Work environment		✓			
		✓			Social interaction		✓			

Figure 15.6 Some questions from a survey – respondent 81

Frequency distributions

A frequency distribution groups respondents into the subcategories into which a variable can be divided. Unless you are not planning to use answers to some of the questions, you should have a frequency distribution for all the variables. Each variable can be specified either separately or collectively in the frame of analysis. To illustrate, they are identified here

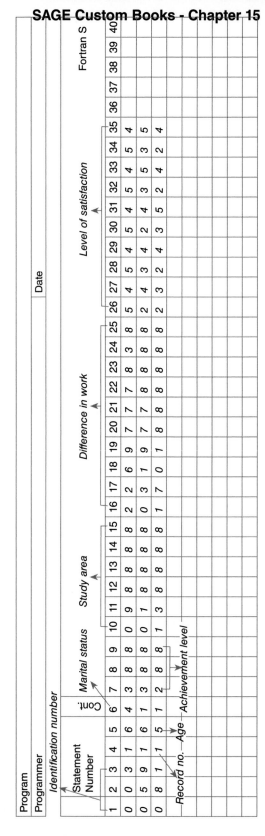

Figure 15.7 An example of coded data on a code sheet

separately by the names used in the code book. For example, the frame of analysis should include frequency distributions for the following variables:

- AGE;
- MS;
- TEDU (TEDU1, TEDU2, TEDU3 – multiple responses, to be collectively analysed);
- STUDY (STUDY1, STUDY2, STUDY 3 – multiple responses, to be collectively analysed);
- DIFWK (DIFWK1, DIFWK2, DIFWK3, DIFWK4, DIFWK5 – multiple responses, to be collectively analysed);
- JOBSTA, JOBSTB;
- JOBSATA, JOBSATB;
- MOTIVA, MOTIVB.
- etc.

Cross-tabulations

Cross-tabulations analyse two variables, usually independent and dependent or attribute and dependent, to determine if there is a relationship between them. The subcategories of both the variables are cross-tabulated to ascertain if a relationship exists between them. Usually, the absolute number of respondents in each cell, and the row and column percentages, give you a reasonably good idea as to the possible association.

In the study we cited as an example in this chapter, one of the main variables to be explained is the level of satisfaction with jobs before and after redeployment. We developed two indices of satisfaction:

1. satisfaction with the job before redeployment (JOBSATB);
2. satisfaction with the job after redeployment (JOBSATA).

Differences in the level of satisfaction can be affected by a number of personal attributes such as the age, education, training and marital status of the respondents. Cross-tabulations help to identify which attributes affect the levels of satisfaction. Theoretically, it is possible to correlate any variables, but it is advisable to be selective or an enormous number of tables will result. Normally only those variables that you think have an effect on the dependent variable should be correlated. The following cross-tabulations are an example of the basis of a frame of analysis: JOBSATA and JOBSATB by AGE, MS, TEDU, STUDY, and DIFWK (these determine whether job satisfaction before and after redeployment is affected by age, marital status, education, and so on); and JOBSATA by JOBSATB (this will reveal whether there is a relationship between job satisfaction before and after redeployment). You can specify as many variables as you want.

Reconstructing the main concepts

There may be places in a research instrument where you look for answers through a number of questions about different aspects of the same issue, for example the level of satisfaction with jobs before and after redeployment (JOBSATB and JOBSATA). In the questionnaire there were 10 aspects of a job about which respondents were asked to identify their level of satisfaction before and after redeployment. The level of satisfaction may vary from aspect to aspect. Though it is important to know respondents' reactions to each aspect, it is equally important to gauge an overall index of their satisfaction. You must therefore decide, before you actually analyse data, how you will combine responses to different questions.

In this example the respondents indicated their level of satisfaction by selecting one of the five response categories. A satisfaction index was developed by assigning a numerical value to the response given by a respondent. The numerical values corresponding to the categories ticked were added to determine the satisfaction index. The satisfaction index score for a respondent varies between 10 and 50. The interpretation of the score is dependent upon the way the numerical values are assigned. In this example the higher the score, the higher the level of satisfaction.

Statistical procedures

In this section you should list the statistical procedures that you want to subject your data to. You should identify the procedures followed by the list of variables that will be subjected to those procedures – for example, regression analysis (JOBSATA on JOBSATB); multiple regression analysis (JOBSATA on AGE, EDUCATION and MS; JOBSATB on AGE, EDUCATION and MS); and analysis of variance. Similarly, it may be necessary to think about and specify the different variables to be subjected to the various statistical procedures. There are a number of user-friendly programs such as SPSS and SAS that you can easily learn.

Analysing quantitative data manually

Coded data can be analysed manually or with the help of a computer. If the number of respondents is reasonably small, there are not many variables to analyse, and you neither are familiar with a relevant computer program nor wish to learn one, you can analyse the data manually. However, manual analysis is useful only for calculating frequencies and for simple cross-tabulations. If you have not entered data into a computer but want to carry out statistical tests, they will have to be calculated manually, which may become extremely difficult and time-consuming. However, the use of statistics depends upon your expertise and desire/need to communicate the findings in a certain way.

Be aware that manual analysis is extremely time-consuming. The easiest way to analyse data manually is to code it directly onto large graph paper in columns in the same way as you would enter it into a computer. On the graph paper you do not need to worry about the column number. Detailed headings can be used or question numbers can be written on each column to code information about the question (Figure 15.8).

To analyse data manually (frequency distributions), count various codes in a column and then decode them. For example, in Figure 15.8, the age of two respondents is coded 6 and one is coded 5. This shows that out of the three respondents, one was between 40 and 44 years of age and the other two were between 45 and 49. Similarly, responses for each variable can be analysed. For cross-tabulations two columns must be read simultaneously to analyse responses in relation to each other.

ID	Age	MS	Education			Study area			Difference in work					Status		Satisfaction	
			1	2	3	1	2	3	1	2	3	4	5	Before	After	Before	After
03	6	4	3	8	8	09	88	88	22	69	77	78	38	5	4	5	4
59	6	1	3	8	8	01	88	88	03	18	77	88	88	2	4	3	4
81	5	1	2	8	8	13	88	88	17	01	88	88	88	2	3	2	4

Figure 15.8 Manual analysis using graph paper

If you want to analyse data using a computer, you should be familiar with the appropriate program. You should know how to create a data file, how to use the procedures involved, what statistical tests to apply and how to interpret them. Obviously in this area knowledge of computers and statistics plays an important role.

Data processing in qualitative studies

How you process and analyse data in a qualitative study depends upon how you plan to communicate the findings. Broadly, there are three ways in which you can write about your findings in qualitative research:

(1) developing a narrative to describe a situation, episode, event or instance;
(2) identifying the main themes that emerge from your field notes or transcription of your in-depth interviews and writing about them, quoting extensively verbatim; and
(3) in addition to (2) above, also quantifying, by indicating their frequency of occurrence, the main themes in order to provide their prevalence.

CODING IN
QUALITATIVE
RESEARCH

Editing, as understood for quantitative studies, is inappropriate for qualitative research. However, it is possible that you may be able to go through your notes to identify if something does not make sense. In such an event, you may be able to recall the context and correct the contents, but be careful in doing so as inability to recall precisely may introduce inaccuracies (due to recall error) in your description. Another way of ensuring whether you are truly

PROCESSING DATA   317

reflecting the situation is to transcribe the interviews or observational notes and share them with the respondents or research participants for confirmation and approval. Validation of the information by a respondent is an important aspect of ensuring the accuracy of data collected through unstructured interviews.

For writing in narrative form there is no analysis per se; however, you need to think through the sequence in which you need or want to narrate. For the other two ways of writing about the findings, you need to go through content analysis, as mentioned earlier. Content analysis means analysing the contents of interviews or observational field notes in order to identify the main themes that emerge from the responses given by your respondents or the observation notes made by you. This process involves a number of steps:

Step 1 Identify the main themes. You need to carefully go through descriptive responses given by your respondents to each question in order to understand the *meaning* they communicate. From these responses you develop broad themes that reflect these meanings. You will notice that people use different words and language to express themselves. It is important for you to select the wording of your themes in a way that accurately represents the meaning of the responses categorised under a theme. These themes become the basis for analysing the text of unstructured interviews. Similarly, you need to go through your field notes to identify the main themes.

Step 2 Assign codes to the main themes. Whether or not you assign a code to a main theme is dependent upon whether or not you want to count the number of times a theme has occurred in an interview. If you decide to count these themes you should, at random, select a few responses to an open-ended question or from your observational or discussion notes and identify the main themes. You continue to identify these themes from the same question till you have reached saturation point. Write these themes and assign a code to each of them, using numbers or keywords, otherwise just identify the main themes.

Step 3 Classify responses under the main themes. Having identified the themes, the next step is to go through the transcripts of all your interviews or your notes and classify the responses or contents of the notes under the different themes. You can also use a computer program such as NVivo, ATLAS.ti or MAXQDA for undertaking this thematic analysis. You will benefit from learning one of these programs if your data is suitable for such analysis.

Step 4 Integrate themes and responses into the text of your report. Having identified responses that fall within different themes, the next step is to integrate them into the text of your report. How you do so is mainly your choice. Some people, while discussing the main themes that emerged from their study, use verbatim responses to keep the 'feel' of the responses. Others count how frequently a theme has occurred, and then provide a sample of the responses. It entirely depends upon the way you want to communicate the findings to your readers.

Content analysis in qualitative research – an example

APPROACHES TO
CONTENT ANALYSIS

The above four-step process was applied to a study recently carried out by the author to develop an operational service model, based upon the principle of family engagement. The information was predominantly gathered through in-depth and focus group discussions with clients, service providers and service managers. After informal talks with a number of stakeholders, a list of possible issues was drawn up to form the basis of discussions in these in-depth interviews and group discussions. The list was merely a guiding framework and was open to inclusion of any new issue that emerged during the discussions. Out of the several issues that were identified to examine various aspects of the model, here the author has taken only one to show the process of identifying themes that emerged. Note that these themes have not been quantified. They are substantiated by verbatims, which is one of the main differences between qualitative and quantitative research. The following example shows perceived strengths of the family engagement model (FEM) as identified by the stakeholders during in-depth interviews and focus groups. Information provided in Figure 15.8 serves as an example of the outcome of this process.

Example — Developing themes through content analysis

Perceived strengths of the model

The framework developed for the perceived strengths of the model is based upon the analysis of the information gathered, which suggested that the various themes that emerged during the data collection stage reflecting strengths of the model can be classified under four perspectives. The following diagram shows the framework that emerged from the analysis.

Perceived strengths from the perspective of the family

This section details the perceived strengths of the model from the perspective of the family. Keep in mind that the sequential order of the perceived strengths is random and does not reflect any order or preference. Also, the naming of these themes is that of the author, which to the best of his knowledge captured the 'meanings' of the intentions of the research participants.

Empowerment of families

Almost everyone expressed the opinion that one of the main strengths of the model is that it empowers families and clients to deal with their own problems. The model provides an opportunity to families to express their feelings about issues of concern to them and, to some extent, to take control of their situations themselves. It seems that in 'preparing a plan for a child under this model, the family of the child will play an extremely important role in deciding about the future of the child, which is the greatest strength of the model'. One of the respondents expressed his/her opinion as follows:

> Oh, the family engagement model actually gives the power back to the family but with the bottom line in place, like the Department's bottom lines, they have to meet them. Oh ... the old model would have been black and white; kids remain in Mum's care, he [the father] would have supervised contacts with kids and it all would have been set up ... the family engagement model was about pulling them in the whole family then coming up with the solutions as long as they reach the Department's bottom line. They actually have to come up and nominate what they were willing to do ... He [the father] returned home, which was much better ... If they have relapse we bring them back in and we talk about it, get them back on track, make sure they were engaging with the services ... In the old method, kids just would have been removed and kids would have gone into the Department's care ... It is more empowering to the family, and it is much easier to work with the family at that level than you are standing over and telling them that you have to do this and this, and holding it against them that if you do not do,

(Continued)

(Continued)

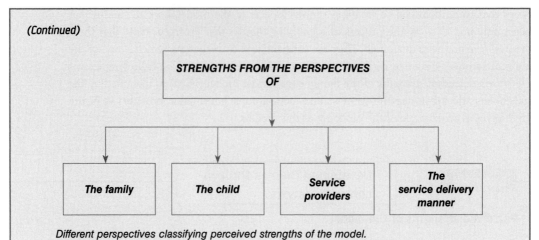

Different perspectives classifying perceived strengths of the model.

well, the kids are out. It is much, much better for the families. You've got more opportunity to work with the family at that level, rather than being on the outside dictating.

Another participant said:

I think this model empowers the family a lot more ... you are having meetings all the time. You give them the bottom line, and they develop their own strategy ... I think it empowers the family when they come back ... because they are developing their plan, they are using their own network and resources ... I think it is empowering.

Yet, according to another respondent: 'it allows them to feel that they can make some decisions ... They are able to work with the Department and that their voices or views are as valid as the Department's.'

Building of capacity of families

Another advantage that came out of the discussions is that the process adopted as a part of the FEM makes clients aware of community resources which, in turn, help them to build their capacity to deal with a situation effectively and independently. As one participant pointed out:

They know that, ok, if something goes wrong in this aspect of their life, they know they can go there for support, they do not need to be calling us ... they may have resolved their own issues ... that is really empowering.

Another participant said: 'under this model, a family has taken a much stronger role in bringing about change as compared to the case conference approach.'

Acknowledgement of positives in families

One of the strengths of the approach is that it acknowledges the strengths of families. The model is primarily based upon designing interventions based on the strengths and positives of a situation rather than on the negatives. 'In the old model the strengths were not acknowledged to a large degree and certainly not of the parents.' During one of the focus groups, a participant expressed the view that:

> The family engagement model starts with the strengths of the family, so bringing the family in at an earlier stage, and trying to get them to help make decisions about what is going to happen to children who are in crisis ... so ... it is involving more people, their extended family, and getting them to come up with a plan.

In another focus group, a respondent said:

> It is only because you actually do work with that strength-based approach and you acknowledge it. It is a huge part of what happens. You can actually say to somebody that you are doing so well, it is great to see the change in you, and even though you personally have nothing to do with those changes, you say, well done ... it is so good to see you looking so well ... You get to a point in a process where you are no longer seen as an outsider, you are no longer seen as a prescriptive organisation, but you are seen as a supportive organisation which is actually assisting that person in the process ... This Department has not been good in acknowledging change, we have not been.

Collaborative decision making and solutions

Another strength pointed out by many is that solutions pertaining to a child are now developed in close collaboration with the family, extended family and other appropriate stakeholders, which makes them (decisions and solutions) more acceptable and workable. In one of the focus group interviews a participant expressed this strength of the model as follows:

> They come up with answers, they got it. You are up front with the family. It gives the family a very clear idea what exactly is expected of them ... this is what they have done, what are the concerns of the Department ... So by having family support meetings, you are telling the family this is what we feel is happening with the child and these are the things that cannot happen to your children, what we intend to do about it in the future to be able to have them back or to improve their environment ... it is straight in front of them, not behind their back ... Previously I know of a case where a family was not involved in any of the discussions and they did not understand why their children were removed from them.

Many participants felt very positive about this collaborative approach. They felt that 'having a family support meeting clearly tells them what has happened, what are the intentions of the Department, and how the Department is going to work with them'. Another participant in one of the focus group discussions added:

> There are differences between how the meetings are held but, I guess, oh, sometimes to get the family to develop, and remind them of the bottom line, rather than us saying, 'This is what I want to happen'. I mean, obviously in the discussion of the general situation, you make things clear, but you let the family take the responsibility to develop their own plan.

A respondent in an in-depth interview expressed the opinion that, now, 'We are identifying the members of the extended family. Once upon-a-time we just had parents; now you have to go around and search and get them all together to make a decision.'

Yet another respondent, talking about the strengths of the model, said 'now we approach very differently.' According to him/her:

(Continued)

(Continued)

> We inform you, we advise you, that the children are at risk ... whatever with the children, we want to sit down and work with you. Throughout this process we want to work with you, and also, plans have been set up. We want you to be a part of that.

It appears that, under this model, decisions are made not by a single individual, but by all those involved. According to one respondent, 'you are sharing responsibility with other agencies and family members; it is not only your decision, it is the decision of everybody.'

Keeps families intact

Some respondents also felt, that in certain cases, 'The children may not even be taken from the family so quickly'. It seems there is a greater attempt to keep the children in the family. One participant said: 'I am actually working with quite a few kids where they are trying to keep the family together.' Another participant added that 'The apprehension rate has come down substantially.'

Perceived strengths from the perspective of the child

A greater focus on children

Many family workers as well as team leaders felt that the whole approach is a lot more focused on children. The approach is child centred and, at every step, concerns for children form the core of an intervention: 'it is a lot more child-focused as well. Rather than focusing on the parents, it is focusing on how we are going to make this child safe, and how we are going to achieve that.'

Returns children to their parents quicker

Some respondents felt that the new approach helped children to get back to their parents quicker. In one of the focus group discussions, one participant said:

> I think it gets the children back to their parents quicker because at the meeting it identifies strong people in the family that can support the parents to keep their kids. So what I found in the office is that some of the kids get back to their parents quicker than through the Case Conference. The Case Conference is every year ... what the families have to jump through by the end of the twelve months at the next meeting ... here it is none of that. It is a strong person, how you are going to support the Mum to keep getting the kids back ... what you do need ... sometimes the kids go back, just like that.

Prevention of removal of children

Some respondents felt that the model actually prevented kids from being removed from their families. According to one participant, 'that is the big advantage of this model; to prevent kids from being removed'.

Perceived strengths from the perspective of service providers

Greater job satisfaction

Almost every service provider said that their work after the introduction of the model had become 'much more satisfying' because 'it is enabling workers and clients'.

Easier for the workers to work under the model

Many respondents felt that 'initially it is more work for a worker but, in the long run, it is less work because of the shared responsibility'. According to one participant:

> As a case worker, I remember the days when I had to really work so hard to meet so many people and do so many things individually and all the responsibility was on my shoulders … but now there is a shared responsibility … you have to do the ground work but when it is done the long term engagement is easier because there are more people involved and they in part make the decisions.

Decline in hostility towards the Department

Another advantage that some respondents pointed out was a decline in hostility among families towards the Department. It was pointed out that though it depended upon the circumstances, there was a feeling that, on the whole, hostility among clients towards the Department had declined. They also felt that though, in the beginning, there might have been hostility, working under the new model, in most situations, made that hostility disappear. In some situations, an increase in hostility was possibly attributable to a situation such as the apprehension of a child. Most respondents were of the opinion that, as compared to the Case Management model, they had experienced far less hostility towards them while working under the new approach.

Increased trust in the staff by clients

Another advantage some workers saw in the new approach was that they felt that clients had started trusting them a lot more. A participant in one of the focus groups described his/her feelings as follows:

> They call us now, I do not have to go and look for them. They are calling me now and asking what is this? … which means they are taking an interest. They are not sitting back and saying, oh well, they are going to tell us or not tell us.

Better rapport with families

Because of the increased number of contacts, it appears that staff were able to build more congenial and trusting relationships with families. In a focus group, one of the respondents said, 'I think the relationship is more respectful and trustful'. Another respondent said:

> Family relationships are a little bit better, and a family also understands that a DCD worker is not someone who goes to homes and removes their children … how horrible people we are, but, by interacting with them they actually understand that we are people at work, and that we are not going to do these things, that is the old way of doing. We are not going to remove a child without saying anything. We have communication with them.

Develops better understanding by workers of the family dynamics

'One of the strengths that I have seen is that it allows the social worker to feel the family dynamics, to think about the dynamics and it allows the families to participate in whatever they want to', said a participant of a focus group.

(Continued)

(Continued)

Fewer aggressive clients

Another obvious difference between the two models, according to some respondents, was fewer aggressive clients. One respondent said:

> There are far less aggressive clients here as compared to other places. I think it is partly because of the approach. Here you very rarely see people who get agitated, it is much more controlled, and it is a calmer atmosphere.

Develops a sense of ownership of a case

One of the advantages of the FEM as pointed out by various respondents was that under the model, 'you feel the case belongs to you; you "own" a child'. Because of this, according to some participants, there was a greater affiliation between the family worker and the child.

Greater community interaction

Another advantage pointed out by family workers was that the model resulted in their having a greater interaction with community agencies and, consequently, had more knowledge of their community and the services available in it. This was primarily because of restructuring under the family engagement model whereby family workers were allocated particular geographical areas, called, 'patches': 'you also develop really nice working relations with those people. You are working together collaboratively towards the goals, and I think, that is really a great benefit', said one participant. There was 'a lot more linking with other agencies' under the model. Not only was the interaction between community agencies increased but, it appears, clients had also started making more use of community agencies.

Greater knowledge about community members

Another benefit of working under the FEM and within a 'patch' was that family workers got to know a lot more community members. According to one respondent, 'The relationship with people in your community is much stronger and widespread.' Another respondent said:

> After a certain time you get to know who lives on what street, family links between people, especially, when you are working with Aboriginal families. Family links are so important, and knowing who is dealing with whom ... knowing who is in the area, what resources you have, makes your job a lot more effective.

Greater control over personal values by workers

Another advantage identified by some respondents was that, with the new model, 'case workers own values and morals cannot be imposed'.

Perceived strengths from the perspective of the service delivery manner

An open, honest and transparent process

The whole process is open to all stakeholders. 'All the cards are on the table', said one participant, and another expressed the opinion that: 'The case worker may be honest, but, I guess, the process, how it was done, was not'. One respondent said that one of the good things about this model was that 'everyone knows what is going on'. According to a respondent:

> Another good thing about these family meetings is that there is the parents, there is the family. The parents might have been telling us one thing or a part of the story and Jaime, another part of the story, not telling Uncle Jimmy ... so it is good in a way that everyone knows what is going on. The whole information is there for everyone that is there. So they cannot push it to us and push it to the family. That is another good thing: they all get the same information, and we get and give the same information to them ... and it is amazing the plan they want to come up with ... it is based upon the information given to them.

Another respondent in a focus group said:

> And you are actually fighting the parents about the guardianship of the child: at the end of the day that is what you are doing, and, I think, just to have the transparent working relationship within the family engagement model actually makes that process a lot easier because everything is out in the open and when it comes up in the court, they are not going to be surprised.

Greater informality in meetings

Family meetings under the FEM are far less formal: 'The family members and others are encouraged to say whatever they want to. They can interrupt and stop the chairperson any time, if they disagree. They can even come back later.' 'What is important is that the minutes are written up, and the family gets a copy of the minutes so that they can go back home and read the minutes. They can come back to us.'

More frequent review of cases

Many people felt that the model provided an opportunity to review cases more frequently which helped them to achieve goals more quickly and, if an intervention was not working, it helped them to change the intervention. As one participant pointed out, 'Changes in the plan to reflect the changes in the family dynamics are undertaken frequently.' Hence, under the model, 'The plan for a child is continually being reviewed.' There seemed to be a lot more flexibility in terms of changing a plan under the model.

Increased honesty, transparency and accountability

Some respondents also felt that, because of the transparency and accountability of the process, simply working within the parameters of the model had helped to keep workers honest and accountable. According to one participant, 'From a practice viewpoint, it allows the social worker to be honest, accountable and to be transparent.'

A fairer approach

Many respondents felt that the FEM was fairer, as it was open, participatory and empowered a family.

Goals set for clients are more attainable and workable

According to one of the participants of a focus group: 'I think the plan of family engagement meetings is more attainable and more workable ... what they are actually capable of doing. We are not setting what they are not

(Continued)

(Continued)

going to achieve, so they are not going to fail.' In addition, it seems, because families were involved in developing a plan, they had a feeling of ownership, and hence they attained the tasks set out in it. Another participant was of the opinion that: 'if you are a part of the solution, then you actually have an investment in making the change.'

Equality in relation to expression of opinion

Some respondents felt that the model provided freedom of expression to parties. All involved were free to express their opinions, and they were encouraged to share their views. As long as the bottom line was met, their opinions were taken into consideration in developing a strategy.

A less chaotic process

As one participant observed: 'it is far less chaotic, just the perception of what was going on. They [referring to workers in the CMM] felt a bit chaotic because work was coming in all the time and they were holding on to cases. Here it is more organised', one participant observed. With the old structure, 'case workers were very stressed; they were not operating particularly well'.

A less stressful approach

Many participants felt that the new approach was less stressful because of its many benefits. It was less stressful for them, and for families, as well as children. In one of the focus groups, a participant expressed his/her feeling in the following words:

> You do not feel that I hate to go to this home ... how are they going to react, what are they going to say to me, or how should I leave or how should I protect myself? You do not have to have those stresses now; it is a calmer situation, it is a happier situation and that is good for the kids, not only for us, but for the kids ... it is actually the kids who also benefit from the approach.

Fewer conflicts with families

Many respondents felt that ongoing conflicts with families were far fewer after the introduction of the new model.

Equality regarding choice of a facilitator for meetings

Another strength was that some participants thought that under the new model facilitation work was not only confined to case managers. Under the model, anyone could become a facilitator.

Increased reflection on practice

Some people also felt that the model provided an opportunity to reflect on practice, thus helping them to improve it.

Total responsibility for cases

Some also pointed out that workers have the total responsibility for cases which seemed to be much better from a number of viewpoints. As pointed out by one person, 'under the model, a field worker is responsible for the total intervention, from A to Z. You do everything in a patch.'

> **Compliance with government's child placement policy**
>
> One of the participants pointed out that the model actually complied with the government's legislative obligation to place Aboriginal and Torres Strait Islander children with their families. According to this participant:
>
> > The model actually meets, for Aboriginal and Torres Strait Islanders child placement principle which is now enshrined in our legislation, where it actually states that children will be placed with family, extended family, immediate community and extended community and a non-Aboriginal person is a last resort ... So this model actually meets that.

Data analysis in mixed methods studies

In mixed methods studies you need to combine a number of data analysis procedures depending upon the way data was collected and the way you want to communicate your findings. Suppose you are interested in finding out the changes in the number of tourists coming to an area or country and how do they feel about their visit. To do so you might collect data either from secondary sources, that is, from the records kept by say the Department of Immigration or through cross-sectional surveys over a period of time to provide information on the number of tourists coming in a year. By analysing these numbers you can estimate the change in the number of tourists over a period of time. This type of analysis that helps you to study the trend in the number of students is quantitative in nature. Further, suppose you found out about their attitudes towards the facilities and stay in the area from some respondents through in-depth interviewing. The data collected through in-depth interviewing can be better subjected to content analysis which is qualitative in nature. In mixed/multiple methods studies, as you use two or more methods either belonging to the same or different research paradigms, mostly the methods used in data collection and your intention about the way you want to communicate your findings determine the way the data should be analysed. If the data is collected by two methods which belong to the two paradigms, you need to use different methods for its analysis appropriate to the way the data was collected.

The role of statistics and computers in research

The role of statistics in research is sometimes exaggerated as you do not have to have a sound statistical knowledge in the designing of a research study (though it may help indirectly). Knowledge of statistics plays a significant role only when you have collected the required information, adhering to the requirements of each operational step of the research process. Up to data collection the role of statistics is limited; it acquires its importance thereafter. This does not mean that without statistics you cannot conduct a research study. You can conduct a perfectly valid study without using any statistics. The use of statistics depends entirely upon the type of study you are conducting, how you want to communicate your findings, who are going to be your readership, the convention in your academic area (some departments place a lot of emphasis on the use of statistical procedures and others do not), and the requirements of your department. Once data is collected you encounter two questions:

1. How do I organise this data to understand it?
2. How to understand what the data means?

In a way, the answer to the first question forms the basis for the answer to the second. Statistics can play a very important role in answering your research questions in such a manner that you are able to quantify, measure, place a level of confidence on the findings, assess the contribution each variable has made in bringing out change, measure the association and relationship between various variables, and help predict what is likely to happen in the light of current trends.

From individual responses, particularly if there are many, it becomes extremely difficult to understand the patterns in the data, so it is important for the data to be aggregated and summarised. It is in this process of aggregation and summarisation that the statistics play a very important role. Simple aggregations such as frequency distribution and cross-tabulation tables and some simple statistical measures such as percentages, means, standard deviations and coefficients of correlation can reduce the volume of data, making it easier to understand. In computing summary measures, it is possible that some information is lost, making it possible to misinterpret the findings. Hence, caution is required when interpreting data.

Statistics also play a vital role in understanding the relationship between variables, particularly when there are more than two. With experience, it is easy to 'read' the relationship between two variables from a table, but not to quantify this relationship. Statistics help you to ascertain the strength of a relationship. They confirm or contradict what you read from a piece of information, and provide an indication of the strength of the relationship and the level of confidence that can be placed in findings. When there are more than two variables, statistics are also helpful in understanding the interdependence between them and their contribution to a phenomenon or event.

Indirectly, knowledge of statistics helps you at each step of the research process. Knowledge of the problems associated with data analysis, the types of statistical test that can be applied to certain types of variable, and the calculation of summary statistics in relation to the measurement scale used play an important role in a research endeavour. However, you can also carry out a perfectly valid study without using any statistical procedures. This depends upon the objectives of your study.

Computers in research can play a very significant role in many ways. In the modern age you can hardly imagine anyone who is computer illiterate. Almost everyone would use a computer for word-processing. All your research activities, from writing a research proposal to completion of dissertation, can be typed and saved on a computer. You will often need to go through a number of drafts to incorporate the development of new thoughts and improvement of your written communication, and computers can help you make additional changes without redoing everything.

VIDEO TUTORIALS
ON SPSS

There are a number of statistical packages, such as IBM SPSS Statistics , SAS and NVivo, that will make it very easy for you to carry out simple or complex data analyses.

Another advantage of computers is in displaying your data the way you want and changing the presentation to better suit your written communication style. Most programmes can help you to present you data the way you want it with extreme ease.

328   **RESEARCH METHODOLOGY**

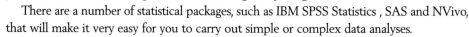

It will pay you to learn the program(s) you are likely to use. In the long run it will save you a great deal of time and money.

Summary

In this chapter you have learnt about data processing. Irrespective of the method of data collection, qualitative or quantitative, the information is called 'raw data' or simply 'data'. The processing of data includes all operations undertaken from collection to analysis either manually or by computer. Data processing in quantitative studies starts with editing, which is basically 'cleaning' your data. This is followed by coding, which entails developing a code book, pre-testing it, the actual coding, and verifying the coded data. In this chapter we have provided a prototype for developing a code book, detailing descriptions of how to develop codes for open-ended and closed questions, and a step-by-step guide to coding data, taking an example from a survey. The chapter also includes detailed information about content analysis. An extended example of content analysis is provided. The chapter also deals with how to treat data for narrative and thematic styles of writing.

Though the development of a frame of analysis continues until you have finished the report, it helps immensely in data analysis to develop this before you begin analysing data. In the frame of analysis the type of analysis to be undertaken (e.g. frequency distribution, cross-tabulation, content analysis), and the statistical procedures to be applied, should be specified.

Computers primarily help by saving labour associated with analysing data manually. Their application in handling complicated statistical and mathematical procedures, word processing, displaying and graphic presentation of the data analysed saves time and increases speed. Statistics are desirable but not essential for a study. The extent of their application depends upon the purpose of the study. Statistics primarily help you to make sense of data, 'read' the data, explore relationships and the interdependence between variables, ascertain the magnitude of an existing relationship or interdependence and place confidence in your findings.

FOR YOU TO THINK ABOUT

- Refamiliarise yourself with the keywords listed at the beginning of this chapter, and if you are uncertain about the meaning or application of any of them revisit them in the chapter before moving on.
- What procedures can you set in place to ensure the accuracy of the information obtained in both quantitative and qualitative studies?
- Thinking of examples from your own area of study, consider the advantages and disadvantages of having used open-ended or closed questions when you come to process your data.
- Assess the role of statistics for a study in your area of interest.

(Continued)

PROCESSING DATA   329

(Continued)

Now, as you have gone through the chapter, try answering the following questions:

- In terms of data processing, what are the advantages and disadvantages of closed and open-ended questions?
- In undertaking content analysis for descriptive information, what considerations would you keep in mind when developing themes?
- Critically examine the applications of statistics with particular reference to quantitative and qualitative research.

Want to learn more? Visit
http://www.uk.sagepub.com/kumar4e
or scan this QR code to gain access to a range of online resources to support your study including practice quizzes, videos, weblinks, flashcards, and journal articles.

16

DISPLAYING DATA

In this chapter you will learn about

- ■ Methods of communicating and displaying analysed data in quantitative and qualitative research
- ■ How to present your data in tables
- ■ Different types of graphs and how to use them to represent your data

Keywords

area chart, bar diagram, bivariate, cumulative frequency polygon,

data display, frequency graph, line diagram, pie chart,

polygon, polyvariate, scattergram, table, univariate.

At the end of this chapter, you should have an understanding of

- Different ways of communicating data
- The anatomy of a table and types of tables
- Different graphics presentations

Methods of communicating and displaying analysed data

Having analysed the data that you collected through either quantitative, qualitative or mixed/multiple method(s), the next task is to present your findings to your readers. The main purpose of using data display techniques is to make the findings easy and clear to understand, and to provide extensive and comprehensive information in a succinct and effective way. Broadly, there are two styles of writing in research: firstly, a descriptive and narrative style; and secondly, an analytical style with factual information incorporated in the text. The descriptive and narrative style is more prevalent in qualitative studies and the analytical in quantitative studies. However, in practice you may mix them if the data permits. The choice of a particular style should be determined primarily by the type of writing style the data gathered lends itself to, your impressions/knowledge of your likely readership's preference, your familiarity with research methodology and statistical procedures, your own writing style, and your impression as to which style of writing would communicate the findings more effectively to the readership.

Because of the nature and purpose of investigation in qualitative research, text becomes the dominant and usually the sole mode of communication. In quantitative studies the text is very commonly combined with other forms of data display, the extent of which depends upon your familiarity with them, the purpose of the study and what you think would make it easier for your readership to understand the content and sustain their interest in it. Hence as a researcher it is entirely up to you to decide the best way of communicating your findings to your readers. Within these two approaches there are many ways of presenting information. If your readers are likely to be familiar with 'reading' data, you can use complicated methods of data display; if not, it is wise to keep to simple techniques.

Although there are many ways of displaying data, this chapter is limited to those more commonly used. There are many computer programs that can help you with this task. In this chapter we confine the communication and display of analysed data to the following four methods: text; tables; graphs; and statistical measures.

Text

Text is by far the most common method of communication in both quantitative and qualitative research studies, and perhaps the only method in the latter. It is, therefore, essential that you know how to communicate effectively, keeping in mind the level of understanding, interest in the topic and need for academic and scientific rigour of those for whom you are writing. Your style should strike a balance between academic and scientific rigour on the one hand, and attracting and sustaining the interest of your readers on the other. Of course, it goes without saying that a reasonable command of the language and clarity of thought are imperative for good communication.

Your writing should be thematic: that is, written around the various themes of your report; findings should be integrated into the literature citing references using an acceptable system of citation; your writing should follow a logical progression of thought; and the layout should be attractive and pleasing to the eye. Language, in terms of clarity and flow, plays an important role in communication. According to the Commonwealth of Australia *Style Manual* (2002: 49):

> The language of well-written documents helps to communicate information effectively. Language is also the means by which writers create the tone or register of a publication and establish relationships with their readers. For these relationships to be productive, the language the writer uses must take full account of the diversity of knowledge, interests and sensitivities within the audience.

Tables

Structure

Other than text, tables are the most common method of presenting analysed data in quantitative studies. According to the *Chicago Manual of Style* (1993: 21), 'Tables offer a useful means of presenting large amounts of detailed information in a small space'. According to the Commonwealth of Australia *Style Manual* (2002: 46), 'tables can be a boon for readers. They can dramatically clarify text, provide visual relief, and serve as quick point of reference.' It is, therefore, essential for beginners to know about their structure and types. Figure 16.1 shows the structure of a table.

A table has five parts:

1. Title – This normally indicates the table number and describes the type of data the table contains. It is important to give each table its own number as you will need to refer to the tables when interpreting and discussing the data in the text of the report. The tables should be numbered sequentially as they appear in the text. The procedure for numbering tables is a personal choice. If you are writing an article, simply identifying tables by number is sufficient. In the case of a dissertation or a report, one way to identify a table is by the chapter number followed by the number of the table within the chapter – the procedure adopted in this book. The main advantage of this procedure is that if it becomes necessary to add or delete a table when revising the report, you only need to change the table numbers for that chapter rather than for the whole report.

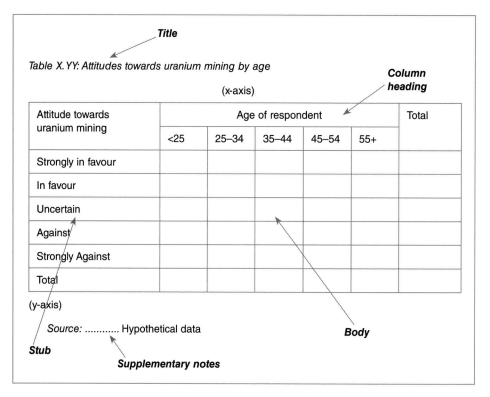

Figure 16.1   The structure of a table

The description accompanying the table number must clearly specify the contents of that table. In the description identify the variables about which information is contained in the table, for example 'Respondents by age' or 'Attitudes towards uranium mining'. If a table contains information about two variables, the dependent variable should be identified first in the title, for example 'Attitudes towards uranium mining [dependent variable] by gender [independent variable]'.

2. Stub – The subcategories of a variable, listed at the head of each row (the left-hand column of the table). According to the *McGraw-Hill Style Manual* (Longyear 1983: 97), 'the stub, usually the first column on the left, lists the items about which information is provided in the horizontal rows to the right.' The *Chicago Manual of Style* (1993: 331) describes the stub as 'a vertical listing of categories or individuals about which information is given in the columns of the table'.

3. Column headings – The subcategories of a variable, listed along the top of the table. In univariate tables (tables displaying information about one variable) the column heading is usually the 'number of respondents' and/or the 'percentage of respondents' (Tables 16.1 and 16.2). In bivariate tables (tables displaying information about two variables) it is the subcategories of one of the variables displayed in the column headings (Table 16.3).

4. Body – The cells housing the analysed data.

5. Supplementary notes or footnotes – There are four types of footnote: source notes; other general notes; notes on specific parts of the table; and notes on the level of probability (*Chicago Manual of Style* 1993: 333). If the data is taken from another source, you have an obligation to acknowledge this. The source should be identified at the bottom of the table, and labelled by the

word 'source', as in Figure 16.1. Similarly, other explanatory notes should be added at the bottom of a table.

Types of table

Depending upon the number of variables about which information is displayed, tables can be categorised as:

- univariate (also known as frequency tables) – containing information about one variable, for example Tables 16.1 and 16.2;
- bivariate (also known as cross-tabulations) – containing information about two variables, for example Table 16.3; and
- polyvariate or multivariate – containing information about more than two variables, for example Table 16.4.

Table 16.1 Respondents by age (frequency table for one population – hypothetical data)

Age	No. of respondents
<20 years	2 (2.0)
20–24	12 (12.0)
25–29	22 (22.0)
30–34	14 (14.0)
35–39	17 (17.0)
40–44	10 (10.0)
45–49	11 (11.0)
50–54	9 (9.0)
55+	3 (3.0)
Total	100 (100.0)

Note: Figures in parentheses are percentages.

Table 16.2 Respondents by age (frequency table comparing two populations – hypothetical data)

Age	Population A	Population B
<20	2 (2.0)	1 (0.6)
20–24	12 (12.0)	17 (10.9)
25–29	22 (22.0)	23 (14.7)
30–34	14 (14.0)	18 (11.5)
35–39	17 (17.0)	26 (16.7)
40–44	10 (10.0)	16 (10.3)
45–49	11 (11.0)	18 (11.5)
50–54	9 (9.0)	27 (17.3)
55+	3 (3.0)	10 (6.4)
No response	0 (0.0)	0 (0.0)
Total	100 (100.0)	156 (100.0*)

Note: Figures in parentheses are percentages (*these sum to 99.9 due to rounding).

Table 16.3   Respondents by attitude towards uranium mining and age (cross-tabulation − hypothetical data)

Attitude towards uranium mining	Age					
	<25	25–34	35–44	45–54	55+	Total
Strongly in favour	(0.0)*	(5.5)	(14.8)	(35.0)	(100.0)	
	0	2	4	7	3	16
	(0.0)†	(12.5)†	(25.0)†	(43.6)†	(18.6)†	(100.0)†
	(0.0)*	(8.3)	(18.5)	(20.0)	(0.0)	
In favour	0	3	5	4	0	12
	(0.0)	(25.0)	(41.7)	(33.3)	(0.0)	(100.0)
	(0.0)*	(0.0)	(7.4)	(20.0)	(0.0)	
Uncertain	0	0	2	4	0	6
	(0.0)	(0.0)	(33.3)	(66.7)	(66.7)	(100.0)
	(14.3)*	(19.4)	(3.7)	(0.0)	(0.0)	
Against	2	7	1	0	0	10
	(20.0)	(70.0)	(10.0)	(0.0)	(0.0)	(100.0)
	(85.7)*	(66.7)	(55.6)	(25.0)	(0.0)	
Strongly against	12	24	15	5	0	56
	(21.4)	(42.9)	(26.8)	(8.9)	(0.0)	(100.0)
Total	(100.0)*	(100.0)	(100.0)	(100.0)	(100.0)	(100.0)
	14	36	27	20	3	100

* =column percentage; † = row percentage.

Table 16.4   Attitude towards uranium mining by age and gender (hypothetical data)

Attitude towards uranium mining	Number of respondents												
	<25		25–34		35–44		45–54		55+		Total		
	F	M	F	M	F	M	F	M	F	M	F	M	T
Strongly in favour	0	0	1	1	3	1	5	2	3	0	12	4	16
In favour	0	0	1	2	3	2	3	1	0	0	7	5	12
Uncertain	0	0	0	0	1	1	2	2	0	0	3	3	6
Against	1	1	4	3	1	0	0	0	0	0	6	4	10
Strongly against	4	8	17	7	8	7	2	3	0	0	31	25	56
Total	5	9	23	13	16	11	12	8	3	0	59	41	100

Types of percentage

The abilities to interpret data accurately and to communicate findings effectively are important skills for a researcher. For accurate and effective interpretation of data, you may need to calculate measures such as percentages, cumulative percentages or ratios. It is also sometimes important to apply other statistical procedures to data. The use of percentages is a common procedure in the interpretation of data. There are three types of percentage: 'row', 'column' and 'total'. It is important to understand the relevance, interpretation and significance of each. Let us take some examples.

Tables 16.1 and 16.2 are univariate or frequency tables. In any univariate table, percentages calculate the magnitude of each subcategory of the variable out of a constant number (100). Such a table shows what would have been the expected number of respondents in each subcategory had there been 100 respondents. Percentages in a univariate table play a more important role when two or more samples or populations are being compared (Table 16.2). As the total number of respondents in each sample or population group normally varies, percentages enable you to standardise them against a fixed number (100). This standardisation against 100 enables you to compare the magnitude of the two populations within the different subcategories of a variable.

In a cross-tabulation such as in Table 16.3, the subcategories of both variables are examined in relation to each other. To make this table less congested, we have collapsed the age categories shown in Table 16.1. For such tables you can calculate three different types of percentage – row, column and total – as follows:

- Row percentage – This is calculated from the total of *all* the subcategories of one variable that are displayed along a row in different columns, in relation to only *one* subcategory of the other variable. For example, in Table 16.3 figures in parentheses marked † are the row percentages calculated out of *the total* (16) of all age subcategories of the variable age in relation to only one subcategory of the second variable (i.e. those who are strongly in favour of uranium mining) – in other words, one subcategory of a variable displayed on the stub by all the subcategories of the variable displayed on the column heading of a table. Out of those who are strongly against uranium mining, 21.4 per cent are under the age of 25 years, none is above the age of 55 and the majority (42.9 per cent) are between 25 and 34 years of age (Table 16.3). This row percentage has thus given you the variation in terms of age among those who are strongly against uranium mining. It has shown how the 56 respondents who are strongly against uranium mining differ in age from one another. Similarly, you can select any other subcategory of the variable (attitude towards uranium mining) to examine its variation in relation to the other variable, age.
- Column percentage – In the same way, you can hold age at a constant level and examine variations in attitude using column percentages. For example, suppose you want to find out differences in attitude among 25–34-year-olds towards uranium mining. The age category 25–34 (column) shows that of the 36 respondents, 24 (66.7 per cent) are strongly against while only 2 (5.5 per cent) are strongly in favour of uranium mining. You can do the same by taking any subcategory of the variable age, to examine differences with respect to the different subcategories of the other variable (attitudes towards uranium mining).
- Total percentage – This standardises the magnitude of each cell; that is, it gives the percent age of respondents who are classified in the subcategories of one variable in relation to the subcategories of the other variable. For example, what percentage of the total population is constituted by those who are under the age of 25 years and are strongly against uranium mining?

It is possible to sort data for three variables. Table 16.4 (percentages not shown) examines respondents' attitudes in relation to their age and gender. As you add more variables to a table it becomes more complicated to read and more difficult to interpret, but the procedure for interpreting it is the same.

The introduction of the third variable, gender, helps you to find out how the observed association between the two subcategories of the two variables, age and attitude, is distributed in relation to gender. In other words, it helps you to find out how many males and females constitute a particular cell showing the association between the other two variables (attitude towards uranium mining and age of the respondents). For example, Table 16.4 shows that of those who are strongly against uranium mining, 24 (42.9 per cent) are 25–34 years of age. This group comprises 17 (70.8 per cent) females and 7 (29.2 per cent) males. Hence, the table shows that a greater proportion of female than male respondents between the ages of 25 and 34 are strongly against uranium mining. Similarly, you can take any two subcategories of age and attitude and relate these to either subcategory (male/female) of the third variable, gender.

Graphs

GRAPHS IN SPSS

Graphic presentations constitute the third way of communicating analysed data. Graphic presentations can make analysed data easier to understand and effectively communicate what it is supposed to show. One of the choices you need to make is whether a set of information is best presented as a table, a graph or text. The main objective of a graph is to present data in a way that is easy to interpret and interesting to look at. Your decision to use a graph should be based mainly on this consideration: 'A graph is based entirely on the tabled data and therefore can tell no story that cannot be learnt by inspecting a table. However, graphic representation often makes it easier to see the pertinent features of a set of data' (Minium 1978: 45).

Graphs can be constructed for every type of data – quantitative and qualitative – and for any type of variable (measured on a nominal, ordinal, interval or ratio scale). There are different types of graph, and your decision to use a particular type should be made on the basis of the measurement scale used in the measurement of a variable. It is equally important to keep in mind the measurement scale used in the measurement of a variable when it comes to interpretation. It is not uncommon to find people misinterpreting a graph and drawing wrong conclusions simply because they have overlooked the measurement scale used in the measurement of a variable. The type of graph you choose depends upon the type of data you are displaying. For categorical variables you can construct only bar charts, histograms or pie charts, whereas for continuous variables, in addition to the above, line or trend graphs can also be constructed. The number of variables shown in a graph is also important in determining the type of graph you can construct.

When constructing a graph of any type it is important to bear the following points in mind:

- A graphic presentation is constructed on two axes: horizontal and vertical. The horizontal axis is called the 'abscissa' or, more commonly, the x-axis, and the vertical axis is called the 'ordinate' or, more commonly, the y-axis (Minium 1978: 45).
- If a graph is designed to display only one variable, it is customary, but not essential, to represent the subcategories of the variable along the x-axis and the frequency or count of each subcategory along the y-axis. The point where the axes intersect is considered as the zero point for the y-axis. When a graph presents two variables, one is displayed on each axis and the point where they intersect is considered as the starting or zero point.

338   RESEARCH METHODOLOGY

- A graph, like a table, should have a title that describes its contents. The axes should also be labelled.
- A graph should be drawn to an appropriate scale. It is important to choose a scale that enables your graph to be neither too small nor too large, and your choice of scale for each axis should result in the spread of axes being roughly proportionate to one another. Sometimes, to fit the spread of the scale (when it is too spread out) on one or both axes, it is necessary to break the scale and alert readers by introducing a break (usually two slanting parallel lines) in the axes.

The histogram

A histogram consists of a series of rectangles drawn next to each other without any space between them, each representing the frequency of a category or subcategory (Figure 16.2). Their height is in proportion to the frequency they represent. The height of the rectangles may represent the absolute or proportional frequency or the percentage of the total. As mentioned, a histogram can be drawn for both categorical and continuous variables. When a histogram is based upon a continuous variable you can interpret the trend exhibited by it, but the same cannot be done if it is based on a categorical variable as you can arrange categorical variables in any order. Therefore when interpreting a histogram you need to take into account whether it is representing categorical or continuous variables. Figure 16.2 provides three examples of histograms using data from Tables 16.1 and 16.4. The histogram in Figure 16.2b is effectively the same as that in Figure 16.2a but is presented in a three-dimensional style.

The bar chart

The bar chart or bar diagram is used for displaying categorical data (Figure 16.3). A bar chart is identical to a histogram, except that in a bar chart the rectangles representing the various frequencies are spaced, thus indicating that the data is categorical. The bar chart is used for variables measured on nominal or ordinal scales. The discrete categories are usually displayed along the x-axis and the number or percentage of respondents on the y-axis. However, as

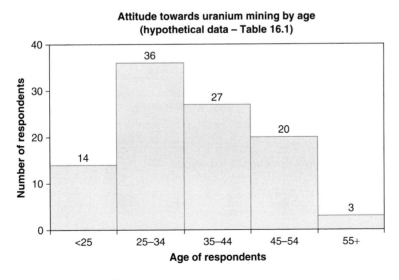

Figure 16.2a   Two-dimensional histogram

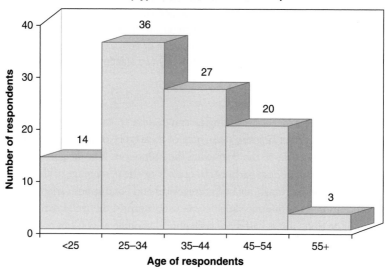

Figure 16.2b   Three-dimensional histogram

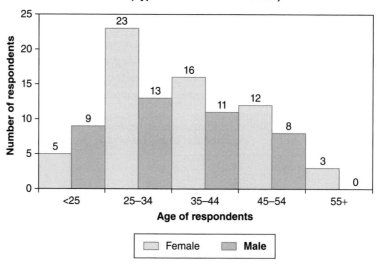

Figure 16.2c   Two-dimensional histogram with two variables

STACKED BARS
GRAPH IN SPSS

illustrated, it is possible to display the discrete categories along the y-axis. The bar chart is an effective way of visually displaying the magnitude of each subcategory of a variable.

The stacked bar chart

A stacked bar chart is similar to a bar chart except that in the former each bar shows information about two or more variables stacked onto each other vertically (Figure 16.4).

340   **RESEARCH METHODOLOGY**

The sections of a bar show the proportion of the variables they represent in relation to one another. The stacked bars can be drawn only for categorical data.

The 100 per cent bar chart

The 100 per cent bar chart (Figure 16.5) is very similar to the stacked bar chart. In this case, the subcategories of a variable are converted into percentages of the total population of the

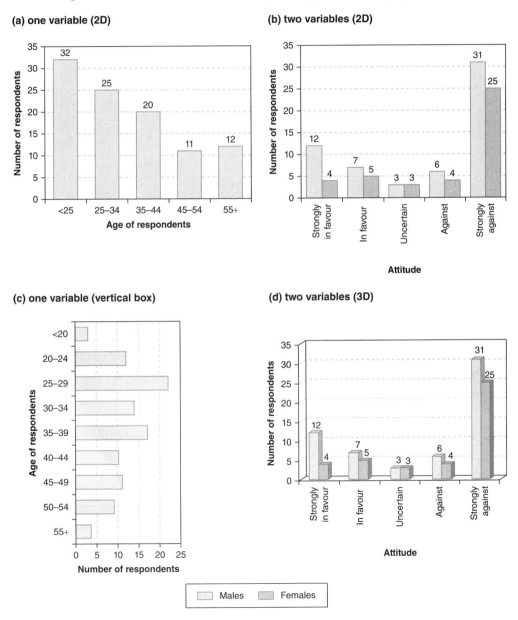

Figure 16.3   Different types of bar chart

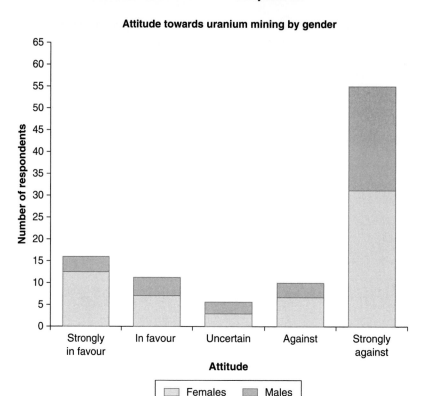

Figure 16.4 The stacked bar chart

subcategory and drawn as a stacked bar chart. Each bar, which totals 100, is sliced into portions relative to the percentage of each subcategory of the variable.

The frequency polygon

The frequency polygon is very similar to a histogram. A frequency polygon is drawn by joining the midpoint of each rectangle at a height commensurate with the frequency of that interval (Figure 16.6). However, there is one problem in constructing a frequency polygon, that is, what to do with the two categories at either extreme if they are open-ended (e.g. if one is less than 15 and the other over 60). How do we draw a trend line for these extremes? To overcome this you imagine that the two extreme categories have an interval similar to the rest and assume the frequency in these categories to be zero. From the midpoint of these intervals, you extend the polygon line to meet the x-axis at both ends. A frequency polygon can be drawn using either absolute or proportionate frequencies.

The cumulative frequency polygon

The cumulative frequency polygon or cumulative frequency curve (Figure 16.7) is drawn on the basis of cumulative frequencies. The main difference between a frequency

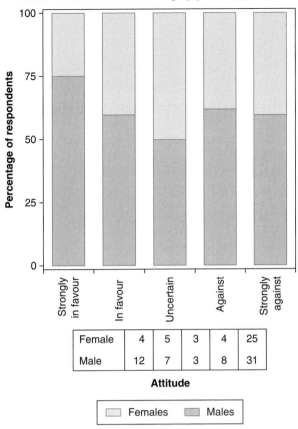

Figure 16.5   The 100 per cent bar chart

polygon and a cumulative frequency polygon is that the former is drawn by joining the midpoints of the intervals, whereas the latter is drawn by joining the end points of the intervals because cumulative frequencies interpret data in relation to the upper limit of an interval. As a cumulative frequency distribution tells you the number of observations less than a given value and is usually based upon grouped data, to interpret a frequency distribution the upper limit needs to be taken.

The stem-and-leaf display

The stem-and-leaf display is an effective, quick and simple way of displaying a frequency distribution (Figure 16.8). The stem-and-leaf diagram for a frequency distribution running into two digits is plotted by displaying digits 0 to 9 on the left of the y-axis, representing the tens of a frequency. The figures representing the units of a frequency (i.e. the right-hand figure of a two-digit frequency display) are displayed on the right of the y-axis. Note that the stem-and-leaf display does not use grouped data but absolute frequencies. If the display is rotated 90 degrees in an anti-clockwise direction, it effectively becomes a histogram. With this technique some of the descriptive statistics

DISPLAYING DATA   343

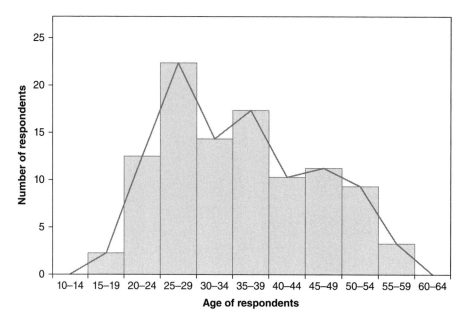

Figure 16.6   The frequency polygon

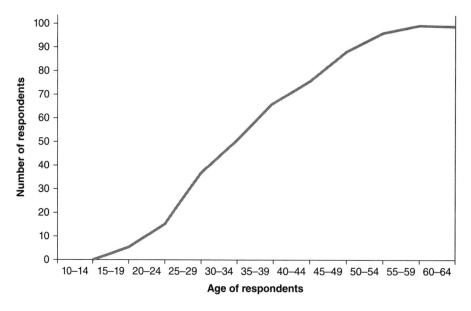

Figure 16.7   The cumulative frequency polygon

relating to the frequency distribution, such as the mean, the mode and the median, can easily be ascertained; however, the procedure for their calculation is beyond the scope of this book. Stem-and-leaf displays are also possible for frequencies running into three and four digits (hundreds and thousands).

344   RESEARCH METHODOLOGY

1	89
2	000111222222334455555556667777788899
3	001112223333334455555666677777889
4	112223333444555566779
5	000113355667

Figure 16.8   The stem-and-leaf display

The pie chart

The pie chart is another way of representing data graphically (Figure 16.9), this time as a circle. There are 360 degrees in a circle, and so the full circle can be used to represent 100 per cent, or the total population. The circle or pie is divided into sections in accordance with the magnitude of each subcategory, and so each slice is in proportion to the size of each subcategory of a frequency distribution. The proportions may be shown either as absolute numbers or as percentages. Manually, pie charts are more difficult to draw than other types of graph because of the difficulty in measuring the degrees of the pie/circle. They can be drawn for both qualitative data and variables measured on a continuous scale but grouped into categories.

The line diagram or trend curve

A set of data measured on a continuous interval or a ratio scale can be displayed using a line diagram or trend curve. A trend line can be drawn for data pertaining to both a specific time (e.g. 1995, 1996, 1997) or a period (e.g. 1985–1989, 1990–1994, 1995–). If it relates to a period, the midpoint of each interval at a height commensurate with

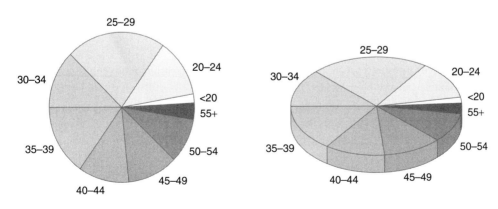

Figure 16.9   Two- and three-dimensional pie charts

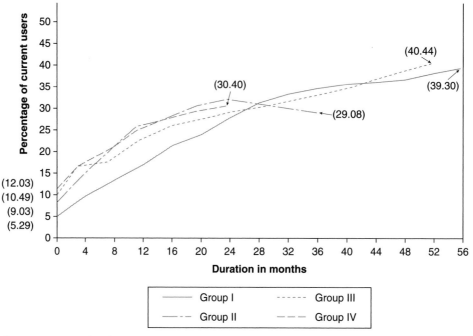

Figure 16.10   The line diagram or trend curve

each frequency – as in the case of a frequency polygon – is marked as a dot. These dots are then connected with straight lines to examine trends in a phenomenon. If the data pertains to exact time, a point is plotted at a height commensurate with the frequency. These points are then connected with straight lines. A line diagram is a useful way of visually conveying the changes when long-term trends in a phenomenon or situation need to be studied. For example, Figure 16.10 clearly shows the trends in the number of current uses of methods for contraception over a period of five years among four study populations receiving four treatment modalities comprising different combinations of maternal and child health, nutritional supplements and family planning services. The same information could not have been depicted with such clarity by a table.

The area chart

For variables measured on an interval or a ratio scale, information about the subcategories of a variable can also be presented in the form of an area chart. This is plotted in the same way as a line diagram but with the area under each line shaded to highlight the total magnitude of the subcategory in relation to other subcategories. For example, Figure 16.11 shows the number of male and female respondents by age.

SCATTERPLOTS
IN SPSS

The scattergram

When you want to show visually how one variable changes in relation to a change in the other variable, a scattergram is extremely effective. Both the variables must be measured

346   **RESEARCH METHODOLOGY**

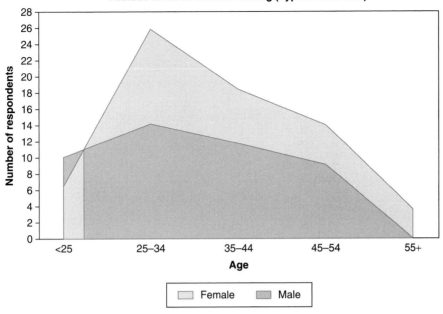

Figure 16.11   The area chart

either on interval or ratio scales and the data on both the variables needs to be available in absolute values for each observation – you cannot plot a scattergram for categorical variables. Data for both variables is taken in pairs and displayed as dots in relation to their values on both axes. Let us take the data on age and income for 10 respondents of a hypothetical study in Table 16.5. The relationship between age and income based upon hypothetical data is shown in Figure 16.12.

Table 16.5   Age and income data

Respondent	Income	Age
A	25,500	24
B	46,000	50
C	30,500	36
D	55,000	45
E	27,000	29
F	35,000	38
G	40,000	37
H	52,000	48
I	47,000	41
J	38,000	47

DISPLAYING DATA   347

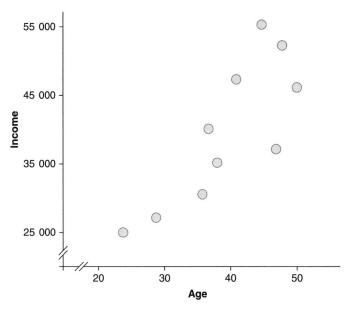

Figure 16.12   The scattergram

Statistical measures

The importance of statistics in research, particularly in quantitative studies, is unquestionably immense. The role of statistics lies in first describing data in aggregated and summary form to enhance its understanding and meaning, to establish whether or not there is a relationship between two variables and, if so, to quantify the magnitude of the relationship. Placing a degree of confidence in the findings is another function of statistics. Many academic disciplines are extremely particular about the integration of statistics into research reports and place immense importance on the application of statistical measures to research findings.

STATISTICS BOOKS

The exclusion of statistics from this book is not an indication of the author's lack of appreciation for statistics, but of the difficulty in accommodating such a vast area in one text. Because of its vastness, the author thought it better for the reader to refer to texts specifically written on statistics.

Though statistical measures are extremely effective in communicating findings in a precise and succinct manner, you can conduct a perfectly valid study without using any statistical measure. However, their use in certain situations is desirable and in some it is essential.

There are many statistical measures, ranging from very simple to extremely complicated. At one end of the spectrum you have simple descriptive measures such as the mean, mode, median, and at the other there are inferential statistical measures such as analysis of variance, factorial analysis and multiple regressions.

Because of its vastness, statistics is considered a separate academic discipline, and before you use these measures you need to learn about them.

348   **RESEARCH METHODOLOGY**

Use of statistical measures is dependent upon the type of data collected, your knowledge of statistics, the purpose of communicating the findings, and the knowledge base in statistics of your readership.

Summary

Research findings in both quantitative and qualitative research are usually conveyed to readers through text. In qualitative research this is more or less the sole method of communication. However, in quantitative studies, though text is still the dominant method of communicating research findings, it is often combined with other forms such as tables, graphs and statistical measures, which can make the research easier to understand. What you use should be determined by what you feel comfortable with and what you think will be easiest for readers to understand. Tables have the advantage of containing a great deal of information in a small space, while graphs make it easy for readers to absorb information at a glance.

Usually, a table will have five parts: title, stub, column headings, body and supplementary notes or footnotes. Depending upon the number of variables about which information in a table is stored, there are three types of table: univariate (frequency), bivariate (cross-tabulation) and multivariate.

To interpret a table, simple arithmetic procedures such as percentages, cumulative frequencies or ratios can be used. You can also calculate simple descriptive statistical procedures such as the mean, the mode, the median, the chi-square test, the *t*-test and the coefficient of correlation. If you have statistical knowledge, advanced statistics can be applied.

Statistics are not included in this book for two reasons: to maintain a sharp focus on research study design; and because the vastness of the subject of statistics would have made this book difficult for beginners in research.

While there are many types of graphs, the common ones are: the histogram, the bar diagram, the stacked bar chart, the 100 per cent bar chart, the frequency polygon, the stem-and-leaf display, the pie chart, the line or trend diagram, the area chart and the scattergram. The choice among these depends upon your purpose and the measurement scale used to measure the variable(s) being displayed. Some graphs are difficult to draw by hand but can be readily done by computer.

FOR YOU TO THINK ABOUT

- Refamiliarise yourself with the keywords listed at the beginning of this chapter, and if you are uncertain about the meaning or application of any of them revisit them in the chapter before moving on.
- Identify two specific examples where you could use a table rather than just text to communicate findings and two examples where graphs would be better.
- Construct a hypothetical bivariate table, within the context of an area of interest. Calculate different types of percentages and interpret the data.

(Continued)

(Continued)

Now, as you have gone through the chapter, try answering the following questions:

- What are the different ways you can communicate your research findings?
- Ideally, a table has a number of parts. Explain them.
- What are the different types of percentage? What functions do they perform in data interpretation?
- What are the different types of graph? Discuss their application in relation to measurement scales.

Want to learn more? Visit
http://www.uk.sagepub.com/kumar4e
or scan this QR code to gain access to a range of online resources to support your study including practice quizzes, videos, weblinks, flashcards, and journal articles.

STEP VIII

WRITING A RESEARCH REPORT

This operational step includes one chapter:

- Chapter 17: Writing a Research Report

17

WRITING A RESEARCH REPORT

In this chapter you will learn about

- How to write a research report
- How to develop a draft outline for your research report
- Writing about variables
- Different referencing systems
- How to write a bibliography

Keywords

association, bibliography, intellectual rigour,

non-spurious relationship, outline, referencing,

spurious relationship, variable, verifiability.

At the end of this chapter, you should have an understanding of

- How to develop an outline of a research report
- How to integrate the hard data into your report
- Drawing inferences and conclusions
- Different referencing systems

Writing a research report

CONVENTIONS IN ACADEMIC WRITING

The last step in the research process is writing the research report. Each step of the process is important for a valid study, as negligence at any stage will affect the quality of not just that part but the whole study. This last step is the most crucial as it is through the report that the findings of the study and their implications are communicated to your supervisor and readers. Most people will not be aware of the amount and quality of work that has gone into your study. While much hard work and care may have been put into every stage of the research, all readers see is the report. Therefore, the whole enterprise can be spoiled if the report is not well written. As Burns (1997: 229) writes, 'extremely valuable and interesting practical work may be spoiled at the last minute by a student who is not able to communicate the results easily'.

In addition to your understanding of research methodology, the quality of the report depends upon such things as your written communication skills and clarity of thought, your ability to express thoughts in a logical and sequential manner, and your subject knowledge base. Another important determinant is your experience in research writing: the more experience you acquire, the more effective you will become at writing a research report. The use of statistical procedures will reinforce the validity of your conclusions and arguments as they enable you to establish if an observed association is due to chance or otherwise (i.e. whether a relationship is spurious or non-spurious) and indicate the strength of an association so readers can place confidence in your findings. The use of graphs to present the findings, though not essential, will make the information more easily understood by readers. As stated in the previous chapter, whether or not graphs are used depends upon the purpose for which the findings are to be used.

The main difference between research and other writing is in the degree of control, rigour and caution required. Research writing is controlled in the sense that you need to be extremely careful about what you write, the words you choose, the way ideas are expressed, and the validity and verifiability of the conclusions you draw. What most distinguishes research writing from other writing is the high degree of intellectual rigour required for research writing. Research writing must be absolutely accurate, clear, unambiguous, logical and concise. Your writing should not be based upon assumptions about knowledge of your readers regarding the study. Bear in mind that you must be able to defend whatever you write should anyone challenge it. Do not use ornamental and superficial language. Even the best researchers make a number of drafts before writing up their final one, so be prepared to undertake this task.

The way findings are communicated differs in quantitative and qualitative research. As mentioned earlier, in qualitative research the findings are mostly communicated in a descriptive or narrative form written around the major themes, events or discourses that emerge from your findings. The main purpose is to describe the variation in a phenomenon, situation, event or episode without making an attempt to quantify it. One way of writing a qualitative report is described in Chapter 15 as a part of the content analysis process. On the other hand, the writing in quantitative research, in addition to being descriptive, also includes its quantification and numerical analysis of data. Depending upon the purpose of the study, statistical measures and tests can also become a part of the research writing to support the findings.

Developing a draft outline

Before you start writing your report, it is good practice to develop an outline ('chapterisation'). This means deciding how you are going to divide your report into different chapters and planning what will be written in each one. In developing the chapterisation, the subobjectives of your study or the major significant themes that emerged from content analysis can provide immense guidance. Develop the chapters around the significant subobjectives or themes of your study. Depending upon the importance of a theme or subobjective, either devote a complete chapter to it or combine it with related themes to form one chapter. The title of each chapter should be descriptive of the main theme, communicate its main thrust and be clear and concise. This is applicable to both types of research.

The following approach is applicable to both qualitative and quantitative types of research, but keep in mind that it is merely suggestive and may be of help if you have no idea where to start. Feel free to change the suggested format in any way you like, or if you prefer a different one, follow that.

The first chapter of your report, possibly entitled 'Introduction', should be a general introduction to the study, covering most of your research proposal and pointing out the deviations, if any, from the original plan. This chapter covers all the preparatory tasks undertaken prior to conducting the study, such as the literature review, the theoretical framework, the objectives of the study, the study design, the sampling strategy and the measurement procedures.

To illustrate this, two examples are provided below for projects referred to previously in this book: the study on foster-care payments and the family engagement model. The first chapters of these reports could be written around the subheadings below. The subsequent structure of these reports is quite different. Keeping in mind the purpose for which family engagement evaluation was commissioned, the report was divided into three parts: the Introduction, the perceived model, and conclusions and recommendation.

Attitudes towards foster-care payments: suggested contents of Chapter 1
Chapter I Introduction

- Introduction
- The development of foster care
- Foster care in Australia
- Foster care in Western Australia
- The Department of Community services
- The out-of-home and community care programme
- Current trends in foster-care placement in Western Australia
- Becoming a foster carer
- Foster-care subsidies
- Issues regarding foster-care payment
- Rationale for the study
- Objectives of the study
- Study design
- Sampling
- Measurement procedure
- Problems and limitations
- Working definitions

Family engagement – A service delivery model: suggested contents of Chapter 1
Part one: Introduction

- Background: the origin of the family engagement idea
- Historical perspective
- The perceived model
    - Conceptual framework
    - Philosophical perspective underpinning the model
    - Intended outcomes
- Objectives of the evaluation
- Evaluation methodology

(Note: In this section, the conceptual framework of the model, its philosophical basis, perceived outcomes as identified by the person(s) responsible for initiating the idea, and what was available in the literature, were included. It also included details about evaluation objectives and evaluation methodology.)

The second chapter in quantitative research reports should provide information about the study population. Here, the relevant social, economic and demographic characteristics of the study population should be described. This chapter serves two purposes:

1. It provides readers with some background information about the population from which you collected the information so they can relate the findings to the type of population studied.
2. It helps to identify the variance within a group; for example, you may want to examine how the level of satisfaction of the consumers of a service changes, for example, with their age, gender or education.

The second chapter in a quantitative research report, therefore, could be entitled 'Socioeconomic-demographic characteristics of the study population' or just 'The study population'. Taking the example of the foster-care payment study, this chapter could be written around the subheadings below.

As qualitative studies are mostly based upon a limited number of in-depth interviews or observations, you may find it very difficult to write about the study population.

Attitude towards foster–care payments: suggested contents of Chapter 2
Chapter 2 The study population

- Introduction
- Respondents by age (Information obtained in response to the question on age should be presented here. Consult 'Writing about variables', the next section of this chapter.)
- Respondents by gender (Follow the suggestions made under 'Writing about variables' (see below) for the rest of the variables.)
- Marital status of the study population
- Ethnicity of respondents
- Study population by number of children
- Average annual income of the study population
- Study population by type of dwelling
- etc.

The title and contents of subsequent chapters depend upon what you have attempted to describe, explore, examine, establish or prove in your study. As the content of each project is different, these chapters will be different. As indicated earlier, the title of each chapter should reflect the main thrust of its contents.

The outline should specify the subsections of the chapter. These subsections should be developed around the different aspects of the theme being discussed in the chapter. If you plan to correlate the information obtained from one variable with another, specify the variables. Plan the sequence for discussion of the variables. In deciding this, keep in mind the linkage and logical progression between the sections. This does not mean that the proposed outline cannot be changed when writing the report – it is possible for it to be significantly changed. However, an outline, even if extremely rough, will be of immense help to you. Again, let us take the study on foster-care payment and the family engagement model as examples:

Attitudes towards foster-care payments: suggested contents of Chapter 3
Chapter 3 Attitudes towards the present level of payment for foster care

- Introduction
- Attitudes towards adequacy of payment for foster care (Responses to questions on the adequacy of foster-care payment should be presented here.)

- adequacy by age (Cross-tabulation, i.e. responses to the question on adequacy of foster-care payment is examined in relation to the responses to questions on age.)
- adequacy by marital status (Cross-tabulation, i.e. responses to the question on adequacy of foster-care payment is examined in relation to the responses to questions on marital status.)
- adequacy by income of the family (Cross-tabulation, i.e. responses to the question on adequacy of foster-care payment is examined in relation to the responses to questions on income.)

- Aspects of foster care not covered by the payment
- Major costs borne by foster carers
- Effects of the current level of payment on the family
- Reasons for increasing the payment

  - proposed level of payment

- Conclusions

(Note: Cross-tabulations can be included for any variable where appropriate.)

Family engagement model: suggested contents of Chapter 2
Part Two: The perceived model

- The philosophy underpinning the model
- Development of the model
- The model in practice
- Perceived differences in practice before and after the introduction of the model
- Perceived strengths of the model
- Perceived weaknesses of the model
- Skills required for effective functioning under the model
- Replication of the model
- Reasons for change to the new model
- Training

  - How should staff be trained?
  - Training provided

- Name of the model
- Determinants of successful implementation of the model
- Indicators of success of the model
- What could have been done differently?
- What needs to be done to improve the model?
- Role of Community Development Funding officers
- Advantages and disadvantages of the Case Management model
- Satisfaction of staff with the model
- The model and departmental vision, philosophy, ethos, principles
- Attitude of clients towards the model
- Attitude of community agencies towards the model
- The model and changes in the selected indicators

(Note: In this section, findings about different aspects of the model as identified through in-depth interviews and focus group discussions were detailed.)

358   RESEARCH METHODOLOGY

Family engagement model: suggested contents of Chapter 3
Part Three: Conclusions and recommendations

- Conclusions
  - General
  - Specific to the model
- Recommendations
  - General
  - Specific to the ... office

This type of outline provides direction in your writing. As mentioned earlier, as you start writing you will certainly change it, but you will find it none the less helpful in your write-up.

Writing about variables

Having developed a chapter outline, the next step is to start writing. Although researchers vary greatly in the ways in which they organise their writing, the following guidelines and format may prove helpful for beginners.

When writing about the information obtained in response to a question (variable), write as if you were providing answers to the following questions:

- Why did you think it important to study the variable? What effects, in your opinion, may this variable have on the main variable you are explaining? (*This is where you provide your own rationale for studying the variable.*)
- In the case of a cross-tabulation, what relationships have other studies found between the variables you are analysing? (*This is where the literature review is integrated into the findings of the study.*)
- What did you expect to find out in terms of the relationship between the two variables? (*If you have formulated a hypothesis, state it here.*)
- What has your study found out? (*Provide the hard data from your study here, as tables, graphs or text.*)
- What does the data show? (*Interpret the findings of your analysis.*)
- What conclusions can you draw? How do the conclusions drawn from your study compare with those from similar studies in the past? Does your study support or contradict them?
- What explanation can you provide for the findings of your study?

The above is only a suggested format for ordering your thoughts, not a list of subheadings. You may wish to change the suggested order to make the reading more interesting. Below is an example of writing about a variable, 'Adequacy of payment for foster care', from Chapter 13:

- Why did you think it important to find out if foster-care payments are adequate? What effects, in your opinion, could the adequacy or otherwise of payment for foster care have on the quality of foster care?
- What have other studies in your literature review said about the adequacy of foster-care payments?
- What did you expect to find out from your study population in terms of its feelings about the adequacy of foster-care payments? If you formulated a hypothesis, you should specify that here.

For example, H_0: Most foster parents would consider the current level of foster-care payments to be adequate.

- What did you find out about the adequacy of foster-care payments? What proportion of the study population said they were adequate? What proportion said they were inadequate? Provide a table or graph showing the distribution of respondents by their response to the question regarding the adequacy of foster-care payments.
- What does your data show about the adequacy of foster-care payments? What are the main findings of your study? How do these findings compare with those of other studies you found in your literature review? Does your study support or contradict them?
- What conclusions can you draw about the adequacy of the amount of payment for foster care?
- What explanation can you provide for the observed findings? Why do you think those who said that foster payments are either adequate or inadequate feel that way?

In the suggested format for writing about information obtained from questions, notice that the literature review is integrated with the findings and conclusions. The extent of the integration of the literature with findings mostly depends upon the level at which you are writing your dissertation (bachelor's, master's or PhD) – the higher the level, the more extensive the literature review, the greater its integration with your findings, and the more careful and confident you need to be about your conclusions.

Writing in qualitative research is more descriptive and narrative than analytical, hence you need to use your imagination in terms of placement of information, linkage between the thoughts and flow of language to make the writing interesting to read and meaningful in conveying the findings.

The suggested format is organised around the main themes of the study. There are other formats. Some researchers write everything under one heading, 'The findings'. This format is appropriate for a research paper, because it is short, but not for a research report or dissertation. Other writers follow the same order as in the research instrument; for example, findings are discussed under each question that was asked of the respondents in an interview or a questionnaire. However, this means that the reader needs to refer continuously to the instrument for each question. This format is segmental, lacks linkage and integration, and may not place findings into perspective.

REFERENCING
SYSTEMS

Referencing

Your report must follow an acceptable academic style of referencing. There are many styles in use in academic circles and the choice of a referencing system varies from one academic discipline to another. You need to know which system is preferred by your department and the university. You should spend some time learning about it. Whichever system you decide to use, make sure you are consistent in its use. According to Butcher (1981: 226), there are four referencing systems from which to choose:

1. the short-title system;
2. the author–date system (also known as the name–year system, Harvard system or parenthetical referencing system);

3. the reference by number system (also known as the Vancouver system);
4. the author–number system.

According to Butcher (1981: 167), 'The first of these is used in most general books, the second mainly in science and social science books; the third and the fourth less frequently'. Butcher (1981) and the various style guides mentioned in this book provide plenty of examples for you to follow.

Writing a bibliography

Again, there are several well-established systems for writing a bibliography and your choice is dependent upon the preference of the discipline and university. In the social sciences some of the most commonly used ones are (Longyear 1983: 83):

CITATION TUTORIAL

- the Harvard system;
- the American Psychological Association system;
- the American Medical Association system;
- the McGraw–Hill system;
- the Modern Languages Association system;
- the footnote system.

To learn about these systems and styles, consult the references provided at the end of this book or consult your library.

Summary

Writing your report is the most crucial step in the research process as it communicates the findings to your research supervisor and readers. A badly written report can spoil all the hard work you have put into your research study.

Styles of research writing vary markedly among researchers but all research reports must be written clearly and concisely. Furthermore, scientific writing requires intellectual rigour and there are certain obligations in terms of accuracy and objectivity. Reports can be written in different formats, and this chapter has suggested one that research students have found to be helpful.

Writing in quantitative and qualitative research differs to the extent that in qualitative research your style is descriptive and narrative, whereas in quantitative research, in addition to being descriptive, it is also analytical and every assertion is supported by empirical evidence gathered through the investigation.

There are different ways of referencing and of writing a bibliography. You need to choose a system that is acceptable to your discipline and university.

Before you start writing the research report, develop an outline of the different chapters and their contents. The chapters should be written around the main themes of the study and for this your subobjectives are of immense help. When providing specific information about variables, the write-up should integrate the rationale for studying the

WRITING A RESEARCH REPORT　　361

variables; the literature review; the hypothesis, if any; findings; conclusions drawn; and possible explanations for the findings.

The suggested format can be described as thematic writing – writing organised around the significant themes of your study. Within a theme the information is provided in an integrated manner following a logical progression of thought.

FOR · YOU · TO · THINK · ABOUT

- Refamiliarise yourself with the keywords listed at the beginning of this chapter, and if you are uncertain about the meaning or application of any of them revisit them in the chapter before moving on.
- A literature review is an integral part of research writing. Reflecting on examples from your own area of interest, explore how you might be able to integrate your research findings with your literature review when it comes to writing your report.

Now, as you have gone through the chapter, try answering the following questions:

- Describe some of the differences in writing a report in quantitative and qualitative research.
- What are the different referencing systems? Detail the referencing of the system that is used in your academic field or at your university.
- What are the different styles of writing a bibliography? Detail the one used in your discipline or at your university.

Want to learn more? Visit
http://www.uk.sagepub.com/kumar4e
or scan this QR code to gain access to a range of online resources to support your study including practice quizzes, videos, weblinks, flashcards, and journal articles.

CHAPTERS FROM
RESEARCH METHODS,
STATISTICS, AND
APPLICATIONS

By
Kathrynn A. Adams,
Eva K. Lawrence

CHAPTER 18

THINKING LIKE A RESEARCHER

Imagine yourself lying on your back in the grass (or in a lawn chair, if you prefer). Stare up into the sky, let your mind wander, and let some of the myriad questions you have about the world come to you. Do not try to answer them, just focus on the kinds of questions that come to mind.

If you are like most students in the social and behavioral sciences, many of your questions are about culture, politics, education, values, or behavior. For example, you might wonder how people develop certain attitudes, why people or animals behave in certain ways, and what interventions might help change behaviors or attitudes. We expect that these questions came pretty easily to you because we have found that curiosity is a key characteristic of students who have opted to focus their studies on the social and behavioral sciences.

Through your studies, you have begun to develop a knowledge base in your discipline. Perhaps this knowledge inspired some of the questions you just generated, and with some additional thought you might be able to apply your knowledge to help answer some of those questions. Perhaps you know this already, but it is worth pointing out that almost all that knowledge you have gained through your coursework was generated through research.

Now you find yourself taking a Research Methods course within your discipline. Perhaps you signed up out of interest, or maybe the course was required or recommended. You may approach the course with excitement, trepidation, or indifference. Regardless of why you are taking the course or how you feel about it, we bet that this will be one of the most influential courses you ever take.

We would even wager that learning about research methods and statistics will change the way you think about the world. We hope you will continue to nurture your curiosity and occasionally stare up in the sky with a sense of wonder. What will change is that you will come to understand the process by which we know what we know in the social and

1

2 • RESEARCH METHODS, STATISTICS, AND APPLICATIONS

behavioral sciences, you will learn to generate more in-depth questions that build on this knowledge, and you will develop the tools to systematically investigate those questions you generate. In other words, you will learn to think like a researcher.

> **IN THIS CHAPTER, YOU WILL LEARN**
>
> - The connection between thinking critically and thinking like a researcher
> - How to think critically about research ethics
> - How to take a scientific approach
> - The steps in the scientific process
> - Basic research terms that we will expound on in later chapters

● CRITICAL THINKING

Critical thinking is essential to all academic pursuits and is therefore an omnipresent term in higher education. We hesitate to use the term here for fear that you have already heard critical thinking defined so many times that the mere mention of it will cause your eyes to glaze over. Bear with us, because although critical thinking is at the heart of what it means to think like a researcher, it is often misunderstood even by those who tout its importance.

One problem is that critical thinking is often equated with criticism. Criticism can be one of the tools used in critical thinking, but simply being critical is not the same as thinking critically. Another problem is that critical thinking is often equated with critical-thinking skills. Critical-thinking skills are used when thinking critically, and are certainly important, but skills alone do not define critical thinking. Moreover, skills are something you have or gain, while critical thinking is something that you do.

Critical thinking is an action that requires dynamic engagement with information or ideas. It involves carefully analyzing that information based on current knowledge, as opposed to relying on personal opinion or beliefs. Additionally, both the knowledge used and the thinking process itself are carefully scrutinized in order to identify and avoid biases. Thinking critically in any academic pursuit and thinking like a researcher are parallel paths. Where they diverge is that researchers think by doing. That is, researchers think critically as they plan, carry out, and evaluate the results of research studies.

● THINKING CRITICALLY ABOUT ETHICS

When researchers plan and carry out their research study, they must carefully consider the ethics of their study. Conducting an ethical research study is more than simply doing the right thing and avoiding doing the wrong thing. Although there are some clear dos and don'ts, ethical decisions are often not that simple. Researchers must consider ethics at every stage of the research process, and consequently we will introduce ethics in this chapter as well as discuss ethical issues throughout the book.

Ethics Codes

An ethics code both guides ethical decision making and delineates the ethical standards that must be followed. Current international and federal ethics codes for human research were created in response to some horrific research conducted in the name of science. Two of the most infamous are the Nazi medical experiments and the Tuskegee syphilis study.

During World War II, the Nazis tortured and murdered an estimated six million Jews along with millions of others who did not fit into the "Aryan race." After the war, a series of military tribunals, called the Nuremberg Trials, were held to try to bring justice to those responsible for carrying out these crimes against humanity. Among those prosecuted were physicians who had conducted medical studies on prisoners of Nazi concentration camps. The prisoners were forced into studies that included amputations, sterilization, and exposure to poison, disease, and hypothermia. In response to such atrocities, the Nuremberg Code was created in 1947 as the first ethical code of conduct for research (Grodin & Annas, 1996; Karigan, 2001). In 1964, the principles of this code were updated and clarified in the Declaration of Helsinki. This declaration has been updated and revised over time and currently serves as the international code of ethics for biomedical research (Karigan, 2001). It states that the rights of the individual must take precedence and that the individual must give their consent, preferably in written form, to participate in biomedical research (World Medical Association, 2008).

Another prime example of unethical research, conducted by the United States Public Health Service, began in 1932 and continued until 1972, even after the enactment of both the Nuremberg Code and Declaration of Helsinki. The Tuskegee syphilis study examined the long-term effects of syphilis without the consent of the patients suffering from the disease. In fact, the men who participated in the study were led to believe they were receiving free health care when instead the syphilis diagnosis and treatment were intentionally withheld. This study went on for 40 years, and only stopped due to public pressure resulting from a newspaper investigation that revealed the true nature of the study (Karigan, 2001). As a result, the Belmont Report was crafted as a guide for the ethical treatment of patients who participate in medical research in the United States. The Belmont Report serves as the basis for the current United States Federal Policy for the Protection of Human Subjects, also known as the "Common Rule" (U.S. Department of Health and Human Services, 2009).

The Nazi and Tuskegee research are extreme examples of what can happen when researchers do not think critically about ethics. Before you assume that all the ethical concerns relate to medical research, consider that some of the most influential social psychology experiments put participants under great emotional duress. Participants in Milgram's (1963) obedience study were told to administer increasingly strong shocks to another person, and were ordered to continue if they hesitated. In reality, the other person was part of the study and not shocked at all, but the participants believed they were inflicting pain on another person and consequently demonstrated great discomfort and emotional stress. Participants

4 • RESEARCH METHODS, STATISTICS, AND APPLICATIONS

in Zimbardo's (1972) Stanford prison experiment were randomly assigned to play the role of guards or prisoners in a mock jail. Within a few days, some of the guards exhibited cruel behaviors toward the prisoners and some of the prisoners became docile or depressed. Zimbardo found himself transformed from an unbiased researcher into the role of prison supervisor. It took an outside observer to point out the cruelty of the experiment and convince Zimbardo to stop it (TED, 2008).

These social science studies contributed greatly to our understanding of social phenomena, but was the negative impact on participants worth it? What about studies that ask participants to disclose intimate details of their personal life, give participants false information, observe participants without their consent, or provide a placebo treatment to participants in need of help? And what about studies with animals?

Some of these questions are more relevant to some fields than others, and because of these differences researchers in the social and behavioral sciences follow the ethics code of their specific discipline's professional organization (see Figure 1.1 for help finding the ethics code for your discipline). Some disciplines, such as political science, use the Federal Common Rule to guide their research (American Political Science Association, 2008). Psychology, sociology, and anthropology have their own ethics codes for research that are either stricter than the Common Rule or more specific to their discipline. For example, the American Psychological Association (APA; 2010a) and the American Anthropological Association (AAA; 2009) have codes of ethics that address animal research, but this type of research does not occur and thus is not addressed in the ethical guidelines for sociology or political science. The AAA guidelines for animal research are much less detailed than the APA's because anthropology researchers do not conduct medical, physiological, or neurobiological research with animals but psychology researchers might.

| Figure 1.1 | Find Your Discipline's Ethics Code |

We summarize key ethical principles and standards for social and behavioral science research in this chapter, but it is worth your while to familiarize yourself with the full ethics code of your discipline. Not only do these codes address research ethics, but they also provide ethical guidelines for the full range of professional activities relevant to the discipline.

You can find your discipline's ethics codes by searching on the national association website. The web addresses for several social science disciplines appear below:

American Anthropological Association: http://www.aaanet.org/committees/ethics/ethicscode.pdf

American Educational Research Association: http://www.aera.net/EthicsCode.htm?terms=ethics http://www.tccd.edu/Documents/About%20TCC/Institutional%20Research/AERA_Code_of_Ethics.pdf

American Political Science Association: www.apsanet.org/media/PDFs/ethicsguideweb.pdf

American Psychological Association: www.apa.org/ethics/code/index.aspx

American Sociological Association: www.asanet.org/images/asa/docs/pdf/CodeofEthics.pdf

Ethical Principles

Ethical principles are moral values and ideals. Table 1.1 lists the ethical principles from several different codes of ethics, and you will notice the common principles espoused by the different organizations. These principles do not explain how to behave, but rather serve as guidelines in ethical decision making. For example, APA's first ethical principle is beneficence and non-maleficence. Applied to research, this means that the researcher must carefully weigh the potential benefits of the study with the potential risk to human participants or animal subjects. Research does not necessarily have to benefit the participants directly, but the question under study should have broader importance to humans or animals. Based on this principle, it is clearly not appropriate to study something just because you find it interesting or because the results may benefit you personally. Moreover, the potential benefits of a study should clearly outweigh the possible harm imposed on human participants or animal subjects. See Practice 1.1 to identify risks and benefits of a study, and consider ways to minimize risks.

Ethical Standards

Ethical standards are specific rules or obligations that promote the ethical principles. The ethical standards for research with human participants address informed consent, the appropriate use of deception and incentives, and confidentiality.

Table 1.1	Comparison of Ethical Principles

Belmont Report (serves as the basis for the Federal Common Rule)	American Anthropological Association (AAA)	American Educational Research Association (AERA)	American Psychological Association (APA)	American Sociological Association (ASA)
• Respect for persons • Beneficence • Justice	• Responsibility to people and animals with whom anthropological researchers work and whose lives and cultures they study • Responsibility to scholarship and science • Responsibility to the public	• Professional competence • Integrity • Professional, scientific, and scholarly responsibility • Respect for people's rights, dignity, and diversity • Social responsibility	• Beneficence and nonmaleficence • Fidelity and responsibility • Integrity • Justice • Respect for people's rights and dignity	• Professional competence • Integrity • Professional and scientific responsibility • Respect for people's rights, dignity, and diversity • Social responsibility

6 • RESEARCH METHODS, STATISTICS, AND APPLICATIONS

Informed Consent

If we are to treat people with respect, then we typically should not study them without their **informed consent**. There are a few situations when a researcher may dispense with informed consent, such as when the study involves observations in natural and public situations and the participants cannot later be identified. Once you start manipulating situations, interacting with participants, making audio or visual recordings of participants, or asking them to complete questionnaires, informed consent is almost always necessary.

> *Informed consent:* An ethical standard by which potential participants are informed of the topic, procedures, risks, and benefits of participation prior to consenting to participate.

Informed consent implies that potential participants have a clear understanding of what the study is about, who is conducting the research, what they are being asked to do, how long it will take, and benefits and risks of participation *before* becoming part of a study. If you plan to record the participant, the participant must agree to be recorded and understand how the video or audio recordings will be used. Participants should also know that they can decline or withdraw from the study at any time without negative repercussions.

What if you wanted to study participants who cannot legally give their consent to participate? If a study involves anyone under 18 or otherwise under the legal guardianship of someone else, the legal guardian must give consent for that person to participate. The participants should still be informed of the study and asked to participate, and can refuse even if their guardian gave permission. See Practice 1.1 to apply these concepts.

Informed consent may be given verbally, although it is wise to also obtain written consent. Researchers often craft an informed consent form that potential participants read prior to giving their consent with their signature. The form helps ensure that all participants receive the information necessary for them to make an informed choice to participate or not.

An informed consent form should include the following information:

1. The purpose of the research or topic of study.

2. What participants will do and how long it will take.

3. Possible benefits of participation, including any incentives provided by the researchers.

4. Any potential risks to participation, including physical or emotional pain or discomfort as well as any risks to confidentiality.

5. Steps that will be taken to safeguard the participants' confidentiality.

6. The right to decline to participate and the right to withdraw from the study after it begins.

7. Verification that declining or withdrawing will not negatively impact the participants and they will still receive any incentives promised by the researcher.

8. The names and contact information of the researchers and supervisors.

9. A place for the participant (and legal guardian of the participant, if applicable) to sign and date the form, thus giving their informed consent for participation.

PRACTICE 1.1

THINKING CRITICALLY ABOUT ETHICS

Consider the following research proposal:

Early initiation of sexual activity is a risk factor for teenage pregnancy and sexually transmitted disease, and is also highly correlated with drug use, delinquency, and school failure. This study seeks to understand the sexual experiences of middle school students. A letter will be sent home to the parents outlining the goals and procedures of the study. Parents who do not want their child to participate in the study can sign and return a form. Children of parents who do not return this form will be asked to complete an anonymous survey asking them to rate their frequency of specific sexual activities (kissing, petting, oral sex, sexual intercourse), the age at which they first engaged in each of these activities, and the approximate number of partners they have had for each activity.

1. What are the benefits of this study?

2. What are the potential risks to participation? How can the researcher minimize these risks?

3. What is wrong with the informed consent process? How would you change it?

Answers to Practice Questions are in Appendix A.

An example informed consent form appears in Figure 1.2. Note that this consent form is for a simple and anonymous questionnaire and involves compensating participants with extra credit. An informed consent form should be tailored to the individual study and may contain more or less of the detail provided in the example. In particular, if a study might cause any emotional or physical distress, or involves asking very personal questions that the participant might deem sensitive or intrusive (such as questions about illegal behavior or their sex lives), then more detail about the nature of the study and procedures should be provided so that the participants can make an informed decision about their participation.

Debriefing

If the study involves any risk or deception, the researcher should include a **debriefing** in order to reduce or mitigate any longer-term effects on the participants. In most cases, debriefing occurs right after the participant completes the study. This is especially important when participation might result in physical or emotional distress because discussing the study immediately afterwards can help assess and reduce the distress, and the researchers can identify an appropriate follow-up plan for those who may need additional help.

Figure 1.2	Example Informed Consent Form

Informed Consent

The study in which I have been asked to participate is about my views about cell phone use in public. If I choose to participate, I will be given a brief questionnaire that should take about 10 minutes to complete.

I understand that in order to participate in this study, I must be at least 18 years old.

I understand that I will receive a small number of extra credit points for participating in this study but beyond that it is unlikely that I will directly benefit from participation. However, the knowledge gained from the study will help us better understand people's attitudes toward cell phone use.

There are no anticipated risks to participation. I understand that my responses are anonymous in that I will not put my name on the questionnaire. Any results will be reported in aggregate form so that my individual responses will not be identifiable. If I sign this consent form, it will be kept in a secure location that is separate from my completed questionnaire. However, my name will be reported to my professor if I wish to earn extra credit for participation.

I understand that I can withdraw from this study and I can refuse to answer any question in the questionnaire by simply leaving that item blank. If I choose to withdraw completely or not answer certain questions, I will not be penalized and I will still receive the extra credit.

If I have questions about the study or wish to find out the results of the study, I can contact Dr. X in the Department of Psychology at the University of Y: (xxx) xxx-xxxx.

I have read and understood this information, and I agree to participate in the study.

Name (Print) _____

Signature _____

Date _____

Debriefing: Clearing up any misconceptions that the participant might have and addressing any negative effects of the study.

What if you wanted to assess participants' natural responses to situations? In some cases, fully disclosing the purpose of a study may lead the participants to respond quite differently than if they did not know the purpose of the study. Likewise, in some cases explaining exactly what the participant will be asked to do may interfere with the research. Thus, researchers must determine how informed the consent must be in order for the study to both be ethical and yield meaningful results.

Deception

During the informed consent process, you do not need to disclose all the details of the study, such as what you expect to find or that some participants will be exposed to different conditions. Most researchers agree that withholding this type of information is not considered deception (Hertwig & Ortmann, 2008). But what if you intend to mislead or downright lie to your participants? These actions are clearly deceptive, and their use is a very controversial issue in research.

There are two primary arguments against the use of deception. First, deception may harm participants by embarrassing them, making them feel uncomfortable, or leading them to mistrust others (Baumrind, 1985; Fisher & Fryberg, 1994). Second, deception may harm the field by increasing suspicion of research and decreasing the integrity of the individual researcher and the entire research community (Baumrind, 1985; Kelman, 1967). Moreover, deception may invalidate research results even in studies that do not use deception. In a review of empirical research, Hertwig and Ortmann (2008) found evidence that participants who suspected that a study involved deception responded differently than participants who were not suspicious.

Others argue that deception should be allowed under certain circumstances. It may be essential in creating and studying a rare occurrence (e.g., emergencies) and eliciting genuine responses from participants (Hertwig & Ortmann, 2008). Additionally, some claim that deception has only a negligible effect on participants' well-being and the credibility of the field (e.g., A. J. Kimmel, 1998).

The acceptability of deception varies by discipline. The code of ethics for anthropologists states that "anthropologists should never deceive the people they are studying regarding the sponsorship, goals, methods, products, or expected impacts of their work" (AAA, 2009, p. 3). Likewise, researchers in experimental economics have essentially banned the use of deception. On the other hand, deception remains a relatively common practice in social psychology and marketing research (Hertwig & Ortmann, 2008).

The ethics codes for political science (per the Common Rule, U.S. Department of Health and Human Services, 2009), educational research (AERA, 2011), psychology (APA, 2010a), and sociology (ASA, 1999) allow for the use of deception in some situations. For example, the APA ethics code (2010a) specifies that deception is allowable under the following conditions:

1. The use of deception is necessary and justifiable given the potential benefits of the study.

2. The study is not expected to cause any physical pain or significant emotional distress.

3. The researchers debrief participants as soon as possible regarding the deception.

In some situations, debriefing participants on the true nature of the study immediately after their participation may contaminate the study. In cases where the potential participants know each other, those who have completed the study and been debriefed could tell future participants about the deception. In these cases, it is acceptable to wait until all data are collected before debriefing participants (assuming that there was no physical risk and minimal emotional risk. If such risk exists, deception would not be ethical).

10 • RESEARCH METHODS, STATISTICS, AND APPLICATIONS

The bottom line is, even if your discipline allows for the use of deception, the pros and cons of using deception warrant serious consideration. If you decide to use deception, special care must be taken to minimize potential harm to the participants and to the integrity of the field. You may also want to check to see if some of your participants suspected the deception and evaluate how that suspicion impacted your results (Hertwig & Ortmann, 2008).

Incentives for Participation

Researchers sometimes offer an incentive for participation in order to recruit participants. This may sound reasonable; after all, the participants are investing a certain amount of time and effort. The challenge is that an incentive can be coercive. For example, if someone offered you $1,000 to complete a 15-minute interview about your sex life, you might feel like you could not pass up that amount of money even if you felt uncomfortable being asked about your sex life.

Incentives can be particularly problematic if the study requires that participants meet certain criteria (e.g., nonsmoker, HIV positive). What if a participant lies about his or her medical history in order to qualify? Such incidents may invalidate the study results and worse, result in serious health complications for the participant (Ripley, 2006). Even though the participant is the deceptive one in these situations, the researcher still has an ethical responsibility because the participant was influenced by the monetary compensation.

At what point does an incentive become coercive? It depends both on who the target population is and the amount of time and effort involved in the study. Paying someone a fair wage for their time seems like a reasonable action, although the potential for coercion will depend on the participants' economic and cultural contexts. Additionally, paying participants for their time might lead the participants to believe that they must complete the study in order to receive payment. Remember that the participants have the right to withdraw from the study at any time, and withdrawing does not mean forfeiture of any incentive promised to them. The incentive is provided to the participants for showing up for the study, not for completing the study.

There are no hard-and-fast rules for incentives, although there are a few helpful guidelines:

1. Researchers should carefully consider who their potential participants are and not offer incentives that they would have a difficult time refusing.

2. The incentive should not be contingent on the participant completing the study.

Confidentiality

Researchers should respect participants' dignity and right to privacy, and as such data and results from research should always be confidential. **Confidentiality** occurs when responses and results from an individual participant are private. Keep in mind that confidentiality does not imply anonymity. **Anonymity** occurs when it is impossible for anyone, including the researcher, to link a participant to his or her data. Anonymity is not feasible when a researcher is planning to test participants at several time points or match participants' self-report with other information such as school or court records (with the appropriate consent, of course). Both confidentiality and anonymity require vigilance on the part of the researcher, and we will discuss specific strategies in later chapters.

Confidentiality: A participant's responses are kept private although the researcher may be able to link the participant with his or her responses.

Anonymity: No one other than the participant can link the participant to his or her responses.

THE SCIENTIFIC APPROACH ●

Ethics is one of many considerations when conducting a research study. Researchers must also consider how to design a study that yields meaningful results and decide on the most appropriate analyses given the research questions. Although ethics, research design, and statistical analyses have their unique issues and processes, all of these fit within the broader scientific approach.

The scientific approach is a specific type of critical thinking that involves approaching a topic with a genuine desire to understand it, identifying and minimizing biases that interfere with this understanding, avoiding overly simplistic explanations, and following a systematic method to study the topic.

That sounds easy enough, but taking the scientific approach actually requires a fair bit of risk and willingness to critically evaluate results regardless of our personal beliefs. Several questions arise when considering the scientific approach. Are we willing to subject our personal beliefs to science? Are we open-minded enough to pay attention to evidence that contradicts our belief systems? Can we truly be unbiased about a subject we feel passionately about? What might we lose by taking a scientific approach?

It is much easier to avoid the scientific approach and instead rely solely on personal beliefs and experiences. It does not take a lot of effort or thought to fall back on what an authority figure told you, or to base decisions on a significant event in your life, or to follow the advice of someone you trust. We might even say that these tendencies are our default. And let's face it, people can lead full and happy lives without ever challenging this default. See Figure 1.3 for a humorous perspective on this.

So why would anyone want to take a scientific approach? Not only does the scientific approach necessitate risk—it does not feel good to have our personal beliefs challenged or to be shown that our beliefs are inaccurate, it also takes more effort: falling back on our defaults is quite easy. In his book *Predictably Irrational: The Hidden Forces That Shape Our Decisions,* Ariely (2009) argues that we often make irrational decisions based on these defaults. Moreover, in their book *New World, New Mind: Moving Toward Conscious Evolution,* Ornstein and Ehrlich (2000) suggest that our nonscientific default served an evolutionary purpose, but that in today's society this default way of thinking and making decisions is insufficient for dealing with modern problems. In fact, they argue that many modern problems are the direct results of relying on our defaults.

The Scientific Approach and Decision Making

One reason we might take a scientific approach is that it can help us make better decisions, both individually and as a society. Take cell phones as an example. If we only relied on our

12 • RESEARCH METHODS, STATISTICS, AND APPLICATIONS

Figure 1.3	Not Your Scientific Approach

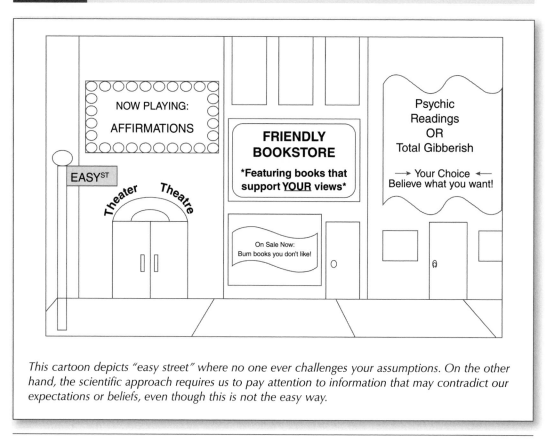

This cartoon depicts "easy street" where no one ever challenges your assumptions. On the other hand, the scientific approach requires us to pay attention to information that may contradict our expectations or beliefs, even though this is not the easy way.

Source: Eva K. Lawrence

default, we might assume that driving while talking on a cell phone is the same as driving while talking to someone in the car, and that the only problem with talking on a cell phone is that one of your hands might be occupied by holding the phone. Along those lines of thinking, using a hands-free device should solve the problem. Some states have even implemented laws outlawing hand-held cell phones while driving but allow hands-free devices (Governors Highway Safety Association, 2011).

However, research consistently demonstrates that talking on a cell phone—regardless if it is hand-held or hands-free—leads to greater distraction and a higher likelihood of getting into an accident than talking with someone in the car (Caird, Willness, Steel, & Scialfa, 2008; Ferlazzo, DiNocera, & Sdoia, 2008; Strayer & Johnston, 2001). The problem with talking on a cell phone while driving does not appear to be an issue that your hands might be occupied, but rather that your attention is divided between two different contexts (and thus is not solved by using a hands-free phone). As you are driving, the person you are talking to may be in an office, or cuddled up on the couch, or driving in a totally different environment. As such, that person does not know to stop talking if a car skids in front of you or to quiet down if you are driving in bad weather.

On the other hand, if you are talking to someone who is in the car with you, that person shares the same context with you. In fact, there is research evidence that having one passenger in the car can actually help you drive more safely because the passenger tends to adjust the conversation according to the current driving conditions (Chalton, 2009; Drews, Pasupathi, & Strayer, 2008). If state legislators were to take a more scientific approach, they would base their decisions on this research and ban the use of any type of cell phone while driving. At this point, however, no state has done so (Governors Highway Safety Association, 2011).

The Scientific Approach and Knowledge

Being able to make an informed decision is a good argument for the scientific approach. However, the scientific approach does not always lead directly to a decision. Take academic honesty as an example. Academic honesty is of particular importance to anyone involved in education. If a student is discovered to have plagiarized, that student receives consequences that can severely impede his or her college career. It may not matter to the academic system if the student was intentionally dishonest or if the student did not understand the rules of plagiarism, in much the same way that a person who speeds will get a ticket even if she did not notice the posted speed limit sign.

A professor who discovers plagiarism may simply report the student and stop there. This is not a scientific approach because she is simply following the rules without further thinking or investigation. If the professor were to take a scientific approach, that professor might dig a little deeper and try to discover knowledge and beliefs that students have about plagiarism, in what situations students are more or less likely to plagiarize, and what strategies are most effective in preventing plagiarism. The end result for the student who plagiarized may be the same, and the policy itself will likely not change. However, the professor's knowledge of plagiarism has increased. Perhaps in the future, the professor can use this knowledge to help students avoid plagiarism, even though it might not affect her decision to report students who plagiarize.

Another advantage to the scientific approach, then, is that it increases our knowledge base. This increased knowledge might not have an immediate effect, but it may serve as a foundation for future research that has real-life applications. For example, earlier research on plagiarism has suggested that plagiarism is more common than anyone would like to believe (Lim & See, 2001; Roig, 1997, 2001). Because of this initial research, other researchers wanted to find out more about why students might plagiarize and found that sometimes students plagiarize due to a lack of knowledge and skill as opposed to actively trying to be deceitful (Culwin, 2006; Landau, Druen, & Arcuri, 2002). Building on that research, there have been several studies examining educational interventions that are effective in improving students' knowledge and skills (Belter & du Pré, 2009; Estow, Lawrence, & Adams, 2011; Schuetze, 2004).

| Figure 1.4 | Plagiarism: A Bad Idea! |

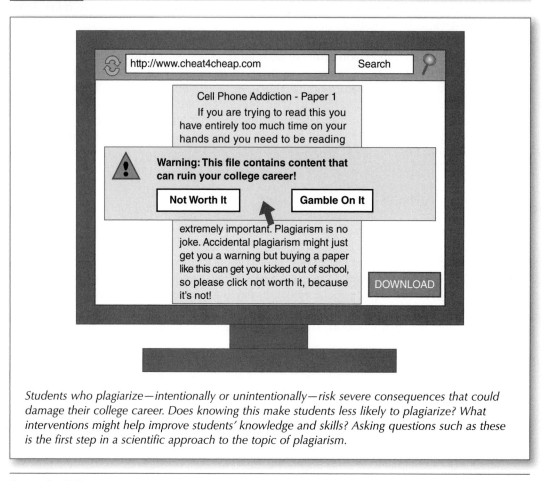

Students who plagiarize—intentionally or unintentionally—risk severe consequences that could damage their college career. Does knowing this make students less likely to plagiarize? What interventions might help improve students' knowledge and skills? Asking questions such as these is the first step in a scientific approach to the topic of plagiarism.

Source: Sandi Coon

The Scientific Method: Defined and Refined

Taking a scientific approach can improve our decision making, and it can help us develop a deeper understanding of a topic. Students often enter the social and behavioral sciences because they are curious about what makes people act in certain ways, or they want to know how best to help others, or they are interested in how our brains work. These are all questions that lend themselves to the scientific approach. In order to investigate these questions scientifically, one must use the scientific method.

Science engenders a sense of certainty among most students. To many, science = hard facts. Many people do not think of the social and behavioral science disciplines as sciences—or they refer to them as "soft sciences"—because there is so much uncertainty associated with these disciplines. However, science is not about facts. Science is about process. The processes of science are referred to as the scientific method—and *method* is what makes something a science. More specifically, science must include a transparent method that can be evaluated and replicated by others.

You probably remember first learning about the scientific method in your elementary school science courses. Every year young students across our country diligently memorize the steps to the scientific method. Again, the focus on these seemingly hard-and-fast rules of science engenders certainty. If you follow the steps to the scientific method, you get the answer or prove something, right? Well, not exactly. You will rule some things out (or disprove them), you will get some answers, but you will likely generate more questions than answers using the scientific method.

Moreover, the scientific method is not strictly linear, but rather is a cycle. If you complete one step, it may lead you to the next, or it may lead you to rethink an earlier step. And then when it looks like you are finished, the process takes you back to the beginning for you or another researcher to begin again.

To use a physical analogy, when we talk about steps of the scientific method we are not talking about steps in a staircase that we go up once, never backtracking or revisiting previous steps. Rather the steps are more like the ones we experience when we are using a stair-stepping machine such as those found in health clubs. Some of these machines have steps that cycle around and therefore we are constantly revisiting previous steps, just as we do in the scientific method. In the scientific method we might even skip a step and come back to it later (imagine skipping a step on an exercise machine). Keep this in mind as we outline the steps of the scientific method.

Also keep in mind that as we outline the scientific method we introduce some key concepts that we will expound on in later chapters. We present them here so that you can form a big picture of research from start to finish, and so that you understand the concept within the larger context of the scientific method.

OVERVIEW OF THE RESEARCH PROCESS (A.K.A. THE SCIENTIFIC METHOD)

Step 1: Identify Your Topic

Your professor may simply assign a research topic, but when you have a chance to choose your own topic it is worthwhile to spend some time thinking carefully about a good topic.

What makes a good topic? First, you want to choose a topic that piques your interest. Perhaps you read something interesting for a class, or heard a news story about an unusual event or behavior, or have some personal observations that you want to test. Personal experiences and observations are a good starting point for selecting a topic, but be careful when you choose a topic that interests you. Interest here means something you are interested in finding out more about—not something that you already have an established belief or opinion about that you are not willing to examine in an unbiased manner.

Although finding an interesting topic is a good first step, you want to avoid a few pitfalls. As a student, you probably have limited time and resources. Do not choose a topic that

16 • RESEARCH METHODS, STATISTICS, AND APPLICATIONS

requires participants who you will need special permission to recruit (e.g., children or individuals with psychological disorders) or one that requires equipment that you do not already have. If you are doing the research for a class project and the professor is requiring you to use a certain type of research design (such as an experiment—see step 4), then be sure your research topic is one that lends itself to that type of design.

You need to think ahead a little at this point to consider participants and design; however, you do not want to be too specific with your topic. Have some questions you are interested in examining, but wait until you read past research to develop specific hypotheses or design the specifics of your study.

Throughout this book, we will draw on research on the topics of academic honesty and technology to demonstrate how different research concepts and processes apply within specific research areas. You might wonder how we chose these two very different topics. We provide an explanation in Application 1.1 and 1.2. For additional help selecting your topic, go to Practice Box 1.2.

APPLICATION 1.1

Step 1: Identify a Research Topic—Focus on Academic Honesty

As college professors, the authors of this book are keenly aware of and interested in the topic of academic honesty. One situation in particular piqued one of the author's interests in this topic, and helped to narrow the topic from academic honesty to plagiarism. A student copied several sentences from the textbook to answer a question on an assignment. The student did not put quotes around the words she took from the book, but did cite the source. The professor explained to the student that this was plagiarism and rather than reporting the incident to the academic dean asked the student to re-do the assignment. The student was quite incensed and did not believe that her actions constituted plagiarism. She was so angry that she went to the dean, who politely told the student that what she had done was indeed an act of plagiarism and recorded this act as part of the student's disciplinary record. This student was so sure that she had not plagiarized that she ended up unintentionally turning herself in for an academic honesty violation.

Although the action clearly constituted plagiarism, the student did not plagiarize intentionally. This raises many questions: what do students believe plagiarism is? How do we raise students' awareness of what plagiarism is and help them avoid it? If a student commits plagiarism, how does that impact our perceptions of the student?

At this point we have a specific topic, but we are just playing around with different research questions. In order to further narrow our topic, we must move on to our second step—to find and read past research on the topic of plagiarism. See Application 1.3 for more on how we developed a study on this topic.

APPLICATION 1.2

Step 1: Identify a Research Topic—Focus on Technology Use

New technology seems to pop up every day, and the use of technology impacts the ways that we relate to each other and the rules we have about what the appropriate use of technology is. Cell phone use is something that particularly interests us (the authors). Students seem to always have their cell phone on them and their phones sometimes ring in class or worse, students might text a friend during class (something the authors think constitutes inappropriate use of technology, although the question remains as to how or if these actions affect student performance).

Some questions that pique our interest are: What are the social rules about cell phone use—and do these rules change based on age? What constitutes problematic cell phone use?

As researchers we should not get too specific until we find out some of the research that's been done on the topic. Reading past research will help us further refine our topic.

PRACTICE 1.2

TAKING A SCIENTIFIC APPROACH IN IDENTIFYING A RESEARCH TOPIC

1. Select a research topic that you might be interested in examining.

2. What, if anything, have you read or heard about from scientific sources like research articles or research summaries, conference presentations, or even class textbooks or lectures that are based on research (rather than personal opinion)? Do not just fall back on the default of relying on personal experience or information gained from friends, family, or the media—take a scientific approach instead.

3. Come up with a list of questions on this topic that interests you. These questions can build off of your answer for question 2 and you can also add other questions based on observations or experiences. Try to come up with at least 10.

   a. Which of these questions do feel you already "know" the answer to or have a strong feeling about? These might not be good to examine because the scientific approach requires that you approach a question in an unbiased manner.

   b. Which of these questions are not testable? In other words, you would not be able to adequately define the constructs or the question is more philosophical than scientific (such as "what is the meaning of life?").

(Continued)

18 • RESEARCH METHODS, STATISTICS, AND APPLICATIONS

(Continued)

c. Which of these questions necessitate special equipment or special populations that you do not have access to?

d. If you are thinking about a research question as part of a class assignment: Did your professor tell you that you will need to select a topic that lends itself to a certain type of design (descriptive, correlational, or experimental)? If so, which of your questions do not lend themselves to the required design?

4. Cross off or modify any of the questions that you identified in A through D, above. Keep in mind that these questions are not necessarily bad ones, they just are not appropriate for you to conduct a study on at this point in your research career.

What questions remain on your list? These might serve as a good place to start.

Keep in mind that your research question will change as you read more research in this area.

Step 2: Find, Read, and Evaluate Past Research

Reading and evaluating past research is one of the most crucial steps in research. You should do it early in the process, but keep in mind that you will likely need to keep going back to the research literature while you design, conduct, and write up your study. In other words, this is not a step you can simply check off and move on. Remember we told you these steps were not linear, but rather are steps that you may need to revisit. Reading the research literature on your topic is something you should plan to do throughout the research process. We discuss this in more detail in Chapter 2.

Step 3: Further Refine Your Topic and Develop a Hypothesis or Research Question

The topic you started with might be very different from the one you decide on after you have read past research. Change is a good thing and suggests that you are truly involved in the process of science—process, after all, implies change.

When you have a good handle on what past research has found, you will want to develop a **testable hypothesis** that is based on this research. A common definition of a hypothesis is that it is an educated guess. For our purposes, this means that a hypothesis is a prediction based on past research. A testable hypothesis means that it can be disproven. A belief in true love, angels, or countless other things that cannot be disproven may be very worthwhile on a personal level, but such beliefs are not testable and thus not suitable research questions. On the other hand, we could test the idea that having a belief in true love improves the quality of intimate relationships.

> *Testable hypothesis:* An educated prediction that can be disproven.

Similarly, the statement that a continued reliance on cell phones will lead to the destruction of humankind is not testable. We cannot disprove that statement because it is based on a prediction of a single future event that no researcher will survive to study. With modification, however, we can make this statement testable: Reliance on cell phones is related to the incidence of distracted driving. That is not nearly as exciting as our first statement, but much more focused and testable.

Step 4: Choose a Research Design

You will want to design a study that tests your hypothesis, is feasible for you to carry out given your time and resource constraints, and is ethical. Keep in mind that there is no perfect study and you cannot examine all the factors that interest you in one study. One of the most basic decisions is the type of research design to use.

There are three basic types of research designs: descriptive, correlational, and experimental. A single study may have multiple hypotheses that are tested with one or more of these designs. The type of design depends largely on the goal of the research. Just like it sounds, descriptive research simply describes a sample or a population. Correlational and experimental research designs examine relationships among variables, with experimental research testing a causal relationship. There is also something called a quasi-experimental design in which some, but not all, of the requirements for an experiment are met. We will go into depth on each of these designs in later chapters, but we provide some basic information so that you can begin to familiarize yourself with these designs.

> *Descriptive research:* Research design in which the primary goal is to describe the variables, but not examine relationships among variables.
>
> *Correlational research (or correlational design):* Research design in which the relationship among two or more variables is examined, but causality cannot be determined.
>
> *Experimental research (or experimental design, or experiment):* Research design that attempts to determine a causal relationship by manipulating one variable, randomly assigning participants or subjects to different levels of that manipulated variable, and measuring the effect of that manipulation on another variable.
>
> *Quasi-experimental research (or quasi-experimental design, or quasi-experiment):* Research design that includes a key characteristic of an experiment, namely, manipulation of a variable. However, it does not have all the requirements for an experiment in that there is no random assignment to the levels of the manipulated variable. Because there is no random assignment, a quasi-experiment cannot demonstrate causation.

20 • RESEARCH METHODS, STATISTICS, AND APPLICATIONS

All designs will have variables you measure, manipulate, or control. A **variable** is something that varies in that it has at least two possible values. Gender is a variable because the categories can be male, female, or transgender. On the other hand, male is not a variable because the category does not vary. Similarly, the description of being an excellent driver does not vary. To make it a variable, we would need to discuss it in terms of the degree of excellence in driving (from 1 to 10, for example).

Variable: A factor in a research study that has two or more possible values.

Descriptive research describes the who, what, when, where, and how, but does not examine relationships among the who, what, when, where, and how. Descriptive research can be exploratory in nature. It is often used to examine phenomena in more depth or to examine an area of research that is either new or needs updating. For example, given that texting on cell phones is a relatively new feature, a descriptive study is warranted to examine who uses the text messaging feature, what the purpose of the text is (e.g., business, fun, flirting), when texting is and is not appropriate, and how many times a day a person texts.

Correlational research examines the relationship between two or more variables but does not test causality. A correlational study tests the degree to which behaviors, events, and feelings co-occur with other behaviors, events, and feelings. For our cell phone use topic, instead of simply describing who uses the text messaging feature, we might go a step further and ask if there is a relationship between frequency of text messaging and other variables such as age, socioeconomic status, mood, and personality. For example, one correlational study found that college students who were anxious were more likely to choose to text someone rather than call them (Reid & Reid, 2007).

We can use correlational research to predict scores, but we cannot use correlations to explain why the scores occurred. A correlational design cannot determine **causation**, in that it cannot show that one variable caused the effect on another variable. If a correlation exists between two variables, it is possible that one variable caused the change in the other but it is also possible that the relationship exists for other reasons. For example, in the study examining the relationship between texting and anxiety, it might be that anxiety leads to greater likelihood of texting *or* that texting increases anxiety. Or, there might be a third variable that is impacting the results. Texting might be related to playing video games, and it may be playing video games that actually causes the anxiety, not the texting. In order to test causality, an experiment should be conducted.

Experimental research examines the relationship between two or more variables and, if properly conducted, can demonstrate causation. An experiment goes beyond prediction to an explanation of a relationship between two variables. At its most basic, an experiment consists of one **independent variable (IV)** and one **dependent variable (DV)**. An experiment tests the effect of the IV on the DV.

Causation: Relationship between cause and effect, in that one variable is shown to have caused the observed change in another variable.

Independent variable (IV): The variable that is manipulated in an experiment.

Dependent variable (DV): The variable that is measured in an experiment and is expected to vary or change based on the IV manipulation.

An experiment requires that:

a. The experimenter systematically manipulates the IV.

b. The experimenter randomly assigns participants to receive different levels of the IV.

c. The experimenter measures the effect of the IV manipulation on the DV.

For example, following is a simple experiment to see if texting increases a person's level of anxiety: We would have two levels of the IV—texting for 2 hours vs. no texting (a "control" group); we would randomly assign participants to one of the two levels of the IV. The texting group would sit and text for 2 hours and the no-texting group would sit and read for 2 hours. After the 2 hours are up, we would give all the participants a measure assessing their self-reported current level of anxiety and we might also check their heart rate as a physiological measure of anxiety.

In some cases, it is not feasible to conduct an experiment and a quasi-experimental design might be chosen instead. **Quasi-experimental research** includes manipulation of an IV but no random assignment to IV level. For example, what if we did not have the resources to randomly assign participants to text or read for an extended period of time? We might instead use pre-existing groups of participants as our comparison groups. We could have one class section of introductory psychology text during the class period and another section read, and then check all the students' heart rates at the end of class. However, a quasi-experiment cannot demonstrate causation. In our example, the two classes were likely different prior to beginning the study and we cannot be sure that any observed differences in heart rate were caused by texting.

Test your understanding of descriptive, correlational, and experimental research designs by completing Practice 1.3. By the way, we realize that you might be tempted to skip over these practice exercises in the chapters or ignore the application boxes. We think taking the extra time will be worth your while, however. We base this on research findings that active repetition of material through practice and application is associated with better learning and retention than simply reading and rereading a text (Fritz, 2011).

Step 5: Plan and Carry Out Your Study

Before you carry out your study, you will need to get approval to do so. Your professor is the first person who will need to OK your study, and he or she will want to make sure you have

---

PRACTICE 1.3

IDENTIFYING DIFFERENT TYPES OF RESEARCH DESIGNS

1. Why would an experiment not be appropriate to investigate the relationship between ethnicity and health? What would be an appropriate research design?

2. The president of a university wants to understand how the beauty of the campus influenced the incoming class of students' decision to enroll in the university. What would be the most appropriate research design?

3. Briefly outline a study to examine the impact of Facebook on mood. What would be the most appropriate research design?

See Appendix A to check your answers.

---

designed a sound study that conforms to the ethical principles and standards of your discipline. Broadly speaking, your study should not harm others and should maintain the dignity and respect of those involved in the study.

You will want to be sure that the benefits of your study outweigh any harm or inconvenience that your participants might experience. Even doing a quick survey can be harmful to participants if it evokes strong emotions or personal reactions. Moreover, unless you are conducting a naturalistic observation, your study will be intrusive (even if it is only a minor intrusion) and will likely require that the participants take time to help you (even if it is just a few minutes). That is why one of the first criteria that your professor will use in evaluating your study is that it has merit—meaning that the study makes sense given past research. Asking people to participate in a study that is not based on past research and contributes nothing to our (or your) knowledge base is unethical because the benefits do not outweigh the potential harm that might be done.

In addition to having your professor OK your study, you will likely need to have your study approved by your college or university's Institutional Review Board (IRB). The IRB reviews research conducted by both students and faculty to ensure that the study has merit and therefore the research is justified. The IRB also ensures that the study complies with the ethical standards of the federal Common Rule (introduced earlier in this chapter) or stricter standards set forth by the institution. Remember also that your discipline-specific code of ethics may be stricter or more specific than the Common Rule, and therefore your professor may have required that your study meet the ethical standards of both the IRB and your discipline. Careful planning about selecting and recruiting participants and how exactly you will carry out your study is necessary before you submit a proposal to your professor and the IRB. In some cases, you may want to conduct a pilot or preliminary test for your measures and procedures, and this would also require pre-approval by your professor and the IRB.

There are many specific ethical standards to follow, and as you engage in the approval process for your professor and IRB it is easy to forget to think critically about why these ethical standards are important. Remember that these standards are not simply tasks to check off in order for you to get approval to complete your project. Instead, the ethical principles behind the standards should guide every step of your research process (see Figure 1.5).

Who Will You Ask to Participate in Your Study?

One of the key decisions in how you will carry out your study is to determine who your population of interest is. Is your study about males, females, or both? Are you only interested in college students, and if so, does it matter if they are traditional-aged students or not? Once you have determined who your population is, you will need to collect data from a sample of that population. Ideally, the sample should be representative of the population. We will discuss sampling procedures in detail in Chapter 4.

What Are the Procedures for Your Study, and What Materials Will You Use?

After you decide how you will get participants, you need to decide what your participants will actually do or what you will do with or to the participants. Your procedures should be consistent with the research design you chose and your hypothesis. You should consider the impact of your procedure and materials on the participants and avoid any procedures that unduly stress your participants. And, you will want your procedures and materials to be consistent with past research in the topic area.

How you will measure your variables is a key consideration at this point in the planning process. The measurement instruments you use will serve to operationally define your variables, which you might recall from earlier in the chapter is essential in eventually testing your hypothesis. Some of the most common ways to measure your variables are observations, interviews, and questionnaires. Other ways to measure your variables include physical tests such as those for heart rate, skin conductance, and temperature. There are also behavioral measures such as how much money a person spends, how long it takes to complete a task, turning off a light or not, and so on. Finally, you can measure your variables without ever interacting with a person or animal by examining records such as medical or school records, historical documents, or data collected by others.

A measure is a tool that can be used in all the different research designs. Unfortunately, students often assume that certain measures are associated only with certain designs. The most common mistake is that observations, interviews, and questionnaires are only used in descriptive research. Although these are measures commonly used in descriptive research (and we will discuss them in more detail in Chapter 4, which focuses on descriptive designs), these types of measures can be used in all the different research designs. For example, we might use observations in a descriptive study examining how people use their phones by watching and recording people texting and talking in a public area. We could also use observations in a correlational or experimental study. For a correlational study, we might observe people's use

Figure 1.5 Ethical Principles Should Guide the Entire Research Process

Consider Ethical Principles

- What are the benefits of the study for individuals, society, and the discipline?
- How can you be sure that the benefits of the study outweigh any risks to the participants or subjects?
- How can you ensure that human participants' rights are upheld, and they are treated with dignity and respect? Or, how can you ensure that animal subjects will be treated humanely?
- How will you maintain competence, objectivity, integrity, fairness, and responsibility?

↓

Identify Ethical Standards That Apply to Your Study and Develop Procedures to Adhere to Those Ethical Standards

↓

Draft a Research Proposal

In the proposal, it should be clear how you will uphold the ethical principles by:

➤ Designing a study that will help to answer a question of importance to individuals or society and advance disciplinary knowledge

➤ Minimizing risk to animal subjects or human participants

➤ Adhering to ethical standards

➤ Following additional procedures that demonstrate responsibility toward subjects/participants, society, and science

↓

Submit the Proposal to Your Professor and Your College/University IRB

Revise Based on Feedback, Resubmit If Necessary

↓

If the study is approved, uphold the ethical principles and follow ethical standards as you interact with subjects/participants, manage and analyze data, and write up results

of phones in a public area and see if there are differences in use related to age or gender. For an experiment, we might randomly assign participants to either overhear a cell phone conversation or overhear a face-to-face conversation and then observe how people react to each of these conditions.

Step 6: Analyze Your Data

Throughout the course of this book you will learn about different types of analyses to help you test different types of hypotheses and research questions. By the end, you should develop a set of tools that will help you test your hypotheses or provide answers to your research question. Be aware that students sometimes confuse types of research design with types of statistical analyses. It does not help matters that researchers have used "descriptive" and "correlational" to describe both designs and statistics. But try to keep them separate. You may have heard the old adage "correlation does not mean causation," and that refers to cor-relational design. Causality is a function of research design, not the type of statistics you use to analyze the design.

Ideally, you should choose the best analysis based on your hypothesis or research ques-tion. Each analysis is like a tool, and you would not want to use a hammer when a screw-driver is more appropriate for the job. However, beginning researchers will have a limited number of tools, and you might find yourself needing to limit the types of hypotheses you develop in order to run analyses that you know how to do. Even by the end of the course, you will only have learned about a few (albeit key) analyses. It is appropriate for beginning researchers to modify their hypotheses and questions to those that they can actually test given the tools they have; just keep in mind that there is a whole world of analyses out there that can answer much more complex questions than you will be able to ask in this beginning Research Methods course.

Step 7: Communicate Results

Once you have carried out and analyzed your data, you will need to consider what the results mean, how they fit or do not fit with past research, what the limitations of your study are, and how a future study might build on yours to address some of these limitations.

Research should be a transparent process, and thus it is important that you make your results public so that others may learn from and build on your study. Remember that a key, ongoing step to the scientific method is reviewing past research. Thus, communicating your results feeds back into the process of science. For a student, this does not necessarily mean that you have to publish your results in a research journal. That is a possibility, but it is more likely you will share your results with your professor and your classmates, and perhaps present your study to other students within and outside your college or university.

Writing a research report is one of the basic ways to communicate your results to others, and we go into more detail on how to do that in Appendix B. When you write a report you have to put the study into context and you will need to explain your study in your own words.

26 • RESEARCH METHODS, STATISTICS, AND APPLICATIONS

The process of writing and revising the report will help you figure out how to effectively communicate your study and its results to others.

Writing in your own words is critical to your own learning and to others understanding your work. After all, no one will be able to understand your study if you cannot explain it clearly and concisely yourself. Writing in your own words is also an important ethical issue. If someone plagiarizes the work of others, then they essentially steal someone's ideas and hurt the credibility of the entire field.

You may think you know what plagiarism is and how to avoid it, but plagiarism is more than just passing off someone's entire work as your own. Plagiarism also includes incorrect citation of others' work. You are expected to build on past research, which will require you to summarize and paraphrase the work of others. You should do so in your own words, and whenever you describe others' work you need to cite the appropriate source. Test your understanding of plagiarism by completing Practice 1.4.

PRACTICE 1.4

IDENTIFYING AND AVOIDING PLAGIARISM

The following was taken directly from Schuetze (2004):

"Increased student confidence in their ability to avoid plagiarism would hypothetically result in an inaccurate perception that they are fully knowledgeable about the complexities involved in proper citations in scientific papers" (p. 259).

Indicate if each of these statements would or would not be considered plagiarism:

a. Increased student confidence in their ability to avoid plagiarism might result in an inaccurate belief that they are fully knowledgeable about the complexities involved in proper citations (Schuetze, 2004).

b. Student confidence in their plagiarism avoidance skills might lead to false perceptions that they understand the intricacies of proper citations.

c. One danger of increasing students' confidence in avoiding plagiarism is that they may overestimate their ability to correctly cite sources (Schuetze, 2004).

d. Increased student confidence in their ability to avoid plagiarism might theoretically result in an incorrect belief that they are completely knowledgeable about the intricacies of proper citations in papers (Schuetze, 2004).

See Appendix A to check your answers.

PROOF AND PROGRESS IN SCIENCE ●

You will sometimes hear people refer to a research study with a statement such as "this research proves that . . . ," but "proof" is an inaccurate term to describe results of a research study. A single research study only examined a portion of the population and only examined the topic in one very specific way, and there can never be complete certainty that the results will generalize to other participants or methods. Not only will a single study not prove something, neither will an entire body of research. Proof means that there is 100% accuracy, whereas with research there is always some probability of error. It is impossible to study everyone in a population, and even if that were possible the measures and methods will never be perfectly accurate. The impossibility of proof will make more sense when you learn more about measurement and statistics in later chapters.

If research does not prove something, then how do we ever know anything in the social and behavioral sciences? How do these disciplines progress? When researchers at the graduate and post-graduate level (and even sometimes undergraduate level) complete a study, they typically submit a research report for publication in a scholarly journal or book, submit their work to present at a conference, or both. Other researchers in the field review and critique the work to help ensure that the study is important enough to be shared publicly and that the methods by which the study was conducted are sound. Once the work is made public, it becomes part of the larger body of knowledge in the field. Future research can then build on this knowledge, and those results will support, refute, or refine the findings of the original study.

Although we never prove something, when research findings consistently demonstrate a certain pattern we feel confident that the pattern is likely one that will generalize to other samples and methods. For example, psychotherapy outcome research has consistently demonstrated that therapy is effective (e.g., Seligman, 1995; Shapiro & Shapiro, 1982; Smith & Glass, 1977). Research cannot prove that therapy has been or will be effective for everyone, but the body of research supporting the efficacy of therapy suggests that if someone is experiencing psychological distress there is a good chance that therapy can help.

Once there is sufficient evidence that we feel confident of the validity of a pattern, researchers begin to ask deeper and more complex questions. For example, psychotherapy researchers have moved beyond the basic question of "does therapy work?" to the more sophisticated questions of "what type of therapy works, for whom, under what conditions, and administered by what type of therapist?" These questions were first posed by Kiesler back in 1971, and therapy outcome research has been chipping away at these questions ever since.

You will get a better sense of how knowledge in a field progresses when you dive into a research topic and start finding and reading research on that topic. Some classic theories and research studies will be cited often, as well as more recent studies that have built on those theories and studies and helped to refine our knowledge of the area. Current research will pose more in-depth questions, and the results of those studies will inspire additional questions, and the cycle will continue. See Application 1.3 for an example of the research process from start to finish.

APPLICATION 1.3

The Scientific Method: Plagiarism Study Example

Step 1: Identify a Topic

As educators, we are interested in how we might help students understand and avoid plagiarism.

Step 2: Find, Read, and Evaluate Past Research

We found an article by Schuetze (2004) that demonstrated that a brief homework assignment can help reduce plagiarism.

Step 3: Refine Topic and Develop a Hypothesis

The study by Schuetze (2004) started us thinking about what we already do in our Research Methods and Analysis class. We give a homework assignment early in the semester to assess students' knowledge of plagiarism, and we then discuss issues of plagiarism in class and also have those students who did not do well on the assignment meet with one of our teaching assistants.

We also always choose a research topic for the semester and students do several studies based on this topic throughout the semester. There is research evidence that such a themed-methods course allows for deeper understanding of material (Marek, Christopher, & Walker, 2004).

Based on this past research, we hypothesized that students who were in a plagiarism-themed research course would demonstrate better knowledge of plagiarism and would have better paraphrasing skills that would help them avoid plagiarism than students who were in a research course with a different theme.

Step 4: Design the Study

Ideally, we would do an experiment to show that the plagiarism-themed course caused improvements in students' knowledge and skills. However, this was not practical or ethical because we cannot randomly assign students to class. Instead, we did a quasi-experiment, which is a design that includes some—but not all—of the procedures for an experiment. We compared students from one semester when we chose plagiarism as our theme to students from another semester when we chose a different theme for the course. We manipulated the theme for the course, but did not randomly assign. Thus, we have some characteristics of an experiment but not all of them.

Step 5: Carry Out the Study

Our participants were students who signed up for the course. All the students received the plagiarism homework at the beginning of the semester and soon afterwards all the students received instruction and one-on-one feedback as needed. Throughout the semester the students in the plagiarism-themed course did a variety of assignments on the topic of plagiarism, including an article analysis, descriptive study, and experiment. Students in the non-plagiarism-themed course did the same assignments but had gender stereotypes as their course theme. All the students did another plagiarism assignment at the end of the semester.

Step 6: Analyze the Data

We compared the first and second plagiarism homework assignments for those in the plagiarism-themed course with those in the non-plagiarism-themed course. We found that those who were in the plagiarism-themed course showed more improvement on the homework assignment than those in the non-plagiarism-themed course.

Step 7: Communicate Results

We wrote up a report based on our study and submitted it for publication to the journal *Teaching of Psychology*. Several reviewers and the editor of the journal gave us feedback, and we went through many revisions based on this feedback.

The article was accepted for publication and appeared in print in 2011. It is now part of the larger body of research on the topic of plagiarism. Other researchers can integrate the knowledge gained from the study, critique and improve upon the method, and build on the findings in their own research studies.

Both an early version and the final publication version of this paper appear in Appendix B.

CHAPTER RESOURCES

KEY TERMS

Define the following terms using your own words. You can check your answers by reviewing the chapter or by comparing them with the definitions in the glossary—but try to define them on your own first.

Anonymity

Causation

Confidentiality

Correlational research
(or correlational design)

Debriefing

Dependent variable (DV)

Descriptive research

Experimental research (or experimental design, or experiment)

Independent variable (IV)

Informed consent

Quasi-experimental research (or quasi-experimental design, or quasi-experiment)

Testable hypothesis

Variable

30 • RESEARCH METHODS, STATISTICS, AND APPLICATIONS

DO YOU UNDERSTAND THE CHAPTER?

Answer these questions on your own and then review the chapter to check your answers.

1. What is critical thinking, and how does it apply to research?

2. What are ethical principles and ethical standards?

3. Why is informed consent important from an ethical perspective?

4. What are the arguments for and against deception?

5. What are the problems with using incentives, and how might researchers minimize these problems?

6. Why is confidentiality important from an ethical perspective? How is it different from anonymity?

7. What are the risks and benefits of the scientific approach?

8. How does the scientific method relate to the scientific approach?

9. What are factors to consider when choosing a research topic?

10. Why is reading and evaluating past research important in the scientific method?

11. What makes a hypothesis testable?

12. What are the three primary types of research design? What are the similarities and differences among the different designs?

13. What are the ethical issues to consider when choosing a research design, planning a study, and carrying out a study?

14. What is plagiarism?

15. Why is plagiarism an important issue in research and writing?

CHAPTER 19

BUILD A SOLID FOUNDATION FOR YOUR STUDY BY FINDING, READING, AND EVALUATING PAST RESEARCH

I f you have started to think like a researcher, then likely you will start to see opportunities for research studies everywhere you turn. For example, watching the nightly news might make you imagine a study comparing different types of news media. Or arguing with your significant other might inspire a study idea about communication styles. You may start developing hypotheses or even begin to design and think about how you will carry out your imagined studies.

We certainly do not want to squash your enthusiasm, but as you might recall from Chapter 1, if you went directly from topic to hypothesis development or study design you would be missing one of the most important parts of the research process—finding, reading, and evaluating past research on your topic. As interesting and unique as your ideas may be, it is almost impossible that someone else has not done research on them or a similar topic. Reading and evaluating past research will help you build a solid foundation for your study, and the study you end up designing after a thorough review of the research literature will be much stronger than one designed without this work.

In order to read and evaluate past research, you first need to find it. Time and time again we have students complain that they cannot find any research on their topic. One student even claimed that there had been no research conducted on test anxiety among college students even though this is an extremely popular topic and there have been hundreds of published studies that have examined this topic in different ways. The student's failure to find

31

relevant research does not mean that he or others who struggle with finding research on a topic are lazy or unintelligent or computer illiterate. On the contrary, the student from this example was intelligent, hard-working, and tech savvy. The problem was that he was using inappropriate strategies to search for information. The first step in developing an appropriate strategy is to understand the different types of sources available and to discern which ones are most useful. Then you need to find and read past research, and build on and cite that research as you design your own study.

IN THIS CHAPTER, YOU WILL LEARN

- The difference between a primary and secondary research source
- How to identify scholarly works
- How to find different types of scholarly works
- The parts of a primary research article
- Ways to build on past research to develop your research study
- The basics of APA format

● TYPES OF SOURCES

Primary Versus Secondary Sources

Generally speaking, a primary source is the one closest to the original source of information whereas a secondary source is at least one step removed from the original source of information. What constitutes the original source of information varies by discipline. In the humanities disciplines such as English and history, the information under study is a historical event or creative work. A primary source in these disciplines is a firsthand account of a historical event or an original creative manuscript.

On the other hand, the original source of information in the social and behavioral sciences is a research study. To a social or behavioral scientist, a **primary research source** is a report of a research study in which data were collected and analyzed, and a **secondary research source** is a review or discussion of previous research that does not include a report on an original research study. We will use these more specific social and behavioral scientist definitions of primary and secondary sources in this chapter.

Primary research source: The authors report the results of an original research study that they conducted.

Secondary research source: The authors review research but do not report results of an original study.

Chapter 2 *Build a Solid Foundation for Your Study* • 33

Scholarly Versus Popular Sources

A **scholarly work** can be a primary or secondary source and must meet all of the following criteria:

- The goal of the work is to advance knowledge and scientific study in the field.
- The author(s) have expertise in the field.
- The work is written for an audience with knowledge in the field, as opposed to the general public.
- The work builds upon other scholarly sources that are clearly cited.

Scholarly works can also be understood in contrast to popular works. **Popular works** are those that serve to educate or entertain a general audience that includes those without specialized training or expertise in the field. Examples of popular sources include *Wikipedia* and other websites, online blogs, educational pamphlets or fact sheets, some books including textbooks, and articles in newspapers or magazines—including *Psychology Today* and *Scientific American*. Popular works may be written by experts in the field or by journalists or others without specialized knowledge or training in an area. Popular works may refer to and cite scholarly sources, or the work might be the personal opinion of the author. Popular works may even be primary sources when the work includes results of surveys and opinion polls the authors conducted, but the results may be questionable if the goal of the work is to entertain or to support the opinion of the author.

Popular sources can provide basic information on a topic, offer support that a topic is relevant and timely, and give you some ideas for research topics and questions. However, when developing a research study, you will want to build primarily upon scholarly sources.

Scholarly works: A work designed to advance knowledge in a field, written by someone with expertise in that field for others with knowledge of the field, that cites and builds upon other scholarly sources.

Popular works: A work designed to entertain or educate and that was written for those who do not necessarily have any knowledge in the topic area.

● TYPES OF SCHOLARLY WORKS

In this section, we will outline different types of scholarly work. Understanding these different types of sources will help you further discern the quality and usefulness of different sources. You will then have the opportunity to test your understanding of the distinction between scholarly and popular sources, and evaluate the quality of these different sources by completing Practice 2.1.

Articles in Academic Journals

There are thousands of journals devoted to publishing scholarly work in the social and behavioral sciences. However, most articles that are submitted for publication in academic journals are not published. There are several reasons for this. First, each academic journal has its own focus or specialty area (e.g., *Cognitive Psychology, American Journal of Sociology, Journal of Teacher Education, Child Development, Law and Human Behavior, Journal of Computer-Mediated Communication*) and editors only publish articles that align with their journal's content and scope. Second, most academic journals are print media and therefore have limited space. Finally, most journals employ a peer review process in order to ensure that they only publish articles that are of high quality and help to advance scholarship in the field.

Peer Review Process

Remember that scholarly works are written by those who have expertise in the topic area. The **peer review** process, then, involves the review of the work by other experts in the field. When a journal editor, who is a leading expert in the field, receives an article he or she makes an initial decision on whether the article is an appropriate fit for the journal and of high enough quality to warrant further review. If so, the editor sends the article to at least two other experts to review. These reviewers make recommendations to the editor to accept or reject the article, or as is more likely the case, to withhold the final decision until after the author of the article has made some recommended revisions and resubmitted the article. Almost all the articles that are eventually published have gone through several revisions based on the critique and advice of experts in the field.

> *Peer review:* Process in which scholarly works are reviewed by other experts in the field.

Why is any of this information relevant to you? One reason is it provides some insight into the process and progress of science that we discussed in Chapter 1. The importance of review and revision will also be relevant as you begin writing your own papers (and you might take some solace in the fact that it is not just students whose works are so vigorously critiqued). In more practical and immediate terms, understanding the journal review process can give you one way to evaluate the quality of an article. Generally speaking, articles published in academic journals represent the best work in the field. However, the presence and rigor of the peer review process varies depending on the journal.

As you become more familiar with the academic journals in your discipline, you will realize that some journals are more selective than others. Journals published by a discipline's professional organization (e.g., American Political Science Association [APSA], American Psychological Association [APA], American Sociological Association [ASA]) tend to be the most rigorous. For example, in 2009, 76% of the manuscripts submitted for publication to a journal published by the APA were rejected (APA, 2010b). Online-only journals tend to be less selective, and there are even some journals in which authors pay to have their work published.

Information on the publication format and review process for specific journals is provided on the journal's website, and you will likely be able to find the journal's rejection or acceptance rate online as well.

Academic Journals Publish Both Primary and Secondary Sources

Academic journals only publish scholarly work, but you should not assume that an article in an academic journal is a primary source. On the contrary, journal articles can be either primary or secondary sources. In fact, several high-quality journals, such as *Psychological Bulletin,* only publish secondary research articles.

Primary Sources in Academic Journals. Recall that a primary source in the social sciences is a report of an original research study. When such a source is published in an academic journal, it is referred to as a **primary research article (or empirical journal article)**. What is sometimes confusing to students is that a primary research article typically provides a summary of past research, just as secondary sources do. The difference is that a primary research article will also include details about the method and results of at least one study that was conducted by the article author(s). Some primary research articles include the method and results of several related studies.

Because primary research articles are firsthand accounts of a study that have been reviewed and accepted by experts in the field, they are the best sources of information on a topic. It is therefore important that you know how to identify which articles published in an academic journal are primary research articles. Some ways to determine this is to see if the authors used phrases such as "this study examined" or if they provide some detail about data collection such as how the participants were recruited or the total number of participants. If you cannot find this type of information, it is likely that the article is not a primary source. More information about reading a primary journal article appears later in this chapter.

The types of studies reported in an empirical article vary quite a bit. The design described in a primary research article may be descriptive, correlational, experimental, or a combination of these. The purpose of the study may be to test a theory or expand basic knowledge in an area, or it may be to evaluate the effectiveness of a program or technique, or the purpose may be to describe the development and evaluation of a measurement scale or assessment tool.

> *Primary research article (or empirical journal article):* Report of the method and results of an original research study (i.e., a primary research source) that is published in an academic journal.

Secondary Sources in Academic Journals. Recall that a secondary source in the social sciences is a review or discussion of previous research that does not include information about a new and original research study. The most common types of secondary sources found in academic journals are literature reviews and meta-analyses.

36 • RESEARCH METHODS, STATISTICS, AND APPLICATIONS

A **literature review** summarizes the findings of many primary research articles but does not report the method or results of an original study. A **meta-analysis** is a more statistically sophisticated version of a literature review in that a meta-analysis uses the statistical results and sample sizes of past studies to synthesize results. Like a literature review, it does not report the method or results of a new study and is therefore considered a secondary source. Both literature reviews and meta-analyses identify common findings in past research as well as inconsistencies or gaps. As such, reading a recently published literature review or meta-analysis is very useful in helping you understand what research has already been conducted and what research should be conducted in the future. Moreover, they provide an excellent resource to help you identify past research in a topic area.

Although useful, the information provided in a review of past research should not be used in lieu of reading the original sources. Whereas a primary research article describes the method and results of a study in anywhere from one page to upwards of 20 pages, a review or meta-analysis will summarize the article in as little as one sentence. The authors of reviews and meta-analyses select only the information that is most relevant to their own article and consequently the summary will provide an incomplete, and in some cases even incorrect, picture of the actual study.

Once in a while you will run across a commentary in an academic journal. **Commentaries** are brief responses about a published article that usually involve a critique of a study or review. They can be very interesting to read if you have read the research article that is the topic of commentary. In this case, you might use the commentary as a source for your study or to generate research questions.

Literature review: Review of past research without a report of original research.

Meta-analysis: A type of review in which the statistical results of past research are synthesized but no original data were collected or analyzed.

Commentaries: Critique or comments about a published research article.

Other Types of Scholarly Work

Conference Papers or Posters

Professional conferences provide a forum for researchers to present their scholarly work (both primary and secondary) in the form of a paper or poster presentation. It can take a year or more for a research article to be published in an academic journal, whereas the works presented at conferences are recent or even in progress. Therefore, these types of scholarly work often represent cutting-edge research. Some professional organizations post the full papers and posters from their conferences online, and some researchers provide the work to conference attendees. More typically, only the titles and summaries are available and you would need to contact the authors directly to obtain the full work. Aside from being relatively hard to come by, the conference review process is not as rigorous as the review process for an academic journal and consequently these works should not be the main sources for your study.

Unpublished Manuscripts

Unpublished manuscripts include articles that have been accepted for publication in an academic journal but are not yet published (in press), are currently under review for publication, have not been submitted for publication, or were rejected from an academic journal. It is unlikely that you will even know that such a manuscript exists unless you see it cited in another source, you have the inside scoop from a professor, or you happen to find a reference to it or the full document online. Assuming that you are able to identify, find, and read the full article, articles that are in press have gone through the review process and can be used and evaluated just as published articles. Other types of unpublished manuscripts should be used judiciously, paying special attention to the quality of the work.

Scholarly Books

Scholarly books are written by experts in the field and are typically published by professional organizations or universities. One important indicator of a scholarly book is that the content is based on past research that is clearly cited. You should also check to make sure the authors do not make sweeping generalizations based on research evidence and do not seem to use research only when it supports their personal opinion. A book can be a primary source if it also describes a new original research study or program of studies. The time lag from implementation to publication of studies within scholarly books is often lengthy, and you should be aware that more recent work on a topic can probably be found in journal articles.

Theses and Dissertations

Theses and dissertations are part of the graduate school requirements for a master's degree and doctorate, respectively. Most often they are original research studies and thus primary sources, but some are reviews or meta-analyses. The full manuscripts are book length, and they are only available via interlibrary loan from the library of the university where the work was completed. Consequently, they require time to obtain and read. Although the review process for a thesis or dissertation is usually quite involved (as any graduate student will tell you), in general it is not as rigorous as the journal review process.

Undergraduate Research

There are forums available for undergraduate students to share their original research, including research conferences (e.g., National Conferences of Undergraduate Research [NCUR], Undergraduate Research Conference [URC]) and undergraduate research journals (e.g., *Journal of Undergraduate Research and Scholarly Excellence, URC Undergraduate Research Journal, The Undergraduate Research Journal of Psychology*). The review process for undergraduate research is much less rigorous than other research, as it should be. Reading these works can give you some great ideas and inspiration, but be judicious in using them as sources for a research study.

Figure 2.1	Types of Sources

Is the source scholarly or popular?

Popular Sources: Primary or secondary sources designed to entertain or educate, such as magazine or newspaper articles, websites, textbooks, etc.

Scholarly Sources: Works designed to advance knowledge in a field that are written by experts in that field.

Use infrequently (if at all) in order to:
• Obtain ideas for your research topic.
• Build a case for the importance of a research topic.

Is the scholarly source a primary or secondary research source?

Secondary Research Source: Reviews research but does not report results of an original study, such as review articles and meta-analyses.

Primary Research Source: Reports results of an original study.

Use to:
• Identify patterns and gaps in past research.
• Identify primary research for you to find and read.

The majority of your sources should be recent primary research articles published in academic journals.

Use to:
• Understand the current state of knowledge in the field.
• Understand how past researches have examined your topic.
• Identify limitations in past research.

PRACTICE 2.1

ARTICLE COMPARISON

Read excerpts from the following three articles about the use of technology to enhance classroom interaction and learning. As you read each excerpt, consider these questions:

1. Which sources are primary? Explain.

2. Which sources are scholarly? Explain.

3. How might each article be useful in taking a scientific approach to the topic? Based on the information provided, what are the limitations of each source?

Article 1:

Gabriel, T. (2011, May 12). Speaking up in class, silently, using social media. *New York Times*. Retrieved from http://www.nytimes.com

Excerpt: "Wasn't it just the other day that teachers confiscated cell phones and principals warned about oversharing on Myspace? Now, Erin Olsen, an English teacher in Sioux Rapids, Iowa, is among a small but growing cadre of educators trying to exploit Twitter-like technology to enhance classroom discussion" (p. 1).

Article 2:

Zepke, N., & Leach, L. (2010). Improving student engagement: Ten proposals for action. *Active Learning in Higher Education, 11,* 167–177. doi:10/1177/146978741037960

Excerpt: "Since the 1980s an extensive research literature has investigated how to improve student success in higher education focusing on student outcomes such as retention, completion, and employability. A parallel research programme has focused on how students engage with their studies and what they, institutions and educators can do to enhance their engagement, and hence success. This article reports on two syntheses of research literature on student engagement and how this can be enhanced" (p. 167).

Article 3:

Dallaire, D. H. (2011). Effective use of personal response "clicker" systems in psychology courses. *Teaching of Psychology, 38,* 199–204. doi:10.1177/0098628311411898

Excerpt: "Though personal response 'clicker' systems can enhance student engagement and learning, little research has examined characteristics which affect learning. In the current study, 151 students reported how their instructor used clickers, their experience of clicker-related hindrances, perceived benefits of using clickers, and their grades. Results show that more clicker uses interacted with students' perceived benefits of clickers to predict grades" (p. 199).

See Appendix A to check your answers.

40 • RESEARCH METHODS, STATISTICS, AND APPLICATIONS

Abstracts

Abstracts are one-paragraph summaries of scholarly works. They are not complete works, but rather part of a conference presentation or research article. We mention them here because abstracts are very easy to find online and are very brief, and consequently students are often tempted to use them as sources. Beware that reading the abstract of a work is not sufficient! Rather, if you find an abstract that interests you, you will need to find and read the full text of the work in order to cite it as well as understand the research the abstract summarizes.

● STRATEGIES TO IDENTIFY AND FIND PAST RESEARCH

Searching Library Databases by Topic

Searching online databases through your college or university library system is the most efficient and effective way to identify past research on a topic. These databases are catalogs of articles published in academic journals, chapters in scholarly books, dissertations, and other scholarly sources. Some databases also catalog nonscholarly sources, so be careful not to assume that all the work you identify through a database is scholarly.

A search of one of the online databases will yield a list of the titles of sources that meet the search criteria and other basic information such as the author(s), source (e.g., name of journal), and year published. By clicking on any of the titles in the list, you can view a more detailed record including a brief summary (the abstract) and a list of keywords associated with the source. Most databases also provide a link to the full text for at least some of the sources listed.

Identify the Appropriate Databases to Search

Choose one or more databases to search based on your discipline, your topic, and whether or not the database is available via your college or university library website. Table 2.1 lists databases commonly used in the social and behavioral science fields. In psychology, for example, PsycINFO is the most comprehensive database and will help you identify research articles relevant to your topic. It covers psychology as well as related disciplines such as anthropology, education, and sociology. PsycArticles is a psychology-specific database that provides the full text of journals published by the American Psychological Association. PsycArticles can be useful when you need to narrow your search to only high-quality psychology articles that are available at a click of a button. However, PsycINFO is the preferred database because it covers those articles available in PsycArticles as well as many others.

Even if you are studying a particular discipline, you may find the databases for other areas quite useful. For example, a psychology student may end up doing a study related to sports, and therefore might want to use both PsycINFO and SPORTDiscus. Likewise, a student in sociology focusing on health issues might find using both SocINDEX and MEDLINE to be a good way to identify relevant research articles. There are also databases that span a wide range of disciplines, as shown in Table 2.1.

Table 2.1	Databases Used in the Social and Behavioral Sciences	

Database	Field(s)	Is the Full Text Available for the Sources Listed in the Database?
Academic Search Premier	Multidiscipline	Some
AnthroSource	Anthropology	Some
Criminal Justice Periodical Index	Criminal Justice	Some
Communication and Mass Media Complete	Communications	Some
EconLit	Economics	Some
ERIC	Education Studies	Some
JSTOR	Multidiscipline	Some
MasterFILE Premier	Multidiscipline	Some
MEDLINE	Health and Medicine	Some
Project MUSE	Multidiscipline	All
PsycArticles	Psychology	All
PsycINFO	Psychology and related fields	Some
SocINDEX	Sociology	Some
Social Sciences Citation Index	Social Sciences	None
Social Sciences Full Text	Social Sciences	All
SPORTDiscus	Sports Studies	Some

Conducting the Database Search

Keyword Searches. Identifying the appropriate keywords for your database search is a critical step. We recommend that you take some time to brainstorm some words and phrases associated with your topic, try them out, and then make adjustments as necessary to obtain lists of sources relevant to your topic.

Sometimes you will hit on some good keywords right away, other times you will get too few or too many results. Too few hits are obviously a problem, but you do not want too many hits either because it will be too tedious to look through them all in order to identify those that are relevant to your topic. Finding the right keywords is like finding the key that unlocks past research, and sometimes it simply takes trial and error (along with time and patience) to hit on the right words.

Following are some strategies to identify appropriate keywords and phrases:

1. It may sound obvious, but if a keyword yields zero results, check first to be sure you spelled the word correctly. Unlike Google or other online searches, the library database will not ask you if you meant to type something else nor will it automatically complete words or correct errors.

42 • RESEARCH METHODS, STATISTICS, AND APPLICATIONS

2. If available in the search engine, try the thesaurus function to get keyword ideas. You might also use a print or online thesaurus.

3. If your topic is discussed in one of your textbooks, see what terms they use and try them.

4. If you are able to identify a few relevant sources, check what keywords are listed for them.

5. Try broadening your terms if you are getting too few results. For example, instead of searching for the keywords "unintentional plagiarism," try just "plagiarism."

6. Try narrowing your terms if you are getting too many results that are not related to your topic. For example, instead of searching for the keyword "honesty," try "academic honesty," "plagiarism," and "cheating."

Start Broad. When you are just beginning to search for articles on your topic, you will want to keep your search broad. Use keywords associated with your topic but also search for research on related topics. For example, if you are interested in cell phone use in the classroom, do not limit your initial searches to only research about cell phones. Instead, you might find it helpful to identify research about other types of technology used in classrooms (e.g., laptops, clickers, PowerPoint) and issues associated with cell phone use in the classroom (e.g., classroom rules and etiquette, multitasking). Likewise, if you are interested in the topic of plagiarism, search also for other issues that might relate to academic honesty such as "cheating," "test taking," "deception," "faking," and "student misconduct."

There are several reasons why you will want to keep your initial searches broad:

1. To identify the keywords that lead to the results that are most relevant and interesting to you. Once you identify these keywords you can use them as you narrow your search.

2. To give you a sense of the research done in your topic. You will not read all of the research you find during these initial, broad searches, but reading the titles and some of the abstracts will give you an idea of what types of studies are out there. You may also want to file away some studies that are not directly related to your topic but might help you build a broader context for your study.

3. To help you fine-tune your topic. Skimming over the titles and abstracts, you may find that there are other important variables related to your topic that you had not considered before. Or, you might find an interesting article that entices you to veer off in a direction different than you had initially planned. Or, you might realize that there are many studies similar to the way you initially conceptualized your study, and therefore you need to delve a bit deeper in order to create a unique study.

Narrowing Your Search. Next you will want to narrow your search to identify those articles that are most directly related to your revised topic that you will find and read now. For example, you could limit your search to articles that are English only (unless you are bilingual) and published in a peer-reviewed journal. You might also limit your search to only those articles published recently (e.g., within the past 10 years). This does not mean that you can only use new studies to create your study and write your paper. However, the foundation for your study should be recent research, with older studies providing a broader context for your study such as a historical or a theoretical perspective. You certainly do not want to base your study only on old articles, as demonstrated in Figure 2.2.

Other ways to narrow your search are to combine or add keywords. You might use "and" to combine the keywords that led to the most relevant results. You might also try finding a recent review or meta-analysis to provide you with an overview of your topic by using "review" or "meta-analysis" as keywords (e.g., "cell phone use and review" or " . . . and meta-analysis"). You might combine your topic keywords with other behaviors and traits associated with your topic (e.g., "cell phone use and academic performance") or with keywords relating to the population you are most interested in examining (e.g., "cell phone use and college students"). If you know you will have to do an experiment on a topic, it is a good idea to read at least one article that describes an experiment, thus you can try using "experiment" as another keyword. Keep in mind that this does not mean that all the studies you use must be with the same type of sample or the same type of study design, but it will be good to find at least a few examples to build upon. In Application 2.1, we provide an example of how we searched for articles on our topic of cell phone use.

More Search Strategies

Use One Source to Find Others

If you have at least one research article related to your topic, you can use the reference section of the article to find additional sources. Many of the library databases will allow you to click

Figure 2.2	Focus on Recent Sources

Some older, classic studies may be useful to provide the theoretical or historical context for your research study. However, focus primarily on recent sources.

Source: Eva K. Lawrence

APPLICATION 2.1

Database Search for Cell Phone Topic

Topic

The *New York Times* article (see excerpt from article in Practice Exercise 2.1) raised some interesting questions about the use of technology in the classrooms such as: Can using cell phones as part of the class structure improve student engagement and learning? Will using cell phones in this way increase or decrease inappropriate or off-task use of cell phones in class?

Initial Searches

First we would list keywords associated with cell phones and other types of technology that may be used in classrooms for academic and nonacademic purposes.

Our initial keyword list: Cell phone, mobile phone, text, laptops, social media, computer mediated communication, twitter, backchannel, digital streaming, powerpoint, clickers

We would conduct databases searches using these keywords to see what types of results we obtain and make modifications if necessary.

For example: If we enter "text" as a keyword in PsycINFO we would get over 50,000 results. However, most of these are not about texting on cell phones, instead many are about textbooks, writing skills, and language. We would be able to find some relevant sources if we looked harder, but wading through 50,000-plus results is an onerous task.

Instead, we might try "text message" to obtain a more workable number of results (149 at the writing of this book), most of which appear to be relevant. Examining the keywords listed for our relevant results provides some additional keywords that we can use, including "SMS message" and "electronic communication."

These initial, broad searches will help us identify the keyword searches that are most successful and identify new keywords. The results for these searches will likely overlap quite a bit.

At this point, we are simply reading titles and abstracts to get an idea of the research conducted in the area. We take note of the following types of articles:

- Those that are directly related to our topic. By doing so we find a few articles about the effective use of cell phones and other technology in the classroom, including those identified in Practice 2.1.

- Those that might be useful to consider later in the research process such as articles about trends in cell phone use and gender differences in patterns of use. We make note of these articles but do not plan to find and read these types of articles yet.
- Those that strike our interest and help us to fine-tune our topic. When we began the search we were most interested in the effective use of cell phones in the classroom. However, we came across some interesting articles about the disruptive nature of cell phones in the classroom and we decide to veer our searches more in this direction.

Narrowing the Search

Once we have identified some of the best keywords, we can narrow the search to find only those articles we will actually be able to read (those in English). We also limit our search to those published in a peer-reviewed journal during the last 10 years.

We narrow our search further by combining our most effective keywords (text message, cell phone, etc.) with others specific to class behavior and performance (e.g., disruptive behavior, incivility, classroom rules, classroom etiquette).

At this point we want to find a few of the most recent and relevant articles to read. As we develop our study and write our research paper, we will want to read some of those we found in our broader searches and we will likely need to make additional, more targeted searches when we advance in the process.

For now, however, we have accomplished our goal of obtaining some basic ideas of the research literature and identifying those that we want to find and read right now.

on a link that will give you a list of the references. If that is not an option, obtain the full text of the article and manually browse the paper and reference section to identify sources relevant to your topic.

With just one research article, you can also find more recent articles that cited it. This is an especially good strategy because it will show you how others have used the article to build a case for your research. Some databases have a "times cited in this database" link that will take you to a list of all the articles within your chosen database that referenced the article. If that is not an option, you can go to the Social Sciences Citation Index to find articles that cite the work.

If you were to examine the reference sections of several articles on your topic, you might notice that some references are used in most of the articles. These are the influential works in the topic area that you will want to find and read. Paying attention to these works will help identify some classic research on the topic and the older articles (more than 10 years) that still have an impact today and that you will want to read and cite for your study.

Search by Author

As you begin finding relevant articles, you will notice certain authors will be cited in many articles and you may notice several articles in your topic by the same author. Researchers

46 • RESEARCH METHODS, STATISTICS, AND APPLICATIONS

typically develop an area of specialization and author several articles on the same subject. If you find a few names that keep popping up, try doing a library search by the author's name. The author's affiliation, or the institution where he or she worked at the time the article was published, is usually provided by the library database. You could go to the institution's website and search for the author's name to see if he or she provides a list of recent publications. In some cases, it may even be appropriate to e-mail an author and ask for recent publications and you may even obtain some manuscripts that are in press or under review. At early stages of the search process contacting the author directly is not worthwhile to you, and may be needlessly burdensome for the author, but it can be very useful as you fine-tune your study.

Search Relevant Journals

Just as you will notice the same references and authors appearing in your searches, you will find the journals that publish articles on your topic. If you are in the early stages of the research process, it may be worthwhile to do a database search by the journal and limit your search to the last few years. You can scan through the list of titles to see if there are any relevant articles. You might even visit a university library that carries the hard copies of the recent issues of the journal and physically flip through the last year or so of the journal. This is a great way to generate ideas for research at the early phases, and you often come upon articles that strike your interest that you might not have found otherwise.

What About Google Scholar and Other Internet Searches?

Google Scholar (www.scholar.google.com) can be a useful search tool for research, if you use it correctly. It is not very helpful if you are at the beginning stages of research and are simply typing in keywords. If you search by author, however, you might be more successful. Google scholar can also be useful in finding the full text of a specific article you have identified. As far as general Internet searches go, we would recommend avoiding them altogether. You are unlikely to find many scholarly sources doing a basic Web search, and you will likely waste a lot of time.

Find the Full Text of a Source

Most databases will provide links to the full text for at least some of the sources they list (see Table 2.1), and the links available will depend upon your college or university's library subscription. This is of course the easiest way to find the full text—you do a search in a database and click on the full-text link and poof, like magic, a PDF or HTML document will appear. It is so easy that it is tempting to only use those databases that always provide the full text (such as PsycArticles or ProjectMUSE) or to set limits in other databases so that the only results you receive are those that have full-text links. Not surprisingly, these limits will limit your findings and you may even end up like those students we mentioned at the beginning of the chapter who claimed that there is no research on their topic. For example, at the time of writing this chapter a search in PsycINFO using the search term "cell phones" yielded 354 results, and 85 of these results were available in full text (which may be higher or lower had the search been made through a different college or university library system). A similar search in PsycArticles, however, yielded only 11 results.

What do you do if an article is not available with a click of a button doing a database search? Many libraries subscribe to some sort of journal finder in which you enter the name of the journal, or click on a link, and it will show you if the journal is available online or as a hard copy in the school library. Be sure you check if the year and issue is available online or in the library because your library may only have subscribed to the paper version of the journal up to a certain date and may have canceled its subscription or moved to only online versions after a certain date. You could try finding the article online by doing a search in Google Scholar or by going to the author's website if he or she has one. If neither applies, you might see if a nearby college or university has the article available and make the trek there. Interlibrary loan is another option, although you can expect to wait up to several weeks to receive the article. If the article is an essential one and you have exhausted all the other means of obtaining the full text, you could contact the author directly to request the article.

Now practice your new knowledge of identifying relevant articles and finding the full text by completing Practice 2.2. There are no right or wrong answers for this practice, but it will help you gain familiarity with the search process. If you are new to this process it may take you a while and be somewhat frustrating, but with practice this process becomes easier and faster.

PRACTICE 2.2

FIND RESEARCH ON YOUR TOPIC

1. What library databases are used most commonly within your discipline? What other databases might be useful to search for research articles on your topic?

2. Do a search for relevant and recent research articles (published in the last 10 years) using the databases you identified. Doing this search will help you identify appropriate articles as well as help you refine your research topic. It should take several hours if you do it correctly!

   a. What keywords and phrases were most *and* least successful in finding relevant articles? Explain your answer.

   b. What other search strategies were helpful for finding relevant articles such as searching by author, looking at reference lists, etc.?

3. Skim over the titles and summaries of some of the articles you found. What can you learn about the way other researchers have considered your research topic? Consider the keywords they used, about how much past research has been done, and different ways the topic has been examined.

4. Identify a few of the most relevant and interesting articles. Figure out how to obtain the full text of these articles.

● READING AND EVALUATING PRIMARY RESEARCH ARTICLES

Format of Unpublished Manuscripts Versus Published Research Articles

Unpublished manuscripts, including student papers, look much different from the articles published in academic journals. When you write your own research papers, your professors will ask you to adhere to a specific style such as APA. Although established by the American Psychological Association, APA style it is not restricted to psychology. In fact, most of the social science disciplines adhere to APA Style. The most recent version of APA Style is detailed in the sixth edition of the *Publication Manual of the American Psychological Association* (2010b), and a condensed APA guide appears in Appendix B. In this appendix, you will see an example of a paper we wrote in its unpublished, manuscript form and in its final, published form.

The primary research articles published in academic journals will vary in length, writing style, the way references are cited, and the headings they use or do not use to organize the article. Many journals use APA format, although others use Modern Language Association (MLA) format or develop their own hybrid format. However, the overall flow and organization of primary research articles will be strikingly similar. Once you understand the basic format, you will know what to expect while reading the article and you will have a good idea of where to look for certain information.

Remember:

- Primary research articles that you read in academic journals will have a very different appearance from the research papers you will write.
- The content and flow of published articles can serve as a model for your own writing, but you should format the paper according to the guidelines of your discipline (such as those outlined in APA's *Publication Manual*).

Organization of Primary Research Articles

Following the title and authors, all published primary research articles will include the following sections (although the names may be slightly different based on the journal format, and some sections may be combined): abstract, introduction, method, results, and discussion. Do not assume that having one or more of these sections ensures that the article is a primary source. A primary research article contains all these sections, but secondary sources may or may not have several or all of these sections. All scholarly works will provide a list of references and most have an abstract. The excerpts from the two scholarly works back in Practice 2.1 are from the articles' abstracts, but you might recall that only the third article was a primary source. Meta-analyses and some review articles will contain a method section describing the selection criteria for the sources they used, and many will have a discussion or conclusions section. Remember that what makes a primary research article unique is that it describes one or more studies that the authors conducted, and you will need to find evidence that a study was conducted within the article's abstract or method to verify that the article is a primary one.

The following sections describe the key parts of a published primary research article and explain what types of information you will find in each. We also provide some tips for reading and evaluating the sections. The best way to understand how to read and evaluate primary research articles is to have the full text of at least one in front of you. Here, we use examples from two articles that we found in PsycINFO using the keywords "cell phone" and "classroom":

- The first one is titled "Costly Cell Phones: The Impact of Cell Phone Rings on Academic Performance." It was written by End, Worthman, Mathews, and Wetterau and published in the journal *Teaching of Psychology* in 2010.
- The second is titled "Predicting and Curbing Classroom Incivility in Higher Education." It was written by Nordstrom, Bartels, and Bucy and published in 2009 in *College Student Journal*.

Test your library skills to see if you can find the full text of these articles through your college or university library database. To quickly narrow down the results, search by each of the article titles. At our college, the full articles were available directly through both PsycINFO and ERIC. Depending on your college or university library system, you may need to take additional steps to obtain the full article.

We are serious. Stop reading and go find the full text of the End et al. (2010) and the Nordstrom et al. (2009) articles (or *at least one* of these). Doing so will help test your library skills, and furthermore we will use them in the following sections. Go now.

OK—now that you have the articles (You do have them, right?), read on about the different parts of a primary research article. Compare the description of each section to what appears in the research articles.

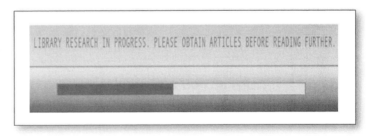

LIBRARY RESEARCH IN PROGRESS. PLEASE OBTAIN ARTICLES BEFORE READING FURTHER.

Title

The title is a brief description of the study and will usually include the key variables examined in the study. Most titles are pretty dry and straight-forward. Some authors choose to let a little creativity shine through in the title, but if this happens they also include a more direct description (usually set off by a colon). After scanning through lists and lists of titles from a library database, most students come to appreciate the utilitarian nature of titles. The title should tell you very quickly whether or not the article is related to your topic. See Application 2.2, which evaluates the titles of the two articles that we asked you to find.

50 • RESEARCH METHODS, STATISTICS, AND APPLICATIONS

Authors

The authors are typically listed right after the title. If there are multiple authors, the author list is usually organized by the degree each contributed, with the first author as the person who was most responsible for the work. This will be important if you decide to use and cite the article. You will want to appropriately credit the authors, and they put some effort in deciding who would be listed first, second, and so on. Therefore do not change the order of authors when you cite the source.

For example, to cite the first example in an APA-style paper (see Appendix B for more information about citations and references):

The first time you cite the article:

End, Worthman, Mathews, and Wetterau (2010) *or* (End, Worthman, Mathews, & Wetterau, 2010)

Later citations:

End et al. (2010) *or* (End et al., 2010)

Paying attention to the authors will also help you identify who the key players are in a certain field. As you delve into a research topic, you will start to notice that many of the authors have published multiple articles on the same topic. As you read further into the article, you may also notice that certain authors are cited by others. You can use this author information to find other relevant articles on your topic.

APPLICATION 2.2

Titles of Two Articles About Disruptive Cell Phones

Title of End et al. (2010) article:	Title of Nordstrom et al. (2009) article:
"Costly Cell Phones: The Impact of Cell Phone Rings on Academic Performance"	"Predicting and Curbing Classroom Incivility in Higher Education"
Notice that this title starts with a little flair with the phrase "costly cell phones," but the more precise topic of the article is provided after the colon. If the title was only "Costly Cell Phones," we might imagine that the article was about the monetary cost of cell phones and may even have assumed that it was not directly relevant to our interest in classroom behaviors.	This title is more direct. It does not specifically mention cell phones in the title because the authors are examining a wide range of possible classroom behaviors. The article's abstract will give us more information about what exact behaviors were examined.

Abstract

The abstract is a one-paragraph summary of the entire article. In a PDF or print version of a published article, the abstract is often set off from the rest of the paper by being in a smaller font, centered, or italicized. In an HTML version of the article, the abstract is the first paragraph. Some journals use a heading to identify the abstract, such as "Abstract," "Overview," or "Summary" but others do not (including our two examples).

The abstract will give you an idea of the purpose of the study (or studies if multiple ones are described), who the participants were and what they did in the study, and the key results. Most often the information contained in the abstract will verify that you indeed have a primary research article (see Application 2.3 for examples). Additionally, like the title, the abstract will help you determine how relevant the article is for your study but will provide a little more detail to help you decide if it will be worthwhile to read the full article. If you cite an article, you must read the full article and not rely solely on the brief information provided in the abstract.

APPLICATION 2.3

Abstracts

The abstracts from both the examples verify that the articles are primary sources.	
The first phrase in End et al. (2010) is "College students participated in a study…" (p. 55).	The third sentence in Nordstrom et al. (2009) contains the phrase "Data from a survey of undergraduate students…" (p. 74).
Additionally, both example abstracts provide a very brief overview of the method, key results, and implications of the study. Read the rest of the article to get the full picture of the study.	

The abstract of a primary research article will also provide some clues as to the research design of the study. Recall that we introduced you to the different types of research designs in Chapter 1. Review these concepts by answering the review questions that follow.

REVIEW OF KEY CONCEPTS:
DISCERNING A STUDY'S DESIGN FROM THE ABSTRACT

Read the Abstracts and Method sections from End et al. (2010) and Nordstrom et al. (2009) articles that we asked you to find.

What type of research design is represented by each of these studies?

If you are not sure, review the key characteristics of different research designs (descriptive, correlational, and experimental) from Chapter 1.

(Continued)

(Continued)

End et al.'s (2010) abstract provides a clue that the study was an experiment. Do you know what that clue is and why it helps us identify the research design? What are the independent and dependent variables (IV and DV)?

Answer:

The clue is in the second sentence, "Researchers assigned 71 participants to either the ringing condition... or the control condition..." (p. 55). A key characteristic of an experiment is assignment of participants to conditions, although we would want to verify that the participants were randomly assigned to ensure that it is a true experiment.

Consequently, we turn to the Method section. In the first sentence of the procedure section, we find the statement confirming that this study is in fact an experiment that used random assignment: "Researchers randomly assigned 32 (12 men, 20 women) participants to the ringing condition and 39 (11 men, 28 women) to the nonringing condition" (p. 56).

Note that the other information included in the article about the number of participants, the hypothesis, and the results are not unique to an experiment. Other types of designs will also have these characteristics.

The independent variable (IV) is the one that is manipulated (or the one to which conditions are assigned). In this study, cell phone ringing is the IV. The dependent variable is measured following exposure to the IV condition. In this study, there are two DVs: performance on a multiple-choice test and content of the students' notes. We would need to read the Method of the article to better understand the procedures of the IV manipulation and how the authors measured the DVs.

What type of research design did Nordstrom et al. (2009) use? What information in the abstract helped you to answer this question?

Answer:

This study is correlational. The summary of the results revealed that there was a relationship between certain traits (consumerism and narcissism) with uncivil classroom behaviors. Both correlational studies and experiments examine relationships, but correlational studies do not examine causation.

How do we know causation is not examined and therefore this study is not an experiment? To have an experiment, the researcher must randomly assign participants to an independent variable condition. It is impossible to determine if a consumerist orientation or narcissism caused uncivil behaviors because we cannot manipulate these traits or randomly assign participants to be consumerists or narcissists.

We are able to discern the basic procedures from the abstract and obtain more detailed information from the Method section.

Introduction

The Introduction begins right after the abstract. Published articles usually will begin this section without a heading. Some journals will have a section labeled "Introduction" followed by a longer section called something like "Literature Review" and then a "Current Study" or "Hypotheses" section, and it might appear that the Introduction ends before the Literature Review section. However, for our purposes and to follow APA format, all these sections represent the Introduction.

The purpose of the Introduction is to provide the rationale for the study. Reading the Introduction will give you insight into the authors' thinking about the topic and the reason they conducted the study. It will also give you a sense of some of the past research in this area.

Introductions range in length and vary in content, but most Introductions follow the same general organization. Understanding this organization can help you efficiently read the Introduction of a variety of studies (see Application 2.4 for a comparison of the content and organization of the Introductions for our two example articles on cell phones in the classroom). Moreover, you will notice that authors organize their introduction in order to build a case for their study. In particular, take note of the following:

1. The Introduction begins by introducing the topic and giving the reader an idea for why the topic is an important one to study.

   - The authors might identify a problem or make an observation, which can be as simple as noting the amount of research already done on the topic.
   - The beginning of the Introduction allows the authors a bit more leeway in terms of creativity as well as the types of sources used. We have seen Introductions that begin with a nursery rhyme or a quote from a famous person. Popular sources such as *Time* magazine or CNN may be used to help develop a case that a topic is important, or recent statistics from website sources may be used to identify trends or emphasize the importance of researching the topic.

2. The review of past research makes up the majority of the Introduction.

   - Remember that reviews are secondary sources that can provide you with a brief summary of past research but should not be used in lieu of reading the original, primary source. In other words, do not cite information from the Introduction of a research article; instead, track down and read the primary source before citing information from it.
   - Some articles will begin the review of past research in the first paragraph of the introduction, citing scholarly sources as a way to introduce the importance of a topic. Others authors will begin the review of past research in the second or third paragraph. The review of past research may be as little as one paragraph or as long as several pages. The review may be subdivided based on the content of the research reviewed in each subsection.
   - As the authors explain the research that has been done that supports their own study, they will often make note of the research that is absent, sparse, or inconsistent. In this way, the authors build a case for the need for their own study.

3. The end of the Introduction will focus on the study the authors conducted.

- The authors may explicitly state or imply how their research study will improve upon past research and how their study is unique. For example, they may be using a different method, studying different types of participants, comparing alternative explanations, examining different ways that one variable impacts another, or examining variables that might impact the relationship between variables.
- The hypotheses for the study are typically near or at the very end of the Introduction. The hypotheses should come as no surprise because all the previous content of the Introduction was building a case for these hypotheses. In the case of exploratory research where the authors do not have set hypotheses, the author will instead state some research questions. Some articles contain both hypotheses and exploratory questions.

Method

The Method explains the method used to test the hypotheses or to help answer the research questions. The Method will include information about the participants (or animal subjects), the measures or materials used in the study, and the procedures of the study. The authors will usually divide this information among subsections in the Method, but the exact number, names, and order of these subsections will vary based on the article.

Participants or Subjects. At minimum, you will find information about the total number of human participants or animal subjects in the Method. Ideally, you will also find information about the characteristics of the participants such as age, gender, and ethnicity. Information about the participants or subjects will help you evaluate the results of the study, and we will discuss some ways to do this later in the chapter.

Measures and Materials. Researchers operationally define their variables by selecting specific measures and materials. Measures can be evaluated in terms of their reliability and measurement validity, and we will discuss both of these in more depth in Chapter 3. Generally speaking, reliability refers to how consistent the measure is. Authors often cite past research that used or developed the measure to support the measure's reliability, or the authors may have evaluated a measure's reliability themselves. However, some authors do not provide any information about reliability of the measures.

The basic definition of measurement validity is the extent to which a measure actually measures what the researcher says it does or the extent to which a manipulation manipulates what the researcher says it does. You can do a simple evaluation of the validity of the measure based on the types of questions or the materials used to measure or manipulate a variable. For example, you might evaluate the question "have you ever used a cell phone in class for nonacademic purposes?" as having decent measurement validity if the authors had meant to measure *self-reported* inappropriate cell phone use in class, but poor measurement validity if the authors had intended to measure *actual* inappropriate cell phone use.

As you progress in the research process, you will need to find ways to measure and/or manipulate variables in your own study. Reading the Method section will provide you with some ideas on how other researchers operationally define the variables and will cite sources

APPLICATION 2.4

Compare Introductions of End et al. (2010) and Nordstrom et al. (2009)

The authors of both articles begin their introductions by stating a problem or observation.	
The End et al. (2010) introduction begins with a little pizzazz. The authors provide a scenario in which a cell phone rings in the middle of a lecture. They then clearly state the problem under investigation—that "students who experience a cell phone intrusion . . . might be unable to identify the disrupted lecture content, and thus their learning could be impaired" (p. 55).	Nordstrom et al. (2009) do not begin their introduction with a scenario, example, or reference to popular sources. Theirs is a more typical beginning to an Introduction, where the authors state some observations and problems relating to the topic.
	In this case, Nordstrom et al. note in the first paragraph that researchers have been interested in the topic of entitlement, and that entitlement in education is problematic in that "students take on a passive learner role while faculty bear more responsibility for student learning" (p. 74). The second paragraph of the Introduction links entitlement to the more specific problem under study—that is, incivility in the classroom.
The majority of both Introductions involve a review of past research and identification of gaps in the research.	
The second paragraph of End et al. provides research evidence that noise disrupts student learning. The authors note that past research has not examined noise coming from inside the classroom. The authors imply that this is an important area for investigation because while professors have little control over environmental noises such as trains, they could put an end to in-class noises.	Nordstrom et al. (2009) begin the review of past research in the first two paragraphs as they introduce the concepts of entitlement and incivility in the classroom.
The beginning of the third and final paragraph brings the focus to cell phones and provides research evidence that cell phones ringing in the classroom is considered problematic and is pervasive.	In the third paragraph, the authors note a gap in past research in that incivility has not been well researched in higher education.
	The authors then subdivide the Introduction into three sections. Each of these subsections focuses on research support for a possible reason for incivility in class: attitudes, consumerism, and narcissism.
Both articles include hypotheses in the Introduction, although they are found in different parts of each article's Introduction.	
End et al. follow a more traditional organization where the hypotheses are stated at the end of the Introduction.	Nordstrom et al. state their hypotheses after each section reviewing research relevant to the hypothesis. They also include additional research questions at the end of the Introduction.

where you can find a measure to use in your study. Some articles will even provide the complete measure or materials such as a script or scenario that you can use or adapt in your study (and appropriately cite the creator of the measure or material, of course).

Procedure and Design. The Procedure describes the steps the authors followed in the study. A general rule of thumb is that the Procedure section should contain enough information that the reader (you) could replicate the study. You may still have some questions about the details of how the study was conducted, but you should have a good idea about how it was carried out. The description of how the study was conducted is generally listed in the order in which the participant experienced them.

The procedures will help you identify the exact research design (or designs) utilized in the study. In some cases, the authors may include a separate Design subsection to explain the logic behind the procedures to help you understand why the authors did what they did. In all cases, the design of the study should be linked with a specific hypothesis. For example, if the authors hypothesize that one variable will have an effect on (or cause a change to) another variable, then the design utilized to test the hypothesis should be experimental because that is the only design that can test causation.

Results

The Results section is typically the most technical section of the article and the most difficult to understand, especially at first. As you become more comfortable with statistics, Results sections will start to make a lot more sense. However, even if you are reading a research article for the very first time you may be surprised by how much you can understand if you try. By this point in your academic career, you should know some basic statistics such as percentages and means. If you devote some time and energy to reading the Results, you will gain familiarity with some of the more advanced statistics and you will see how they are used to test hypotheses, even if you cannot yet decipher what every single number or statistical notation means.

The main focus of the Results is the results of analyses used to test the hypotheses or help answer the research questions. Take note when the authors state that a result was statistically significant and determine if the results support one of the hypotheses. We will talk more about statistical significance in Chapter 6, but for now simply know that **statistical significance testing** is used to help reduce the likelihood that the results were obtained purely by chance. Researchers do not want to report spurious patterns or relationships, but they do want to be able to identify patterns and relationships in their data that, in fact, exist.

> *Statistical significance testing:* A process to reduce the likelihood that the results were obtained by chance alone.

You might also examine the means, percentages, or other numbers associated with the statistically significant result so that you have some understanding of how the authors tested the hypotheses. Tables or graphs can be very useful in summarizing these results, and you should pay special attention to these when they are available.

Discussion

The Discussion (also named Conclusions in some journals) will usually begin with an explanation of the results without the technical language. It will also put the results into context—usually first stating if the results support or do not support the hypotheses and then explaining how the results fit or do not fit with past research. The Discussion will also suggest what the larger implications and applications of the study might be, point out limitations of the study, and offer suggestions for future research that may address limitations and expand upon the results of the study.

The Discussion is a good place to get an overview of the results of the study and to generate ideas for your own research. However, do not rely on it exclusively to understand the results. The Discussion is the authors' interpretation of the results, and you may come up with your own explanation based on a thorough reading of the Results section. It would be good practice to read through the results and write out some of the key conclusions, and then compare these to what the authors say. Or you might read the Discussion first, and then try to figure out how the authors came to their conclusions based on information they provide in the Results section.

Following are three questions to consider when evaluating the results of a study. The authors may address one or more of these in their Discussion section. Even if they do not, you can consider these questions as you evaluate a research study.

1. *Did the study have enough power?* Power refers to the ability to find statistically significant patterns and relationships in the data when they exist. We will discuss power in more detail in Chapter 6, but for now simply know that the stronger the pattern or relationship and the larger the sample, the more power the study has and the greater likelihood of finding statistically significant results.

How do you use this information in evaluating the power of a study? If you have a study that did not find significant results, it is possible that a pattern or relationship does exist but there was not enough power to detect it due to a small sample size or because the way the research measured or manipulated the variables was not strong enough. If you have a study that found significant results with a relatively small sample, the pattern or relationship must have been relatively strong in order for the results to meet the criteria for statistical significance. Likewise, studies with very large samples are able to detect very small patterns or relationships and the strength of the pattern or relationship should be carefully considered when evaluating the results.

> *Power:* The ability to find statistical significance when in fact a pattern or relationship exists. Sample size and the strength of the relationship between two or more variables are two factors that impact a study's power.

2. *If the authors hypothesized a relationship between variables, did they utilize a design and procedures that helped to demonstrate causation?* If the authors conducted a correlational study, they cannot demonstrate causation and therefore the study cannot help explain why a relationship exists. An experiment helps to demonstrate causation through random assignment, manipulation of an independent variable (IV), and measurement of a dependent variable. These basic requirements of an experiment help improve the study's **internal validity, or the extent to which one can demonstrate that one variable (the IV) caused a change in another variable (the DV). We will discuss internal validity in more depth in later chapters.

Internal validity: The extent to which you can demonstrate a causal relationship between your IV and DV.

3. *How strong is the external validity of the study?* **External validity** is the extent to which a study's results can be generalized to other samples, settings, or procedures. If the study's authors utilized first-year college students as participants, the external validity could be impacted because the results may not generalize to more advanced students or individuals who are not in college. Similarly, if the authors conducted the study in a controlled laboratory it is not clear whether or how the results would generalize to a real-world situation. We will discuss external validity in more depth in the next chapter.

External validity: The extent to which the results of a study can be generalized to other samples, settings, or procedures.

References

All the sources cited within the article will be listed in a References section or in footnotes throughout the article. The References section is a good place to look to identify other research on your topic. You will also notice that the number of references listed is quite high given the length of the article. For example, the End et al. (2010) article has 11 references and Nordstrom et al. (2009) has 33. Most of the references will be cited in the Introduction, and a few new ones may be cited in the Method and Discussion. This demonstrates the importance of building a study on past research, including past methodology, and evaluating the results within the context of past research.

Shape of a Primary Research Article

Once you gain familiarity with the way a primary research article is organized, you will notice that most share a similar shape. This shape is often described as an hourglass in that a primary research article is organized so that it starts broad, moves to the more narrow or specific, and then gets broad again. See Figure 2.3 for a depiction of this organization.

| Figure 2.3 | Shape of a Primary Research Article |

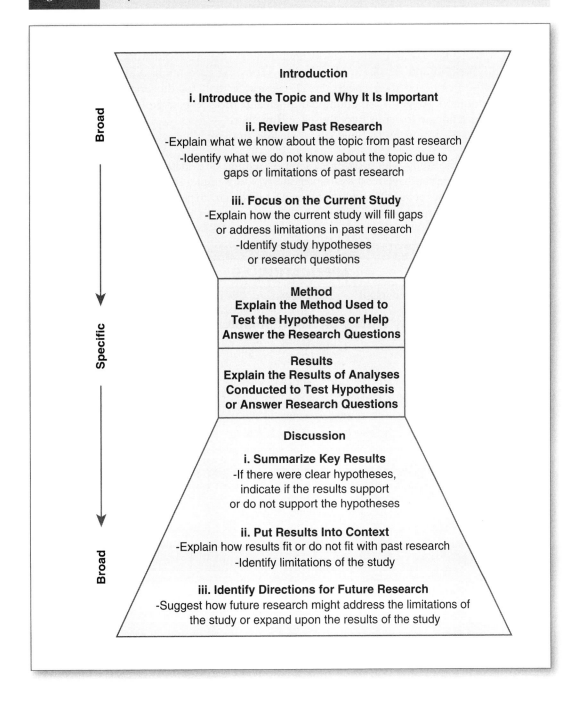

60 • RESEARCH METHODS, STATISTICS, AND APPLICATIONS

● DEVELOP STUDY IDEAS BASED ON PAST RESEARCH

Once you begin to find and read primary research articles on your topic, you might find yourself overwhelmed with information. We recommend that you find one or two recent articles that you find interesting and that include methodology that you can understand. Carefully evaluate the method and results to identify limitations that you might address or questions that the study raises, and then check the Discussion section for the limitations and future research the authors suggest. Use additional articles to provide background information and help build the rationale for your hypotheses and method.

Following are some ways to build on a research study:

1. Replicate the study with a different sample, setting, or measure. Do this if most of the past research you have read examines one type of sample, setting, or measure and you have reason to believe (based on other past research) that the results may be different if conducted with another sample, in another setting, or using another measure.

APPLICATION 2.5

Replicate Study With a Different Sample, Setting, or Measure

Sample

The participants in both the End et al. (2010) and Nordstrom et al. (2009) were of traditional college age. We might wonder if the results would be different for adult students. We might think that the ways that adults learn and interact in class would vary from traditional-aged students, and would want to see if there is research to support this idea (so we would return to the databases for a search of research on adult learners). If we find evidence for this, we could replicate one of the studies with a sample of adult students or better yet, we could include both traditional and adult students to compare the results.

Setting

End et al. conducted their experiment in a tightly controlled, but artificial situation. In their Discussion section, they noted their use of a videotaped lecture as a potential limitation. Students would be able to ask a professor to repeat information from a live lecture that was disrupted with a cell phone ring, but they were unable to do this with the videotaped lecture. We might try to replicate this study using a live lecture while trying as much as possible to maximize internal validity (e.g., have the lecturers practice and carefully follow a script; have the lecturers automatically repeat information that was disrupted in the ringing condition and have them repeat the same information in the no-ring condition). We might even have observers code the students' reaction to the cell phone ring and keep track of how many questions or comments were made by students during each lecture condition. We could use this information as another variable that might help us explain our results.

Measure

Nordstrom et al. measured cell phone incivility by asking students to report how often they engaged in a wide range of specific uncivil classroom behaviors including vulgarity and using a cell phone. We might wonder if students over- or under-report their incivility. We could do additional research on the use of self-report measures and identify situations or constructs in which participants' self-reports may be biased. If we find evidence to question the use of self-report for the construct of incivility, we could conduct a study that uses peer report or classroom observations instead.

2. Conduct an experiment based on a quasi- or non-experimental study. Do this if causation has not been consistently established by past research, or it has not been consistently established with the population you are examining. Be sure that it is both possible and ethical to conduct an experiment to help establish causation among the variables.

APPLICATION 2.6

Conduct an Experiment Based on a Quasi- or Non-Experimental Study

Nordstrom et al. (2009) found that participants who reported more supportive attitudes toward incivility in the classroom were more likely to report engaging in such uncivil behaviors. They used a non-experimental approach, a correlational design, to examine the relationship between attitudes toward incivility and uncivil behaviors.

We cannot randomly assign some participants to have attitudes supporting classroom incivility. However, we can conduct an experiment that examines ways to change attitudes about incivility and participation in uncivil behaviors. Such a study would not be able to establish a direct causal link between attitudes and behaviors.

For example, we might see what impact education about the problem of incivility (the IV) has on attitudes and behaviors (the DVs). Before moving forward with this study, we would need to find and read past research about how education or knowledge impacts attitudes and behaviors in general and incivility more specifically.

3. Conduct a similar study with a different outcome or dependent variable. Do this if you find research evidence supporting the new relationship you plan to examine.

APPLICATION 2.7

Conduct a Similar Study With a Different Outcome or Dependent Variable

End et al. (2010) examined the impact of cell phone rings on test performance whereas Nordstrom et al. (2009) examined the relationship among personality characteristics, attitudes, and a range of uncivil classroom behaviors including using cell phones during class.

There are ways we might build off of both of these studies, for example:

1. We could conduct a study like Nordstrom et al. in which we ask students about their attitudes and behaviors but focus more specifically on cell phone use. Building off of End et al.'s study, we could include several questions about a cell phone ringing in class during a lecture, or during group work, or during an exam. We could also ask if the student thinks others should turn off or silence phones during class, and how often the participants themselves do those behaviors.

   We could also add another variable about personal observations of cell phone use in class. We would then gauge the range and frequency of participants' experiences and how that relates to their own behaviors and attitudes.

2. We could conduct a study much like End et al. in which a confederate's cell phone rings in class (or doesn't ring). We could then examine how that experience impacts participants' attitudes toward uncivil behaviors in the classroom, including cell phone use.

   If we decided to go this route, we would want to build a rationale that experiencing others' cell phone use in class impacts attitudes toward that use. That would necessitate finding additional research, or perhaps conducting the study described above first to help determine if there is a link between experience with classroom cell phone use and attitudes toward that use.

4. Examine how another variable might impact results. Do this if you have research evidence to suggest that results may depend on another variable.

APPLICATION 2.8

Examine How Another Variable Impacts Results

End et al. (2010) found that students who experienced a cell phone ringing during a video lecture fared worse on a test than those who did not experience the ringing. But did all students in the ringing condition fare equally poorly, or did their level of impairment vary based on other factors?

In particular, we might expect that a cell phone ring especially affects those with attention problems. We could pull in past research about attention problems including the vast literature on attention deficit hyperactivity disorder (ADHD) to build a case for a study examining individual differences in distractibility.

Another option is to examine how personality affects how someone reacts to a ringing cell phone. Nordstrom et al. (2009) found that those with higher levels of narcissism reported that they were more accepting of uncivil classroom behaviors. We could test whether a ringing cell phone in fact less negatively impacts narcissistic individuals.

ETHICS TIP GIVE CREDIT TO YOUR SOURCES AND AVOID PLAGIARISM

Accuracy

- Just because information appears in an article, it does not mean that that article is the original (primary) source for that information—be sure you accurately cite the original source.
- Take time to understand the findings of a research study or other source so that you can accurately summarize them.

Avoid Plagiarism

- Be sure you know what plagiarism is (see Chapter 1 for a refresher).
- As you take notes, summarize and paraphrase the article in your own words. This takes more time, but it helps ensure that you understand the information before you write it down in your notes.
- If you must directly quote an article as a short cut for taking notes, be sure the direct quotes are in quotation marks—that way you will not look back at your notes and assume the words are your own.

64 • RESEARCH METHODS, STATISTICS, AND APPLICATIONS

● APA FORMAT FOR REFERENCES

Because giving proper credit is so critical to avoiding plagiarism, we will briefly describe how to format references at the end of your paper. A more detailed APA format guide appears in Appendix B, and for the most accurate and detailed information you should of course go to the original source—the sixth edition of the *Publication Manual of the American Psychological Association* (2010b).

If you are like many students who struggle with getting the details of APA formatting just right, you might wonder why APA format matters at all. The main rationale for adhering to APA format, or any formatting style, is that the consistency helps readers quickly identify the information they need. As you get more comfortable reading primary research articles, you will come to appreciate that you can find information such as the hypotheses, method, and results in the same place within most articles. Likewise, when you want to read more about a study cited in an article, the consistency in the reference list will help you quickly identify the information you need to find the article using your library's databases.

- What to include in a reference for a journal article:
  - Author(s) names (last name followed by initials)
  - Date of publication, in parentheses
  - Article title
  - Journal title and volume
  - Do not include issue number unless the journal begins numbering each issue with page 1.
  - Page numbers of article
  - doi number, if available
- Formatting the reference:
  - Do not indent the first line of the reference, but indent all subsequent lines of that reference (this is called a "hanging indent").
  - For articles with multiple authors: Keep the order of authors the same as it appears in the article, separate the authors by commas, and use both a comma and an ampersand (&) before the last author.
  - For the article title, capitalize only the first letter of the first word, the first word after a colon or other punctuation, or proper names.
  - For the journal title, capitalize the first letter of all the main words (e.g., not "of" or "and").
  - Italicize the journal title and the volume number.
  - Put a period after the parenthesized date, after the article title, and after the page numbers, but not after the doi number.
  - Use a comma to separate the title, volume, and page numbers. To indicate page range, use an en dash (–) instead of a hyphen (-).
  - Put a space after any punctuation (except following the colon after "doi").

Look at Figure 2.4 for an example reference, with key points noted, for the Nordstrom et al. (2009) article. Then practice writing a reference using APA format by completing Practice 2.3. Finally, put it all together to complete Practice 2.4 to apply what you have learned about reading and referencing a research article on your own topic.

Figure 2.4	Example APA-Formatted Reference With Notation

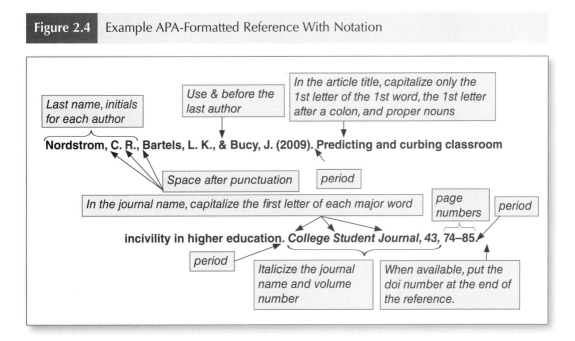

Last name, initials for each author

Use & before the last author

In the article title, capitalize only the 1st letter of the 1st word, the 1st letter after a colon, and proper nouns

Nordstrom, C. R., Bartels, L. K., & Bucy, J. (2009). Predicting and curbing classroom

Space after punctuation

period

In the journal name, capitalize the first letter of each major word

page numbers

period

incivility in higher education. *College Student Journal, 43,* 74–85.

period

Italicize the journal name and volume number

When available, put the doi number at the end of the reference.

PRACTICE 2.3

WRITE A REFERENCE USING APA FORMAT

Put the following information into an APA-style reference:

- Article title: Costly Cell Phones: The Impact of Cell Phone Rings on Academic Performance
- Journal title: Teaching of Psychology
- Authors: Christian M. End, Shaye Worthman, Mary Bridget Mathews, and Katharina Wetterau
- Date: 2010
- Volume: 37
- Page numbers: 55 to 57
- doi number: 10.1080/00986280903425912

See Appendix A to check your answer.

PRACTICE 2.4

READ, EVALUATE, AND REFERENCE A PRIMARY RESEARCH ARTICLE ON YOUR TOPIC

1. Choose a primary research article on your topic (or revised topic) that you think is most like a study you might like to do. Find the full text of the article.

2. Answer the following based on the article, using your *own words* (do not copy answers directly from the article).

   a. What is the rationale for the study? (hint: look in the Introduction)

   b. What is/are the hypothesis(es) or research questions examined? (hint: the hypotheses or research questions are usually toward the end of the Introduction)

   c. Describe the method used to test the hypothesis(es) or answer the research question(s). (hint: look in the Method)

   d. What were the results of the study? (hint: look in the Results).

   e. What future research do the author(s) suggest? (hint: look in the Discussion)

3. What are some of the ways you might build on this study? (Consider your answer to 2e, and see pp. 60–63 for more ideas.)

4. Write the reference for the article in APA format.

CHAPTER RESOURCES

KEY TERMS

Define the following terms using your own words. You can check your answers by reviewing the chapter or by comparing them with the definitions in the glossary—but try to define them on your own first.

Commentaries	Popular works
External validity	Primary research article (or empirical journal article)
Internal validity	
Literature review	Primary research source
Meta-analysis	Scholarly work
Peer review	Secondary research source
Power	Statistical significance testing

DO YOU UNDERSTAND THE CHAPTER?

Answer these questions on your own and then review the chapter to check your answers.

1. What is the difference between a primary and secondary source?

2. What is the difference between scholarly and popular works?

3. Why is the peer review process important?

4. Describe the different types of articles that can be found in academic journals.

5. How can you tell if a journal article is a primary source?

6. Describe scholarly sources that are not found in academic journals.

7. How would you find conference papers or posters, dissertations, or unpublished manuscripts? What are the pros and cons of these types of sources?

8. What databases are most applicable to your discipline and topic?

9. Explain how you would conduct a key-word search on your topic.

10. How else might you find relevant research on your topic?

11. List and briefly describe the purpose of each section in a primary research article.

CHAPTER 20

THE CORNERSTONES OF GOOD RESEARCH

Reliability and Validity

Consider the following scenario:

Twins, Chris and Pat, both want to lose weight and agree to begin a weight loss program, URN CHRG. They intend to stay on the diet for 6 weeks and agree that whoever loses the most weight will win from the other twin a month's membership at a local athletic club. The twins each purchase inexpensive scales to monitor their weight at their individual apartments. They agree to weigh every 5 days and to record the weight. Pat finds that his weight seems to go up and down, sometimes showing weight loss and sometimes showing weight gain, even though he reports that he is diligently following URN CHRG's weight loss program. In contrast, Chris's recorded weight continuously decreases. At the end of the 6 weeks, they meet at the doctor's office for an official weigh-in. Although they both expect that Chris will weigh less, the doctor's scale shows that in fact Pat weighs less than Chris. The figure on the next page reflects the results of the weigh-ins by the twins.

How could this happen when according to the home scales Pat weighed more?

If you think the answer may be related to the "cheap" scales they bought, then you would be correct. Yet, psychologists want to know more than just that the weight on the cheap scales is different from the doctor's scale. And like good psychology students who understand the research process, Chris and Pat want to investigate exactly what the problem is with their scales. They each bring their scale to the doctor's office and Pat finds that each time he steps

68

on his scale to compare the number to the doctor's scale, the weight varies as much as 10 pounds. Chris finds that he consistently weighs 5 pounds less on his scale than on the doctor's scale. The issues of consistency and accuracy are what we refer to as *reliability* and *validity*.

IN THIS CHAPTER, YOU WILL LEARN

- The definition of reliability and validity
- How to evaluate the reliability and validity of a study
- How to operationally define constructs with qualitative and quantitative measures
- How to identify different scales of measurement
- Different types of measures, including questionnaires and unobtrusive measures
- How to assess the reliability and validity of measures

RELIABILITY AND VALIDITY BROADLY DEFINED ●

Reliability means consistency and **validity** means accuracy. Both reliability and validity are critical factors in research. You can see from the everyday example at the beginning of the chapter why we need reliable and valid measures in order to accurately describe variables and show results. If we do not have reliable and valid measures, the results of our research will not be meaningful or useful in describing behavior or the factors that influence behavior. As the title of this chapter states, validity and reliability are the foundation of good research.

Pat's Scale:	Chris's Scale:
Week 1 — 154	156
Week 2 — 142	155
Week 3 — 164	154
Week 4 — 150	153
Week 5 — 158	152
Week 6 — 152	151

Doctor's Scale
Pat: 149.0   Chris: 155.0

Reliability: Consistency of findings or measures.

Validity: Accuracy of findings or measures.

We typically consider reliability and validity from two perspectives: (a) in regard to the results of the whole study (study level), and (b) in regard to how we measure specific variables (measure level). We will consider each of these perspectives in detail.

● RELIABILITY AND VALIDITY AT THE STUDY LEVEL

Study Reliability

The **reliability of a study** refers to the expectation that we will find similar results when we repeat a study. In research we are seeking to identify general patterns of behavior. If similar studies find different results, this suggests that we have not found a pattern in which we can have confidence. **Replication**, or repeating a study, is one way to test the reliability of a finding from a study and can be literal or conceptual. A literal replication occurs when we repeat a study in an identical manner, using the same variables and procedure and a similar sample. Most of the time we do not re-do a study in exactly the same form, and instead conduct a conceptual replication by examining the same patterns or relationships in a slightly different way or by including additional variables.

> *Reliability of a study:* How consistent the results are across similar studies.
>
> *Replication:* Conducting the same study with new participants (literal replication) or conducting a study examining the same patterns or relationships but with different methods (conceptual replication).

For example, in studying how to reduce plagiarism, researchers have found that hands-on experience is more effective than providing explanations or resources about academic dishonesty (Belter & du Pré, 2009; Culwin, 2006; Estow et al., 2011; Schuetze, 2004). Of the research we just cited, Schuetze (2004) completed the earliest study with a single homework assignment; Belter and du Pré (2009) required students to show 100% mastery on a quiz about plagiarism, proper citation, and penalties for violations. Students in Culwin's (2006) study completed an essay assignment that was assessed for non-originality; students then received feedback about the violations and discussed academic integrity. Estow et al. (2011) examined the effect of using plagiarism as a research topic for an entire course and included among the many student assignments a survey of attitudes toward and knowledge about plagiarism and an experiment that examined the effect of student plagiarism and intent on ratings of severity of punishment and mood of professor.

Although each of the studies examined a different type of "hands-on experience," they all found similar results that plagiarism was better understood and avoided following the hands-on experience and thus the conceptual replications were successful in demonstrating reliability of the findings of Schuetze's (2004) study. In other words, the hands-on experience had a reliable effect on reducing plagiarism. This is the reliability that we seek from studies, that the results can be replicated or repeated in future studies.

If the studies examining hands-on experience had not found the same results, we would question the reliability of the Schuetze study and would then be skeptical of her results. However, just because we find consistent or reliable results across several studies does not guarantee that those results are accurate.

Note that:

- Results of a study *cannot* be valid unless they are reliable.
- Results of a study *can* be reliable but not valid.

In other words, reliability is a prerequisite for validity but reliability alone is not sufficient to demonstrate validity. The validity of a study refers to how accurate the results are and is examined in two ways: **internal validity** and **external validity**.

> *Internal validity:* The degree to which we can say that we found an accurate relationship among variables, in that changes in one variable are caused by changes in another variable.
>
> *External validity:* The degree to which we can say that the results of a study are accurate for different types of people in different settings assessed with different procedures.

Internal Validity

Internal validity applies when the researchers are interested in examining a causal relationship. If a researcher wants to determine that *A* causes *B*, then he or she must manipulate *A*, measure *B*, and control for all the other extraneous variables that could have an effect on *B*.

REVIEW OF KEY CONCEPTS: INDEPENDENT AND DEPENDENT VARIABLES

1) *If* A *is the variable that is manipulated, and* B *is the variable that is measured, which is the independent variable (IV) and which is the dependent variable (DV)?*

2) *What type of research design uses IVs and DVs to demonstrate a causal relationship?*

3) *What is the other key ingredient of this type of design?*

You are correct if you said A *is the IV and* B *is the DV, and that an experiment is the specific type of research design that examines a causal relationship through manipulation of the IV and measurement of the DV. Random assignment to groups is the other key factor in experiments.*

In reality, it is very difficult to control for every possible extraneous variable in a study. Therefore, internal validity is the extent to which we can say that the result from a study is, in fact, caused or determined by the manipulation of the independent variable rather than some other factor. We want to be confident that our findings are directly related to the independent variable, and this is why researchers examining causality use an experimental design to reduce the chances that something other than the independent variable caused changes in the dependent variable. Internal validity is also why we use control groups to show that when only one factor (the independent variable) is changed, the outcome (the dependent variable) is affected or changed.

72 • RESEARCH METHODS, STATISTICS, AND APPLICATIONS

Let's apply this information about internal validity to Schuetze's (2004) study. Students in both the experimental and control sections of developmental psychology heard a presentation and received a handout describing plagiarism and how to avoid this academic violation. Students in the experimental group also completed a homework assignment early in the semester that required them to identify statements requiring citations within a brief manuscript. These students received feedback on the assignment and discussed correct citations in class. A comparison of the experimental and control groups on a homework assignment later in the semester that required students to identify where citations belonged showed that the experimental group who had completed a previous assignment performed significantly better than the control group who received similar information but did not complete the earlier assignment. Note that the students were in the same type of class and received similar information about plagiarism. The only difference was the homework assignment, which allowed the experimental group to practice the information they gained from the plagiarism presentation and handout.

We might question the internal validity of the study (that the hands-on experience influenced the skill in correctly citing sources) if the study had included obvious differences between the experimental and control groups other than the citation practice. For example, what if the researcher had obtained participants from two different types of classes, one with more advanced psychology majors and one with first-year students or had used two different assignments to judge the ability to correctly use citations (and thus avoid plagiarism)? In each of these cases a factor besides the additional homework assignment could be responsible for the results. In the former case, the more advanced students will have taken more psychology classes than the first-year students and been exposed to more information about citing sources in psychology papers. In the latter case where two different assignments were used, one of them might be more difficult than the other, which could account for the differences in citation skill. A factor that is not controlled by the researcher and that systematically influences the results is called a **confound**. Confounds or threats to the internal validity of a study come in many forms and will be discussed in detail in Chapter 8.

> *Confound (or confounding variable):* A variable that is not the focus of the research study, but affects the variables of interest in the study.

External Validity

External validity refers to the ability to generalize the results of a study to other settings, other samples, and other methods. Findings about social situations, attitudes, behaviors, and the factors that impact them are of little use if they apply only to the specific participants in the study. Even if the results are replicated with other participants and produce reliable results, we might question the external validity of the results if all the participants represent a specific group. Additionally, we would wonder about the external validity if studies were conducted primarily within one setting or used one procedure such as when research is primarily completed with small samples of college students in a laboratory-like setting.

External validity of any particular study is a matter of degree. The more diverse the sample and the more realistic the setting and procedures, the greater the likelihood that the results will generalize beyond the particular people and setting of your study. Limiting your sample to college students or to a laboratory setting does not mean that the study has no external validity. It simply means that we do not know if the results would generalize or not, and that future research is needed to replicate the study with other samples and in other settings. Remember there is no perfect study, and it is not feasible to examine all types of participants in all different settings using all different types of procedures.

For example, we wonder if the homework assignment used by Schuetze (2004) in a developmental psychology course is applicable to other classes within other disciplines (economics or history, for example) or to different age groups (high school students, for example). Citation skill was measured in the Schuetze study and found to increase with practice. Hopefully other skills related to avoiding plagiarism (paraphrasing, for example) could be increased with hands-on practice. You can see why a researcher might spend her lifetime researching a single topic as there is much work that can be done to test the external validity of one study.

Practice 3.1 gives you the opportunity to test whether you understand the concepts of validity and reliability at the study level. If you are not able to correctly identify these examples, you may want to review the previous pages.

PRACTICE 3.1

DISTINGUISHING BETWEEN EXTERNAL VALIDITY, INTERNAL VALIDITY, AND RELIABILITY AT THE STUDY LEVEL

Read the following examples and determine whether they are related to external validity, internal validity, or reliability at the study level.

Cobb, Heaney, Corcoran, and Henderson-Begg (2010) found that student satisfaction in a British University with using texting in class was very high, especially among more timid students. A faculty member at your institution decides to implement a texting system in his classroom to see if he obtains the same results with students at a U.S. university.

End, Wortham, Mathews, and Wetterau (2010) found that cell phone ringing during a presentation decreased scores on a multiple-choice test on the lecture material and disrupted students' note taking of material during the ringing for the experimental group in comparison to a control group's test scores and lecture notes. Suppose you find that not only did the cell phone ring in the class for the experimental group but that the cell phone owner answered the call and walked out of the class talking loudly as she exited the room. What aspect of the experiment does this new information call into question?

(Continued)

(Continued)

Estow et al. (2011) examined the topic of plagiarism as a research theme throughout one semester in two different sections of Research Methods. Students completed different assignments that used plagiarism as the focus. The results were the same for both experimental sections in terms of increased understanding of plagiarism and improved paraphrasing skills relative to a control group of students studying research methods but using a different theme.

See Appendix A to check your answers.

Balancing Internal and External Validity

Tension always exists between internal and external validity because the greater the internal validity, the harder it is to achieve external validity. Internal validity is established by tightly controlling the experimental situation which then may decrease the probability that the results will generalize beyond the specific situation defined by the study. However, if the experimental setting and procedure are too uncontrolled in order to better represent circumstances in "real life" where a multitude of factors can vary, the internal validity of the study may be so compromised that one is unable to obtain significant results or is unable to identify which factor or factors have created differences in the dependent variable.

Thus, researchers must find a balance between the internal and external validity so that they are confident that the IV is responsible for the changes in the DV and that the findings are relevant to other situations and populations. Due to their particular interest, researchers may choose to focus more on one type of validity than the other. For example, if the researcher is examining the effect of a new variable or a new procedure, he may focus on internal validity or increased control within the study in order to increase his chances of finding significant results. Another researcher may be more interested in finding out how well a finding established in one setting generalizes to other settings. For example, there have been studies in the classroom demonstrating cell phones are distracting and decrease learning (End et al., 2010; Froese et al., 2012; Wood et al., 2012) so a researcher might test if personal cell phone use will decrease productivity in an office setting. This second researcher may focus on external validity by completing the study in a setting that does not allow for the rigid controls that are possible in the laboratory. You should be starting to see how many legitimate possibilities exist for research within a particular area and how each study can add to our knowledge about the effect of an IV on a DV in slightly different and valuable ways.

In Application 3.1, two studies are reviewed in terms of how they balance internal and external validity. You then will have an opportunity to practice your new skills in Practice 3.2.

APPLICATION 3.1

Balancing Internal and External Validity in Cell Phone Research

Let's return to the two studies we had you find in Chapter 2:

Internal Validity	
End et al.'s study is an experiment and therefore internal validity is a primary focus. Efforts to maximize internal validity are described in the Method, including: 1. The IV condition was the only factor that varied across the groups. 2. Participants were randomly assigned to the IV condition to help ensure that the groups are similar prior to exposure to the IV manipulation (ring or no ring). 3. A videotaped lecture was used to ensure that the lecture content was exactly the same for all participants.	Nordstrom et al.'s study is not an experiment and therefore establishing a causal relationship and having strong internal validity is not a focus. Even so, maintaining some level of control is important in all studies, not just those that examine causal relationships. Notice that Nordstrom and her colleagues were careful to keep the measures and procedures the same across participants.
External Validity	
Efforts that End et al. took to increase internal validity may reduce the external validity of the study. In particular, as the authors themselves note in the Discussion section, results based on a videotaped lecture may or may not generalize to a live lecture. The sample size was relatively small (71 participants) and consisted of students who were participating for credit, likely for an introductory-level psychology course. We might wonder how these results would generalize to other samples of students—particularly those who in a real class situation would be earning a grade rather than research credit. The authors try to address this issue by providing an incentive for students to take good notes and do well on the test, but we cannot be sure that this incentive is similar to the incentive of getting a good grade in a class. Finally, given that the majority of the sample was of traditional college age and White, we might wonder how these results would generalize to adult, non-White college students.	Nordstrom et al. had a large sample, but like the End et al. study, the students were participating for credit for an introductory psychology course, and the majority of the students were traditional-aged college students and White. Therefore, we might question how well the results would generalize to different samples.

76 • RESEARCH METHODS, STATISTICS, AND APPLICATIONS

PRACTICE 3.2

ASSESSING THE BALANCE OF INTERNAL AND EXTERNAL VALIDITY IN A STUDY FROM YOUR TOPIC

Consider an article you have recently read.

- Can you describe how the authors of that article addressed internal and external validity?
- What trade-offs did they make in order to achieve an acceptable balance between internal and external validity?

● RELIABILITY AND VALIDITY OF MEASUREMENT

The second way in which reliability and validity are of concern to researchers involves individual measures or variables. Recall that in the scenario at the beginning of this chapter Chris and Pat each had problems with their scales and therefore could not accurately assess their weight. One of these scales suffered from poor measurement reliability and the other had poor measurement validity.

> *Measurement reliability:* Consistency of a measure.
>
> *Measurement validity:* Measurement is accurate in that it measures what it purports to measure.

Measurement reliability concerns the consistency of measurement—in this case, a scale should register the same weight for the same person, especially when one steps on the scale again within a few minutes' time. Pat's scale registered his weight as heavier and lighter within a few minutes, causing us to question the consistency or reliability of his scale in assessing weight.

Measurement validity concerns the ability of an instrument or factor to accurately measure (or assess) what it is supposed to measure. Even though Chris's scale seemed to show a consistent weight loss, the weight shown was not valid as it was 5 pounds lighter than Chris's real weight as reflected on the doctor's scale. This example demonstrates how a measure can be reliable or consistent (Chris's weight was shown as 5 pounds lighter each time) without being valid.

Remember:

- A measure *cannot* be valid unless it is reliable.
- A measure *can* be reliable but not valid.

Sometimes we question validity because we are not sure that the measure in fact represents the variable we are studying. For example, suppose Chris decided to measure his weight loss by how loose his jeans felt. Instead of weighing on a scale, he decided to try on the same pair of jeans every 5 days and found that over 6 weeks' time, the jeans became looser. His jeans may feel less tight with each successive wear, but he may not be measuring weight loss. Instead, he may be measuring the stretch of the jean fabric. Thus, his "measure" of weight (fit of jeans) is not a valid one. In order to be valid, a measure must both be reliable and accurately reflect the variable in question.

CONSTRUCTS AND OPERATIONAL DEFINITIONS ●

In order to assess the reliability and validity of any measurement instrument, we must clearly define the measures we are using. Although in the social and behavioral sciences we sometimes measure variables that are concrete and well defined, such as weight, time, or cost, we are often examining **constructs** that are more abstract, such as personal opinions, achievement, community support, attention, or self-efficacy. Constructs are variables that cannot be directly observed nor do we have physical tests that directly assess them. As researchers we have to develop ways to define and measure these abstract constructs. For example, plagiarism as a construct can be broadly defined as claiming ownership for another's ideas, written material, or work. But this definition is not specific enough because there are multiple ways in which one could measure plagiarism according to this definition.

We use **operational definitions** to explicitly define abstract constructs for a specific study. For example, Schuetze (2004) used citation errors to assess plagiarism. Other researchers have focused on paraphrasing in addition to proper citation (Belter & du Pré, 2009; Estow et al., 2011). Most people would agree both improper citation and paraphrasing constitute plagiarism but can also think of other ways one might measure plagiarism (verbally taking credit for another's idea, or cutting and pasting or copying material from another source). In research we must always provide clear definitions of the variables in our studies, and we must be able to defend or explain the rationale for the operational definitions we use. Sometimes the major criticism of a study is the operational definition of variables.

> *Construct:* A concept that cannot be directly observed or measured.
>
> *Operational definition:* The explicit explanation of a variable in terms of how it is measured or manipulated.

Deciding How to Measure Your Constructs

As a researcher you have many options in terms of operationally defining, or measuring, constructs. One of your first global decisions regarding constructs involves deciding whether to use **qualitative** or **quantitative measures**.

Qualitative Measures

Qualitative measures are non-numerical while quantitative measures are numerical. For instance, suppose you are interested in the construct of frustration and decide to observe people's response to having someone get in front of them while they are waiting in line to vote. You could operationally define frustration as a frown, an opening of the mouth and raising of eyebrows, a downturn of the mouth, or a verbal comment to the person who broke in line. In order to get a qualitative measure of frustration you could have two observers write down the different responses they saw the participant make immediately following the breaking-in-line incident. Many times the written descriptions by the two observers would then be coded or examined for trends in order to see whether the observers recorded similar responses to breaking in line and whether there are similarities across the participants' responses. In order to evaluate the descriptions, we would read the observers' descriptions of their observations of all the participants. We would look for similar terms or similar behaviors that were described. We might even find that there is a consistent pattern of responses that begins with a raising of the eyebrows and circle of mouth, then a wrinkled brow followed by staring at the "line breaker," and a downturn of the mouth. We could use numbers (1 = *raising of eyebrows*) or letter codes (F = *frown*) for each of these behaviors and determine how many and in what order they appeared in the observers' descriptions.

> *Qualitative measure:* Non-numerical assessment.
>
> *Quantitative measure:* Numerical measure.

Quantitative Measures

Alternatively, you could quantitatively measure frustration by having the two observers rate from 1 to 5 (1 = *no response;* 5 = *very frustrated*) how frustrated the participant was following the breaking-in-line incident. You can see that both measures require some interpretation of the participant's behavior by the observers but the qualitative measurement will result in a lot of text to be interpreted and judgments will be required as responses by different participants are compared. The quantitative measurement will produce a numerical value for each participant that can be averaged without needing interpretation.

We sometimes mistakenly believe that numerical data is "better" or more valid than narrative information because numbers have an agreed-upon meaning (e.g., a quantity of 1 has a specific value such that 2 is larger than 1 and smaller than 3 by the same amount). We forget that interpretation can be required in the measurement of numerical data, such as occurred in our example above when the observers rated frustration on a 5-point scale. Even when we rate our own behavior on a numerical scale, we are required to interpret what a value, say 3, means according to our behavior, attitude, or emotion.

Some quantitative measures do not require as much interpretation as our example of rating frustration. A good example is when we operationally define dependence on one's cell phone as the number of minutes spent on the cell phone during the last month (as indicated on the cell phone bill). Regardless of the variables we are studying in research, we most often rely on quantitative measures because of the ease of understanding and analyzing numerical data. We should always remember, however, that some interpretation is often involved in obtaining the numbers we analyze.

Scales of Measurement

Data are also measured according to four scales of measurement that vary by four attributes, which determine the preciseness of the scale of measurement. **Identity** means that each number is unique. **Order** reflects that numbers have a sequence and can be identified as occurring before or after other numbers in the sequence. Numbers that have **equal intervals** have the same quantity or interval between each number. Finally, a **true zero** exists when a variable has a real rather than an arbitrary zero point. The four scales of measurement are described below from least to most precise.

Identity: Each number has a unique meaning.

Order: Numbers on a scale are ordered in sequence.

Equal intervals: The distance between numbers on a scale is equal.

True zero (or absolute zero): The score of zero on a scale is a fixed point.

Figure 3.1	Quantitative Measures

Researchers often require that participants quantify their feelings, attitudes, or behaviors by assigning a number to a variable rather than providing a verbal description of it. Can you name a few advantages and disadvantages of this tendency to use quantitative rather than qualitative data?

Source: Sandi Coon

Social and behavioral science research employs the four scales of measurement with varying frequencies. The type of statistical analyses employed depends on the type of measurement scales to be analyzed. Thus, it is important that you are able to identify and understand the differences between the scales of measurement.

Nominal Scales

Nominal scales represent categories. Although numbers are used to represent categories within a nominal scale, the numbers have no numerical value. If you were to assign a numerical value to a category, a higher score would not necessarily mean that there was more of some quality. Therefore, nominal scales only have identity, but do not have order or any of the other scale properties.

Demographic data, such as gender, ethnicity, and marital status, each represent a nominal scale. For example, you may code different types of marital status using numbers, such as 1 = *single,* 2 = *married,* 3 = *divorced,* but the numbers have no value or order. In this case, 1 representing "single" is not greater or less than 2 representing "married." You can count the frequency within each category but you do not perform mathematical operations on the numbers—you may have a larger number (or frequency) of single than

| Table 3.1 | Scales of Measurement |

Measurement Scale	Used to Measure ...	Properties				Example
		Identity?	Order?	Equal Intervals?	True Zero?	
Nominal	Categories	✓				Types of cars
Ordinal	Rankings	✓	✓			Rankings of football teams
Interval	Ratings	✓	✓	✓		7-point Likert-type scale (*strongly disagree* to *strongly agree*) assessing agreement with the law banning texting while driving
Ratio	Quantity	✓	✓	✓	✓	Amount of time studying for your last Research Methods test

married or divorced participants in a study, but there is no average marital status, for example. Another example of a measurement using a nominal scale is political affiliation where 1 = *Democrat,* 2 = *Republican,* 3 = *Green Party,* 4 = *Independent.* A question that is answered with Yes/No or True/False is also an example of a nominal scale.

Example 3.1	Nominal Scale of Measurement

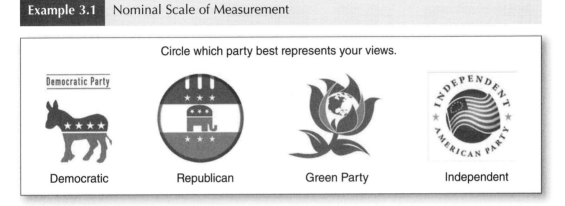

Source: Democratic and Republican Party logos: © Can Stock Photo Inc./gknec; Green Party logo: Scott McLarty, mclarty@greens.org; Independent Party logo: independenceforever@live.com

Ordinal Scales

Ordinal scales represent rankings. This scale of measurement includes numbers that have order so that each number is greater or less than other numbers. However, the interval between the numbers in an ordinal scale is not equal.

Track and field races are scored on an ordinal scale. Think of the results of a 50-yard dash with 12 runners. The runners will cross the finish line in such a manner that we can identify who came in first, who came in second, who came in third, all the way until the 12th or last-place finisher. In this case, each runner's finish (first, second, third, etc.) is represented by a number (1, 2, 3, etc.) that tells us the order of the runners. What we do not know is the time or interval between each of the runner's placement. For example, the runner who came in first may have been far ahead of the second and third runners, who came in very close to one another. Like nominal data, ordinal data cannot be manipulated mathematically because there are no fixed intervals between scores.

Nominal scale: A scale of measurement where numbers represent categories and have no numerical value.

Ordinal scale: A scale of measurement with numbers that have order so that each number is greater or less than other numbers but the interval between the numbers is not equal; also called rankings.

Example 3.2	Ordinal Scale of Measurement

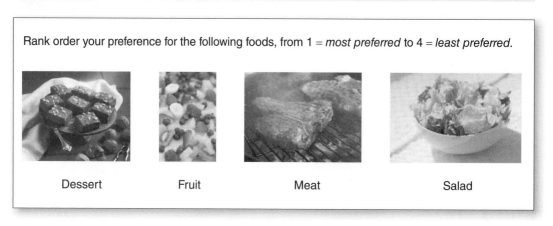

Rank order your preference for the following foods, from 1 = *most preferred* to 4 = *least preferred*.

Dessert   Fruit   Meat   Salad

Source: Dessert: © Getty Images/Jupiterimage; Fruit: Pink Sherbet Photography; Salad: © Getty Images/Medioimages/Photodisc

Interval Scales

Interval scales are ratings that have both order and equal intervals between values on the scale. The limiting factor for interval scales is that they do not have a true zero. We make assumptions that the interval scale begins at one (or zero sometimes) and represents one extreme of the construct we are measuring, but there is no true point that represents that there is absolutely zero of the quality measured, or an absence of the concept.

Temperature is a good example to illustrate the lack of a true zero. On the Fahrenheit scale, 32 degrees is freezing while on the Celsius scale, 0 represents freezing. We have 0 degrees (it's cold!) on both scales, but it is an arbitrary value that has a different meaning on each of the two scales. In addition, even though both scales have a zero point, there is still temperature at 0, so the scales lack a "true" zero where there is an absence of the variable.

Most of you have probably taken a questionnaire where you were asked to rate how satisfied you were with some service or product that you had recently used or bought. The possibilities may have ranged from 1 = *Very dissatisfied* to 5 = *Very satisfied,* and you could have chosen any value between 1 and 5 to represent your satisfaction from very low to very high. This type of scale is used frequently in the social and behavioral sciences. It is called a **Likert-type scale** named after the psychologist, Rensis Likert, who invented the scale. The interval between each of the values (one) is considered to be the same so that the distance between 2 and 3 is considered the same as the distance between 4 and 5. This quality allows us to perform mathematical operations and statistical analysis on the values from an interval scale. Interval scales can have as few as 3 values and as many as more than 100.

This content has been removed for permissions reasons.

Ratio Scales

Ratio scales measure quantity. This scale of measurement has the qualities of an interval scale (order and equal intervals) plus it has a true zero. Traditional quantitative measures such as distance, time, and weight are ratio scales. We do not need to develop a measurement scale to assess these variables as there are already well-established mechanisms for them (e.g., clocks, scales). Our example at the beginning of the chapter of the use of a scale to measure weight demonstrates a ratio scale (as well as the importance of reliability and validity of our measures!). We use ratio scales to measure reaction time, such as how quickly a person responds to the ringing of her cell phone. We may also operationally define a variable using a ratio scale. For example, we may define cell phone dependence by how long it is between phone calls (made or received) during a one-hour period. Although ratio is the most precise scale of the four scales of measurement, we use interval scales more frequently to measure social science concepts.

| Example 3.4 | An Everyday Example of Ratio Scale of Measurement |

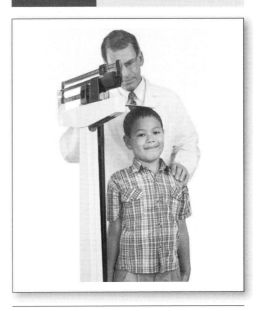

Source: © Can Stock Photo Inc./forestpath

Interval scale: A scale of measurement that has both order and equal intervals between values on the scale.

Likert-type scale: A commonly used type of interval scale response in which items are rated on a range of numbers (usually between 5 and 7 response options) that are assumed to have equal intervals.

Ratio scale: A scale of measurement where values measure quantity, and have order, equal intervals, and a true zero.

PRACTICE 3.3

IDENTIFYING SCALES OF MEASUREMENT

Assume that you want to examine plagiarism among college students.

Can you identify the four scales of measurement among the items below?

1. I believe plagiarism is a serious problem among college students.

1	2	3	4	5
Strongly Disagree		*Neither Disagree Nor Agree*		*Strongly Agree*

2. Have you ever plagiarized? Yes_____   No _____

3. Rank the seriousness of the following problems among college students

   (1 = *most serious*, 8 = *least serious*).

   _____Alcohol consumption   _____Use of illegal drugs

   _____Stress from school   _____Financial problems

   _____Plagiarism   _____Stress from family

   _____Depression   _____Learning problems

4. How many times have you observed cheating during a test while at college? _____

5. Please provide the following information:

   Gender:_____   Age:_____   Ethnicity:_____

6. Academic Year in School (circle one):

   First year   Sophomore   Junior   Senior

More Practice: Can you think of examples of each scale of measurement using "driver aggression" as your variable?

● TYPES OF MEASURES

Regardless of the scale of measurement used, researchers have many choices in terms of how they will collect data in their study.

Questionnaires

A common method is to use what we call a **questionnaire**. This measure is exactly what you might assume: Participants respond to a question or questions regarding a particular topic, variable, trait, attitude, and so on. Each question, or item, on a questionnaire consists of a stem and a response. The stem can be a statement, question, or single word that describes or lists an attitude, belief, behavior, emotion, or characteristic. Those completing the measure are asked to provide a response to each stem.

A single item can be used to represent a construct, such as one question that assesses education level, for instance. Alternatively, multiple items can be grouped around a particular theme such as opinions about a topic (recycling) or self-assessment of a trait (optimism) and a **scale score** computed based on the items. Many constructs are multidimensional (think about recycling), and the scale measuring them may be composed of different subscales each of which has several items related to them. In terms of a scale assessing recycling, there may be items that focus on attitudes toward recycling, items that focus on behavior, and items that focus on knowledge. All items on the scale are related to recycling, but there are subscales assessing attitudes, behavior, and knowledge.

The **response format** for questionnaires can be broken into two general types of formats, **open-ended** and **closed-ended response formats**. An open-ended response format allows respondents to provide their own answers, and because it is non-numerical it is a type of qualitative measure. Closed-ended response formats are typically quantitative measures that provide options that the respondents select from and can vary from dichotomous options (two choices such as Yes/No or True/False), to multiple choice, to Likert-type rating scales. Dichotomous options are always in the **forced-choice response format** in that there is no neutral response. Rating scales may or may not be forced-choice depending on whether or not there is a middle, or neutral, response option. For example, a Likert-type scale with the four response options of *strongly disagree, disagree, agree,* and *strongly agree* is a forced-choice response format in that it requires the respondent to either disagree or agree to some degree, while a Likert-type scale with five response options of *strongly disagree, disagree, neutral, agree,* and *strongly agree* allows the respondent the option to maintain a neutral stance.

Each type of response has advantages and disadvantages. Open-ended responses must be categorized and thus the interpretation of such responses can be time-consuming and complicated. In addition, it can be difficult to compare the unique responses of each person. The benefit of open-ended responses, however, is that respondents can provide their own thoughts or ideas rather than having them limited to what the scale lists. Open-ended response formats are commonly used in interviews or pilot studies where we want to solicit people's spontaneous responses and look for similarities among them. Closed-ended responses provide specific and limited answers about an attitude, characteristic, or situation, so compiling frequencies or scores for each respondent can be done quickly. The listed responses, however, may not represent the respondents' thoughts or may lead them to an answer that they would not have provided on their own. Because of the ease of scoring and clarity of responses, most questionnaires use closed-ended response formats.

Questionnaire: A document, presented in hard-copy or on the computer, consisting of items that assess one or more constructs.

Scale score: The score that is computed from items assessing a particular construct, most commonly a sum or average of the numbers representing responses to individual items in the document.

Response format: The type of response, either participant generated or choice from among listed options, required by items on a questionnaire.

Open-ended response format: Item on a scale that requires the respondents to generate their own answers.

Closed-ended response format: Item that provides a limited number of choices from which respondents must select.

Forced-choice response format: Response format in which there is no neutral, or middle, option.

Many questionnaires have been developed to assess various constructs (e.g., intelligence, self-esteem, depression, locus of control, liking, loving, attachment style, cell phone problem use). Next, we describe four scales that have been used in social science research that demonstrate different response formats.

Examples of Different Response Formats for Questionnaires

The Classroom Critical Incident Questionnaire uses an open-ended response format and consists of five items (Brookfield, 1995). The scale was developed to capture the views of students about the essential events or occurrences in a class. The responses are collected at the end of a class as a way to assist the teacher in evaluating how a class is going. The teacher reads the responses and attempts to identify themes or commonalities within the responses, which are then shared with the class at the beginning of the next meeting.

Table 3.2a	Example of Questionnaire With Open-Ended Response Format

The Classroom Critical Incident Questionnaire—*Please take about 5 minutes to respond to the questions below about this weekend's class.*

At what moment in class this weekend did you feel most engaged with what was happening?

At what moment in class this weekend were you most distanced from what was happening?

Source: Brookfield, S. D. (1995). *Becoming a critically reflective teacher.* San Francisco, CA: Jossey-Bass.

A second scale, called the Rotter Internal-External (I-E) Locus of Control Scale, uses a dichotomous response format and assesses whether people hold an internal or an external perspective (Rotter, 1966). Those with an internal perspective are more likely to consider themselves responsible for events and consequences while those with an external perspective believe that their environment or others control events and consequences. Each item on the I-E scale consists of a pair of statements, one that represents an internal view and one that represents an external view. Respondents are required to select one statement from the pair that better reflects their view. This response format is referred to as a "forced choice." The full measure has 23 items, and a scale score is computed by adding up the number of external responses so that scores on the scale can range from 0–23, with higher scores reflecting more external views.

Table 3.2b	Example of Questionnaire With Forced-Choice Response Format

Rotter's Locus of Control—*Please circle the a or b statement in each pair that best represents your view of the world. There are no right or wrong answers; we are just interested in your view of the world.*

1. a. Children get into trouble because their parents punish them too much.
   b. The trouble with most children nowadays is that their parents are too easy with them.
2. a. Many of the unhappy things in people's lives are partly due to bad luck.
   b. People's misfortunes result from the mistakes they make.

Source: Rotter, J. (1966). Generalized expectancies for internal versus external control of reinforcement. *Psychological Monographs General and Applied, 80,* 1–28.

The SMS Problem Use Diagnostic Questionnaire (SMS-PUDQ) assesses the problematic or overuse of SMS, otherwise known as text messaging (Rutland, Sheets, & Young, 2007) and employs the commonly used Likert-type response format. The scale consists of eight statements that are rated by respondents on a 10-point scale according to how much a statement is like them (1 = *not true at all,* 10 = *extremely true*). The eight items are divided into two subscales, Pathological Use (5 items) and Problem Use (3 items). Subscales are determined by a statistical analysis, called factor analysis, which examines which items are responded to similarly or seem interdependent. Once items are identified as related, the researcher decides on a descriptive name for each subscale. In this case, five of the items seemed more troublesome and disruptive to everyday functioning and hence the name Pathological Use was used for that subscale, while the three items in the Problematic Use subscale suggest excessive texting but to a degree that is not so disruptive to other activities. The SMS-PUDQ is short and was found to have only two subscales, but longer questionnaires may have as many as five or six subscales. Other scales or questionnaires used in research may represent a construct as a whole such as Rotter's I-E Locus of Control Scale, which was described above. Occasionally, researchers use only one subscale of a measure because that subscale seems more relevant to their research question than the entire scale.

Table 3.2c	Example of Questionnaire With Likert-Type Response Format

SMS Problem Use Diagnostic Questionnaire (SMS-PUDQ)—*Mark the number below each item that best describes you and text messaging.*

1. I feel restless, moody, depressed, or irritable when attempting to control, cut back, or stop SMS use.

1	2	3	4	5	6	7	8	9	10

Not true at all   *Extremely true*

2. I use SMS longer than originally intended.

1	2	3	4	5	6	7	8	9	10

Not true at all   *Extremely true*

Source: Rutland, J. B., Sheets, T., & Young, T. (2007). Development of a scale to measure problem use of short message service: The SMS Problem Use Diagnostic Questionnaire. *CyberPsychology & Behavior, 10,* 841–843.

Scales sometimes contain items that are worded in opposite ways in order to increase the probability that the respondent is paying attention to the actual content of each item. For example, the Self-Control Scale developed by Tangney, Baumeister, and Boone (2004) consists of 36 statements that respondents rate on a 5-point Likert-type scale in terms of how much the statement is like them, where 1 = *not at all* and 5 = *very much.* Of the 36 items, 23 are written to represent lack of self-control, for example "I have a hard time breaking bad habits." The remaining 13 items are written to represent self-control, such as "I am good at resisting temptation." In order to have the self-control scale scored so that higher scores represent more self-control, the 23 items that represent lack of self-control are *recoded* so that each "1" becomes a "5," each "2" becomes a "4" and so on. After recoding, all lower ratings reflect low self-control and all higher ratings represent high self-control.

Table 3.2d	Example Questionnaire With Items That Need Recoding

Self-Control Scale—*Using the scale provided, please indicate how much each of the following statements reflects how you typically are.*

	Not at all	Very much
1. I am good at resisting temptation.		1-------2-------3-------4-------5
2. I have a hard time breaking bad habits.		1------ 2-------3-------4-------5

Source: Tangney, J., Baumeister, R., & Boone, A. (2004). High self-control predicts good adjustment, less pathology, better grades, and interpersonal success. *Journal of Personality, 72,* 271–322.

Observational and Unobtrusive Measures

A second global category of measures is called **observational** and **unobtrusive measures**. We often assess these measures outside the laboratory, although they also can be used in lab studies. Observational measures are just what they imply; we observe an overt behavior, gesture, or facial expression of a person. The people or person being observed may or may not be aware that they are being observed. Observational measures are different from questionnaires in that the person does not report their behavior, attitude, or emotion; these measures are observed and recorded by others or equipment. The variable to be measured must be operationally defined so that it is explicit enough for observers to determine its presence/absence or level of intensity. The observers who record the behavior should be trained so that their observations are valid (measure the behavior as it is operationally defined) and consistent (reliable) across the two observers.

Unobtrusive measures sometimes are taken in order to make objective judgments about behavior that people may not accurately report, either deliberately or because they are unaware of their behavior. People are unaware of the measurement at the time it is taken and usually unaware that they have participated in a study. The rationale for unobtrusive measures is not to deceive people but to obtain a valid measure of some factor that people may not report accurately due to concerns about the acceptability of the behavior or due to their lack of attention to their behavior. Webb, Campbell, Schwartz, and Sechrest (1966) wrote a book, *Unobtrusive Measures: Nonreactive Research in the Social Science*, documenting the usefulness of such measures as a supplement to questionnaires and surveys that rely on self-report and arguing for their advantages in many situations. They noted such measures as examining carpet wear (how often the carpet needed cleaning or replaced) in front of museum exhibits in order to determine the most popular exhibit and examining the number of empty beer, wine, or liquor bottles in people's trash in order to determine the amount of alcohol consumed at home. In the first case, people may not pay attention to or remember every exhibit they visit and so asking them about their favorite exhibit may not accurately reflect their actual visitation pattern. In the second case, people may under-report the amount of alcohol they drink (for obvious reasons) and so the number of empty bottles may better reflect the amount of alcohol consumed in their home. A selection of different days and different homes could provide a valid measure of alcohol consumed in a particular area or neighborhood. In addition, sampling at least some of the same houses twice could provide a measure of reliability of the measure.

Observational measure: A measure that is rated by observers and sometimes made without the awareness of the person performing the behavior.

Unobtrusive measure: A measure that is made of behaviors or situations without disturbing the naturally occurring behavior or situation in order to reduce changes that might occur if there was awareness of measurement.

90 • RESEARCH METHODS, STATISTICS, AND APPLICATIONS

● ASSESSING RELIABILITY AND VALIDITY OF YOUR MEASURE

Remember from the discussion of weight at the beginning of the chapter that we want our measure to produce consistent scores given consistent circumstances. Correlation is the statistic that is used to assess reliability—you probably learned about correlation in your introductory course when the methods of your discipline were covered, and learned that a perfect positive correlation equals 1.0 and means that the scores increase or decrease together in a totally consistent pattern. In testing reliability, the closer the correlation is to 1.0, the more reliable the scores on the scale are. There are different types of reliability that can be assessed and are relevant, depending on the situation. You will learn more about when and how to compute correlations in Chapter 7.

Assessing Reliability

Internal Consistency

Internal consistency is used to assess the reliability of scales or subscales. Internal consistency only applies to scales (also called measures) that have multiple items that are meant to be combined into a single score (or subscale scores). Internal consistency means that there is consistency in the way that the participant or observer responded to the multiple items on the scale. We would not want items included in the scale score that do not assess the same variable or which are responded to differently than the other items on a scale.

One common way to compute the internal consistency of a scale is **Cronbach's alpha (α)**, which computes the correlation between responses to all of the items in a scale. In the SMS-PUDQ (see Table 3.2c), we would expect that people would respond similarly (although not necessarily identically), to "I have repeatedly made unsuccessful efforts to control, cut back, or stop SMS use" and "I feel restless, moody, depressed, or irritable when attempting to cut down or stop SMS use." So if a person rated the first item as very much like them, we would expect them to also rate the second item as very much like them. Cronbach's checks for this consistency among all items in a scale. In order for a scale to be considered internally consistent, an alpha of .70 or higher ($\geq$.70) is desired, although slightly below that is usually considered acceptable.

Cronbach's analysis can tell us the intercorrelations among items and also how alpha would be affected (increased or decreased) if we delete an item. This latter information is important because when alpha is less than .70, we can sometimes delete one or two items in a scale to reach the .70 standard. The scales mentioned above were found to be highly reliable. The self-control scale showed an alpha of .89 with two different samples of college students and the SMS-PUDQ showed a Cronbach's alpha of .84 for the Pathological Use subscale and a .87 for the Problematic Use subscale.

Split-half reliability also assesses the internal consistency of the scale. The split-half reliability is a simple correlation of the sum of the scores of half the items to the sum of the other half of the items. However, do not be fooled by the name "split-half" and assume that simply correlating the first and second half of the items is sufficient. Sometimes items become more difficult or respondents become fatigued or bored or change in other ways from the beginning to the end of a scale. Such changes would decrease the correlation between the first and second halves of the scale, so in order to check the consistency of answers throughout the scale researchers typically correlate responses to the even and odd items.

Internal consistency: The consistency of participant responses to all the items in a scale.

Cronbach's alpha (α): Test used to assess the internal consistency of a scale by computing the intercorrelations among responses to scale items; values of .70 or higher are interpreted as acceptable internal consistency.

Split-half reliability: Correlations between the responses to half the items on a scale to the other half (usually even-numbered items correlated with odd-numbered items); values of .70 or higher are considered to denote acceptable reliability.

Test-Retest Reliability

We are sometimes concerned with the consistency of scale scores over time, and in these cases we compute the **test-retest reliability**. People take the measure, wait some period of time, and retake the measure. The total scores for each person for each administration of the scale are then correlated. This type of reliability is particularly relevant for the Self-Control Scale as it was intended to measure the trait of self-control, which should be stable over time. When the scale was first being developed, a sample of college students took the Self-Control Scale a second time approximately three weeks after they completed it the first time. The test-retest reliability was quite high, $r = .89$, showing that the students scored very similarly on the scale both times they completed it. Test-retest reliability is the only type of reliability that can be assessed for a single item that is used to measure a variable. For example, I might ask a class of college students to rate their average self-esteem one day and then to rate it again a week later. Although self-esteem may vary somewhat over time, we would expect that those with high self-esteem would rate themselves higher on both occasions than those with low self-esteem.

Alternate Forms Reliability

Alternate forms reliability is similar to test-retest reliability in that the respondent takes a measure twice. In the case of alternate forms, however, there is more than one form of the measure and the forms are considered to be equal in their ability to measure a construct. Using alternate forms of a scale is one way to avoid practice effects that can occur when one uses the same test or scale to establish reliability. When students take a test such as the SAT more than once, they do not take the exact same test but an alternate form. Each version of the SAT is considered equal in terms of its difficulty and accuracy in measuring the students' mastery of knowledge. One would expect a high positive correlation between two forms of the SAT for a sample of high school seniors.

92 • RESEARCH METHODS, STATISTICS, AND APPLICATIONS

Inter-Rater Reliability

Inter-rater reliability is used when at least two different observers or raters make independent judgments, meaning that they do not know each other's codes or scores. Inter-rater reliability is computed by correlating the different raters' scores. We expect to obtain a very high correlation or agreement (.90 or higher) in order to establish the reliability of the observation measure. In one study (Cramer, Mayer, & Ryan, 2007), trained graduate student observers recorded information about cars leaving a parking structure. Among the information recorded was the gender of the driver, whether the driver was using a cell phone, and whether passengers were present. Inter-rater reliability was assessed by having pairs of observers make the first 50 observations together. There was very high agreement between the pairs of observers on all three measures: 95.9% agreement about the gender of the driver, 98.9% agreement between observers about the use of a cell phone by a specific driver, and 99% agreement about whether passengers were present.

Test-retest reliability: A measure of the stability of scores on a scale over time.

Alternate forms reliability: The relationship between scores on two different forms of a scale.

Inter-rater reliability: A measure of agreement between different raters' scores.

Assessing Validity

In addition to showing reliability, we also expect scales assessing constructs to be valid or to accurately measure what we say they are measuring. Remember that scales can be reliable without being valid, so it is important to test both reliability and validity. Like reliability, there are different types of validity.

Figure 3.2 Types of Reliability of Individual Measures

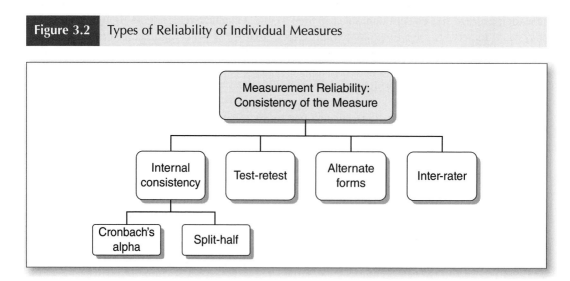

Face Validity

The public commonly uses **face validity** to judge whether something measures what it is supposed to measure. For example, someone may tell us that movie *A* is more popular than other movies because the number of tickets sold for movie *A* at their local theater is greater than the number of tickets sold for other movies. The number of tickets sold may be a valid measure of movie popularity, or we may find out that all local high school students were required to see movie *A* or that a local person stars in movie *A* and everyone wanted to see her in the movie rather than the movie itself. Researchers are suspicious of face validity because it is untested and sometimes based on only one person's opinion or view.

Construct Validity

Construct validity concerns whether a measure is reflective of the hypothetical construct of a variable. It is a general sense of what the variable means. So self-control must be defined in a way that reflects the attitudes, behaviors, and emotions associated with the construct. Several types of validity help us to determine whether our scale has construct validity.

Face validity: Whether a particular measure seems to be appropriate as a way to assess a construct.

Construct validity: Whether a measure mirrors the characteristics of a hypothetical construct; can be assessed in multiple ways.

Content validity is related to the items that make up a scale. Do the items in the scale accurately reflect the construct we are attempting to measure? Are all aspects of the construct represented among our items? Researchers may consult with experts in the field or use a theory that is related to the construct or examine past research on the construct to develop items to measure a particular construct. In the case of the SMS-PUDQ, Rutland et al. (2007) began with a model of addiction (Griffiths, 2005), which included several characteristics of addiction such as withdrawal, tolerance, relapse, mood modification, and compulsivity. They also reviewed past research on the development of the Mobile Phone Problematic Use Scale (MPPUS), which used the same addiction model but focused on cell phone use rather than texting. Finally, they studied research that had examined other types of technology addiction (Internet, for example). Based on all of this information, they developed items for their scale that were meant to assess problematic text messaging. For instance, the item "I use SMS longer than originally intended" was meant to represent compulsivity, which is part of Griffiths's addiction model and fit with the past research on problematic use of cell phones and other technologies. In developing the items for their Self-Control Scale, Tangney et al. (2004) examined existing scales that measured self-control and past research on the construct. Their scale included items assessing the factors related to self-control as identified by past research (e.g., achievement, impulse control, interpersonal relationships). There is no statistical test to assess content validity, but experts or those scrutinizing scales may criticize or praise a scale for its coverage of the construct the scale is intended to measure.

Convergent validity assesses the relationship of a scale to an existing measure of the same or a similar construct that has already shown adequate validity. Convergent refers to the fact that we expect the new scale to be positively correlated to the existing measures or to accepted measures. For example, Rutland et al. (2007) found that scores on the SMS-PUDQ were significantly related to self-reported minutes spent in a week sending and receiving text messages as well as scores on the MPPUS. Likewise, the convergent validity of the Self-Control Scale was established by finding that college students' scores on the scale positively correlated with the factors identified in past research as related to self-control, including higher grades, fewer eating and alcohol problems, and more positive interpersonal relationships.

Not only do we expect our scale to positively correlate with related behaviors or scales, but we also expect scale scores to negatively correlate or have no correlation with scales assessing unrelated or different constructs. This type of validity is called **divergent validity**. For example, we would not want or expect a scale assessing problematic texting use to correlate with optimism. We sometimes include such correlations in order to demonstrate the distinctiveness of a scale or to show that a scale does not measure a different construct. Using the scales we have been discussing, we would not expect the Self-Control Scale to be positively correlated with the SMS-PUDQ, which measures a lack of control regarding texting. In fact, scores on these scales might be negatively correlated.

> *Content validity:* Inclusion of all aspects of a construct by items on a scale or measure.
>
> *Convergent validity:* Positive relationship between two scales measuring the same or similar constructs.
>
> *Divergent validity:* Negative or no relationship between two scales measuring different constructs.

The final type of construct validity we might measure is **criterion validity**, which relates scores from a scale to a behavior that represents the construct measured by the scale. There are two types of criterion validity: **concurrent validity** and **predictive validity**. These two types of validity differ only in timing of the behavior. Concurrent validity establishes a relationship between a scale and a current behavior, while predictive validity establishes a relationship between a scale score and a future behavior. For instance, SAT scores from the fall could be correlated to seniors' high school cumulative GPA to show concurrent validity of the SAT. The same SAT scores could be correlated to seniors' first-year college GPA to establish predictive validity. Using the SMS-PUDQ, we could correlate scores with minutes texting the same day to establish concurrent validity or texting minutes reported on their phone bill the next month to establish predictive validity. We would expect that those who have problems of overuse according to the SMS-PUDQ would have texted more at both times (at the current time and next month) than those who scored lower on the SMS-PUDQ.

> *Criterion validity:* Positive correlation between scale scores and a behavioral measure.
>
> *Concurrent validity:* Positive correlation between scale scores and a current behavior that is related to the construct assessed by the scale.
>
> *Predictive validity:* Positive relationship between scale scores and a future behavior that is related to the construct assessed by the scale.

Figure 3.3	Types of Validity of Individual Measures

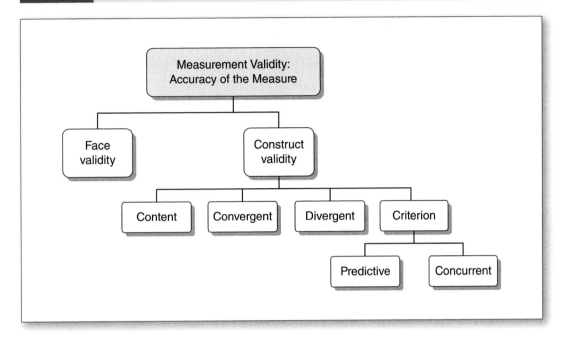

ETHICS TIP	USING APPROPRIATE MEASURES TO GET MEANINGFUL RESULTS

According to ethical guidelines, all studies should be designed to increase our knowledge about behaviors, situations, or theories. This means that researchers have a responsibility to use only those measures or procedures that will produce meaningful results. If you (or anyone) conduct research that includes unreliable or invalid measures or employs procedures full of confounds so that you cannot generalize the results or even make sense of them, you have violated the ethical standards for research. You would be wasting participants' time if you collect data with an unreliable measure or one that is not explicitly defined and valid. Likewise, you have wasted participants' time if you cannot make judgments about the results of your study because there are multiple likely explanations for your findings.

Researchers depend on the good will of society in terms of providing willing participants and in supporting legitimate research. Studies that cause suspicion about the usefulness or benefits of social and behavioral studies harm more than just the researcher conducting the meaningless research. Carefully selecting valid and reliable measures is a first step in fulfilling your ethical responsibilities as a researcher.

PRACTICE 3.4

YOUR RESEARCH TOPIC AND RELIABILITY AND VALIDITY

Find a research article on your topic. Choose one variable from the article and answer the following questions.

- How is the variable operationally defined or measured?
- What scale of measurement is the variable?
- What evidence is provided about the measure's reliability?
- What evidence is provided about the measure's validity?

● USING DATA ANALYSIS PROGRAMS

Once you collect data, you can use some type of software to organize the data and to check the reliability of your scale or measure. In our text, we will provide examples from the *Statistical Package for the Social Sciences* (IBM SPSS Version 21), which is widely used by psychologists to analyze data.

Entering Data

All statistical programs have a specific format to follow in entering data. Be sure that you follow the format for the program you are using.

1. Find out how your statistical program treats missing data. Do you leave blank the space when an item was not answered, or is there a particular code for missing data, such as M or 0?

2. It is unethical to eliminate any piece of data because it is not what you expected or does not fit your hypothesis. You should discuss with your professor the possibility of eliminating data that seems to suggest the participant misunderstood what was being asked or did not take the study seriously.

3. Decide on codes for non-numeric data; for instance, code females as "1," males as "2."

4. Be careful to enter your data accurately, as a mistake in data entry will affect the outcome (even if just a little) of any statistical analysis using those data and can affect the

meaning of your results. It is always a good idea to check the accuracy of the entire data file once you have completed entering all the data.

Computing Scale Scores

Many measures in research require that you add or in some way manipulate the individual responses before computing a total scale score.

Do you need to recode? One of the most common manipulations we have to perform on data items is to recode some of the items on a scale. Before recoding you must understand how total scores are interpreted for your scale—what do high or low scores imply? You will need to identify whether or which items on the scale do not fit (seem to imply an opposite direction) the stated interpretation. These items will need to be recoded before you can add all the items for a total score on the scale. For example, high scores on the Self-Control Scale (Tangney et al., 2004) are interpreted as signifying high self-control. The scale consists of 36 items which are rated by participants in terms of how much they are like them (1 = *not at all* and 5 = *very much*). Eleven of the items are worded so that a "5" means high self-control ("I refuse things that are bad for me"), while 23 of the items are worded so that a "5" means low self-control ("I am lazy"). The 23 items will then need to be recoded. Follow the directions for your statistical package, which will tell you how to change a response of "1" to "5," a response of "2" to "4," leave "3" as "3," change a response of "4" to "2" and a response of "5" to "1."

Add the scores for a total score: After recoding, you are now ready to compute a total score by adding all of the original items that did not need to be recoded and those that were recoded. Be sure that you include each item (either the original or the recoded score) only once. In our example of the Self-Control Scale, you will sum 11 unaltered ratings from items that did not need to be recoded and 13 recoded ratings to obtain the total self-control score.

Computing Internal Consistency

In many statistical software packages, the internal consistency of multi-item scales can be easily computed using Cronbach's alpha. Remember that Cronbach's examines the consistency of responses within the scale, so that you will use the items that fit the interpretation of the scale (those items that do not need recoding) and the recoded items rather than all of the original items. So computing the internal consistency uses the same values as computing the total scale score. The difference is that one operation (computing the total score) adds the items and the other operation (computing the internal consistency) calculates the correlation among items.

The internal consistency for your sample should be reported when you describe a scale in the Materials or Apparatus section within the Method section in your report.

PRACTICE 3.5

EXAMPLES FROM THE LITERATURE

Review the following excerpts from journal articles. As you do so, consider the following questions:

- What is the purpose of the described scale?
- What do I learn about the development and format of the scale/questionnaire?
- What do I learn about the reliability of the scale?
- What do I learn about the validity of the scale?

Article 1.

This content has been removed for permissions reasons.

Article 2.

Campbell, S. (2006). Perceptions of mobile phones in classroom: Ringing, cheating, and classroom policies. *Communication Education, 55,* 280–294.

An original self-report survey containing 27 items was used to assess attitudes about mobile phone use in college classrooms and demographic information. The attitudinal items were loosely grounded in the literature reviewed above. For these items, participants were asked to respond using a 5-point Likert-type scale with response options ranging from *strongly agree* to *strongly disagree*. …

Prior to data collection, a pilot study with 31 participants was conducted to help with instrument development. Written comments were solicited from the pilot participants to evaluate item clarity. A preliminary factor analysis and Cronbach's alpha scores were used to assess the strength of the relationship among variables in each factor.... A Cronbach alpha of at least .70 was used to further determine whether an item should be retained in the scale subsequent to factor analysis. Six items were removed from the analysis for not meeting these criteria. The remaining 14 items yielded four interpretable factors for attitudes about mobile phone use in college classrooms and policies. (p. 284)

See Appendix A to check your answers.

CHAPTER RESOURCES

KEY TERMS

Define the following terms using your own words. You can check your answers by reviewing the chapter or by comparing them with the definitions in the glossary—but try to define them on your own first.

Alternate forms reliability	Face validity
Closed-ended response format	Forced-choice response format
Concurrent validity	Identity
Confound (or confounding variable)	Internal consistency
Construct	Internal validity
Construct validity	Inter-rater reliability
Content validity	Interval scale
Convergent validity	Likert-type scale
Criterion validity	Measurement reliability
Cronbach's alpha (α)	Measurement validity
Divergent validity	Nominal scale
Equal intervals	Observational measure
External validity	Open-ended response format

100 • RESEARCH METHODS, STATISTICS, AND APPLICATIONS

Operational definition	Reliability of a study
Order	Replication
Ordinal scale	Response format
Predictive validity	Scale score
Qualitative measure	Split-half reliability
Quantitative measure	Test-retest reliability
Questionnaire	True zero (or absolute zero)
Ratio scale	Unobtrusive measure
Reliability	Validity

DO YOU UNDERSTAND THE CHAPTER?

Answer these questions on your own and then review the chapter to check your answers.

1. What is the difference between internal and external validity? How does each type of validity contribute to the research process?

2. How do confounds influence the validity of a study? Give an example of a possible confound in a study.

3. Explain the balance that must be achieved between the internal and external validity of a study.

4. How are operational definitions related to validity and reliability of measures?

5. Distinguish between qualitative and quantitative measures.

6. What are the four scales or measurement, and what qualities distinguish each scale?

7. What scales of measurement are most commonly used in psychological research?

8. What is a questionnaire?

9. What is the difference between open- and closed-ended items? What are the advantages and disadvantages of each type of response?

10. How can we determine if a measure/scale is reliable? Describe the different ways that are possible.

11. What does Cronbach's alpha tell us? What standard/level should alpha achieve?

12. How can we determine if a measure is valid? Distinguish between the different types of validity.

13. What are observational measures?

14. How do we determine if observations are reliable?

15. What are the advantages of unobtrusive measures?

16. Why is it important to identify items that require recoding in a questionnaire?

PRACTICE DATASET

A researcher conducts an extensive survey on the use of texting. She also collects information about the participants' age and gender. Here is the five-question scale she used to measure attitudes regarding texting with one's romantic partner:

Please rate how much you agree with each statement.	Strongly Disagree	Disagree	Neither Agree Nor Disagree	Agree	Strongly Agree
1. Texting allows me to stay in consistent contact with my partner.	1	2	3	4	5
2. Text messages can easily be misunderstood.	1	2	3	4	5
3. Texting is better than cell phones because my partner and I can communicate without others hearing any part of our conversation.	1	2	3	4	5
4. Texting decreases face-to-face contact with my partner.	1	2	3	4	5
5. Almost all of my text messages to my partner are positive.	1	2	3	4	5

She collected data from 10 people; here is a summary of the data:

ID	Age	Gender	Texting Questionnaire				
			Q1	Q2	Q3	Q4	Q5
1	31	Female	5	3	2	2	4
2	19	Male	4	4	3	1	5
3	20	Female	4	1	4	1	4
4	55	Male	3	5	2	1	2
5	21	Female	5	1	5	3	5
6	22	Female	5	2	5	1	5
7	18	Male	4	4	5	2	4
8	19	Male	4	3	4	2	4
9	22	Male	4	2	4	1	4
10	24	Female	5	2	2	2	3

102 • RESEARCH METHODS, STATISTICS, AND APPLICATIONS

1. **Enter** the data. All variables should be numeric, so be sure to code gender as numbers.

2. Look over the questionnaire. You will want all the questions to indicate more positive views of texting with romantic partners. Right now there are some questions that need to be reverse coded. **Recode** the questions you identified so that a score of 1 = 5, 2 = 4, 3 = 3, 4 = 2, 5 = 1.

3. **Compute** the total score on the text-use questionnaire by computing the sum of the five questions. Remember to use the *recoded* variables here, not the original ones.

4. **Compute** the internal consistency for the questionnaire by computing Cronbach's alpha. Comment about your results for internal consistency. What could you do to improve the internal consistency of the questionnaire so that it meets the .70 standard?

CHAPTER 21

DESIGNING A DESCRIPTIVE STUDY

B y now you have learned how to identify a research topic and refine it based on past research. You have also learned how to operationally define the constructs of interest and evaluate the reliability and validity of your measures and study. In this chapter, we will introduce you to the most basic type of study: descriptive research. Descriptive research seeks to answer "who, what, where, when, and how" questions. These questions serve as a way to get more detail about an event or to understand attitudes and behaviors. They serve as an important first step prior to predicting or explaining events, attitudes, or behaviors.

IN THIS CHAPTER, YOU WILL LEARN

- When a descriptive study is appropriate
- Common methods for descriptive studies
- How to evaluate the validity of descriptive research
- How to identify a population and obtain a sample
- Ways to integrate descriptive research with other types of research designs

103

● WHEN IS A DESCRIPTIVE STUDY APPROPRIATE?

Understand Prevalence and Trends

Descriptive research can be used to provide a quick snapshot of the prevalence of a phenomenon. Such studies are quite common among health researchers who want to know the prevalence of a specific type of risk behavior (e.g., smoking) or disease (e.g., cancer). This descriptive research allows for an assessment of the need for intervention and can also be used to target interventions toward those who seem to be at highest risk.

Descriptive research also helps us understand trends in behaviors and attitudes. To serve that end, the Pew Research Center has been collecting and sharing information about a variety of issues impacting American life since the early 1990s. They poll the public about a variety of issues including global attitudes and views of the press and public policies. They also track social and demographic trends. This type of descriptive information helps paint a picture of our changing national and political landscape for policy makers, and can prompt further research on how and why behaviors and attitudes change.

Changing trends can also prompt additional descriptive research. For example, research from the Pew Internet and American Life Project (2011) suggests that 46% of adults and 73% of adolescents in the United States used the Internet in 2000, and this rose to 78% and 95%, respectfully, in 2011. The high rate of Internet use and upward trend have implications for academic honesty, which spurred new descriptive research examining the frequency of cutting and pasting from the Internet into student work (M. McCullough & Holmberg, 2005; Renard, 2000) as well as ways that educators detect plagiarism from the Internet (Batane, 2010; M. McCullough & Holmberg, 2005; Walker, 2010).

Explore a Phenomenon in Depth

Descriptive studies also allow for an in-depth examination of a topic. This type of research can be especially useful for examining a new phenomenon. For example, plagiarism detection software such as Turnitin is a relatively new invention that arose in response to Internet plagiarism. Descriptive studies have been used to investigate these programs' efficacy in detecting plagiarism (Batane, 2010; Walker, 2010) and deterring plagiarism (Batane, 2010; Ledwith & Risquez, 2008), as well as students' views of such programs (Batane, 2010).

Researchers can also use descriptive research to determine if the patterns they found in their study fit with existing research and theories. If not, they may modify the theories or develop new ones that will be tested with future research. In this way, descriptive research serves as an important first step in the progress of science. Before attempting to predict or explain an event, attitude, or behavior, it must first be accurately described.

Examine a Phenomenon in a Different Population

Just because a phenomenon is described in one population does not necessarily mean that the description will fit a different population. Thus, another reason for conducting a descriptive study might be to consider if patterns and prevalence of behaviors and attitudes that are found in one population are similar in a different population. The rationale for such a study is strengthened if there is research evidence suggesting why the prevalence or pattern might be different. For example, Trost (2009) conducted a study to examine the type and frequency of academic dishonesty among Swedish university students. Her rationale for conducting the study was twofold: Past research had suggested that Swedes tend to value honesty and abhor lying to a great degree and that this morality is part of the Swedish identity, and there had not been any research on academic dishonesty conducted with a Swedish population. Thus, she made the case for the need to conduct a descriptive study to document patterns of academic dishonesty in a different population than had been previously evaluated.

REVIEW OF KEY CONCEPTS: EXTERNAL VALIDITY

Can you recall what type of validity is under examination when we wonder if results from one study generalize to a different population? More broadly, this type of validity also deals with questions about whether results from one study will generalize to other participants (or animal subjects), other settings, and other methods.

If you answered "external validity," you are correct! If not, take a minute to review the concepts of validity from Chapter 3. Remember that external validity is not something that a study has or does not have, but instead reminds us to consider how generalizable the results of one study might be to other participants, settings, or methods. Therefore, when we evaluate the external validity of the Pew Internet and American Life Project's report on the prevalence of Internet use in the United States, we do not say that the results cannot generalize to other countries. Instead, we simply wonder if the results might be similar or different in other countries. In accordance with the process of science, the question of external validity might prompt other researchers to examine this question empirically.

PRACTICE 4.1

IDENTIFY A DESCRIPTIVE STUDY BASED ON YOUR TOPIC

1. Come up with a few descriptive questions (who, what, where, when, and how) based on your topic.

2. Choose (or modify) one that has the strongest rationale, in that the research literature suggests that one of the following studies is warranted:

   a. An understanding of prevalence or trends

   b. An in-depth examination

   c. An examination in a different population than has been studied

106 • RESEARCH METHODS, STATISTICS, AND APPLICATIONS

● METHODS FOR DESCRIPTIVE STUDIES

There are many different methods of descriptive research, but keep in mind that none are exclusively used for descriptive designs alone. We introduce methods commonly used in descriptive research here to help paint a clearer picture about what descriptive research entails. These same methods can be used in correlational research and some can be used in experimental research as well. Examples of each of these methods can be found in Applications 4.1 and 4.2, and a comparison of the advantages and disadvantages appear in Table 4.1.

Survey Research

Survey research involves asking people to report on their own attitudes and behaviors. Such self-report can provide insight into how individuals see themselves and allows the researcher to obtain information about people's thoughts and feelings that cannot be directly observed. The disadvantage is that self-report may not be accurate, either because people are deceiving themselves or trying to deceive the researcher.

In particular, self-reports may be inaccurate due to the **social desirability bias**, meaning that participants may respond based on how they want to be perceived rather than how they actually think or behave. See Figure 4.1 for an example of the social desirability bias. There are ways to minimize or at least measure participants' bias toward social desirability. Anonymity of responses can be helpful, as can neutrally worded questions. Some researchers even include questions or scales designed to test the validity of participants' responses. If participants answer in the affirmative to the question "I never lie," there is a good chance that they are in fact lying and may be doing so in their other answers.

> *Survey research:* Interviews or questionnaires in which participants report on their attitudes and behaviors.
>
> *Social desirability bias:* Participants may respond based on how they want to be perceived or what is socially acceptable.

Many use the term *survey* when referring to questionnaires. However, survey research refers to the method used to collect data, and both interviews and questionnaires are tools used in survey research.

Interviews

Interviews are one-on-one conversations directed by a researcher that can take place in person, over the phone, or via e-mail. Anonymity is more difficult with interviews, although the researcher should still carefully guard the participants' confidentiality. (Recall from Chapter 1

Figure 4.1	Social Desirability Bias

People do not always report their true thoughts, feelings, and behaviors. Instead, their responses may be influenced by the social desirability bias in that they report what they think others want to hear, or what they think is socially acceptable.

Source: Eva K. Lawrence

that *anonymity* means that no one knows the identity of the participant whereas *confidentiality* means that the identities are confidential but may be known to the researcher.) A potential lack of anonymity is a clear disadvantage for interviews because it can increase the social desirability bias. Interviews are also subject to **interviewer bias**, in which the interviewer's verbal and nonverbal responses to the participants' answers change how the participants answer subsequent questions. For example, imagine that someone was interviewing you and their eyes got wide and they said "wow, that's horrible" after you provided an honest answer to their question. Their responses would likely impact how you answered the next question. Another disadvantage to interviews is that they are quite time-consuming.

Interviewer bias: The interviewer may provide verbal or nonverbal cues that impact how the participant responds.

Given these considerable disadvantages, you might wonder why anyone would choose to conduct an interview. There are several advantages to interviews, and the decision to conduct an interview necessitates an evaluation of the potential advantages and disadvantages given the specific focus of the research study. The one-on-one nature of an interview may inspire the participant to take the research more seriously, which may in turn increase the response rate as well as the accuracy of the answers. The interviewer is also privy to additional information that might be missed in other formats. Specifically, the interviewer can take note of not only the participant's response but also the manner in which the participant delivers the response. Face-to-face interviews are especially rich sources for observing nonverbal cues such as facial expressions, hand gestures, pauses, and posture. Finally, interviews can allow for question clarification or follow-up questions, although this depends on how structured the interviews are.

Structured interviews include a standard set of questions that the interviewer asks all participants. The interviewer does not vary the order of questions or the manner in which they are asked. The interviewer also has strict guidelines for how to answer any questions that the participant might have. If the participant asks for clarification for what a question means, the interviewer might only be able to repeat the question and explain that the participant has to use his or her own judgment to interpret the question. The rationale for a structured interview is that it ensures that all participants had similar interview experiences and the exact same questions. It also reduces the potential for interviewer bias. Additionally, a researcher can train several novice interviewers to conduct structured interviews.

Semi-structured interviews are much more flexible than structured interviews. The interviewer has a base set of questions or topics that he or she wants to cover, but can prompt the participant for more information, add new questions based on the participants' responses, and clarify questions as necessary. The ability to ask additional questions is a great advantage to the semi-structured interview, and the interviewer may be able to discover new information that he or she had not thought to ask about. However, conducting a semi-structured interview requires more training and practice in order to reduce interviewer bias and a solid knowledge of the research topic in order to formulate neutral follow-up questions during the interview.

Structured interviews: All questions, follow-up questions, and responses by the interviewer are determined beforehand to ensure that all the participants have a very similar experience.

Semi-structured interviews: There is a set of core questions or topics that the interviewer will follow, but the interviewer may prompt for more information, ask follow-up questions, or clarify questions as the interviewer deems necessary.

Questionnaires

Recall from Chapter 3 that questionnaires are measures in which the participants respond to questions on paper or online. Questionnaires allow for anonymity and can therefore reduce social desirability bias. Multiple participants can complete the questionnaire at the same time and thus questionnaires can save a lot of time over interviews. Additionally, administration is easily accomplished by handing out questionnaires in person, sending them through the mail, or e-mailing or posting an online questionnaire. Handing out questionnaires in person is the most work-intensive type of administration, and participants may not believe that their answers are truly anonymous. However, the response rate tends to be higher compared to mailed or e-mailed questionnaires. Additionally, a researcher can help clarify questions if necessary.

Mailed questionnaires were once popular due to the convenience of administration. The response rate for mailed questionnaires, however, is notoriously low and the cost of printing and mailing high. Consequently, most researchers who decide not to hand out questionnaires in person now prefer online administration. The key advantage to online questionnaires over those administered in person is that they allow a researcher to easily and inexpensively reach a large number of people across the world. Additionally, research suggests that online questionnaires yield results similar to those completed in person, although the utility of online questionnaires may vary based on the topic studied (Krantz, 2011).

Observational Research

Observational research involves observing and recording the behavior of humans or animals. Observations may stand alone, or they may supplement other research methods. The key advantage of observations in human research is that observations focus on what people actually do, not what they say they do or what they intend to do. One downside to observations is that they are time-consuming.

Another disadvantage is that observations are prone to **observer bias** in which the observers selectively attend to what they expect or hope to see. Fortunately, there are several strategies to reduce observer bias. Having observers who are **blind**, meaning they do not know what the hypotheses are, can greatly reduce observer bias. It is also wise to have more than one observer. This allows you to compare their observations and test their inter-rater reliability (see Chapter 3 for a review of inter-rater reliability). Observers should be carefully trained on what behaviors to attend to and how different behaviors are operationally defined. Ideally, the observers should practice their observations until their inter-rater reliability is acceptable prior to beginning the actual study. Finally, the more structured the observation, the less room there is for error and bias.

> *Observer bias:* The observers pay closer attention to behaviors that support their expectations or interpret behaviors in ways that support their expectations or lose their focus on the target behavior.
>
> *Blind:* Observers are not informed of the hypotheses in order to reduce observer bias.

Observers record behaviors on an observer code sheet. At its most flexible, this code sheet is simply a piece of paper upon which the observer records a **narrative** account of what the participant did. This can provide a full picture of the participants' behaviors, but the coding for this type of data is most subject to observer bias. A more structured approach is to develop a code sheet ahead of time listing items that operationally define the constructs of most interest to the researcher and that are based on past research. A middle ground would be to have both a structured code sheet but encourage the observer to also narrate any unexpected or noteworthy behavior.

A structured code sheet might include a **checklist** on which the observer identifies key demographic variables, such as gender and ethnicity, and then checks off whether specific behaviors occurred. For example, someone observing a public cell phone conversation might indicate if any of the following behaviors occurred: *spoke on a hands-free device, apologized for the call, left room.* An observer might also record the timing of a behavior such as how long a behavior lasts (**duration**), how long it takes to complete a task (**task completion time**), how quickly a participant responds to a stimulus (**reaction time**), or the time between two tasks (**latency**).

Finally, the code sheet might also include a **rating scale** to assess the intensity of a behavior. For example, loudness of a cell phone conversation can be rated on a scale from 1 to 10, with 10 = *extremely loud,* or on a 3-point scale (*soft, moderate, loud*). Recall from Chapter 3 that a Likert-type scale is a specific type of rating scale in which respondents report their intensity of an experience or their level of agreement. A Likert-type scale might ask the observer to report how much they agree that the cell phone conversation was loud, rated as 1 = *strongly disagree;* 2 = *disagree;* 3 = *neutral;* 4 = *agree;* 5 = *strongly agree.*

Narrative: A detailed account of behaviors or responses.

Checklist: A list of qualities or behaviors that are checked if present.

Duration: How long a behavior lasts.

Task completion time: How long it takes to complete a task.

Reaction time: How long it takes a participant to respond to a stimulus.

Latency: The time between stopping one task and beginning a new task.

Rating scale: A numerical rating of a particular quality.

REVIEW OF KEY CONCEPTS: SCALES OF MEASUREMENT

Can you recall what scale of measurement is represented by each of the following items:

1. Checklist item: _____Person spoke on a hands-free device.

2. Rating: The volume of the conversation was

1	2	3	4	5	6	7
not at all loud						*extremely loud*

3. Duration: The conversation lasted _____ seconds.

Recall that nominal scales are categories, including yes/no answers, that do not have magnitude. Ordinal scales are rankings that have magnitude but no equal intervals. Interval scales are ratings that have magnitude and equal intervals, but no absolute zero. Finally, ratio scales are quantities that have magnitude, equal intervals, and an absolute zero.

If you said the first was a nominal scale (checked or not checked), the second an interval scale, and the third a ratio scale, then you are correct! If you had difficulty with this exercise, be sure to review Chapter 3. These scales of measurement will be important when it comes to figuring out how to analyze data.

Observers may code behaviors that are live or recorded. Recording allows for higher accuracy because the observer can examine the recording many times, and any discrepancy between observers' codes can be investigated by examining the recording. Recording is much more of an invasion of privacy than observing a live situation, and as such has greater ethical implications. The decision to do a live observation or to record the situation also depends on other decisions the researcher makes. Factors which influence the decision are described below.

Covert Versus Overt Observations

In a **covert observation**, the observers do not reveal that they are observing the participants, whereas they do reveal themselves in an **overt observation**. A concern with overt observations is that participants who know they are being observed may change their behavior. This change may be due to the social desirability bias, or it may occur simply because being watched introduces another factor into the situation. Consequently, those who conduct overt observations typically allow the participant some time to acclimate to the situation prior to the start of the study. They may also remove themselves from the situation by watching participants through a one-way mirror, recording the participants, or both.

Covert observation: Observations are made without the participants' awareness.

Overt observation: No attempts are made to hide the observation.

Covert observations are designed to capture the participants' natural and spontaneous reactions to situations. They can be especially important when observing behaviors that are prone to the social desirability bias. There are ethical considerations with watching someone without their awareness, although less so if the observations take place in a public place. If a covert observation was to happen in a private space, deception would have to be employed. For example, an observer might deceive the participant into believing they are there to observe a child's behavior when in fact the parents' behavior is the focus. As discussed in Chapter 1, the use of deception in research is quite controversial, and the risks and benefits of deception must be carefully weighed. Additionally, recording someone without their consent raises serious ethical concerns especially if the person's face or other identifying feature is recorded.

Natural Versus Contrived Observations

Naturalistic observations occur in the participants' (or animal subjects') natural environment and take place without any interference by the observer or researcher. It might involve observing animals or humans in these settings or it could instead involve unobtrusive observations as described in Chapter 3. In unobtrusive observations, the observer examines traces of animal or human behavior, such as tracks or garbage.

Contrived observations are those that are set up for research purposes and might include observing participants' reactions to an event or physical stimulus or asking participants to complete a task or engage in an activity. Contrived observations can occur in a laboratory setting where the researcher has the most control over the setting, but they may also occur in a natural environment such as a home, school, or public place.

> *Natural (or naturalistic) observation:* Observations that occur in natural environments or situations and do not involve interference by anyone involved in the research.
>
> *Contrived observation:* The researcher sets up the situation and observes how participants or subjects respond.

A naturalistic observation of public cell phone use would require the observer to watch and record participants' use and reactions to cell phone conversations. A downside to the naturalistic approach is that the observer has no control over the situation and a long time may pass before the behavior of interest occurs. In this case, naturally occurring cell phone use will vary quite a bit in who sends or receives the call, the volume, and the duration. Moreover, it may take a while for someone to naturally initiate or receive a cell phone call.

A contrived approach could address these issues by creating a situation and then observing people's reactions. For example, a contrived observation of reactions to public cell phone use might involve a cell phone ringing in a public place so that the researcher has control over when the phone rings, for how long, and the type of ring tone. Contrived observations might also employ a **confederate** who appears to be a participant but is actually working with the researcher. In our cell phone example, a confederate may stage a conversation or may react in a predetermined way to a staged conversation.

> *Confederate:* Someone who pretends to be a participant or uninvolved person, but in actuality is working with the researcher and has been told to behave in a particular way.

Nonparticipant Versus Participant Observations

Nonparticipant observation occurs when the researcher is not directly involved in the situation, whereas **participant observation** involves the active involvement of the researcher in the situation under observation. Participant observation may involve a confederate who interacts with participants in a brief task or situation or it might involve a deeper infiltration into a social group, either covertly or overtly. The more involved the participant observation, the greater the chance that the participants will exhibit natural and spontaneous behaviors. This is true even if observation is overt because the participants acclimate to the observers' presence and the personal relationships that develop often engender trust and comfort. Greater involvement of the researchers also blurs the line between researcher and participant. The disadvantage of involvement by the researchers is that they may lose their objectivity as they become more entrenched in the group.

Nonparticipant observation: The researcher or observer is not directly involved in the situation.

Participant observation: The researcher or observer becomes actively involved in the situation.

Archival Research

Archival research involves the analysis of existing data or records. As with all research, it begins with a careful review of existing research followed by the development of a testable hypothesis that builds on past research. The key difference with archival research is that the data have already been collected. Archival research thus has many advantages: A researcher can save time and resources by not collecting data; some archives span a large time frame and the analysis of those data allows for a systematic examination of historical patterns and trends; and finally, there are fewer ethical considerations with certain types of archives including materials that do not directly involve people or animals, data from a study that has already undergone IRB approval, or public records.

Archival research: Analysis of existing data or records.

There are also challenges to archival research. Archival research requires that you identify the appropriate archival source and obtain access. Additionally, you must decide how to use the data to test your hypothesis. The biggest disadvantage to archival research is that the data were not collected with your hypothesis in mind, and as such the data available might not represent exactly what you were hoping to analyze.

Secondary Data

One source of archival research is **secondary data**. These are data that were collected for research purposes by some other researcher or organization. Sources of secondary data include governmental agencies, non-profit organizations, colleges and universities, data repositories, and individual researchers.

Secondary data: Research data that were collected by one researcher or group but analyzed by a different researcher or group.

Some secondary data are relatively easy to access. Data from the Pew Research Center are available for download from the Internet. Data from the National Longitudinal Study of Youth are available upon request and have been the source of over 400 research studies

(NORC, n.d.). The largest repository of social science data is the Dataverse Network created by the Institute for Quantitative Social Science (IQSS) at Harvard University. Researchers upload their data to the network. Anyone can then search the network, and many datasets are available for download or available with permission of the researcher. Sharing data in this way helps to make the process of science as transparent as possible by encouraging replication and verification of research results.

On the other hand, access to other secondary data is limited. Some researchers and institutions prefer not to share their data for fear that the confidentiality of their members or participants might be breached or because they prefer to have control over who analyzes their data and for what purposes.

Additionally, even if you can obtain secondary data, those data may not be coded in such a way that allows you to test your hypothesis. You may instead need to adjust your hypothesis to match the data available. For example, suppose you had originally hypothesized that the use of liquor among adolescents between the ages of 16 and 17 has decreased over the years. However, the secondary data set you are using categorizes age in larger chunks, such as 15- to 18-year-olds, and had data on alcohol use in general instead of the specific type of alcohol. If you wanted to use that data set, you would need to adjust your hypotheses based on the data you actually have.

Records and Documents

Other sources of archival research are the countless records and documents that were not created for research purposes. This includes confidential information such as school or medical records that can be accessed only if consent is given by an individual or institution. Other information is publicly available, including websites, newspaper articles, public records, and historical documents. For example, you might examine patterns of what songs or artists made the Billboard music chart, or you might research the statistics of professional athletes or teams, or you might research the history of the United States through records, media, and pictures preserved by the National Archives and Records Administration. Additionally, you could use information or pictures posted on social media sites such as Facebook and Twitter as the data for a research project.

Because these records and documents were not originally intended for research, they have distinct advantages and disadvantages over other types of data. The advantages are that they allow for the analysis of some behaviors and attitudes that cannot be directly observed, and the records can be used in lieu of a potentially biased self-report or serve as a way to verify self-report. The disadvantage is that the researcher must figure out how to accurately code the data. Not only is this time-consuming, but it also introduces the potential for bias into the coding process if a researcher selectively attends to information that supports the study's hypothesis. This bias can be reduced in similar ways to observational coding: Have people who are blind to the hypothesis code the data, have multiple coders, train the coders well, and check their inter-rater reliability.

Table 4.1	Comparison of Methods	

	Advantages	**Disadvantages**
Survey research (interviews and questionnaires)	• Obtain individual's perspective • Interviews allow a researcher to ask follow-up questions and obtain detailed responses • Questionnaires are easy to administer and many participants can usually be surveyed at the same time	• Potential social desirability bias • Interviews are time-consuming and have the potential for interviewer bias • Questionnaires do not elicit as much in-depth information as can be obtained in an interview
Observations	• Focus on observable behavior rather than self-report, reducing the social desirability bias	• Can be time-consuming to collect and code data • Potential observer bias (this can be reduced if observers are "blind" to hypotheses)
Archival research	• No direct data collection necessary • Archives may span a larger time frame than would be feasible for a single researcher to collect • May have fewer ethical considerations • May allow the study of some behaviors and attitudes that cannot be obtained through surveys or observations	• Data may be difficult to obtain • May need to adjust your hypotheses to match the data you can obtain • May require a lot of time and effort to code the data

ETHICS TIP   KNOW WHEN TO GET INFORMED CONSENT

Informed consent is essential under the following situations:

- There is a possibility that participation in the research will cause the participants harm or distress.
- The study is not anonymous.

(Continued)

(Continued)

- The study uses video or audio recordings and these recordings could be used to identify the participants.
- The study involves observations in nonpublic places.
- The study involves archives that are confidential or that if revealed might place participants at risk.

PRACTICE 4.2

EVALUATE METHODS FOR A DESCRIPTIVE STUDY ON YOUR TOPIC

1. Recall the question you came up with for Practice 4.1 and assess different ways of studying that question and evaluate the following methods:

Surveys

a. Would self-report be a viable method to help answer your question? Why or why not?

b. If yes, what would be the pros and cons of interviews? What would be the pros and cons of questionnaires?

Observational Research

a. Would observations be a viable method to help answer your question? Why or why not?

b. If yes, would you use naturalistic or contrived observations? Would you use participant or nonparticipant observations?

Archival Research

a. Would you be able to obtain secondary data or find records/documents to help answer your question?

b. If yes, what archival records would you use?

2. Of the methods that you could use for your study, which one would you choose? Why?

3. Would you need to obtain informed consent to carry out the study you chose? Why or why not?

VALIDITY IN DESCRIPTIVE STUDIES

> ### REVIEW OF KEY CONCEPTS: MEASUREMENT VALIDITY, INTERNAL VALIDITY, AND EXTERNAL VALIDITY
>
> *Measurement validity is the extent to which the measures used in a study actually measure what they intend to measure.*
>
> *Internal validity is the extent to which you can demonstrate a causal link between your variables.*
>
> *External validity is the extent to which results of one study generalize to other samples, settings, and methods.*

In order to accurately describe something, the measures used must be valid. Recall from Chapter 3 that a measure cannot be valid unless it is reliable. Having all the participants experience the same testing environment can increase reliability of measures in descriptive research as well as having all coders use the same standards. Training any interviewers, observers, or coders and allowing them to practice prior to the start of the study increases validity. Conducting a **pilot study** in which you carry out a study with a smaller sample is a good way to test the measures and work out any kinks prior to conducting the full study.

> *Pilot study:* A preliminary study with a small sample to test measures and procedures.

Increasing a measure's reliability will in turn increase the measure's validity. Other ways to increase the validity of a measure include being sure that each question or code is clear, only assesses one idea at a time, and adequately represents the construct of interest. Many novice researchers begin designing their study by making up their own questions or codes. After all, this appears to be the best way to ensure that they are worded such that they measure exactly what the researcher wants them to measure. Starting from scratch, however, is not the best way to approach measurement validity. Remember that you will want your study to build on past research, and therefore it is important to find out how others operationally defined their variables. Using measures with established reliability and validity helps your research fit in with past research and also saves time in having to create and test your own measures. If such measures are unavailable or do not seem to actually measure what you want, you can use the measures, questions, and codes from past research as a model or edit them to apply to your own research.

Measurement validity is critical to any type of research study. The importance of internal and external validity varies based on the study design. Descriptive research examines the "who, what, where, when, and how," but it does not examine the "why." In other words,

118 • RESEARCH METHODS, STATISTICS, AND APPLICATIONS

descriptive research does not seek to explain what caused a situation, feeling, or behavior. Purely descriptive studies do not examine the relationship among variables. Because of this, internal validity is not a concern in descriptive research. Instead, external validity is of primary concern in descriptive research. Descriptive studies describe the participants, animals, or archives that were part of the study, but the researcher hopes that the findings will apply beyond the study's sample. The external validity of the study depends on who the population of interest is and how the sample was obtained.

● DEFINING THE POPULATION AND OBTAINING A SAMPLE

Who or What Is the Population of Interest?

A **population** is the group of people, animals, or archives that you are interested in examining. Residency, occupation, gender, age, and time frame are some of the characteristics that might define a population. A **subpopulation** is a portion of the population. Both the population and subpopulations are defined by the researcher. For example, a researcher might define the population as all residents within a certain state, and a subpopulation might be defined as women within that state. If the population of interest is women, a subpopulation might be women between the ages of 18 and 24.

> *Population:* The group that a researcher is interested in examining defined by specific characteristics such as residency, occupation, gender, or age.
>
> *Subpopulation:* A portion or subgroup of the population.

It may seem that the best strategy from an external validity standpoint is to define the population as broadly as possible. If you have human participants, it might be tempting to think of your population as all people. This is a serious mistake, however, because the resources required to create a study that could generalize to all people is greater than any researcher, much less a student researcher, can manage. Consequently, you will want to narrow your population of interest.

The smaller and more clearly defined your population, the easier it is to conduct a study that adequately describes that population. You might define your population as students who are enrolled in your Research Methods class this semester. It is possible to conduct a study that included data from each member of the class, in which case you would expect that the results would adequately describe your population and you could draw conclusions about that narrow population.

On the other hand, if your population is too narrowly defined you will be severely limited in the conclusions you can draw. It is unlikely that you would be interested only in students enrolled in the class this semester. Instead, you might want your results to generalize to students who have ever taken the course at your college or university, or even to students who have taken a research course at other institutions. Additionally, although it is possible to collect data on every member of a small, clearly defined population it is also possible that some members of the population will be excluded because they were not present when data were collected, they decided not to participate, or their data were incomplete or contained too many errors.

The problem with collecting data from all members is compounded for larger populations. Take the U.S. census as an example. Every 10 years the U.S. Census Bureau attempts to collect information about how many people are residing in the United States and the residency, ethnicity, and age information of each person. In 2010, the Census Bureau advertised on television, mailed advance letters notifying people of the upcoming census, mailed the census survey itself along with reminders to complete the census, and hand delivered the census to those without postal addresses. Still, 26% of households did not mail back their census forms. Consequently, census workers went door to door to reach those nonresponders. In all, the U.S. government hired over 600,000 people and spent $13 billion for the 2010 census (United States Census Bureau, 2011).

Given the difficulty and expense of obtaining information from every single person or animal in your population, or obtaining every archive, researchers often choose to obtain a sample from the population. A **sample** is a subset of the population that is meant to represent the full population, and **sampling** is the procedure used to obtain the sample. The extent to which a sample actually represents the population is dependent on the amount of bias in the sampling procedure. **Sampling bias** occurs when some members of the population are more likely to participate

| Figure 4.2 | Sampling |

This cartoon illustrates that obtaining information from every participant, subject, or archive in your population is tricky, if not impossible. Consequently, researchers instead obtain a sample of the population.

Source: Eva K. Lawrence

than others. Sampling bias is of particular concern in descriptive research where the primary goal is to describe the population and maximize the study's external validity. As such, it is important that researchers conducting a descriptive study carefully consider how to obtain a sample that represents the population.

Sample: A subset of the population from which data are collected.

Sampling: The process by which a sample is selected.

Sampling bias: When some members of a population are overrepresented in the sample.

How Will You Obtain a Sample From Your Population?

Probability Sampling

Probability sampling (also called random sampling) is any method of sampling that uses **random selection** in which all members of a particular population or subpopulation have an equal chance of being selected. Probability sampling reduces sampling bias and increases the chance that the sample will be representative of the population.

Random selection is one of the most misunderstood concepts by novice researchers. As such, you should work on remembering the following distinctions:

- Random selection does *not* mean haphazard selection.
  - Random is used in everyday language to mean all sorts of things, including haphazard, careless, pointless, or rambling. Be careful, because random selection is none of these things.
  - Random selection requires careful planning to ensure that the sample was chosen only on the basis of membership to a specific population or subset of the population and not other individual characteristics. It also means that each member of the population has an equal chance of being selected.

- Random selection is *not* the same as random assignment.
  - Random selection is a sampling procedure used to ensure a representative population. Random selection can be used in any type of research design, but it is especially important in descriptive research.
  - Random assignment refers to how you assign members of your sample to groups within your study and is only used in experimental designs.

With a small population, random selection might involve writing the names of the members of the population on pieces of paper, putting them in a hat, and then drawing a sample at random. For larger populations, all the names can be listed in a spreadsheet. A computer program such as SPSS can then be used to randomly select a sample or a researcher might use a random numbers table to select the sample (see Appendix C.1).

Random selection can occur with or without replacement. **Random selection with replacement** means that a selected member of the population is returned to the pool of possible participants and thus may be selected into the sample more than once. **Random selection without replacement** means that once a member of the population is selected that member is removed from the pool and cannot be selected into the sample again. Random selection with replacement ensures that each selection is completely independent in that selection of one member does not impact the selection of future members of the sample. This replacement is preferable from a statistical standpoint, but practically speaking most researchers practice random selection without replacement so that a participant is not sampled more than once.

Probability sampling (or random sampling): Sampling procedure that uses random selection.

Random selection: A process of selecting a sample in which all members of a population or a sub-population have an equal chance of being selected.

Random selection with replacement: A selected member of the population is returned to the pool of possible participants so that any member may be selected into the sample more than once.

Random selection without replacement: A selected member of the population is removed from the pool of possible participants so that any member may be selected into the sample only once.

Once the sample has been randomly selected, the researcher's work has only just begun. The researcher must now collect data from members of the sample. If someone refuses to participate or if an archive is missing, the researcher cannot simply select a new participant or archive that is more readily available. This would negate the random selection process and introduce sampling bias.

It is rare that any researcher will be able to obtain data from 100% of the selected sample. There are no hard-and-fast rules for what an acceptable response rate is, and it varies based on the standards set by previous research on the topic. A **nonresponse bias** occurs when the researcher is not able to obtain data from members of the sample, and those who responded differ from those who did not. To limit the nonresponse bias, the researcher must attempt to collect data from as many members selected for the sample as possible. This requires perseverance in sending advance notice and reminders to participants, attempting to reach them in various ways (mail, e-mail, telephone, in person), and perhaps offering incentives if ethically appropriate.

Another strategy is to compare those who responded to those who did not respond to determine if they differ on any key variables (e.g., gender, age, any variable related to the measures collected in the study). This can only be done if you have some data for your non-responders that you collected from other sources, such as public records. Ideally, the differences between responders and nonresponders will be negligible, and this provides evidence that the nonresponse bias was minimal in the study.

122 • RESEARCH METHODS, STATISTICS, AND APPLICATIONS

> *Nonresponse bias:* The extent to which those who were selected and participated in the study differ from those who were selected but did not participate.

Procedures for Probability Sampling. There are several different ways to achieve probability sampling. These include simple random sampling, stratified random sampling, and cluster sampling.

> *Simple random sampling:* A type of probability sampling in which every single member of the population has an equal chance of being selected for the sample.
>
> *Stratified random sampling:* A type of probability sampling that results in the sample representing key subpopulations based on characteristics such as age, gender, and ethnicity.
>
> *Cluster sampling:* A type of probability sampling in which groups, or clusters, are randomly selected instead of individuals.

Simple random sampling is a type of probability sampling in which every single member of the population has an equal chance of being selected for the sample. Table 4.2 outlines the steps for simple random sampling, with an example of each step for a study about academic honesty.

Table 4.2 Simple Random Sampling

Steps in Simple Random Sampling	Example for a Study on Academic Honesty
1. Define the population.	• To make sampling manageable, we define the population as the students currently enrolled in one college.
2. Identify all members of the population.	• Obtain a list of all the students enrolled in the college from the registrar's office.
3. Randomly select a sample from that population.	• Transfer the names to a computer program such as SPSS and then follow the appropriate steps so that the program generates a random sample. Alternatively, use a random numbers table to select the sample.
4. Collect data from that sample. Attempt to both reduce and assess the nonresponse bias.	• Approach students who were selected and attempt to collect data from as many of them as possible. • Continue collecting data, including following up with students using various means and offering incentives for participation, until an appropriate response rate is achieved. • Compare students who responded to those who did not respond on variables obtained through the registrar's office, such as GPA, year in school, and major.

Stratified random sampling is probability sampling that results in the sample representing key subpopulations based on characteristics such as age, gender, and ethnicity. With stratified random sampling, the sample has the same proportion of these groups as are in the population. For example, a researcher might want to stratify their sample based on gender. If the population is 54% female then the sample will also be 54% female.

Stratified random sampling is the standard sampling method for phone interviews conducted by the Pew Research Center. Their sample is stratified based on type of phone, with those with landlines (who may also have a cell phone) sampled at 60% and those who use cell phones exclusively sampled at 40%. This stratification was determined to provide the most diverse sample of adults in respect to age, ethnicity, and socioeconomic status. The landlines are further stratified to ensure proportional representation of different parts of the country, and the cell phone numbers stratified based on both geography and wireless carrier. The sample is selected using random digit dialing (Pew Research Center, n.d.). See Table 4.3 for an outline of the steps in stratified random sampling and an example for a study on academic honesty.

Both simple and stratified random sampling require the researcher to identify all members of the population. For example, if the researcher has defined the population as college students he or she must first identify all the colleges and universities in the world and then obtain a list of the students enrolled. This is obviously difficult and time-consuming. Consequently, researchers who use one of these two sampling techniques tend to define their population more narrowly. For example, a researcher interested in college students might define her population as college students enrolled in one or a few colleges or universities that will allow the researcher access to student records. Alternatively, a researcher may use cluster sampling when it is impossible or impractical to obtain a list of all members of a specified population.

Cluster sampling is a type of probability sampling in which groups, or clusters, are randomly selected instead of individuals. A cluster might be defined as a neighborhood, a school, or a class within a school. See Table 4.4 for the steps in cluster sampling and an example.

How large should your probability sample be? The closer a probability sample comes to including the full population, the more likely that sample will represent the population. Of course, the larger a sample the more time, effort, and expenses are involved. Consequently, it is wise to consider the minimum sample size required in order for the results to represent the population.

To estimate the minimum sample size required for a descriptive study using probability sampling, you must know how large the population is as well as identify both the confidence interval and confidence level. A **confidence interval** is an estimation of the margin of error for your scores, or the range of values within which your scores will fall. Researchers typically aim for a 5% confidence interval. A **confidence level** is a measure of how sure you are that your scores will fall within that confidence interval. Researchers typically choose either a 95% or 99% confidence level.

Confidence interval: An estimation of the range of values within which the scores will fall (margin of error).

Confidence level: A measure of how likely the scores will fall within a stated confidence interval.

Table 4.3 Stratified Random Sampling

Steps in Stratified Random Sampling	Example for a Study on Academic Honesty
1. Define the population.	• We define the population as students currently enrolled in one college.
2. Identify the groups that you want to be proportionately represented in your sample.	• For this research, year in school is an important variable because we might assume that beginning students have had less experience with the academic honor code than more advanced students.
3. Identify all the members of the population and to which strata each member belongs.	• Obtain a list of all the students enrolled in the college from the registrar's office along with their year in school.
4. Divide the population based on the groups you identified.	• Create a database of students for each year: first year, second, third, fourth, fifth, or more.
5. Determine the proportion of the population represented by each group.	• Calculate the total number of students in each year and the total number of students in the college. Find the proportion for each year by dividing the total number of students in each year by the total number of students. $$\%_{\text{first year}} = \frac{N_{\text{first year}}}{N_{\text{total students}}}$$
6. Randomly select a sample from each group in proportions equal to those of the population.	• Use a computer or random numbers table to randomly select a sample from each year that is equal to the proportion of those in the population. For example, if 25% of the students enrolled in the college are first years, 18% second years, 22% third years, 24% fourth years, and 11% fifth year or beyond, then we will want those same proportions in our sample. For a sample of 100, we would randomly select 25 from the first-year database, 18 from the second-year database, 22 from the third years, 24 from the fourth years, and 11 from the fifth years.
7. Collect data from the samples. Attempt to both reduce and assess the nonresponse bias.	• Approach students who were selected, use various strategies to improve the response rate, and continue collecting data until an appropriate response rate is reached for each year in school. • Compare students who responded to those who did not respond on year in school as well as other variables obtained from the registrar's office such as GPA and major.

Table 4.4	Cluster Sampling

Steps in Cluster Sampling	Example for a Study on Academic Honesty
1. Define the population.	• The population is students enrolled in one college.
2. Identify the clusters that will be used for sampling.	• Classes would be good clusters for this study, and we would choose a type of class that most students are required to take or choose a popular class time to ensure that our sample contains a variety of students. For example, we might select all classes that meet during the 1 p.m. period on Tuesdays and Thursdays because this is the most popular time period and contains a variety of classes.
3. Identify all of these clusters within the population.	• We would write down all the classes that meet on Tuesdays and Thursdays at 1 p.m.
4. Randomly select a sample of clusters.	• We would put these classes in a hat and select our sample at random.
5. Collect data from all the individuals within each cluster sample. Attempt to both reduce and assess nonresponse bias.	• We would approach the professors who teach the classes we selected and ask if we could conduct a study with the students enrolled in their 1 p.m. class. • Ideally, we would conduct the study during the class period to help ensure that we would be able to collect data from most of the students in the classes. • To help ensure that all the professors teaching during the 1 p.m. timeslot allow access to their class, we would get administrative support for the study, notify the professors well in advance so that they can plan around the data collection day, and explain the importance of the study. • We will follow up with any students who were absent the day of the study to help ensure that we obtain data from all the individuals enrolled in the 1 p.m. class periods. • To assess the possibility of a nonresponse bias, we would compare the types of students who participated to any who did not participate on the type of 1 p.m. class in which they were enrolled and relevant information that the professor of the class or college was willing to provide such as course grade, year in school, or GPA.

126 • RESEARCH METHODS, STATISTICS, AND APPLICATIONS

For example, suppose we conducted our study of academic honesty and found that 15% of students in our sample reporting that they have plagiarized. A 5% confidence interval would give us a range of 10–20%. If we had a 95% confidence level, we would be 95% sure that between 10% and 20% of students in the population would report that they plagiarized. Before we can say that, however, we need to determine the sample size necessary to establish that confidence interval and confidence level.

The easiest way to calculate the estimated sample size needed to obtain the desired confidence interval and confidence level is to use an online sample size calculator. Creative Research Systems provides a free sample size calculator at www.surveysystem.com/sscalc.htm. Another option is to use the table provided in Appendix C.2, although this table only provides populations of certain sizes and you might need to round your sample size up or down. A third option is to calculate the sample size by hand:

Sample size (*ss*) calculation:

$$\text{Step 1: } ss = .25Z^2 \ / \ c^2 \text{ or } \frac{.25Z^2}{c^2}$$

$$\text{Step 2: New } ss = \frac{ss}{1 + \frac{(ss - 1)}{\text{pop}}}$$

where $Z = Z$ score (1.96 for 95% confidence level and 2.576 for 99% confidence level), c = confidence interval expressed as decimal (e.g., .05 = 5% confidence interval), and pop = population.

For example, for a 2.5% confidence interval and 95% confidence level and population of 5,000:

$$\text{Step 1: } ss = \frac{.25(1.96)^2}{(.025)^2} = \frac{.25(3.84)}{.000625} = \frac{.9604}{.000625} = 1536.64$$

$$\text{Step 2: New } ss = \frac{1536.64}{1 + \frac{(1536 - 1)}{5000}} = \frac{1536.64}{1 + .307128} = 1176$$

Keep in mind a few important points:

- The sample size calculations are only an estimate. The sample size required to best represent the population depends on how homogeneous, or similar, members of the population are. A very homogeneous population requires a smaller sample, whereas a very heterogeneous, or diverse, population requires a larger sample.
- You will likely not obtain 100% of your selected sample. Therefore, you should plan on obtaining a larger sample size to account for this. You can estimate how much larger a sample size you will need based on the response rate of past research. For example, if you expect that you will be unable to collect data from 10% of your selected sample, then you should increase your sample size by 10%.

- The higher your nonresponse rate, the less likely it is that your sample will represent your population.
- Even if you were to obtain 100% of your selected sample, you are never completely sure that the results you obtain from your sample will in fact represent the population. The confidence interval and confidence level demonstrate this point.

APPLICATION 4.1

Examples of Probability Sampling

Study A: Archives With Simple Random Sampling

M. McCullough and Holmberg (2005) used Google searches to examine the prevalence of plagiarism in theses completed for a master's degree.

They defined their population as master's theses that were completed during 2003, that were in English, and that were available online via the WorldCat database. The population consisted of 2,600 theses, of which the authors randomly selected a sample of 260 (10%) to examine for evidence of plagiarism. The nonresponse rate was 19% because some of the full texts could not be retrieved or they were duplicates in the database.

Study B: Questionnaires With Cluster Sampling

Vowell and Chen (2004) compared how well different sociological theories explained cheating behaviors such as copying or allowing someone else to copy work.

They defined their population as undergraduate students enrolled in one university located in the Southwestern United States. They listed all the 11 a.m. to 12:20 p.m. classes and then randomly selected 42 of those classes. The researchers approached the professors teaching the selected classes and asked them to administer a questionnaire during the selected class. The nonresponse rate was 14% because some professors opted to not include their class in the study.

Nonprobability Sampling

Nonprobability sampling (also called nonrandom sampling) is any method of sampling that does not rely on random selection. Sampling bias is a serious concern with nonprobability sampling. Unlike probability sampling, there is no set sample size that can be reached that gives us confidence that a nonprobability sample will represent the population. Even if a researcher was able to obtain a sample from the majority of members of a population, it is possible that the sample would not represent the full population. Take the 2010 census as an example. The 26% of those who did not mail back their census data likely represent those who are poorer and have less stable living environments than the 74% who did respond.

> *Nonprobability sampling (or nonrandom sampling):* Sampling procedure that does not use random selection.

Even though sampling bias is inherent in nonprobability sampling, a majority of studies actually utilize nonprobability sampling. There are several reasons for this:

1. Nonprobability sampling is easier and much less time-consuming than probability sampling. It does not require identification of all members or clusters in a population. Instead of randomly selecting a sample and then trying to obtain data from each member of a sample, the nonprobability sample is defined simply as anyone (or any animal or archive) contributing data to the study.

2. A truly representative sample is an ideal that a researcher strives for but never fully attains. The representativeness of a probability sample is limited in small samples or by nonresponse and chance error. Additionally, the population defined in probability sampling is typically narrow (e.g., students enrolled in one college) and the question remains if the sample represents a broader population (e.g., all college students).

3. There are methods to examine the representativeness of a sample, including comparisons between the sample characteristics or results obtained in one study to the average obtained from other studies (we will talk more about this in Chapter 6). Moreover, the external validity of a study can be tested through replication.

The bottom line is that probability sampling is the best choice when your main goal is to describe a population and you are able to identify all the members or clusters in a population, obtain the appropriate sample size, and minimize the nonresponse rate. If these criteria cannot be met, nonprobability sampling is an acceptable alternative in descriptive research. If your primary goal is not to describe a population but rather examine relationships, as in correlational and experimental designs, nonprobability sampling is a perfectly fine and common method of sampling.

Procedures for nonprobability sampling. There are several different ways to achieve nonprobability sampling. These include convenience sampling, quota sampling, maximum variation sampling, and snowball sampling. Like probability sampling, nonprobability sampling requires that you define your population. However, because you will not need to identify every member or cluster in the population you do not need to be as specific. For our example study of academic honesty, we can simply define the population as U.S. college students.

> *Convenience sampling:* A type of nonprobability sample made up of those volunteers or others who are readily available and willing to participate.
>
> *Quota sampling:* A type of nonprobability sampling that results in the sample representing key subpopulations based on characteristics such as age, gender, and ethnicity.

Maximum variation sampling: A nonprobability sampling strategy in which the researcher seeks out the full range of extremes in the population.

Snowball sampling: A nonprobability sampling strategy in which participants recruit others into the sample.

Convenience sampling is the most basic type of nonprobability sample in which those who were available and willing to provide data make up the sample. Convenience samples may be obtained in a variety of ways, such as advertising for volunteers or asking a group of people in the school cafeteria or outside a grocery store to participate in your study. At the extreme, a convenience sample can be very convenient. You might ask just your friends and family to participate or just those students who attended a school event that you also attended.

It is wise, however, to avoid these types of overly convenient samples because they may overrepresent one group in the population. This is particularly problematic if your sample is composed of those who have similar views on the subject you are investigating. Instead, you should make your convenience sampling a bit more inconvenient by obtaining data from various places at various times of day. See Table 4.5 for more detail about the steps for convenience sampling and an example for a study on academic honesty.

Table 4.5 Convenience Sampling

Steps in Convenience Sampling	Example for a Study on Academic Honesty
1. Define the population.	• Because we do not need to identify all members of the population and we believe we can get a range of responses from students across the country, we define our population as U.S. college students.
2. Decide where and when you will be able to find a sample from your population.	• We would limit our data collection to college campuses because we will be most likely to find college students there (as opposed to a more general location like a grocery store). • We will go to several different locations on one college campus at different times of the day to help ensure that our sample contains a variety of types of students. We may also collect data at nearby colleges or even try to recruit from colleges in other states in an attempt at obtaining a diverse sample of students.
3. Collect data. Screen out those who do not belong to your population.	• Approach potential participants and first make sure that they are students. Ask students if they are willing to participate in the study.

130 • RESEARCH METHODS, STATISTICS, AND APPLICATIONS

Quota sampling is nonprobability sampling that results in the sample representing key subsets of your population, or subpopulations based on characteristics such as age, gender, and ethnicity. The goal is the same as stratified random sampling, but quota sampling is accomplished without random selection. See Table 4.6 for steps in quota sampling and an example.

Table 4.6 Quota Sampling

Steps in Quota Sampling	Example for a Study on Academic Honesty
1. Define the population.	• The population is U.S. college students.
2. Identify the groups that you want to be proportionately represented in your sample.	• We would choose the same groups—year in school—as for our stratified random sample example.
3. Determine the proportion or approximate proportion of the population represented by each group.	• Because our population is all U.S. college students, the information from a single college is not sufficient. Instead, we will look to national data that provides averages and approximations on how many college students are in their first, second, third, fourth, and fifth plus year.
4. Decide where and when you will be able to find a sample of the groups you identified.	• We would limit data collection to college campuses. We would attempt to find students of various years at the public places on campus, and recruit at other colleges in an attempt to diversify our sample.
5. Collect data from each group in proportions equal to those of the population. When you have reached the quota for one group, you can stop collecting data for that group and focus on completing data collection for the rest of the other group(s).	• Approach potential participants and first make sure that they are students. Ask students if they are willing to participate in the study. • Be sure that one of the questions we ask, either before or as part of the study, is their year in school. Keep track of how many students of each year we have, and be sure to keep the proportions equal to those in our population. For example, if our population estimate is 25% first-year students then 25% of our sample should also be first-year students. Likewise, the proportion for other years in the population should be matched in our sample. • If we are unable to find enough students representing a particular year, we may need to focus our efforts on areas where students of that year typically congregate, advertise for volunteers from that year, or ask friends and professors to help us find participants who are in that year of school.

Maximum variation sampling is a sampling strategy in which the researcher seeks out the full range of extremes in the population. The goal is to achieve a representative sample through this purposeful sampling instead of relying on probability. The premise is that the average achieved with maximum variation sampling will approximate the population average. Maximum variation sampling is most commonly used with small samples such as those achieved through interviews. See Table 4.7 for more information about maximum variation sampling.

Table 4.7	Maximum Variation Sampling

Steps in Maximum Variation Sampling	Example for a Study on Academic Honesty
1. Define the population.	• Because obtaining a maximum variation sample takes time and focus and is designed for smaller samples, we define the population more narrowly as those students currently enrolled in one college.

2. Identify the extremes in the population.	• Given our subject of academic honesty, we will want to have a sample with the following characteristics:
	  ○ One student from each year
	  ○ One who is majoring in each of the disciplines on campus (e.g., social sciences, natural science, humanities, etc.)
	  ○ An honors student
	  ○ A student on academic probation
	  ○ A student with an average GPA
	  ○ A student who had violated the academic honor code and one who has not.
	  ○ An international student
	  ○ A student from another state and one from the same state as the college

3. Seek out members of the population that represent various extremes as well as those who represent the average.	• Finding these extremes will be challenging. One option is that we can advertise for volunteers or recruit at public places on campus, having this initial group complete a brief questionnaire along with contact information. We can then use this information to screen for those who meet our criteria. • We might also ask those who have already agreed to participate if they know anyone who would meet a specific criterion (such as an international student).
4. Collect data.	• We will contact those who met our criteria and ask them to participate in our study. If someone refuses, we will simply find a replacement.

In **snowball sampling** the participants recruit others into the sample. Snowball sampling is typically used to seek out members of a specific population who are difficult to find or who might be distrustful of a researcher, such as sex workers, illegal immigrants, the homeless, those who are HIV positive, or drug dealers. The researcher must first identify at least one member of the population who is not only willing to participate in the study but also to help the researcher recruit other participants. If each participant helps recruit several others, the sample will grow exponentially, like a snowball.

Getting your foot in the door to make initial contacts is the first challenge in snowball sampling. It may be that you know someone who could help you, or you may contact someone who already has a relationship with members of the population of interest. For example, if you wanted to conduct a study on the homeless you might first approach the director of a homeless shelter. The director could then recommend homeless adults who might be willing to talk with you, and could even come with you to the initial meeting. Once you develop the trust of a few initial contacts, they too might personally introduce you to other potential participants.

There are unique considerations when using snowball sampling. Because all the participants know each other or have common associates, they will likely have similar views and experiences. Thus, your sample may only represent that small subset of the already narrowly defined population. There are also ethical implications in asking participants to identify others who might not want to be identified. One way to address this issue is to have the participants give your contact information to others and encourage them to contact you directly. If you have established a good reputation within the population of interest by treating participants with respect and keeping their personal information confidential, it is possible that members of the population will seek you out. Another option is for the participant to obtain permission from others for you to contact them, or even bring potential participants to you with their consent. See Table 4.8 for the steps in snowball sampling and an example.

| Table 4.8 | Snowball Sampling |

Steps in Snowball Sampling	Example for a Study on Academic Honesty
1. Define the population.	• Snowball sampling would best be used for a smaller, more hard to reach, subset of the college student population. • For a study on academic honesty, we will define our population as students who have intentionally cheated on their academic work.
2. Identify strategies for recruiting the initial participants.	• We would talk with the judicial board on campus and ask members of that group to help us identify those who were caught cheating, or we might ask professors to refer students who were caught cheating in their class.

Steps in Snowball Sampling	Example for a Study on Academic Honesty
	Since this would be a violation of the students' confidentiality, we would ask the judicial board and professors to contact the students directly and encourage them to contact us or for consent for us to contact them. We might be able to work out an incentive for participation, although we would want to be careful that the incentive was not coercive. • We could also hold a focus group on the topic of academic honesty. We would establish the confidential nature of the discussion and ask if there were any students willing to share their own experiences. We would ask those students who revealed that they had cheated for permission to contact them for a follow-up study.
3. Collect data from the initial participants.	• We would collect data from our initial participants. • We would work on creating a trusting relationship where the participants do not feel judged and feel confident being honest with us. This is important in any research study, but especially so given the topic of our study and our sampling technique.
4. Ask the initial participants to recruit other members from the population, and likewise ask each new participant to help with recruitment.	• We would then ask the initial participants to talk with other students who they know have cheated on assignments and either ask them to contact us or get permission for us to contact them. • The snowball technique will hopefully give us access not only to those who were caught cheating (who we may have recruited exclusively if we relied on the judicial board or professors to recruit participants) but also those who were not caught cheating. • We would continue this process with each new participant until we had a sample of adequate size or we felt that we have reached all the members of the population who we are able to reach.

How large should your nonprobability sample be? What is considered a large sample size is relative. A sample of 50 may be considered large if the population itself is very small and homogeneous, whereas a sample of 500 may be considered small if the population it is drawn from is quite large and heterogeneous. The larger the sample size relative to the population size and heterogeneity, the better external validity the study has because it improves your chances that your results will generalize to other samples. However, because probability sampling was not used, there is no guarantee that even a very large sample will be representative of the population.

On the other hand, sample size is still important when conducting certain types of statistics. We will discuss this in more detail in Chapter 6. In the meantime, aim for as large a sample size as is possible given your resources and time.

APPLICATION 4.2

Examples of Nonprobability Sampling

Study C: Interviews and Observations With Maximum Variation Sampling

Parameswaran and Devi (2006) examined the prevalence and types of plagiarism that occur within engineering labs, and the attitudes and motivations of students regarding plagiarism.

The researchers conducted individual interviews with mechanical and electrical engineering students and made observations of engineering lab sessions.

The population for the interviews was students enrolled in engineering labs at one university.

Maximum variation sampling was used to select 30 interview participants who represented a range of grade-point averages, ethnicities, nationalities, social groups, departments, and years in school.

Study D: Questionnaires With Convenience Sampling

Trost (2009) examined the prevalence of different forms of academic dishonesty among Swedish students.

The population was Swedish university students, and as such the researcher screened out international students. The sample was collected by approaching students at the end of natural sciences, technical sciences, and social science classes at a Swedish university and asking if the students would be willing to complete a questionnaire. A total of 325 were asked to participate and 3 declined.

Table 4.9 presents a summary of the different sampling techniques we have discussed in this chapter.

Table 4.9 Types of Sampling Techniques

Probability (Random) Sampling	Nonprobability (Nonrandom) Sampling
Simple Random Sampling	Convenience Sampling
Stratified Random Sampling	Quota Sampling
Cluster Sampling	Maximum Variation Sampling
	Snowball Sampling

BEYOND DESCRIPTION

What is beyond description? Correlational and experimental designs, of course! These designs go beyond describing phenomena to examining relationships among phenomena. Describing and examining relationships do not have to be mutually exclusive. Although many social science researchers conduct purely descriptive studies, others choose to use multiple research designs within a single study. In fact, in some disciplines such as psychology it is rare for a study to be purely descriptive. It is equally rare that correlational or experimental designs are conducted without first describing the variables of interest.

In particular, descriptive and correlational research often go hand in hand because these are both nonexperimental designs. Social scientists are incredibly curious. When a researcher collects descriptive information examining several variables, and the data are in a form that allows relationships among the variables to be analyzed, and there is research evidence suggesting that there might be a relationship among the variables, it is too tempting to not also conduct a correlational study.

For example, M. McCullough and Holmberg's (2005) primary goal was descriptive in that they sought to determine how much plagiarism could be identified using Google searches. However, they also utilized a correlational design to examine the relationship between plagiarism, institution, and subject matter. This allowed the researchers to determine if plagiarism was more common in certain institutions or for certain subjects. Likewise, Trost (2009) examined the prevalence of different types of academically dishonest acts among Swedish students but also examined the relationship between gender and academic dishonesty. Both of these examples focused primarily on descriptive research but included correlational research as well. We will examine correlational studies in more depth in Chapter 7.

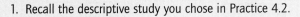

PRACTICE 4.3

DEFINE THE POPULATION AND DECIDE HOW TO COLLECT A SAMPLE FOR YOUR STUDY

1. Recall the descriptive study you chose in Practice 4.2.

2. Who or what is your population of interest?

3. Should you do probability sampling based on the goal of your study? Is it feasible to do probability sampling?

4. Choose a specific sampling procedure and outline how you will obtain a sample from your population.

CHAPTER RESOURCES

KEY TERMS

Define the following terms using your own words. You can check your answers by reviewing the chapter or by comparing them with the definitions in the glossary—but try to define them on your own first.

Archival research

Blind

Checklist

Cluster sampling

Confederate

Confidence interval

Confidence level

Contrived observation

Convenience sampling

Covert observation

Duration

Interviewer bias

Latency

Maximum variation sampling

Narrative

Natural (or naturalistic) observation

Nonparticipant observation

Nonprobability sampling (or nonrandom sampling)

Nonresponse bias

Observer bias

Overt observation

Participant observation

Pilot study

Population

Probability sampling (or random sampling)

Quota sampling

Random selection

Random selection with replacement

Random selection without replacement

Rating scale

Reaction time

Sample

Sampling

Sampling bias

Secondary data

Semi-structured interviews

Simple random sampling

Snowball sampling

Social desirability bias

Stratified random sampling

Structured interviews

Subpopulation

Survey research

Task completion time

DO YOU UNDERSTAND THE CHAPTER?

Answer these questions on your own and then review the chapter to check your answers.

1. What are some reasons to conduct a descriptive study?

2. What is survey research? What are some of the pros and cons of interviews and questionnaires?

3. What types of decisions must be made when conducting observational research?

4. What is archival research? What are possible ways to find archives?

5. Evaluate ethical issues, particularly informed consent, with the different descriptive methods.

6. What are the ways to evaluate validity in a descriptive study?

7. How does a researcher define a population and subpopulations?

8. How is probability sampling different from nonprobability sampling?

9. Describe the different types and procedures of probability sampling and of nonprobability sampling.